SUTTON MODERN BRI

THE AG
APPEASEMENT

Rhiannon
Wade

SUTTON MODERN BRITISH HISTORY

General Editor: Keith Laybourn,
Professor of History, University of Huddersfield

Forthcoming Titles

SUTTON MODERN BRITISH HISTORY

THE AGE OF APPEASEMENT

THE EVOLUTION OF BRITISH FOREIGN POLICY IN THE 1930S

PEIJIAN SHEN

SUTTON PUBLISHING

First published in 1999 by
Sutton Publishing Limited · Phoenix Mill
Thrupp · Stroud · Gloucestershire · GL5 2BU

British Library Cataloguing in Publication Data
A catalogue record for this book is available from the British Library

ISBN 0 7509 2118 8 (hb)
ISBN 0 7509 2119 6 (pb)

Jacket/cover picture: Prime Minister Neville Chamberlain at Heston Airport before departing for his second round of talks with Hitler, 22 September 1938. (Hulton Getty)

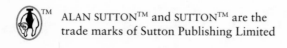

ALAN SUTTON™ and SUTTON™ are the
trade marks of Sutton Publishing Limited

Typeset in 11/14 pt Sabon.
Typesetting and origination by
Sutton Publishing Limited.
Printed in Great Britain by
Redwood Books, Trowbridge, Wiltshire.

*In memory of my parents, who died before
I completed this work, so much of which
stems from their support and understanding.*

CONTENTS

ACKNOWLEDGEMENTS

This book is based on my PhD thesis. In writing it, I have incurred many obligations, and I am happy to take this opportunity to thank all those who have helped in its preparation.

I am particularly grateful to Professor Paul Wilkinson, my PhD Supervisor, in the Department of International Relations at the University of St Andrews, Scotland. I am also thankful to the University of St Andrews itself, which provided research grants and accommodation in the beautiful surroundings of the 'auld grey toon'.

I am also indebted to my friends Clement Boden, Anna Crowe and Marilyn Pollard for their assistance in proof-reading the typescript and polishing up my sometimes rusty English grammar.

Finally, my thanks go to the Institute of Asian Research at the University of British Columbia, Vancouver, which offered me the position of Honorary Research Associate and excellent library facilities to allow me to complete revision of this work.

P.S.

INTRODUCTION

The Second World War was in a real sense partly a resumption of the First World War. Although it restored the balance of power for the time being, the Versailles Treaty did not remove, but only temporarily froze, the problems in the modern world. Within the Versailles Settlement there were three sets of tensions: between the great powers (the aggressive powers and the Western Powers), between the aggressive powers and the weak powers (victim nations and colonies), and between the Western Powers and the weak powers. In the 1930s, the aggressors' ambitions and expansionism not only threatened the survival of victim nations, but also challenged the Western Powers, which finally intensified tensions between the aggressors and the rest of the world, and led to the Second World War.

Versailles itself was ambivalent. On the one hand, it was a product of power politics: five victor powers (Britain, France, America, Italy and Japan) carved up the world at the Paris Peace Conference and utilised the Treaty to legalise their captured interests. However, after four years' bloody struggle, all the powers were exhausted and needed peace no matter what their motives were. The Treaty, therefore, created both principle and mechanism – the Covenant and the League – to maintain world peace. Recognising the victor powers as masters of the world, the League was also a deterrent against the future invasion of victim nations and colonies, which had progressive significance in history. However, given its ambivalence, power politics was the dominant aspect. Placing their own national interests above those of the League, the great powers consistently decided international affairs during the inter-war period, ignoring the rights of victim nations. They would follow the Covenant only when it was in accordance with their desires. This was the basic reason why the League did not work when it faced any challenge.

In the history of the inter-war period, 'the German problem' was the core. As a defeated Great Power but not a victim nation, Germany was seriously weakened by her former European partners. The Versailles Treaty deprived Germany of all her colonies. In Europe, Germany's eastern borders were pushed back, and the Rhineland was occupied by the Allied Army for fifteen years, becoming a demilitarised zone. German–Austrian union was permanently forbidden. According to the Treaty, she had to pay a large sum in reparations, and her army was reduced to 100,000. In addition, she was morally charged with 'war-guilt'. However, Germany had not been deprived of the military and economic potential of a great power: her army maintained a military backbone; the Ruhr, the industrial centre, was still in her hands, and reparations were never fully paid. Although Germany was forced to sign the Treaty, the Germans still resented the perceived injustice of their loss of empire, and wished to recover it.

Of the Great Powers, there were two countries – Italy and Japan – whose territorial demands had not been completely satisfied at the Paris Conference,[1] and they naturally took the German side due to their aggressive ambitions with regard to future adventures. These three were sometimes called the 'have-not' powers.

By contrast, the Western Powers, in particular the British and French Empires, which had grabbed vast colonial interests by invasion and expansion in the previous few centuries, reached their fullest extents by taking over German and Turkish colonies after the First World War. Chatfield, British First Sea Lord, said in 1934: 'We have got most of the world already, or the best parts of it, and we only want to keep what we have got and prevent others from taking it away from us.'[2]

For the Western Powers, the most serious threat came from their 'have-not' partners. One historian analysed this from an economic point of view:

> Much of the economic argument of the 'have-not' powers was understood in the west . . . There was an underlying assumption that Germany and Japan did have real economic claims which had to be respected, and that economic concessions in these areas would go far to eliminating the evident sense of grievance that both powers harboured towards the west.[3]

In general, due to their limited strength, it was not easy for the Western Powers to defend their world-wide interests, which were a little too much to handle. Lord Robert Vansittart, the Permanent Under-Secretary at the Foreign Office, wrote in his memo on 8 June 1935:

> I have long thought the distribution of this limited globe quite untenable, and quite unjustifiable. Like fools we made it far worse at Versailles. What has happened in regard to Japan; what is happening in regard to Italy; and what is about to happen in regard to Germany, should surely confirm this view to anyone with political antennae.[4]

Therefore, British policy-makers were ready to sacrifice weak powers or some of their own secondary interests to satisfy the aggressors as long as the latter did not jeopardise their vital interests. Chamberlain, the Prime Minister, expressed this view fully on 26 November 1937:

> I don't see why we shouldn't say to Germany, give us satisfactory assurances that you won't use force to deal with the Austrians and Czecho-Slovakians and we will give you similar assurances that we won't use force to prevent the changes you want if you can get them by peaceful means.[5]

As the representatives of an imperial power, top British leaders inherently understood and justified the ambitions and expansionism of the aggressors. Chamberlain thought that:

> they [the Germans] want to dominate Eastern Europe; they want as close a union with Austria as they can get, without incorporating her in the Reich, and they want much the same thing for the Sudeten Deutsch as we did for the Uitlanders in the Transvaal.[6]

Hoare, the Foreign Secretary, publicly declared during the Abyssinian crisis that the British Government sympathised with Italy's expansion in Abyssinia.[7] The senior officers in the Foreign Office (FO) found it difficult to persuade the Japanese not to increase their military forces in Shanghai in 1932 because the British had done a similar thing in 1927.[8] How could they possibly oppose the Japanese invasion of Manchuria when they themselves had cut Hong Kong off from China by force?

With no leg to stand on against the aggressors, Cabinet members and senior officers in the FO, in spite of personality differences, took the aggressors' side, with few exceptions, when they formulated foreign policy during the crises of the 1930s. In the autumn of 1937, Henderson, the British Ambassador in Berlin, suggested to Halifax, who was to visit Hitler in November, that Britain should somehow meet German demands in Austria and Czechoslovakia:

> Morally even we cannot deny the right of Germans living in large blocks on the German frontier to decide their own fate . . . We should, even if we don't like it, sympathise with German aspirations for unity, provided all change be based on the clearly established principle of self-determination.[9]

During his visit to Germany, Halifax told Hitler that Britain would not stop Germany from altering the map of Eastern Europe – for example, Danzig, Austria, Czechoslovakia – as long as this was achieved by peaceful means.[10] This accorded with Chamberlain's own line of thinking, as he made clear: 'What I wanted H[alifax] to do was to convince Hitler of our sincerity and to ascertain what objectives he had in mind . . .'[11] Eden greatly admired Halifax's visit too. He himself put forward a proposal to the Cabinet on 1 January 1938 that the British Government should offer Germany the colonies, and search in return for a general settlement.[12] Like his colleagues, he prevented Britain from being involved in a quarrel with Germany over Central and Eastern Europe by declaring that Britain was interested in that region without undertaking any military commitment. He believed that what a taxi driver said about the German occupation of the Rhineland represented public opinion: namely, that the Germans only went into their back garden.[13] He also had sympathy with the Sudeten Germans.

Among the staff of the FO, there was a strong tendency that was prepared to come to terms with Germany, allowing her to expand in Central and Eastern Europe. Vansittart, who was known for his anti-German standpoint, advocated this policy and proposed that they should 'come to terms with Germany at a price'.[14] His successor, Cadogan, offered the same recipe for Government policy-making, although his personal relation with Vansittart was strained. It was, despite a little exaggeration, described thus:

> Almost everyone, Conservatives, Liberals and Labour alike,
> regarded the French notion of keeping Germany permanently as a

second-class power as absurd, and agreed that the Versailles Treaty must be revised in Germany's favour.[15]

On the contrary, British policy-makers had no sympathy with victim nations. Simon (Foreign Secretary 1931–1935) often used the words 'wretched' or 'foolish' to describe the Chinese.[16] He blamed China for denying Japanese interests in Manchuria, which provoked the Japanese invasion. Hoare took the Abyssinians to be 'bad neighbours'. Henderson called the Czechs 'a pig-headed race', who, Chamberlain thought, 'were, in fact, themselves responsible for most of the trouble' during the Munich period.[17] It is apparent that due to her similar aggressive experience, Britain had an inherently intimate relationship with the aggressive powers, which made it impossible for her sincerely to take the victims' side, and help them in their struggle against invasion.

In addition, as leaders of a declining empire which had suffered a great sacrifice during the First World War, without exception, the three prime ministers in the 1930s had a fear of war.[18] All of them believed that Britain was not in a position – financially, economically or militarily – to fight. War would destroy British interests, or even the British Empire. In MacDonald's eyes, war with Japan over Manchuria 'was unthinkable', and even 'a strong protest might lead to war.'[19] Simon did not like the idea of a 'war to end war'. This argument was best explained by Lord Grey, one of the Vice-presidents of the League of Nations Union during the Manchurian crisis: 'I do not like the idea of resorting to war to prevent war . . . It is too much like lighting a large fire in order to prevent a smaller one.'[20] The crucial point of policy-making in Baldwin's Government was to exclude the country from any danger of war. Baldwin often repeated that Britain was not ready for war, and he would not allow the country to be involved in a war if there were 'even one chance in a hundred'. War to him was 'the most fearful terror and prostitution of man's knowledge that ever was known.' It 'could leave nothing in Europe at last but anarchy . . .'[21] Chamberlain was more afraid of war than anyone else, saying that war 'wins nothing, cures nothing, ends nothing', and in the last war there were 'the 7 million of young men who were cut off in their prime, the 13 million who were maimed and mutilated, the misery and the sufferings of the mothers or the fathers . . . in war there are no winners, but all are losers'.[22] Therefore, the top British leaders completely ruled out any possibility of checking aggressors by force.

In brief, due to her imperial nature and fear of war, Britain was more likely to take a standpoint closer to the aggressive powers than to the victim nations during the inter-war crises. This could be said to constitute the subjective root of appeasement.

On the other hand, the international and domestic situation after the First World War offered the background for appeasement. Although Wilson, the American President, was the principal founder of the League, the United States rejected membership, owing to her policy of isolationism. Without American participation, the security of world peace was greatly weakened. Russia, however, was completely excluded from the Settlement until 1934, when she was allowed to join the League. But even after that, her desire to co-operate in collective security was always misinterpreted and rejected by the Western world, particularly by the British Government.

It was apparent that Britain and France were the only great powers in a leading position in the League to maintain the Versailles Settlement. However, in spite of being a dominant power in the European Continent, France had become politically weak during the inter-war period because of internal confusion. She generally followed the British lead in diplomacy in the 1930s. The situation on the British side was not promising either. After the First World War, Britain was completely exhausted, and victory had cost the country her previous supremacy. During the war, total British casualties were about 2,400,000.[23] The war cost £10,000 million, and the National Debt mounted from £650 million (March 1914) to £7,434 million (March 1919).[24] What is more, this island empire, whose life largely relied on overseas trade, lost a great part of her international market. Her Dominions became more and more independent, and would no longer offer her open markets, nor supply her with raw materials as readily as before. Not only were British products challenged by those of Japan and America, but her naval supremacy no longer existed after the Washington Treaty of 1922, by which America gained equal footing with Britain.[25]

In comparison with Japan and America, British industrial production lagged far behind, and had not recovered to the 1913 level by 1927.[26] Yet only two years later, Britain dropped into the abyss of the 1929–32 Depression. During the inter-war period, the British Government was so preoccupied with the problems of a capitalist system – slums, strikes, unemployment and party struggle, etc. – that it had to focus on domestic issues rather than external ones, even though these were graver.

In 1931, Japan invaded Manchuria, becoming the source of war in the world. In 1933, after he came to power in Germany, Hitler immediately announced that Germany withdrew from the Disarmament Conference as well as from the League. In 1935, he openly violated the terms of Versailles by declaring conscription. In 1936, he sent troops to the Rhineland, and in the same year, Italy conquered Abyssinia. Soon, the three aggressors came to conclude their Axis agreement according to their joint ambitions.

The shift in the balance of power not only threatened world peace, but also challenged the British Empire, which had owned vast overseas trade and global colonial interests. However, with her decline, Britain considered only Western Europe as the vital interest she had to insure. In the face of the disturbance in the Far East, the Mediterranean and Europe, the policy-makers would rather make concessions by sacrificing victim nations in order to seek a new settlement with the aggressors. Appeasement was the policy which emerged to meet this requirement.

A brief review of history is necessary. At the time the Japanese invaded Manchuria, Britain was suffering from the abandonment of the Gold Standard. The Labour Government had resigned, and the National Government had recently been formed under the premiership of MacDonald. His defence theory was: 'that arms gave only a false security, that the surest guarantee against aggression was the force of world opinion, that Government should stop worrying about the risks of war and start running risks for peace.'[27] Now the Chiefs of Staff, due to the Far Eastern crisis, warned the Government that 'The Ten Year Rule'[28] was too optimistic and ignored the danger of the situation. With support from the FO, the Chiefs of Staff suggested that rearmament should be put on the agenda. However, when the Cabinet considered their reports, ministers argued that 'acceptance of the Chiefs of Staff report must not be taken to justify increased expenditure on defence without regard to the very serious financial and economic situation.'[29] Until early 1934, MacDonald still wanted to keep his policy of disarmament, although he had reluctantly come to the conclusion that rearmament might be necessary.[30]

Realising that German rearmament was a threat to British as well as European peace, Chamberlain, then Chancellor of the Exchequer, initiated the first expansion of the Air Force in 1934. However, in June he reduced expenditure over five years from the £76 million suggested by the Defence Requirements Committee (DRC) to £50 million because he 'was merely advocating the cheapest way of defence, instead of the best', as he explained later:

> If we were now to follow Winston's advice and sacrifice our commerce to the manufacture of arms, we should inflict a certain injury on our trade from which it would take generations to recover, we should destroy the confidence which now happily exists, and we should cripple the revenue.[31]

MacDonald fully supported his Chancellor's wish to cut down defence expenditure, as minuted:

> He was in entire agreement with the Chancellor of the Exchequer from the financial point of view . . . The whole question had to be considered in the light of the national income and the commitments which would have to be faced . . . The Service Departments must understand that it was not possible to contemplate the bill in full which the General Staff put forward. It was the duty of the General Staff to inform the Cabinet as to the maximum risk and it was the Cabinet's duty to reduce the expenditure involved in accordance with the political situation; and it was the duty of the Chancellor and the Treasury to incur no expenditure which could not reasonably or even possibly be met.[32]

During the election of 1935, Baldwin, the Prime Minister, declared: 'I give you my word that there will be no great armaments.'[33] Until the Spring of 1938, the British policy on rearmament was still 'business as usual', meaning that rearmament had to give way to normal industry and trade. It is therefore no surprise that British rearmament in the 1930s lagged far behind Germany's.

Due to the military weakness caused by the Government's defence policy, the Chiefs of Staff, when asked by the Cabinet about the risk of war, consistently warned that Britain was not ready to be involved in war. (What else could they possibly say?) These warnings were used by the Government as evidence to support and justify their concessions to the dictators. The appeasers repeated that they had to appease the aggressors because the Chiefs of Staff warned that Britain's military force was too weak to fight. In the face of the grave situation created by their own policy, British policy-makers came to a strategic conclusion: Britain could not fight against Germany, Italy and Japan simultaneously, with Germany being the principal enemy. On the other hand, the Government never made any real effort to co-operate with its potential allies. For instance, it never fully backed up France when the latter was prepared to resist German expansion. Because of her strategic position, France placed more emphasis on her allies in Eastern Europe, and was prepared to fight for them if she could rely on British assistance, whereas Britain did not consider Central and Eastern Europe as her vital interests, and hesitated to undertake any new commitments. Moreover, the British Government was afraid that France might go too far and prevent a settlement with Germany. Nor did it whole-heartedly seek co-operation with the United States, as both sides were reluctant to take responsibility in an arrangement against aggression. The British Government particularly feared that co-operation with America would offend Japan and cut across its efforts to improve relations with Italy and Germany. Nor did it sincerely win over assistance from Russia, due to its underestimation of Soviet forces, and a hatred and fear of communism.[34] In fact, it perhaps hated communism even more than Nazism. Baldwin told the Cabinet after Hitler's re-occupation of the Rhineland that the French 'might succeed in crushing Germany with the aid of Russia, but it would probably only result in Germany going Bolshevik.'[35] 'If there is any fighting to be done,' he said to Churchill, 'I should like to see the Bolsheviks and the Nazis doing it.'[36] Chamberlain shared the same attitude, as his Private Secretary Douglas-Home recalled in 1962:

> Chamberlain, like many others, saw Communism as the major long-term danger. He hated Hitler and German Fascism, but he felt that Europe in general and Britain in particular were in even greater danger from Communism.[37]

Being on her guard against the Soviets, Britain was unable to take a firm stand against Germany. Without Russian back-up, the small countries in Central and Eastern Europe, which had been restored or newly created by the Treaty, were widely open to German invasion. Above all, Britain never organised collective security against aggressions in the League, because she was afraid that it would be provocative to the aggressors, who would damage British interests all over the world – interests that Britain had no power to defend. All this further weakened Britain herself and her potential allies, while Germany, Italy and Japan strengthened their Axis.

Under these circumstances, the British Government turned to a conciliatory policy – appeasement – to avoid the challenge. Based on their own assumption, which had never been proved by any substantial evidence, the appeasers believed that Hitler's ambitions were limited. After the Rhineland crisis, the Cabinet maintained its decision that it would search for a settlement with Germany as soon as possible by making concessions. If this settlement could be reached, diplomacy would remove the heavy burden from the national finances, and even disarmament could be expected. Therefore, in the Government's view, appeasement would not only save money, but also save Britain from being challenged.

However, it is a misunderstanding to claim that rearmament was in any case contradictory to appeasement. As a policy, which, in theory, was one of concession but not surrender, appeasement required rearmament to a certain extent for support. Being closely inter-related, appeasement and rearmament offered a premise to each other: appeasement could reduce the financial burden of rearmament, and limited rearmament could enforce the position when concessions were sought. Chamberlain told the Cabinet: 'In our foreign policy we were doing our best to drive two horses abreast, conciliation and rearmament. It was a very nice art to keep these two steeds in step.'[38] This explains why, while British expenditure on rearmament continued to increase slowly from 1934 to 1939, appeasement was a parallel policy, which was brought to a climax.

In short, Britain's economic, political and military decline gave her no confidence in facing the challenge from the 'have-not' powers. She would rather calm them down by paying them a price than check them by coercive means. This could be described as the objective root of appeasement.

In spite of these factors, appeasement was not inevitable because there were practical alternatives, proposed by the Opposition, which were open to the Government. In the 1930s, the Opposition in the House consisted of the Labour Party, Liberal Party and some Conservative dissidents such as Churchill, Eden (after his resignation), Amery and Cecil (Leader of the League of Nations Union). However, opposition to the Government did not necessarily mean opposition to appeasement. For instance, although they sometimes delivered mild criticism, Amery and Eden were generally in agreement with Government foreign policy, and the latter, in particular, supported the Munich initiative.[39]

In other Opposition quarters, the Labour Party advocated the policy of supporting the League and using coercive measures – economic sanctions backed up by military force – against the aggressor. It voted for armaments for 'collective security', though it opposed increasing expenditure for national defence.[40] The Liberals held similar ground. In fact, they co-operated with Labour over most issues of foreign affairs.[41] The League and collective security were also emphasised by Cecil, who was one of the founders of the League. He had seriously criticised the Government's concessions to the aggressors since 1931; however, he did not give very much thought to the alternative course, perhaps because he 'did not, indeed, foresee what a terrible price' they had to pay for appeasement.[42] The most outstanding anti-appeaser in Parliament, however, was Winston Churchill, who proposed both rearmament and collective security action under the League. In November 1936, he appealed for Britain and France, due to their military inferiority to Germany, to 'gather round them all the elements of collective security or . . . combined defensive strength against aggression' under the League.[43] In 1938, he went even further, proposing a 'Grand Alliance' as a deterrent against the German invasion of Czechoslovakia. Despite his anti-communist standpoint, he emphasised the importance of an alliance with Russia.

The weakness of the Opposition had two aspects. First, there were some flaws in their own proposals. For example, Labour and the Liberals opposed rearmament, and they did not press the Government to take action during the Rhineland crisis, although Attlee warned: 'No sympathy for the injustices inflicted on the German people by the Versailles Treaty should blind us to the true nature of the act of the German Government.'[44] Attlee also supported Chamberlain's going to Munich, on condition that 'every member of this House is desirous of neglecting no chance of preserving the peace without sacrificing principles'.[45] Second, although they were loosely connected, the Opposition did not form a solid coalition, and sometimes failed to act jointly in imposing pressure on the Government.[46] In addition, there existed serious divergence between them over some issues. For example, in 1934, the Liberal Leader, Herbert Samuel, sharply criticised Churchill's proposal of increasing the Air Force as 'the language of a Malay running amok . . . the language of blind and causeless panic'.[47] This further weakened their own position.

Among the public, there was loud support for taking a firm stand against the aggressor during the Manchurian crisis. In the Peace Ballot of 1935, there were five questions about peace and war. The result of the 11,559,165-vote poll showed that the majority of the people preferred checking aggression by military and non-military measures.[48] Shortly before the Anschluss, three polls were organised by the British Institute of Public Opinion to test the public's attitude towards the Government's foreign policy. Replies to the question. 'Do you favour Mr. Chamberlain's foreign policy?' were recorded as: Yes 26%, No 58%, No opinion 16%.[49] During the Munich period, Halifax realised, when he telegraphed Chamberlain on 23 September, that 'great mass of public opinion seems to be hardening in sense of feeling that we have gone to limit of concession'.[50] After Munich, in an opinion poll of February 1939, only 28% felt that Chamberlain's policy would work.[51] On the other hand, there was a groundswell in favour of appeasement in the 1930s. However, this has been unduly exaggerated in the past because, according to substantial evidence, it was, to a great extent, engineered by the Government, using various means.[52]

Generally speaking, public opinion in the 1930s was varied, and because of this, it did not exert great enough pressure to alter the conciliatory course the British Government adopted. However, the blame should not be placed on the public, because policy-making was the Government's job. Although the proposals of the Opposition were not perfect, their direction was right. If the policy-makers had listened to and taken on board the correct points, British foreign policy might have pursued a better course. In other words, if the Government had fully co-operated with France, America and Russia, and effectively organised collective security under the League, Britain would have been stronger than her enemies, in spite of her military weakness. The aggressors could have been checked one by one, which would have ruled out the risk of facing three enemies simultaneously. Alternatively, if the Government had speeded up rearmament as quickly as possible, with the sacrifice of some economic benefit, Britain would not have suffered so greatly in the first stages of the Second World War, even if the aggressors had not been checked.

However, all this pressure and criticism had little influence on policy-making. The top British leaders chose appeasement, and insisted on it for almost ten years, even though their policy suffered setbacks time after time. Apart from the roots of appeasement that have been discussed above, the explanation can be found in the following observations.

First, the policy-makers had never really listened to opposing views. MacDonald disliked 'admitting his ignorance of a problem even to the expert'. Baldwin, seeming to rely largely on experts, 'was in reality a dictator. His personality was very strong and almost irresistible.'[53] Chamberlain was unfortunately more stubborn and of a closed mind. He said: 'I am completely convinced that the course I am taking is right and therefore cannot be influenced by the attacks of my critics.'[54] He always felt superior to others, although he knew very little about foreign policy. He liked a 'yes-men' Cabinet, and got it after the resignations of Eden and Cooper. Under his long premiership, he and his closest ministers formed the Inner Cabinet and the Foreign Policy Committee to determine policy. This small circle of politicians turned a deaf ear to any criticism and suggestions from Churchill, the Labour leaders and other critics. They even treated information from secret sources in the same way.[55] Not only did Chamberlain ignore any criticism from outsiders, but he also rejected dissenting views from other ministers. If any or most Cabinet members did not agree with him, Chamberlain would, as he did during Munich, insist on his own course without consulting the others. His colleagues, including Halifax and Hoare, did not oppose him to the extent of resignation because they agreed in principle with appeasement. Any divergence between them and their Prime Minister was only technical. They themselves, like Chamberlain, preferred to listen to what they wanted to hear, no matter whether it was correct or not. Therefore, Henderson's advice, in spite of misleading the Government, was generally welcome, and Wilson, who knew nothing about diplomacy, became Chamberlain's confidential adviser (Halifax also found him useful). As a part of the policy-making mechanism, the FO usually formulated several different proposals to the Cabinet, among which only those along the line of appeasement would be chosen. As for proposals, which might not meet with Cabinet approval, they would be suppressed or abandoned at an early stage of policy-making within the FO. In addition, the FO was only able to *advise* the course: it had no power to compel the Cabinet to accept what it recommended. After all, most senior officers were quite happy with a policy of coming to terms with the aggressors, although sometimes they felt their superiors went too far. The position of the Chiefs of Staff, however, was worse than that of the FO because they could not be sure how much of their advice would be taken into account during policy-making. Their duty, as MacDonald stipulated, was 'to inform the Cabinet as to the maximum risk'.[56] In other words, policy-making was not their business. Strictly guided by the instructions of the Cabinet, they had to investigate the situation from the angle ministers required. Their advice, therefore, generally accorded with their superiors' desires. For example, based on the Government's policy of slow rearmament, they could only advise that Britain was not ready to fight. If they expressed a different opinion (which sometimes they did – for example they suggested accelerating rearmament, and warned about the deterrent value of the Rhineland and the importance of an alliance with Russia), their proposals would be put aside or revised according to the Cabinet's will. Under these circumstances, it was impossible for the appeasers to change their way of thinking.

Second, there was not a single anti-appeaser in the Cabinet in the 1930s. Eden and Duff Cooper were supposed to be anti-appeasers.[57] However, from the Government's documents, it can be clearly shown that Eden was not an anti-appeaser – on the contrary, he was one of the most important founders of appeasement towards Germany, because it was he who formulated the basis for appeasement during the Rhineland crisis while Baldwin was not very interested in diplomacy. Although he had some disagreements with Chamberlain over the issues of Italy and of co-operation with America, Eden shared completely the Prime Minister's views on Germany. Cooper resigned because of mobilisation on the eve of Munich, but he had gone along with the Prime Minister all the way to Munich, although he had sometimes voiced different views. While Halifax and Hoare also sometimes told Chamberlain of their divergence, they co-operated with the Prime Minister quite happily in spite of their differences of opinion, and all the decisions were made with complete agreement from them.[58] Therefore, the divergence between Chamberlain and the principal ministers was between appeasers, not between appeasers and anti-appeasers. It was impossible for a Cabinet composed of appeasers to abandon its own policy.

Third, involvement in the process of pursuing appeasement was a vicious circle:

1   Leaving Japan unchecked in the Far East made it difficult for Britain to concentrate on Europe, which was one of the rationales for European appeasement. On the other hand, in order to come to terms with Germany and Italy, she had to appease Japan further, which, in return, required her to make more concessions in Europe.

2   Policy-makers, against advice from the Chiefs of Staff about the

deterrent value of the Rhineland, acquiesced in Hitler's re-occupation of the Rhineland, and then found that there was nothing they could do to prevent the *Anschluss* because deterrence had been taken away. However, due to their failure to act during the *Anschluss*, they put themselves in a more embarrassing position when they faced the possible German invasion in Czechoslovakia, because Germany, after her successful annexation of Austria, had surrounded Czechoslovakia on three sides. Because of this, the appeasers could more easily justify meeting Hitler's demands at Munich.

3   Appeasement was based on the idea that Britain was militarily and economically weak, and she should not undertake any new commitments. However, this policy caused dissension and discord between Britain and her potential allies: America became more isolated because she felt Britain let her down in the Manchurian crisis. Russia was finally disappointed by Britain, and signed the Soviet–German Pact in 1939 for her own safety. Belgium broke away from the Locarno system. As for the Central and East European countries, some of them had been sold out by Britain, some of them had become Germany's satellite states. This left Britain and France no reliable ally in the East except Poland, which was crushed immediately by Hitler's blitz ('lightning war'). The result of appeasement was not to strengthen Britain, but to make her weaker, which convinced the appeasers that further concessions were the only possible way to hold the situation.

4   Appeasement aimed to reduce the rearmament burden on the national finances. However, the deteriorating situation required increasing expenditure on defence. Slow increases in rearmament were unable to meet the fast-increasing challenge. In order to minimise the danger, the appeasers were in a greater hurry to turn to appeasement. Being caught in this vicious circle, the Government followed the road of appeasement further and further, until war broke out.

In addition, the top British leaders were unaware of the nature of the German Nazis, Italian fascists and Japanese militarists, who were a new phenomenon in modern history. As Thorne put it:

Few of the leading appeasers spoke German or had much knowledge of European history. Few – even Halifax who had at least read History at Oxford – had studied *Mein Kampf*. Many in Britain found it hard to credit that Nazism could be quite as appalling as its enemies declared it to be; it was a movement quite beyond the comprehension of men like Baldwin or Halifax, or those who . . . were experienced in Commonwealth spheres rather than nearer home.[59]

Baldwin confessed that he felt it very difficult to judge Hitler: 'We none of us know what is going on in that strange man's mind.' 'He had never been able to find anyone who could give him really reliable information about Hitler's character and designs.'[60] Chamberlain never believed that Hitler would fight for that 10 per cent if he could be offered 90 per cent of what he wanted. All this blinded the appeasers when they were figuring out the policy.

Appeasement is one of the most controversial subjects in the study of history and international relations. According to the dictionary, it means: 'A policy of making concessions to a potential aggressor in order preserve peace, *spec.* a policy pursued by Britain towards Germany prior to the outbreak of war in 1939.'[61] Most Western historians believe that appeasement started either in 1933, when Hitler came to power, or in 1937, when Chamberlain took over.[62] Some of them trace its roots back to the years of the First World War, or even earlier, to 1854–6, during the Crimean War. At that time, 'the term "appeasement", a good honest word which made its way into modern English from the old French, means the act of soothing or satisfying,' and it is said that this positive meaning was kept until the end of 1938.[63]

Many politicians and scholars are critical of this policy because it encouraged the aggressors in their adventure, which finally led to the Second World War.[64] Since 'Munich' in 1938 represented a climax of 'appeasement', these two terms are often used interchangeably in criticism. Churchill, a principal anti-appeaser in the 1930s, pointed out: '"Appeasement" in all its forms only encouraged their aggression and gave the Dictators more power' . . . 'One of the unhappy consequences of our appeasement policy . . . had been to convince him [Hitler] that neither we nor France were capable of fighting a war.'[65] Attlee, Leader of the Labour Party, condemned appeasement in 1937 when he said: 'the policy of this Government throughout, right on from 1931, had always been to try and appease the aggressors by the sacrifice of weaker States, but the more you yield to the aggressor the greater his appetite'.[66] Many historians considered 'appeasement' and 'Munich' as 'pejorative' words, referring to a policy of 'feckless, cowardly, and counterproductive yielding'.[67] Namier condemns: 'At several junctures it could have been stopped without excessive effort or sacrifice, but . . . appeasers aided Hitler's work.'[68] The denunciation from Margaret George is also very sharp:

> In even the Tory view of the matter there is broad consensus that British foreign policy in the 1930's was an unqualified disaster. Led by the government of Stanley Baldwin and Neville Chamberlain, the British nation pursued the will-o'-the-wisp of peace with Fascism, peace at any price, peace – as one Conservative put it – 'at any cost in humiliation' . . . Britain had lost not only the great goal of peace but in judgment of the world, and in the shamed awareness of her own citizens, she had lost an incalculable amount of prestige and respect.[69]

Appeasement was not only criticised by Western scholars, but also by historians of the former Soviet Union and of China. Apart from general criticism, the Soviets thought that the appeasers deliberately incited Germany and Japan to invade the USSR.[70] Chinese scholars have explored how a weak power could have prevented her own interests from being betrayed by the great powers who adopted appeasement. One of their observations is that a weak power, if she decided to defend her independence, should rely on its own people. While accepting aid from Western Powers, she must not put her destiny into their hands.

Another school of commentators holds an ambivalent attitude, maintaining that appeasement was wrong and ineffective on one hand, and searching for justification for it on the other. Parker analysed:

> Chamberlainite appeasement, it is true, was not a feeble policy of surrender and unlimited retreat . . . His policy meant intervention in continental Europe to induce Hitler's Germany to insist only on expansion so limited that it would not threaten the safety or independence of the United Kingdom. In retrospect this appears a bold, venturesome policy, certain, given the ambitions of Hitler, to lead to an Anglo-German war.

However, he concludes:

> the balance of evidence points to counter-revisionist interpretations. Led by Chamberlain, the government rejected effective deterrence.

Chamberlain's powerful, obstinate personality and his skill in debate probably stifled serious chances of preventing the Second World War.[71]

Nevertheless, appeasers and their supporters, sparing no effort, defend the policy. Their major viewpoints can be listed as follows:

Argument 1: 'The peace of Versailles lacked moral validity from the start.' A.J.P. Taylor comments: 'This was obviously true in regard to the Germans.' Some scholars share, or imply agreement with, this view on the grounds that the harshness of the Versailles Treaty, including 'war-guilt', was unfairly and unequally forced upon Germany, which disturbed the conscience of the British politicians and the public. They justify appeasement because it 'was based nevertheless upon a single premise, national self-determination.' Therefore, Versailles had to be revised in favour of the German side: 'If Germany could be appeased by revision, Europe might yet avoid the chaos.'[72]

Argument 2: Chamberlain's pursuit of appeasement 'in radically different, unsuitable circumstances, may have been the fault of his judgement, but it was certainly not the fault of his intentions. His aim was to preserve peace in Europe. It was an honourable quest.' 'It was Christian to love one's neighbour, and sound business to encourage his prosperity,'[73] Eubank argued, 'For Chamberlain practised appeasement, not out of cowardice or fear, but out of a positive belief that appeasement would open the way to peace for all.'[74]

Argument 3: At odds with the orthodox view that appeasers and their policy were cowardly, stupid, humiliating and shortsighted, some scholars argue that Chamberlain 'was a cultivated, highly intelligent, hard-working statesman'. Appeasement 'was never an apologetic, shy or shameful creed.'[75]

Argument 4: Appeasement is generally accepted as 'the nadir of British weakness', and as 'an inevitable consequence of the British predicament, a realistic attempt to hold the dictators at bay in Europe'.[76] It 'had never meant peace at any price, but the acceptance of limited German advances'.[77]

Argument 5: Munich postponed war and allowed time for rearmament.[78]

Argument 6: Related to the arguments above, appeasement was supported by majority of people in the 1930s, as Hoare argued:

Appeasement did not mean surrender, nor was it a policy only to be used towards the dictators. To Chamberlain it meant the methodical removal of the principal causes of friction in the world. The policy seemed so reasonable that he could not believe that even Hitler would repudiate it.

Appeasement was not his personal policy. Not only was it supported by his colleagues; it expressed the general desire of the British people. This is a fundamental consideration in judging his action.[79]

Argument 7: This is represented by A.J.P. Taylor's approval of Munich:

The settlement at Munich was a triumph for British policy, which had worked precisely to this end; not a triumph for Hitler . . . Nor was it merely a triumph for selfish or cynical British statesman . . . It was a triumph for all that was best and most enlightened in British life; a triumph for those who had preached equal justice between peoples; a triumph for those who had courageously denounced the harshness and short-sightedness of Versailles.

He explains in his 'Second Thought' in *The Origins of the Second World War*:

In 1938 Czechoslovakia was betrayed. In 1939 Poland was saved. Less than one hundred thousand Czechs died during the war. Six and half million Poles were killed. Which was better – to be a betrayed Czech or a saved Pole?[80]

This book will explore whether these arguments hold any water or not. However, further discussion of these points will be left to the Conclusion, after the whole process of appeasement in the 1930s has been reviewed.

Although a huge number of books have been published on the subject in the past few decades, research on appeasement is far from complete. The main shortcoming is twofold. First, Western scholars have a tendency to consider appeasement only as a policy in Europe, rather than a global one. In their studies, few have linked British Far Eastern policy with general appeasement. Since British foreign policy towards Germany, Italy and Japan was an organic whole, neglect of Far Eastern policy in the study of general appeasement results in a one-sided understanding, which makes it impossible to see the whole picture. Second, the previous studies focus mainly on what appeasement is, and when and why it happened. Few describe *how* it was conducted. The author believes that without a thorough survey of the policy-making process, the nature and development of appeasement cannot be fully explored.

In this book, we will first examine the Manchurian crisis, which, in the author's opinion, was the starting point of appeasement on the grounds that:

1 British foreign policy towards the Far East and Europe was an organic whole; as Eden said: 'I did not regard Europe and the Far East as separate problems.'[81] Far Eastern appeasement was in fact one of the fundamental reasons for European appeasement.
2 Japan was the first aggressor in the Far East, and her ambition was nursed by this conciliatory policy. From Manchuria to the outbreak of war, British policy-making followed the same line. There was no fundamental difference between the underlying assumptions of policy towards Japan and that towards European aggressors.
3 The Japanese invasion of China set an example for Mussolini and Hitler. The 1931 crisis was the beginning of the collapse of the League and the prologue to the Second World War.

Based largely on both published and unpublished documents, which are quoted verbatim, this book concentrates on the main process of appeasement within the British Government from 1931 to 1939, setting out a step-by-step survey of policy-formation in the FO and policy decision-making in the Cabinet with the purpose of pin-pointing the origin, evolution and nature of appeasement, the principal policy-makers' viewpoints and activities in policy-formulating and their responsibility for encouraging the aggressive powers and making the Second World War inevitable. The book also studies relations between Britain and other countries such as France, America and the Soviet Union, to explore why their co-operation against aggression resulted in failure.

In addition, the study of public opinion investigates how the Government misled the public and put fetters on the media in order to create a favourable atmosphere for pursuing appeasement. It also points out that there was a big gap between public opinion and policy-making, because throughout the FO and Cabinet documents, there is little evidence to suggest that ministers seriously considered outside opinion. It is understood that the policy was decided by a small political circle, which was almost totally isolated from public opinion, and in particular from those views which opposed the Government's.

Appeasement was an imperial policy for resettling the world between the great powers. It aimed to insure British vital interests while the British Empire was declining, by sacrificing victim nations, acquiescing in invasion or bargaining with aggressive powers so as to reach settlement. Based on imperialist moral standards and political thought, it employed the rule of 'fair play' – equality and justice to Germany and other 'have-not' powers – but this was not applicable to victim nations and colonies, just as freedom in the ancient Roman Empire was the prerogative of its citizens, but not of its slaves. Although this policy was, in the appeasers' eyes, very realistic and reasonable, appeasement failed to achieve any of its aims: settlement with the aggressors, avoidance of war, and separation of Japan, Italy and Germany.

The appeasers must be held partly responsible for the Second World War because their policy encouraged and strengthened the aggressive powers. Although the aggressors' ambitions and expansion were the factors that led directly to the war, these could not have borne fruit without certain conditions. Hitler could not strike before 1935 because German rearmament had only just started. He would not consider taking the risk of war with the Western Powers during the period of the Rhineland on the grounds that Germany was not strong enough to contend with Britain and France. If he had started war in unfavourable conditions, then he would have been defeated sooner and more easily. In other words, without the favourable conditions that were created by appeasement, Hitler might not have successfully launched the Second World War. It is therefore no exaggeration to say that the aggressors' ambitions and expansion, with the help of appeasement, made the Second World War inevitable.

CHALLENGE FROM THE FAR EAST

THE MANCHURIAN INCIDENT AND THE SINO–JAPANESE WAR

Japanese ambitions in China could be traced back to the late nineteenth century. After defeating Russia in the Russo–Japanese War of 1904–5, Japan replaced Russia's dominant role in Manchuria. On 1 January 1915, the Japanese envoy delivered to Yuan Shi-kai, the Chinese President, 'twenty-one demands', which attempted to build up Japanese supremacy in the whole of China. After the mid-1920s, key military officers such as Ishiwara, Nagata, Itagaki and Imamura frequently exchanged views on future territorial designs in Manchuria. By the Autumn of 1930, the Japanese Chiefs of Staff had worked out three alternatives for their Manchurian adventure:

1   to press the local authority headed by Chang Hsueh-liang to concede more rights to Japan;
2   if this failed, the replacement of Chang by a pro-Japanese regime was to be arranged;
3   the final resort was to occupy Manchuria by military operation.

The Kwantung Army took the liberty of carrying out the third plan in September 1931, although the Tokyo Government's decision to act was not officially announced until 1932.[1]

On the night of 18 September 1931, Japanese troops guarding the South Manchurian Railway suddenly attacked Mukden according to 'a carefully prepared plan', using as an excuse the blowing up of a section of the railway, an incident for which it is believed they themselves were responsible.[2] Three days later, China appealed to the League Council under Article 11 of the Covenant. Having discussed the appeal, the Council reached a decision on 30 September that requested both the Japanese and Chinese 'to do all in their power to hasten the restoration of normal relations between them'.[3] On one hand, Japan declared that she had no territorial ambition in China and would withdraw her troops into the railway zone as soon as possible; but on the other hand, she hastened the military operation and occupied the whole of Manchuria by the beginning of 1932. Due to the good offices of the Western Powers, the two disputants started negotiations in February 1933, and signed the Tang Ku Armistice in May which temporarily relieved tension in the Far East, but left the problem unresolved. However, occupation of Manchuria did not satisfy Japan's appetite, and she went further to prepare for total war against China.

On 7 July 1937, Japanese troops initiated the offensive against the 29th Chinese Army garrisoned at Lukouchiao near Peking, which marked the outbreak of the Sino-Japanese War. By the end of 1938, the Japanese controlled a large part of North China and the Yangtze Valley, including many principal cities such as Peking, Tientsin, Shanghai, Hankow, Canton and Nanking (the capital). However, the Chinese never gave up resistance. They moved the capital to Chungking, continuing to fight the Japanese with little help from the Western Powers. It was clear by September 1939 that the war would not bring Japan an easy victory, but exhaustion instead.

During the inter-war period, the Manchurian crisis was the first fundamental challenge to the Versailles Settlement, and the first major test of the League of Nations. If it was the prologue to the Second World War, then the following Sino–Japanese War was the pre-trial of strength between the Axis and the Allies. Since it emerged in 1931, not only had the Far Eastern challenge jeopardised vast British interests in China, but also pushed British policy-making further and further into a blind alley.

Although there has been considerable study into this subject, the nature of British Far Eastern policy has not yet been fully explored. Several arguments have been put forward. First, that British Far Eastern policy was not appeasement, on the grounds that Britain 'made no "Munich agreement" in the Far East', buying off an aggressor 'at the sacrifice of principle'. The policy was that 'Japan somehow had to be accommodated, but at the same time stopped.'[4] The second argument denies that there exists a fundamental relationship between

Far Eastern and European crises, because the Manchurian crisis did not 'cause' Mussolini's conquest of Abyssinia and Hitler's adventures in Europe. The Manchurian incident was 'far away', it 'did not endanger the peace of Europe'.[5] 'Clearly there were links between the situation in Europe and that in the Far East' A.J.P. Taylor says, and then asks: 'but what were they?'[6] This chapter will analyse British Far Eastern policy-making in the 1930s in order to address the above arguments.

THE IMPORTANT BRITISH POLICY-MAKERS IN THE MANCHURIAN EPISODE

In the First National Government formed in 1931, MacDonald, as 'a bookish Premier', was aloof from his colleagues, 'sensitive to unfriendly critics' and 'shrank from exposing his whole mind'. His arrogance was such that he 'disliked admitting his ignorance of a problem even to the expert'. At the same time, he was realistic enough to only want 'to achieve what was practical'.[7] In the Cabinet, he inspired loyalty from his colleagues, although his suspicious nature never allowed him complete trust in them.[8] He relied heavily on Baldwin[9] 'to deal with the economic crisis', and the latter, being in accord with MacDonald on foreign affairs, once said to Thomas Jones[10] that 'he dislikes the Chinese'.[11]

Drawing on his considerable knowledge and skill in foreign affairs, the Prime Minister usually 'used his prerogative of diplomatic intervention freely'. As for the Far Eastern crisis, he thought it was 'unthinkable' to have a war against Japan, and approved of Anglo-Japanese *rapprochement*, though he laid stress on Anglo-American relations.[12]

However, his third premiership since 1931 had been 'a sad diminuendo of failing powers, ebbing authority and gathering derision', partly because of a decline in his health. 'He was already a tired man' with a worsening eye problem that accelerated his failure.[13] At the beginning of the crisis, he gave hardly any precise instructions to the British Delegates to the League, so they did not know what line should be adopted to handle the matter.[14] When the Japanese created the Shanghai incident in early 1932, MacDonald's eye operation kept him away from office for six weeks, although he still supervised foreign policy.[15]

His appointment of Simon as Foreign Secretary surprised many because Simon's 'contacts hitherto had been mostly with the domestic side of the policy'. The decision was made due to 'party exigencies'.[16] From the Cabinet minutes, it seems that he usually took his Foreign

Secretary's advice, although there had been 'fierce disagreements' between them in earlier years.[17]

Simon was a shy and hesitant man.[18] He showed great intelligence when he analysed complicated problems, but he lacked a decisive manner in handling them. Chamberlain and Eden made similar comments on his personality and capability. The former said Simon: 'can always make an admirable speech in the House, to a brief, but . . . the fact is that his manner inspires no confidence, and that he seems temperamentally unable to make up his mind to action when a difficult situation arises'.[19] Although he was not highly admired by his colleagues, Simon never criticised them in his memoirs. Perhaps because of his tact, he got along very well with three prime ministers in the 1930s, and after 1935, when he was not in charge of the FO, he continued to exert his influence on diplomacy as one of the 'Big Four' in the Cabinet,[20] who were dominant in foreign policy-making. During the Manchurian crisis, Simon played a very important part in shaping foreign policy. Like many of his colleagues, he disliked the Chinese, often referring to them as 'wretched' or 'foolish'.[21] He clearly showed his standpoint towards the Sino–Japanese dispute:

> although Japan has undoubtedly acted in a way contrary to the principles of the Covenant . . . This is not a case in which the armed forces of one country have crossed the frontiers of another in circumstances where they had no previous right to be on the other's soil.[22]

At ministerial level, Chamberlain, Eden, Halifax and Cadogan were also crucial conductors of Far Eastern policy, particularly after the beginning of the Sino–Japanese War. Their respective positions on general policy-making will be discussed in the following chapters.

In the Foreign Office, Lord Robert Vansittart, the Permanent Under-Secretary, was one of the most important members, whom Simon generally relied on.[23] His role in policy-making will be explored throughout the following chapters. Regarding to the Far Eastern crisis, Vansittart thought: 'the Chinese had been asking for trouble, and they got it'.[24] In his opinion, Britain was 'incapable of checking Japan in any way' unless America was 'eventually prepared to use force'.[25] As a senior member of the Defence Requirements Committee, he was in a key position to formulate the basis for the Government's policy of accommodation with Japan.

Other officials in the FO, such as Wellesley, the Deputy Under-Secretary, Pratt, the Chief Adviser to the Far Eastern Department, and Orde, Head of the Far Eastern Department, also played an important role in policy-making. All of them justified the Japanese aggression.[26] In addition, some influence on policy-making came from diplomats such as Lord Cecil, the Chief British Delegate to the Council of the League; Drummond, Secretary-General of the League; Lindley and Craigie, the British Ambassadors in Tokyo; Lampson, Minister in Peking, and Lindsay, the British Ambassador in Washington. They reported first-hand information together with their advice to the FO, and put the instructions from the Government into action.

In the early 1930s, British foreign policy was usually set out by the FO and decided by the Cabinet. During the Manchurian crisis, the Cabinet made its decisions generally based on the suggestions from the FO, since it was distracted by domestic problems. Even in the late 1930s, when the Cabinet and its Foreign Policy Committee took over most policy-making towards Europe, the FO was still the key formulator of Far Eastern policy.

THE MANCHURIAN CRISIS
First Phase: September 1931–January 1932

British Policy-making

When the incident occurred, Britain was deep in the economical depression of 1929–32. She was forced off the Gold Standard in 1931, and the number of unemployed steadily increased: 2.5 million by the end of 1930, 2.7 million by the middle of 1931, growing to 3 million in early 1933. Both richer and poorer classes were not very much concerned about the Far Eastern crisis.[27] Although the press revealed some conflicting views, only after the General Election in November did the issue attract more attention from the editorial comments of the principal newspapers such as *The Times*, the *Manchester Guardian*, the *Daily Herald*, the *Daily Express*, the *News Chronicle*, and so on. In the House, debates on the subject in the full sense did not take place until late March 1932.[28] Thorne observed:

Neither the Labour nor the Liberal members of the Government were to display any strong predilection for China's cause as opposed to that of Japan; few of the Tories were to be uncritically pro-Japanese; over the decisive matter of Britain's interests and resources in the area, there was to be unanimity.[29]

MacDonald's First National Government, which had come to power a month earlier, was so preoccupied with domestic problems that the Far Eastern crisis did not command its full attention. The ministers did not discuss the Sino–Japanese dispute in detail until 11 November.[30] Meanwhile, due to 'some disquieting news from Geneva', MacDonald requested Lord Reading, the Foreign Secretary at the time, to attend the Council meeting on 14 October in order to handle the problem. 'We ought to be in a position at the Council to take a leading part on a well thought out policy' he said to Reading.[31] But as a matter of fact, neither the Cabinet nor the FO had any ready-made policy to cope with the situation.[32]

Lindley in Tokyo sent back his point of view:

> that Chinese have followed most exasperating policy in Manchuria . . . to undermine Japanese position which after all rests largely on treaty rights; and to the obvious probability that Japanese action in Manchuria will react favourably on British interests in Manchuria [China].[33]

He further persuaded Lord Reading to press the Chinese for moderation rather than to press the Japanese,[34] but his suggestion was opposed by Lampson in Peking because to counsel the Chinese to be moderate was, in his words, 'like counselling moderation to the hare with the hounds already close on his heels'.[35] Lampson explicitly regarded the Japanese action as 'an instance of brutal application of ruthless force against a weaker neighbour', and thought it might ruin the League.[36] He urged upon Reading that Britain should take some action.[37]

Within the FO, most staff shared Lindley's opinion that they would rather ignore the spirit of the Covenant than offend Japan.[38] Pratt doubted 'whether the strict and academic application of League principles is the best method of dealing with such a situation'.[39] As head of the FO, Reading confessed reluctantly that

> it is difficult for the Council to abandon the principle that disputes may only be settled by peaceful means, and it would seem difficult for the signatories of the Pact of Paris to look on while Japan ignores Article II of that instrument.

The problem was, as he said, 'whether anything can be done in the meanwhile to save the Council from being faced with a deadlock'.[40] The instructions he gave Lindley and Lampson were to pacify both the Chinese and Japanese Governments,[41] and to inquire of the governments in Washington, Berlin, Rome and Paris whether they would take similar action.[42]

At Geneva, the Council adopted a resolution on 24 October that reaffirmed the resolution of 30 September which had fixed 16 November as the date of Japanese withdrawal.[43] Drummond believed that Japan would withdraw her troops soon.[44] Instead Japan extended her military operation in Manchuria, and this made the deadlock more serious.

Faced with this situation, Lindley and Mackillop (of the Far Eastern Department) put forward similar proposals. The former suggested that the League should 'send a commission to Manchuria in order to arrange and supervise the evacuation of the Japanese troops and, at the same time, call upon the Chinese Government to enter into negotiations with the Japanese at once without waiting for the evacuation to begin'.[45] Both Orde and Pratt thought that Japan considered her position in Manchuria more important than her relations with the League. The former did not believe that the Japanese would carry out the Council's resolution by the deadline. He concluded: 'we should work for an ultimate compromise or at least do nothing to prejudice the chances of arriving at one'.[46] Finally, Reading formulated the proposal on 29 October for the League:

if Japanese and Chinese representatives could be got together to discuss evacuation . . ., [the] two Governments might be advised . . . to begin discussion of the point regarding treaty rights. Japan might then be able to effect and excuse complete evacuation by telling her people that she had secured the point about direct negotiation on treaty rights and thus save her face. [47]

On 9 November, Sir John Simon took his seat at the FO, succeeding Reading. The immediate problem he faced was that there was little hope of the Japanese withdrawing their troops by the deadline. Like his colleagues, he believed at that moment that the Japanese 'had no territorial designs', but vital political and economic interests in Manchuria. He told his colleagues that one of the causes of the dispute was that the Chinese had not recognised Japanese interests in

Manchuria, but at Geneva, the Japanese delegate 'had not put his country's case very well'. The Council's decision to make 16 November the deadline was 'a serious step', because 'the League had no means to make the notice effective'. In addition, if the Chinese shifted their appeal from Article 11 to Article 16, sanctions of various kinds, such as restrictions on trade, the withdrawal of the Ambassador and dispatch of an international force to Manchuria, might be suggested, none of which, in his opinion, was practicable. Based on his suggestion, the ministers agreed on a line that the British delegates should pursue: 'the League of Nations should be upheld', but Article 16 of the Covenant was 'not suitable and could not in practice be applied in the present case'. They instructed Simon that he must make every effort to stop the Chinese from shifting the appeal to Article 16. As to Japan, Simon should continue to persuade her to withdraw her troops before negotiations took place, or arrange for discussions on the Treaty situation together with the question of troop withdrawal. In brief, the British policy 'should be one of conciliation, with an avoidance of implied threats'.[48]

The Council meeting of November 'led to nothing', but undermined 'the moral authority of the League'.[49] He realised that before she established her dominant position in Manchuria, Japan would not agree to withdraw any of her troops.[50] Cecil suggested that the Council should not be excessively accommodating to Japan,[51] but Simon was inclined to give up rather than to check the Japanese. He wrote to MacDonald:

> the League cannot as a League confirm the continuance of Japanese troops on Chinese territory and regrets that it is not possible owing to Japanese opposition to reach a unanimous and effective conclusion. This is not satisfactory but if all efforts at adjournment fail it is better than pretending (what nobody believes) that the League is really in a position to control the situation.[52]

As soon as he came back to London, Simon prepared a memo for the Cabinet meeting of 25 November, in which he reported that the League had proposed to appoint a Commission of Enquiry, which could not report until it had finished its investigation in eight or nine months. He consulted his colleagues as to whether the British delegate should take the lead:

Here we have got to weigh the disadvantages against each other. On the one hand the immediate disadvantage to ourselves in losing favour with Japan; and on the other hand the general risk, in which we share, is that the League, in refusing to reaffirm its true function, will lose so much respect as may yet be accorded to it in the face of its failure to enforce its demands upon the parties.

He suggested that 'the Council could do no more than it did on October 24th, namely, to reaffirm its resolution of September 30th' and 'place again on formal record its views as to the obligations of both parties'. This, however, 'would be a confession of complete failure, not veiled even by the despatch of a Commission of Enquiry to the Far East', but he disapproved of the application of Article 15, on the grounds that it introduced a more menacing atmosphere. He thought that it was necessary to 'give a respite of six to nine months during which passion may cool'.

After a short discussion, Thomas, the Dominions Secretary, asked him to pay attention to the attitude of the Dominions, and then the ministers came to a conclusion, which was immediately communicated to Cecil:

Cabinet is opposed to British Representative taking up a special and separate attitude in public session on the ground that it would not be effective and would only cause further heartburnings [sic].[53]

Around the end of the first phase, it was not merely Simon who did not know what steps to take next; neither did the other staff in the FO. Wellesley told his colleagues: 'I feel very certain that no permanent solution of the problem is to be found on a purely juridical basis.'[54] Orde summed up the situation as follows:

It is hard to see what further action can be taken . . . For the rest, it would seem that all we can do is to await the report of the Commission of Enquiry.[55]

Anglo-American Co-operation

British policy-making became entangled with the issue of Anglo-American co-operation from the very beginning. Since the Japanese invasion of China violated the Covenant as well as the Nine Power Treaty and the Kellogg Pact, the Chinese appealed to Washington when they put their case before the League. It was believed that co-operation between Britain and America was essential to a solution of the Far Eastern crisis. Both British and American statesmen emphasised the importance of it during the crisis, but criticised each other afterwards for failure to co-operate.

Soon after the incident of 18 September, Pratt suggested that possible Anglo-American co-operation should be only based on non-coercive principles, rather than economic or military sanctions against Japan.[56]

On the American side, in spite of excluding sanctions, a series of diplomatic activities had taken place to support the League. On 3 November, the American Government delivered a note to the Japanese Government, reinforcing the position taken by the League.[57] Stimson instructed Forbes, the American Ambassador in Tokyo:

> I do not intend to remain inactive and aloof, leaving to the others the whole burden of action. The implication of silence on the part of the United States would be that we were taking sides with Japan . . .

He even warned the Japanese Ambassador on 19 November that he would publish all the documents on the Manchurian crisis between Japan and the United States, which would embarrass the Japanese Government.[58]

While the British policy-makers did not know what to do next, Stimson issued his famous Note of 7 January 1932, in which he declared that the United States did not intend to recognise any situation, treaty or agreement brought about contrary to the Kellogg Pact.[59]

Before despatching the Note, he told Lindsay of his strong hope that the British Government would take similar action.[60] But Wellesley thought that this action was 'premature', and might cause 'considerable irritation quite unnecessarily'. Orde took a similar view.[61] As for Simon, the only thing he was concerned about was how to deal with the House and the American request.[62] Under his instruction, Wellesley prepared information for the press, which was published three days later. It read:

> . . . the Japanese representative at the Council . . . stated on October 13th that Japan was the champion in Manchuria of the principle of equal opportunity and the 'open door' for the economic activities of all nations . . .

In view of this statement H.M.G. have not considered it necessary to address any formal note to the Japanese Government on the lines of the American Government's note . . .[63]

The Americans could not veil their disappointment when they learned of Britain's reaction.[64] The Japanese responded to the Note with an 'ironical tone',[65] and at the same time 'highly appreciated the friendly attitude of His Majesty's Government'.[66]

The Second Phase: January–September 1932

The Shanghai Incident and British Policy

In the first three weeks of January, the situation in Shanghai became very tense. On 18 January, five Japanese were injured in a local clash between some Chinese and Japanese. Although the Mayor of Shanghai had accepted all demands by the Japanese Consul-General, who regarded the reply as satisfactory, Japanese forces suddenly attacked Chapei without any warning on the night of 28 January. However, they were not very successful this time since their offensive met with the indomitable resistance of the 19th Chinese Army. On 29 January, China evoked Article 10 and Article 15 of the Covenant.

The Shanghai incident brought the Far Eastern crisis to another climax, and drew much attention from the British, since Britain had vast interests in this region. There was controversy between the newspapers: one side held the view that if, at the beginning, greater understanding had been shown to the Japanese, and a more flexible attitude adopted, a hopeful result might have been obtained. The other side, represented by the *Manchester Guardian*, insisted that if 'firm action' had been taken against Japan at the outset, the crisis might have been successfully resolved. Its editorial comment on 1 February 1932 said:

it was of vital importance to this country that we should not connive at Japanese aggression . . . It was for their apparent inability to realise the importance of the dispute from this point of view, in its early stages, that Sir John Simon and the representatives of the other Powers on the League of Nations Council were chiefly to blame. Had they then made it clear that they intended . . . to stand by the Covenant it is probable that the dispute could have been settled quietly by diplomatic means.[67]

In the House, some MPs, such as Mander and Cocks, were persistent in urging the Government, following the American example, to send a Note to China and Japan. However, the question was cleverly evaded by the Government.[68] The policy-makers did not want to put any pressure at all on the aggressor. Two days before the Japanese attacked Shanghai, turning a cold shoulder to the American application for joint action,[69] the FO was busy finding a way of co-operating with Japan without rebuffing America. Pratt suggested that Britain should point out to the United States that she could not stop Japan from acting similarly to the way she did in 1927, but what the Western Powers could do was to press the Chinese to meet Japanese demands with regard to suppression of the boycott.[70]

The incident of 28 January caused a certain psychological change in the FO. Simon said: 'the first step taken by Japan in Shanghai ought to be called a wrong step'.[71] Orde drew his colleagues' attention to the fact that 'the Japanese action in all its violence cannot be justified.'[72] Pratt was in accord, and he even went further, agreeing that the Chinese boycott, which he had condemned before, was the only weapon China possessed. However, he warned his colleagues in his memorandums dated 31 January and 1 February:

> unless we were prepared to withdraw altogether from the Far East it might be difficult to escape eventually being drawn into war . . . if we try to avoid this fatal path by protesting and doing nothing more the consequences may yet be much the same.

> There is of course the possibility of the economic collapse of Japan under the combined effect of the Chinese boycott and the Anglo-American severance of relations . . . but it must remain a matter for speculation whether the collapse would be so immediate or so complete as to avert the dangers referred to above.[73]

These memorandums won general agreement in the FO. Vansittart agreed with his estimate of the danger that if Japan continued unchecked, the British position and its vast interests in the Far East would 'never recover'. However, he did not think that there was anything they were able to do to check Japan and protect British interests unless 'the United States are eventually prepared to use force', which was not impossible. But before that moment came, Britain 'must eventually swallow any & every humiliation in the Far East'. Therefore, he strongly recommended:

We can have no longrange, or even shortrange, policy in the Far East. We must live from hand to mouth – an humiliating process – unless we have made up, or cleared, our minds upon the answer. [i.e. the USA had decided to use force.]

Wellesley was also in accord with Pratt, pointing out that: 'the success of our Far Eastern policy and the prosperity of our economic interests are largely dependent on Japanese good will'. But he did not forget to warn his superiors in rank of the serious situation the crisis would lead to:

the development of this very dangerous situation may force our hand . . . we may be dragged by events along a path which may end in war with her.

But I maintain that from a material point of view we have nothing to gain and much to lose by antagonising Japan; and to associate ourselves in pressure from America would definitely have this effect.

The danger, as I see it, lies in a definite Anglo-American anti-Japanese attitude . . . [75]

His memo as well as Pratt's was recommended to the Cabinet for consideration.[76]

In fact, the top British leaders were hesitating to make any decision at that moment, because Lindley in Tokyo warned on 3 February:

The position is now so delicate that a single false step may precipitate catastrophe. I trust therefore that no further action be taken at Geneva or elsewhere . . .[77]

The telegrams the Ambassador sent to Simon certainly discouraged the FO from contemplating any strong measures.[78]

However, Lindley's point of view met with bitter criticism from Lord Cecil, The British Delegate in Geneva, who perceived that although the League had done everything to 'save Japanese susceptibilities', 'they tried one thing and then another to see how far they could go and when they found that in fact there was no strong disposition to stop them they went further and further'. He warned Simon seriously:

If we do not take a vigorous line I am confident that the Japanese will establish themselves as the dominating power in China, and through China in the whole of Asia, with consequences to British interests, the League and world peace which may be of most extreme seriousness.

He suggested that if they decided to adopt a firm line, the Government should impose sanctions on Japan, including withdrawal of the Ambassador in Tokyo and taking 'economic action, with all its consequences, to coerce the Japanese'. But when Simon consulted Wellesley and Vansittart about Cecil's proposal, neither of them wanted to adopt any coercive measures. Vansittart said: 'The less we hear of economic blockades & Art. 16 just now, the better.' He had no doubt that Simon was in accord with him.[79]

The Foreign Secretary was now particularly disturbed by the problem of co-operation with the United States. He told MacDonald and other Cabinet members that if Britain did not act with America, the latter would be rebuffed; however, if she did, America would leave Britain with 'the brunt of the work and of the blame . . . But we cannot afford to upset the United States of America over this,' he explained, adding:

We are in grave danger of falling between two stools – offending Japan without completely satisfying America.

I am afraid that I am not hopeful that we can restrain Japan.[80]

During this period, MacDonald frequently discussed the emergency situation with Baldwin, Simon and the ministers at the head of the three Service Departments, all of whom later made up the Far Eastern Committee with another three Cabinet members under the leadership of the Prime Minister.[81] It was evident that in Cabinet, Pratt and Wellesley's proposals togather with Lindley's advice were taken seriously, but Cecil's suggestion was not welcomed.[82]

On 17 February, a Cabinet meeting regarding the Shanghai incident was held to discuss the problem that the United States requested the British to take joint action in invoking the Nine-Power Treaty. In addition, Simon drew attention to the point that since it was impossible for Britain alone to assume the burden of Japanese resentment, he wanted to show Japan that the appeal of 16 February from the League was not minatory in intention. The appeal reads:

The Secretary of State and, indeed, the whole British Government are wholly opposed to the Council pronouncing judgment in a matter which is not completely before them . . . It is contrary to the first principles of jurisprudence that judgment should be pronounced before the case of the parties has been fully heard. Japan has not yet delivered a statement of her case . . .

Apart from this, he consulted his colleagues about how to answer Mander's question in the House regarding the Government's attitude to the application of Article 16. He suggested hinting that the Government 'had no intention of resorting to sanctions'.

In the course of the discussion, the Cabinet instructed Samuel, the Home Secretary, to 'do his best to induce Mr. Mander to withdraw' his question. If this failed, Simon's reply 'should not be limited to a negative but should explain that the question had been referred to the Assembly, that neither side had yet put in its case; and that any action pre-judging the issue was to be deprecated'.[83]

Meanwhile, the situation at Shanghai seemed to offer the FO an outlet for its policy-making. Pratt argued, in his memo dated 21 February, that if Japan controlled Shanghai with a quick and easy victory, as she had done in Manchuria, it might well prove difficult for British enterprise in China. If the Chinese were successful in their defiance of Japan, all other foreign privileges would be swept away. But the present fighting indicated that the Japanese would win with difficulty, which would avert both these dangers. He concluded:

It is then that the opportunity may occur for the League, under British leadership, to help Japan out of her difficulties and help to build up a new and more stable system of international relationships in the Far East.

His view was generally shared by Orde, Wellesley and Vansittart.[84]

When he received this memo in Geneva, Simon found that both the Chinese and Japanese were in the mood to welcome intervention. He reported to the Cabinet that Britain had taken the chance and put forward her plan for the re-establishment of peaceful conditions in Shanghai. This 'silenced the critics', who complained that Britain was either 'working behind the back of the League', or failing to show herself 'as vigorous as the United States' was prepared to be.[85]

At the end of February, Britain, France and Italy as well as the United States agreed on a joint offer of good offices to end hostilities, and to set up a conference in Shanghai.[86] As a result, with the intervention of the Western Powers, Sino-Japanese negotiations started on 28 February.

Anglo-American Co-operation

A few days before the outbreak of the Shanghai incident, Stimson sent for Lindsay and told him that he was contemplating supporting the Chinese in some way, because if the Japanese conquered China, it would mean disaster for the trade of other powers, especially Britain and the United States. He suggested:

1 a formal and strongly worded intimation to Japan that nothing could justify the entry of any Japanese forces into the International Settlement;
2 reinforcing Anglo-American military forces in Shanghai.

He told Lindsay that he was very anxious to have the co-operation of the British Government in both of these contemplated measures.[87] But when his proposal was discussed at the FO it was immediately ridiculed. Pratt, Orde and Wellesley wrote down their agreed minutes:

> The picture which Mr. Stimson has in his mind . . . is almost entirely an imaginary one, and he has done his utmost to rush us into hasty and ill considered action which would have gravely aggravated the situation in the Far East . . . [88]

Simon instructed the British Ambassador in Washington to inform Stimson of the British proposal: Britain and the United States should press the Chinese Government into suppressing 'mob violence' and restraining 'boycott activities' on one hand, and remind the Japanese of 'the vast concentration of foreign interests in Shanghai and the Yangtsee valley' on the other.[89] A sudden attack by the Japanese on Shanghai had Simon running around in circles: he instructed Lindley to ask the Japanese Government why Chapei was attacked after the Chinese acceptance of Japanese demands, and to state that the British Government could not agree to the International Settlement being used as a military base;[90] but on the other hand, he urged Lindsay to ask the American Government if it would take similar action.[91] On top of this, he had to explain to the Cabinet why, according to *The Times*, there had been a delay in communicating with America.[92]

On the American side, Stimson declared that the United States could not act under Article 15 as a member of the League, but she would collaborate with the members of the League concerned under the Nine-Power Treaty and the Kellogg Treaty.[93]

On 30 January 30, he took the initiative to telephone MacDonald and convey Hoover's suggestion for a direct appeal to the Japanese Emperor from the American President and the King of the United Kingdom for a cessation of hostilities and the beginning of negotiations for a settlement. He told MacDonald: 'we would endeavor to put the appeal in such shape that it would be difficult for them to refuse'. He stressed that the United States would not do it unless Britain could join. This suggestion was 'a very sudden proposal' to MacDonald. However, he agreed to consider it.[94]

Nevertheless, the FO held a negative view of the appeal. It thought the situation had materially changed since that telephone conversation, and the appeal should concentrate on Shanghai and exclude Manchuria.[95] The next day, MacDonald answered Stimson by telephone that the British appeal could be sent only by the Prime Minister to the Japanese Prime Minister.[96] In view of this, Stimson decided that 'the project should be postponed'.[97]

On 31 January the Japanese, due to an unexpected counter-attack by the Chinese Army, turned to the Western Powers for their good offices.[98] Stimson put forward his five-point proposal for a cessation of the conflict, which was generally agreed by Britain, France and Italy.[99] On 2 February, the Four Powers dispatched the proposal to the Japanese Government.[100] But Japan refused it on the grounds that although the first four were acceptable, the fifth point, which connected the Shanghai affair with the Manchurian crisis, was unacceptable.[101]

On the British side, Lindley thought: 'acceptance of four points would be most valuable in any case'.[102] Simon even said: 'If we can get any practical results on one, two, three or four it will be a very good thing.'[103] Two days later he showed Atherton, the American Chargé d'Affaires in Britain, a new British proposal which omitted Manchuria from forthcoming representation to Tokyo in order to continue the good offices.[104] But Stimson did not want to give up the fifth point because, in his opinion, it was essential that there should be a complete cessation of hostilities in China.[105] He disliked the British proposal, and said to Simon: 'I don't think it is dignified to go on negotiating with Japan after she has refused the essence of our proposal.'[106]

On 9 February, Stimson sent for Lindsay and told him that he was contemplating invocation of the Nine Power Treaty. He hoped that the

British Government would take joint action.[107] Two days later, Simon phoned him from Geneva, saying that he had first to consult London.[108] In fact, neither Simon nor Vansittart thought that the moment was ripe, and they preferred to wait and see whether Lampson could achieve anything at Shanghai.[109]

During the following days, there were several phone calls between Stimson and Simon which explored the increasing divergence between the two sides. Stressing that Britain was a member of the League, Simon was inclined to deal with the problem within the system of the League, and to separate the Shanghai affair from the Manchurian crisis, while Stimson emphasised the importance of Anglo-American joint action, and of the fifth point. He tried to persuade Simon that Britain could simultaneously join in two separate actions taken both by the Nine Power Treaty signatories and by the League. Simon seemed quite inclined to follow this argument, but again he had to consult his colleagues first.[110]

Immediately after that, a ministerial meeting was held in MacDonald's nursing home to consider the American proposal. After discussion, ministers concluded:

> the best course would be for the Council of the League to make some measured appeal to Japan, on lines similar to those proposed by Mr Stimson, and to make an effort to synchronise the two.

As a result of the meeting, a message was sent to Geneva suggesting the lines of an appeal to Japan by the League.[111]

But 'to make an effort to synchronise the two' was conditional, according to Atherton's understanding: if the United States got 'all the signatories of the Nine Power Pact to agree to the draft of the Nine-Power proclamation', Britain would join in; otherwise, she would 'content herself with participation in the League appeal', and leave the Americans to take independent action on the Nine Power Treaty.[112]

That evening, Simon telephoned Stimson and turned down the latter's proposal, saying: 'I am not decided whether we can actually join you on the same piece of paper or not.'[113] On 16 February, Vansittart submitted to Atherton a memo which indicated that 'it is thoroughly understood that the question whether other Powers could join in the American document is still in suspense'.[114]

When Atherton told Stimson by telephone about Britain's decision not to go ahead, the latter could not help saying: 'She has let us down.'[115] Since they feared acting alone, the Americans informed the FO: 'there may be no American note'.[116]

Late in February, the Japanese gave a very strong hint that they wished that 'they were well out of the Shanghai affair'.[117] Simon felt it was time for intervention. With a new proposal of good offices, he asked Wilson, the American delegate at Geneva, whether the United States could join them.[118] Being discouraged by his earlier experience, Stimson instructed Wilson to co-operate, but at the same time 'to go a little slow'.[119]

Negotiations between the Chinese and Japanese led to the Armistice Agreement on 5 May, which gradually relieved the tense situation at Shanghai. Meanwhile, the Japanese created their puppet state 'Manchukuo', and the deadlock over the Manchuria problem continued.

The Third Phase: September 1932–May 1933

The Lytton Report and Policy-making

March–September 1932 could be called a 'waiting period' for the Report from the Lytton Commission, which was sent to China for investigation by the League.

When the Lytton Report was published on 1 October, public opinion was generally positive. Attlee, the Labour leader, remarked that this document would create 'a great opportunity to vindicate the authority of the League of Nations'. The Labour Opposition demanded that the Government should make every effort to support the principles of the Covenant. The *Daily Herald* and the *Daily Express* regarded the report as a judgement against the Japanese, and the former's editorial, under the heading 'Guilty!', declared that Japan had been found guilty of a series of aggressive actions.[120] At Geneva, Koo, the Chinese representative, appealed to Cecil that the League should impose some special moral pressure on Japan, such as excluding her from the League or withdrawing ambassadors in Japan. However, the policy-makers shut the door on public opinion. Pratt minuted:

Moral pressure of the kind advocated by Mr Koo would do infinite harm. It would prevent the growth of those influences in Japan which will eventually take the power out of the hands of the younger hotheads now in control and agree to a reasonable settlement of the dispute with China.

This minute met with general agreement from his colleagues, including Vansittart and Orde.[121]

On 10 October, Pratt summarised the main points of the report. His analysis was that the document:

> could easily be taken as a severe condemnation of Japan, but . . . if one looks to the substance below the surface, the balance of right inclines to her side.
>
> It is a fair deduction from the Report that while both parties are to blame, China's failure to set her house in order is the root cause of the present difficulties . . .
>
> In these circumstances . . . an effective beginning should be made with the reconstruction of China and that the two parties should be persuaded to meet in friendly negotiation . . .
>
> The Lytton Report . . . should, however, greatly ease the strain of the present situation, for there will no longer be any excuse for treating Japan as the criminal in the dock, and there can be no question of sanctions or of driving her from the League.

This 'admirable review', Simon found, was very helpful in clearing his own mind.[122] After reading it, Orde did not wish to add anything, except that he wondered if Japan would accept the solution.[123]

Orde's anxiety was not unwarranted. According to Lindley's observation, the report would most probably be rejected by Japan, on the grounds that it assured that the military operation of Japanese troops on 18 September could not be regarded as self-defence, and 'Manchukuo' could not be considered to have been called into existence by a genuine and spontaneous independent movement.[124] At Geneva, Drummond, Secretary-General of the League, presumed that unless Japan accepted the report, the Council could do no more than pass it on to the Committee of nineteen and the Assembly. Then the problem was what the Committee of nineteen should propose to the Assembly which would make a report under Article 15. In these circumstances, he put forward two proposals, of which he favoured the second, namely, the Assembly would adopt the report up to Chapter 8, which described the Manchurian incident. As to Chapters 9 and 10, which referred to principles and to the suggestions for settlement, the Assembly could first consult the Members of the Nine Power Treaty plus the Soviets for the result of their examination, and then it might formulate its final conclusions based on all points of view. In his opinion, this proposal, despite showing the League's weakness, had certain clear advantages: it would force the Americans and Soviets 'to take their responsibilities', gain time, and leave the League 'with the last word'.[125]

Simon wanted his subordinates to be free to give their opinions on these proposals. Being in accord, as usual, Pratt and Orde agreed to an extent with the second proposal, but drew attention to three difficulties, such as the question of recognition of 'Manchukuo', the impossibility of further delay and difficulty in engaging the Soviets. After the exchange of views, Wellesley and Vansittart came to a conclusion, as the former minuted:

We are all agreed on the following points:
1. That Sir E. Drummond's second proposal should be taken as the basis for our proposals.
2. That Russia should be added to the nine Powers.
3. But Mr. Orde's proposal for a further enquiry into the state of feeling in Manchuria would be worth supporting if the Japanese can be induced to put it forward.

But Vansittart did not consider Orde's suggestion workable.[126]

After two revisions considering various opinions from his colleagues, Drummond submitted his final proposal in early November, which included the following steps:

1. adoption of the first eight chapters of the Report;
2. declaration of non-recognition of and non-cooperation with 'Manchukuo';
3. the powers of the Kellogg Pact and of the Nine Power Treaty, including the Soviets, should be invited to a conference;
4. as soon as the result was known, the Assembly could declare that in view of the difficulties experienced by the Chinese Government in its work of reconstruction, which had been increased by the incident of 18 September 1931, the League would take a decision affording China technical assistance.[127]

In late November, the Cabinet twice discussed the policy that Britain should pursue in the League. Simon reported to his colleagues Drummond's proposal, to which he would agree, on the grounds that 'the League can do nothing directly'. But he was afraid that 'the United

States would much prefer to disclaim responsibility by leaving the League of Nations to grasp the nettle itself'.[128] Since the Lytton Report had denied the creation of 'Manchukuo' as the result of 'spontaneous action of Manchurian inhabitants', he did not see how the Council could be expected to do other than pronounce a condemnation of Japan, which might lead to the possibility of Japan leaving the League.[129] Racking his brains for a solution, Simon found a method to ward off the conclusions unfavourable to Japan. He had noticed that 'the Lytton Commission did not recommend the League to do anything in particular'. 'Most of their recommendations were addressed to China or Japan', which was a point he might be able to make some use of.[130] He promised his colleagues that the British delegate would neither take a lead nor commit Britain never to recognise 'Manchukuo'.[131]

Without much discussion, the Cabinet agreed with Simon's conclusion:

> We ought to act as a loyal member of the League . . . the course we take is *pro* League and not *anti* Japan . . . we must strive to be fair to both sides. But we must not involve ourselves in trouble with Japan.

They noticed that the stress was laid on the last sentence.[132]

The Policy of 'a Loyal Member of the League'

In late November and early December, the Council organised a general debate on the Manchurian crisis based on the Lytton Report.[133] Giving a speech on 7 December, Simon mentioned nothing about the two important conclusions of the Report concerning the Japanese invasion, but drew attention to his two observations. The first was a quotation of a passage from Chapter 9:

> the issues involved in this conflict are not as simple as they are often represented to be. They are, on the contrary, exceedingly complicated, and only an intimate knowledge of all the facts, as well as of their historical background, should entitle anyone to express a definite opinion upon them. This is not a case in which one country has declared war on another country without previously exhausting the opportunities for conciliation provided in the Covenant of the League of Nations. Neither is it a simple

case of the violation of the frontier of one country by the armed forces of a neighbouring country . . .

In his second observation, he blamed the Chinese for the existence of an anti-foreign feeling and anti-foreign boycott in China.[134] He argued that the other speakers neglected these factors, and it could not be fairly judged 'unless proper emphasis was laid on those passages in the Report which criticised China'. He concluded from the report that: 'a mere restoration of the *status quo ante* would be no solution'.[135]

Simon's speech was admired by Matsuoka, the Japanese Delegate at Geneva,[136] but criticised by many representatives of other countries, on the grounds that Britain had 'supported and encouraged the Japanese adventures in Manchuria' because the British self-interest lay in not offending Japan.[137]

Although the League had made every effort to accommodate Japan, the Japanese Government finally informed the Committee of Nineteen on 22 January that they had rejected the Committee's resolution of 18 January. Under these circumstances, Pratt advised that Britain had to join in the League's condemnation of Japan and run an equal danger of antagonising Japan. He did not know how to avoid the dilemma, but suggested:

We shall only be able effectively to head off a demand for the expulsion of Japan by showing that we are prepared to join in a dignified but quite unequivocal condemnation of her actions . . . antagonising Japan in this way and to this extent . . . would probably not result in any very great damage to our material interests, whereas if we do not go at least thus far our moral prestige which is the real basis of our position in China would be destroyed . . . Moreover unless we take the bold and simple course of condemning Japan we shall run the far graver risks of weakening the League and alienating America.[138]

In the exchange of views between inner members of the FO, Pratt's proposals met with general agreement. However, Simon and Vansittart, in spite of being generally in agreement with him, thought the weakness in his proposal was that it would be regarded as taking the lead and urging the other powers to follow.[139]

Later, Simon reported to the Cabinet that Britain would continue not to recognise 'Manchukuo' for some time, because the League had adopted non-recognition as its principle. But as soon as the right moment came, Britain would at once reconsider revising her policy. He hoped that the Cabinet could consider rejecting any sanctions under Article 16, and the use of modified pressure: the members of the League could declare that Japan had broken the rules of the League.[140]

At Geneva, the resolution for adoption of the Assembly on 21 February 1933 was under preparation, based on the Lytton Report. Eden and Pratt took part in drafting it.[141] Simon instructed Eden to shape the document following the above lines so that it did not prevent Britain from future revision of her position in accordance with her on-going self-interest.[142] The resolution included condemnation of Japanese violation of the rules of the League, and non-recognition of 'Manchukuo', which was accepted by the Assembly on 24 February, but rejected by Japan.[143]

Anglo-American Co-operation

After the publication of the Lytton Report, Stimson informed Simon that America's first concern was that the authority of the Nine-Power Treaty and Kellogg Pact must be firmly defended. To this end, the United States was prepared to co-operate with other powers, particularly with Britain. He pushed Britain to take a lead, since she was a member of the League as well as one of signatories of the Nine Power Treaty.[144] But from Mellon, the American Ambassador in London, he learned that the British were 'a little too lukewarm to take a vigorous lead'.[145]

On the other hand, the British tried to find out how far the Americans were prepared to go with the League. On 26 October, Simon invited Davis (the American Delegate to the Disarmament Conference) and Atherton to the meeting at the FO. Davis told his British colleagues that the Americans had not thought out any plan, and they wanted the League to handle the matter.[146]

Considering Simon's speech of 7 December 'disconcerting', Stimson warned his British partners that any indication of weakness or too conciliatory an attitude by Britain would encourage Japan. He pointed out seriously that:

> if the British Government shows itself willing neither as a government nor as a member of the League to take a stand on behalf of principles, and if the League, in consequence, dodges the issues and pretends to believe that a committee or commission of

conciliation can, unsupported by a foundation of principles . . . I cannot but doubt whether any useful purpose would be served by our appointing a representative, if asked so to do, to work with such a commission.[147]

He considered adoption of the Lytton Report and non-recognition as a precondition to American participation in the work of a committee of conciliation.[148] Since he was wholly dissatisfied with the draft resolution of 16 December due to its unprincipled character, Stimson instructed Wilson: 'you will not help that breaking of the ice by any sign of weakness. Not a bit. Just the reverse.[149] He wanted Wilson to bear in mind that he must make it very clear he would take a decision of co-operation on the basis of whether the League had acted in the nature of an affirmation of findings of principle – whether the League resolution was in accord with American principles.[150]

In mid-January, the League failed to find any basis for conciliation. Simon sought further American support; but his reluctance to mention the next step left Stimson with the impression that there was no change in British policy. Stimson would rather push the British Government into line backed up firmly by the non-recognition than go along with Britain and make any unprincipled accommodation to Japan.[151] As to participation in the Advisory Committee for Conciliation, the American Government, despite acceptance of the invitation, did not commit itself to anything.[152]

On 27 March, Japan gave preliminary notice of her withdrawal from the League and the Manchurian crisis was left unsettled, although later, the Sino-Japanese Armistice at Tang Ku was signed on 31 May 1933.

THE IMPACT OF MANCHURIA ON DEFENCE POLICY AND STRATEGY IN THE FAR EAST AND EUROPE

The Manchurian episode clearly indicated that Japan had adopted an aggressive strategy in China, which would inevitably result in conflict with the Western Powers. Soon after Shanghai incident, the Chiefs of Staff sounded a serious warning in their report of 17 March 1932:

we possess only light naval forces in the Far East . . . the bases at Singapore and Hong Kong, essential to the maintenance of a fleet of capital ships on arrival in the Far East, are not in a defensible condition. The whole of our territory in the Far East as well as the coast line of India and the Dominions and our vast trade and shipping lies open to attack.

They suggested that 'the Ten-Year Rule',[153] which had served as a guideline for the three-service budget since 1919, was no longer tenable and that defence in the Far East be strengthened. The report was generally agreed by the Committee of Imperial Defence (CID), but the feedback from the Treasury, headed by Chamberlain, was quite discouraging. The Treasurer pointed out: 'in present circumstances, we are no more in a position financially and economically to engage in a major war in the Far East than we are militarily'. He emphasised: 'today financial and economic risks are by far the most serious and urgent the country has to face and that other risks must be run until the country has had time and opportunity to recuperate and our financial situation to improve'. In other words, the Government would rather run the risk of Japanese attack on Hong Kong or Singapore than spoil the economic situation at home. This represented the Cabinet view. When it met to consider the report on 23 March, the ministers, although accepting cancellation of the 'Ten-Year Rule', concluded that this did not mean that the defence budget could be increased without considering the serious economic situation. Furthermore, they decided that there would be an eighteen-month postponement before they put the Chiefs of Staff's suggestions into effect.[154]

The significance of suspending the 'Ten-Year Rule' was very limited, because it did not result in a new defence policy, nor did it lead to a sufficient increase in armament expenditure. In 1932, the three-service budget was cut to the lowest level in the inter-war period. The 1933 budget had only increased by less than 4.3 per cent. The actual expenditure in the following year was lower than that recommended by the Defence Requirements Committee (DRC). Until after October 1933, when Germany withdrew from the Disarmament Conference, the British Government was still immersed in the dream of disarmament,[155] being reluctant to shift from the illusion of disarmament to the reality of rearmament.

On 9 November, the CID considered the Annual Review by Chiefs of Staff, which listed three major commitments – the Far East, Europe and India – repeating the previous view that the Far East 'remains the greatest and most immediate of our commitments'. Chamberlain thought 'it was a mistake' to give priority to the Far East instead of Europe. This 'had gradually poisoned our relations with Japan', he said:

If it were possible to improve our relations with Japan the whole problem in the Far East would be much simplified, and it even might be possible to reduce the Far East in the order of priority. This was one of the reasons which led him to suggest that it might perhaps be unwise to commit ourselves too definitely to an order of priority.

MacDonald and Simon agreed with the view of the Chiefs of Staff, while they also thought Chamberlain's proposal necessary. In the end, the Committee appointed the Defence Requirements Committee, which was composed of Hankey, a secretary of the Cabinet (as Chair), Fisher, Permanent Under-Secretary at the Treasury, Vansittart and three Chiefs of Staff, to investigate the situation.[156]

The DRC started its first meeting on 14 November, and continued to work on its report in the following months. Meanwhile, the Navy Staff warned it that without a strength of two-power standard (a fleet large enough to fight Japan in the Far East, while leaving in home waters sufficient forces to contend with the strongest European power), the Navy could no longer afford to wage war in the Far East and in Europe at the same time.[157] The officials in the FO also put forward a number of memorandums to discuss the Far East situation from various angles. Having been circulated in the FO, this collection of papers was sent to the Cabinet and other departments with Vansittart's covering letter, in which he summed up the conclusion for the basis of future Far Eastern policy:

(1)   It would be inadvisable to tie our Far Eastern policy to either Japan or to the United States, since the former have fundamental aims to which we cannot give support, while the latter are an entirely uncertain factor.

(2)   It is a major British interest not to antagonise Japan, and still more not to be made the spear-head of opposition to her aims . . .[158]

Differing from Hankey and the Chiefs of Staff, both of whom stressed Far Eastern danger, Vansittart advised the Cabinet around the beginning of December:

The order of priorities which put Japan first pre-supposed that Japan would attack us after we had got into difficulties elsewhere. 'Elsewhere' therefore came first, not second; and elsewhere could only mean Europe, and Europe could only mean Germany . . . Our resources were not sufficient to meet a menace from both Japan and Germany, and . . . of the two Germany was the greater menace.

Fisher shared his view completely, and went further, to argue that Britain should be prepared to re-establish Anglo-Japanese friendship even at a cost to Anglo-American relations, including preparations for hostilities against America.[159] His pro-Japanese view was supported by his superior, Chamberlain, who told his colleagues that the United States 'will give us no understanding to resist by force any action by Japan'.[160] However, the DRC as a whole did not accept such an extreme view, but did urge the importance of achieving a *rapprochement* with Japan.[161] In its discussions, the DRC realised that due to the financial situation, it was impossible to maintain a two-power standard navy. Britain was therefore unable to fight a two-front war in both the Far East and Europe. Its conclusion was that if détente in Anglo-Japanese relations could be achieved, it would allow the British Navy sufficient force to concentrate on European and Mediterranean waters.[162]

In its first report of 28 February 1934, the DRC advised:

advantage should be taken of any opportunity to improve our relations with Japan . . . We cannot overstate the importance we attach to getting back, not to an alliance (since that would not be practical politics) but at least to our old terms of cordiality and mutual respect with Japan . . .

It observed that while some improvement of Britain's defence in the Far East had to be made *vis-à-vis* Japan, Germany should be designated as 'the ultimate potential enemy against whom our "long range" defence policy has to be decided.' Faced with the possibility that Britain might be involved in war simultaneously in the Far East and in Europe, détente with Japan would allow Britain to concentrate on Germany. However, a policy of accommodation with Japan should be backed up by a British-reinforced military position in the Far East, 'showing a tooth'. The report went further to calculate that the expenditure on the three services would be £82 million, of which £71 million was to be spent in the next five years.[163]

On 14 March, the Cabinet considered the report for the first time. Chamberlain 'warmly supported' the DRC policy of accommodation with Japan. He hoped to tell Japan that 'we had not linked ourselves with America'. He went on to suggest:

> there should be a Pact of Non-Aggression with Japan for a term of years. This might have to be subject to certain assurances, for example, as to Japan's attitude on China. If we could get a satisfactory bilateral pact it might have a beneficial effect on our relations which would enable us to concentrate on the serious situation that was developing nearer home.

The report gained ample support from some other ministers, but Simon displayed some doubts about whether the attempt to restore friendship would be successful due to a number of difficulties: the issue of 'Manchukuo', Anglo-American relations, and the forthcoming Naval Conference. In particular, he had tried his best to appease Japan during the recent crisis, but in vain. However, he agreed with Chamberlain's suggestion of a non-aggression pact.

MacDonald held some reservations on this policy, because he thought 'it would be regarded in America as an Alliance,' but he did not at all oppose the pro-Japanese course, as he said that 'all were agreed that something would have to be done to improve relations with Japan and get on more confidential terms'. In the end, the Cabinet asked the FO and the Admiralty to give further consideration to improving relations with Japan.[164]

According to Cabinet instructions, Simon dictated the first draft of the memo with the help of Orde, and then Vansittart revised it extensively before submission. After analysing the pros and cons of a pact with Japan, the memo found that 'on the whole, the balance seems to incline on the side of the "cons"' due to various disadvantages, such as the record of the Japanese violation of the Kellogg Pact, the issue of 'Manchukuo', the possible negative attitude of America, Russia and China, and in particular, the League of Nations. After discussing it on 19 March, the Cabinet decided that the proposal for a non-aggression pact with Japan should receive further consideration.[165]

On 2 May, the Cabinet decided to refer the DRC Report to the Ministerial Committee on Disarmament, which, after some discussion, asked Chamberlain to re-estimate the costs of the whole rearmament programme suggested by the DRC. Despite supporting the report, the Chancellor was unhappy with the expensive programme. He drew his colleagues' attention to the following points. First, economic recovery was still the most difficult and urgent task at home, so the country could not bear such a heavy burden of armament. Second, Britain should concentrate on Germany in Europe, instead of the Far East. Third, the best defence against the German threat was a strong Air Force. He argued that the expenditure of £67 million suggested by the DRC for shipbuilding was based on a one-power standard, on the assumption that the country would be fighting only against Japan, not a two-front war both in the Far East and in Europe; since the DRC also concluded that Germany was the ultimate enemy, the logical view should be that Britain must prepare for war against her major enemy – Germany – rather than war in the Far East. His conclusion was that if they made military preparations for confronting the European menace, they must give up any hope of preparing for war against Japan, as he explained in his letter to his sister on 28 July:

> if we are to take the necessary measures of defence against her [Germany] we certainly can't afford at the same time to rebuild our battle-fleet. Therefore we ought to be making eyes at Japan.

Accordingly, he reduced the naval replacement budget from £67 million to £5.5 million, and the deficiency programme from £21 million to £13 million.[166] Although he agreed that the Army was important for defence of the Low Countries if the RAF failed to deter German invasion, he cut the Army deficiency budget from the £40 million recommended by the DRC to £19 million. The RAF obtained substantial support from Chamberlain because a powerful Air Force was considered to be an effective deterrent to German aggression. The Treasurer suggested an increase to £18.2 million for the RAF instead of the £15.7 million advised by the DRC.[167] However, even so, British rearmament of the Air Force generally lagged far behind Germany's in the 1930s.[168] Finally, Chamberlain successfully convinced the Ministerial Committee to accept most of his recommendations, trimming the total DRC budget drastically.

In November 1935, the DRC put forward another rearmament programme for 1936–40, requiring £1,038,500,000, and again the ministers reduced the total expenditure in February 1936 by £22.8 million. All this was fatal to the British rearmament effort in the 1930s, and sowed the seeds of her military weakness. During 1934–6, Germany's gross national product devoted to military expenditure was twice or even three times that of Britain (see Table 1.1).

Table 1.1: Percentage of GNP Devoted to Military Expenditure[169]

	UK	Germany
1934	3	6
1935	3	8
1936	4	13

The DRC's policy of restoring a détente in Anglo-Japanese relations by 'showing a tooth' became a policy of appeasing the aggressor.

Early in July 1934, Clive, the new British Ambassador in Tokyo, reported that Mirota, the Japanese Foreign Minister, had told him that Japan was ready to sign 'non-aggression pacts with England and America'.[170] The Ambassador's report received intensive consideration, both from the FO and the Cabinet. Although they agreed to improve Anglo-Japanese relations in principle,[171] a majority of senior members of the FO, including Vansittart, Orde and Mounsey (an Assistant Under-Secretary), disliked the Japanese idea. Apart from the disadvantages they had explored in their previous proposals, Orde analysed that if as a result of a pact the Government were 'to encourage Japan to fight Russia, we should see the Russian counterpoise to Germany seriously weakened'.[172] His argument explored the importance of Russia as a link between Far Eastern and European developments.

Since the beginning of the Manchurian dispute, there had been an outcry in the international communist movement, considering that the Japanese invasion of China 'represents for the imperialists a prelude to a war of intervention against the Soviet Union'. According to the Soviet view, by appeasing Japan, the Western Powers such as Britain, France and America were encouraging her to go further to launch a war against Russia.[173] Faced with Hitler's regime rising in Europe and Japanese expansion in the Far East, Stalin was disturbed by the possibility of a two-front war.[174] Since 1932, the Soviet Government had mobilized all resources to protect security.

First, through the Comintern, it instructed the communists of the world to support China and defend the Soviet Union. Georgi Dimitrov, Head of the Comintern's West European Bureau in Berlin, stated:

In connection with Japan's military operations in Manchuria the war danger has directly intensified, for these may develop into an attack on the Soviet Union which has long been in preparation.

> We consider it to be absolutely necessary, therefore, that our parties should step up the campaign against the war danger and in defence of the Soviet Union.

His call was responded to by the British, French and other Western communist parties, bearing the major responsibility of preventing the transportation of arms for Japan.[175] The communist's struggle against fascist Japan was closely linked with their campaign against the Nazis in Europe. Under instruction from Moscow, they changed their policy: they no longer considered Western social-democrats to be the enemy, but tried to co-operate with them, forming a united front against world fascism.[176] The Soviet Government was consistently suspicious that the British Conservatives, while appeasing Japan, were encouraging Nazi Germany's expansion to the East.[177] Attempts at an Anglo-Japanese non-aggression pact could be well considered as part of such a plot. Dimitrov instructed the British Communist Party that 'at the present stage, fighting the fascist danger in Great Britain means primarily fighting the "National Government" and its reactionary measures'.[178] The British Left declared that 'if the British Government is in any way involved in an attack on the Soviet Union', they would 'urge a General Strike'.[179]

Second, the Soviet Government made a great effort to break its diplomatic isolation. In 1934, Russia joined the League. With this international organization, the Soviets wanted to work out a system of collective security for their own safety. In addition, they had signed mutual assistance pacts with France and Czechoslovakia based on the same consideration.

Third, although the European menace took more and more priority in the Soviet strategy, they did not relax their vigilance towards Japan. On the one hand, they strengthened their defence capabilities in the Far East,[180] and on the other, they lost no time in easing tensions with Japan. At the end of 1931, they offered to sign a non-aggression pact with the latter, but their suggestion went unanswered. However, since then, there had been negotiations back and forth between the two sides until April 1941, when the two countries finally agreed to a neutrality pact. The Soviets argued in favour of their appeasement towards Japan that 'The Soviet Union signed this pact with an eye to safeguarding its security in the Far East, especially in view of the fact that in the west war with Germany was definitely drawing closer.'[181]

Although there existed in British political circles fundamental misgivings and distrust of communism, the officials in the FO did not recommend a pact with Japan on the grounds that it would raise difficulties in relations with China, Russia and America, particularly undermining Russia's deterrent to German expansion. Orde wrote that the idea of a non-aggression pact ignored 'the prime importance of Russia':

> A pact will increase the chances of a Russo–Japanese war and of a weakening of Russia, and will entail, unless accompanied by unobtainable guarantees for China, violent Chinese resentment against us, a diminution in the authority of the League, and most likely a worsening of our relations with the United States.[182]

Simon, however, showed a great interest in the Japanese approach regarding the non-aggression pact, and said: 'why *not*? . . . It may be a valuable buffer against Japanese naval liberty.'[183] Chamberlain (Acting Prime Minister 8 August–22 September 1934) admired the idea too as he wrote to Simon on 1 September that if Britain could not avoid entering into hostilities with Japan in the East:

> if we had to contemplate the division of our forces so as to protect our Far Eastern interests while prosecuting a war in Europe, then it must be evident that not only would India, Hong Kong, and Australasia be in dire peril but that we ourselves would stand in far greater danger of destruction by a fully armed and organised Germany.

He argued against inconveniences which the FO was worried about:

> it is at least arguable that the Manchukuo affair, except insofar as it served to discredit the League, has not hitherto harmed us and, so long as the open door is maintained, is actually likely to benefit British exporters.

He held quite an optimistic view on signing such a pact:

> I have heard it suggested that . . . the Japanese are now in so aggressive a mood and so much under the influence of ambitious soldiers and sailors that they would not think of tying their hands by any agreement to keep the peace. This view seems to me to give insufficient weight to their anxieties about the Soviet

Government, the only Power which really menaces their present acquisitions or their future ambitions. With Russia on their flank it seems to me that Japan would gladly see any accession of security in other directions.

However, he agreed with Simon's suggestion of seeking Japan's views on a pact.[184]

On 8 October, Simon learned from the Japanese Ambassador that 'putting aside the question of Manchukuo as being a *fait accompli*, assurances on the subject of China inside the Great Wall might reasonably be expected to form a part of any new understanding with Japan . . .'[185] A week later, in their joint memo for the Cabinet, Simon and Chamberlain embodied most points in the latter's letter of 1 September, going to extremes to meet Japanese demands. In fact, they looked for a resolution similar to that of Munich 1938:

> The story of Manchukuo . . . is largely past history, and the important thing, both for China and for ourselves, is that Japanese aggression and penetration should not pass the Great Wall and invade or monopolise China proper . . . If, indeed, Japan were prepared to enter into a new and specific assurance which would guarantee the integrity of China proper, without prejudice to the position on either side as regards Manchukuo, this might provide in the eyes of China something of real value in a special Anglo-Japanese arrangement which otherwise it would be impossible to justify. While it would be difficult to frame the guarantee in such a way as not to amount to a recognition of Manchukuo and an abandonment of the line hitherto taken by the League of Nations . . .

Regarding Russia, the memo says:

> anything which makes Japan feel more secure tends to encourage her in an aggressive attitude towards Russia. It may well be that Russia's admission to the League of Nations will cause Japan to adopt a less aggressive policy . . . Japan's attitude in favour of a definite policy of Anglo-Japanese friendship is in part inspired by the desire to secure our benevolence in the event of Soviet-Japanese relations becoming extremely strained.[186]

However, the situation was so delicate and so serious that the Cabinet was unable to come to a decision due to differences within the

Government. On 24 October, it decided to postpone the consideration of it 'until further progress had been made in the Anglo-Japanese Naval discussion'.[187] The non-aggression pact was frustrated later because of the breakdown of the London Naval Conference. However, Chamberlain believed that a regional pact in the Far East 'would *pro tanto* ease' the British position in Europe and deter future German aggression.[188] He did not abandon the idea until the outbreak of the Sino–Japanese War.

In retrospect, exclusion of co-operation with Russia created a big loophole in British Far Eastern defence strategy. In the face of an increasing threat from Japan, Britain did not have any powerful allies in that region, due to American aloofness and Soviet antagonism. Holding feelings of distrust and hatred against communism,[189] the British Government preferred to seek *rapprochement* with fascist Japan rather than communist Russia, just as it chose Nazi Germany in Europe. Chamberlain even hoped to use Russia and Japan's conflicting interests to help achieve his purposes. There is no doubt that this damaged Anglo-Soviet relations further, which cast a shadow on their possible co-operation against Germany in Europe. Ironically, it was the Soviet Union which successfully came to a deal with Japan in 1941, preventing her Far Eastern border being attacked, while Britain became one of the major targets for Japan, being driven out of the Far East during the Second World War.

HOPELESS STRUGGLE POLICY-MAKING AFTER THE OUTBREAK OF THE SINO–JAPANESE WAR, 1937–9

Since the Lukouchiao incident on 7 July 1937, the Japanese military success not only violated China's integrity and independence, but also jeopardised the Western Powers' interests in China. Having learned their lesson during the Manchurian episode, British policy-makers had no illusions about the Japanese ambition 'to turn North China into a second 'Manchukuo'.[190] Pratt suggested the course the Government should take:

[w]e cannot resist . . . because we are not prepared to use force against Japan.

There is only one thing that might conceivably prevent or at least delay developments . . . namely, the fear that we and the Americans were acting together . . . It may, therefore, be worth

> while trying to get the U.S.A. to join us in asking the Japanese
> Government to clarify their attitude.

His conclusion represented the general opinion of the FO.[191]

On 20 July, Eden, the Foreign Secretary, expressed to Bingham, the American Ambassador in London, that the British Government 'were willing to co-operate with the United States Government in any step', for example taking joint action to offer good offices. They both agreed that 'we could not go to war in the matter'.[192] Next morning, without instruction from his government, the Ambassador put forward his personal proposal to Eden that Britain could ask America to join it in an embargo on Japan. It seemed that Eden was not prepared to go that far, saying that he would first like to know the Americans' attitude towards joint action.[193]

After each of these interviews, Eden had an exchange of views with Chamberlain, the Prime Minister, who was not happy with Bingham's suggestion, but agreed to approach the American Government for joint action with the purpose of averting war in the Far East.[194]

The American reply arrived on 22 July, indicating that they preferred working on 'parallel lines' to taking joint action. Norman Davis, US Ambassador-at-Large, told Lindsay that the 'United States Government was rather reluctant to "get mixed up with all Europe" in the Far East'.[195] When the Cabinet discussed the reply on 28 July, Simon (Chancellor of the Exchequer) recalled that the Americans had put forward proposals for joint representations during the Manchurian episode, but Britain 'had preferred to proceed independently'. Now the situation was reversed. Eden 'could suggest no further action that could usefully be taken'.[196]

On 26 August, the British Ambassador in China was seriously wounded during a machine-gun and bomb attack by Japanese planes.[197] After consultation with Chamberlain, Eden sent a communication to Tokyo, requesting from the Japanese Government a formal apology, suitable punishment of the troublemakers, and a guarantee that it would prevent such incidents happening again.[198]

On 8 September, in the light of an unsatisfactory interim reply from Tokyo, ministers considered the question of whether the Government should withdraw the Ambassador in Tokyo if the Japanese final reply was unsatisfactory. Chamberlain was afraid that the withdrawal of the Ambassador 'would not seriously injure Japan', but would instead place Britain in 'a humiliating and embarrassing position' when it was necessary for the Ambassador to return to Tokyo. He suggested that if the Japanese final reply was unsatisfactory, the British Government should express its 'disappointment and regret' but 'did not consider that it was consonant with our own dignity to press them further'. At the same time, the Government would offer the wounded Ambassador a grant of £5,000 in compensation. 'In this way,' he said, 'the incident could be closed by us with dignity and without loss of prestige.' His suggestion was supported by some ministers. Eden also agreed, but pointed out that the Prime Minister's proposal might make Japan 'sever diplomatic relations with us'. Chamberlain summed up: 'the Government were in no way seeking a quarrel with Japan. On the contrary they would like to reach an amicable settlement of this incident.'[199]

However, Japanese provocation inevitably stirred up discussions in political circles about imposing an embargo on Japan. On 29 September *The Times* contained a letter from Keynes, the economist, who had been the principal Treasury representative at the Paris Peace Conference in 1919, estimating that there were 'at least nine chances in 10' that a threat of economic sanctions against Japan by Britain, America and the other nations would be effective. On the same day, in his letter to Jebb, the First Secretary of the Western Department, Keynes summed up the lessons from the Italo–Abyssinian dispute of 1935–6, and pointed out that sanctions against Italy failed because 'they were never applied to any adequate extent'. However, he emphasized that 'if America will not play . . . we can not proceed'. In the response, Jebb told him that the FO were currently considering the matter.[200] In fact, since the Lukouchiao incident, particularly since Japan's attack on Shanghai, the FO had hardened its attitude. On 23 August, Pratt projected that the hostilities in Shanghai might end in three ways: a stalemate, a Japanese victory, or a Chinese victory. His conclusion was:

A stale-mate or a Japanese victory would . . . be a complete disaster from which British interests in China from the Yangtze valley northwards might never recover, and that a Chinese victory . . . would save British interests from extinction and offer a fair prospect of renewed prosperity in the future . . . Unless, therefore, we are prepared to issue an ultimatum to Japan and back it with sufficient force (the only argument that Japan appreciates) there is nothing we can do to protect British interests.

Orde shared his opinion, reviewing the previous policy towards Japan with a critical commentary:

> In the past the western powers, ourselves included, have treated them gently and with marked forbearance, and it is perhaps not astonishing that as a result they have come to believe that a policy of swagger and bluster can sweep all before it. By all means let us try methods of firmness and standing up for our rights on every possible occasion.

But he 'strongly deprecated . . . running any risk of war with Japan'.[201]

In Cabinet, the question of an embargo was also on the agenda. At the meeting of 29 September, Chamberlain, discouraged by the failure of the embargo on Italy during the Italo–Abyssinian crisis, told his colleagues that 'no-one would give any support to any such proposal'. Eden, however, intended to consider an embargo as 'the last resort' if the Americans were willing to co-operate. But he 'wanted to avoid it if he could'.[202] The next day, on his instruction, Orde drafted a telegram to Washington after discussion with Chamberlain, concluding with the sentences:

> We are prepared to consider with the United States Government any course that may fulfil these requisites; but we can obviously say no more without knowing their views . . .

As he was leaving for Yorkshire, Eden asked Vansittart to take the draft to Chamberlain for his approval. The Prime Minister amended the conclusion part as follows:

> We are not convinced that the sort of action suggested here would be effective but we should be quite prepared to examine it further ourselves or with the United States Government if the latter consider it worth pursuing.

Without further consultation with Eden, the telegram was sent to Washington on 30 September. When he read this version on 2 October, Eden was very annoyed, regarding it 'as an invitation to America to reject the idea'. He immediately instructed Mallet, Counsellor at the Washington Embassy, to explain to the State Department that the question of whether or not an embargo 'would in fact prove effective clearly requires further examination'. It was to be desired that the Americans should join them in such an examination.[203]

In its reply of 5 October, the State Department turned down the British proposal, saying that it would only 'cooperate by pacific methods'. On the same day, President Roosevelt gave a speech in Chicago, revealing the difference in tone. He used the word 'quarantine', referring to a method for protecting the community from 'the epidemic of world lawlessness'.[204]

The fresh light thrown by Roosevelt's speech did not balance the disappointment caused by the American reply, but 'aroused much speculation', both in the FO and in the Cabinet. One typical opinion in the FO was that the 'quarantine' speech 'will certainly create a great moral effect', and that there might be strong pressure on the British Government to follow up his proposal for concerted action. However, an opposite view, represented by Sargent, Assistant Under-Secretary, held that the speech did not represent any real change in policy. Vansittart summed up on 7 October: 'we must see how far we can develop this change of tone in the USA, though we may well be disappointed'.[205]

At the ministerial level, Eden felt that after the President's speech, 'it was hardly possible for the American Government to reject' the British proposal. Chamberlain, on the contrary, expressed strong reservations in his letter to his sister. Roosevelt's speech, he wrote:

> sounded very fierce but when one examined it carefully it was contradictory in parts and very vague in essentials. What does he means by 'putting them in quarantine'? . . . my first impression [is] that the President's pronouncement was intended to sound out the ground & see how far his public opinion was prepared to go but that he himself . . . had no present intention of doing anything that wasn't perfectly safe.[206]

On 6 October, Cabinet held a meeting to discuss Roosevelt's speech and the issue of the embargo. Chamberlain pointed out that whatever the speech implied, it was important for the Government not to give the impression that America 'had offered to co-operate in economic sanctions' but that Britain was 'standing in the way of such action'. He thought that 'some reply ought to be made at once'. On the other hand, he warned the Cabinet of the British dilemma both in Europe and in the Far East:

He could not imagine anything more suicidal than to pick a quarrel with Japan at the present moment when the European situation had become so serious.

He concluded:

that sanctions, if effective, involved the risk of war, and, if they were not effective, were of no value. That was a point which might have to be put to the United States of America, namely, as to whether, in the event of their favouring economic sanctions, they were prepared for the consequences, which might well include co-operating in the defence of our own possessions in the Far East.

Hore-Belisha, the War Secretary, drew their attention to the General Staff's disturbance at the fact that the weak British military presence in the Far East made potential countering of any Japanese attack less viable. In fact, two days earlier, Phillips, Principal Assistant Secretary in the Admiralty, was instructed to write to the FO, expressing their reservations on an embargo:

it would be essential to bear in mind that, in the present unsettled political state of Europe, there would be a serious possibility that, once we became involved in hostilities in the Far East, the opportunity of our military unpreparedness might be seized by Germany or Italy to take advantage of our pre-occupation.

They advised that it should be made clear to the Americans that:

H.M. Government would not be prepared to consider sanctions against Japan unless we were firmly assured, in advance, that we could count on the fullest military support and collaboration of the U.S.A. . . .

Their observation was fully supported by the Air Ministry. Eden did not have any objections to the above arguments either. He said that he 'agreed with' the Prime Minister's view about Roosevelt's speech, and added that some diplomatic action should be taken to explore its implications.[207]

After the meeting, he had a discussion with Vansittart about the American reply, and the latter then brought Chamberlain the draft telegram to Washington, which was prepared in the FO on the lines of previous ministerial discussions. The Prime Minister consulted Halifax

(Lord President), Simon and others over the weekend, and gave Vansittart a copy of the amended notes on 11 October. The next day, Eden sent the dispatch to Washington, re-drafted on the lines of the notes. It read:

> I am somewhat concerned lest public opinion here and in the United States should too hastily and too easily assume that quarantine means economic sanctions without the risk of war . . . It would surely be unjustifiable and therefore highly dangerous to assume that Japan would in her present mood submit to a boycott or to economic sanctions that were effective without seeking to rectify the consequences.[208]

The following day, Cabinet members considered the FO proposal for the forthcoming Nine-Power Conference. A little earlier that day, an inter-departmental meeting had been held to discuss it. Representatives of different departments had expressed such divided views on the FO proposal, which was to a certain extent in favour of imposing an embargo on Japan, that they finally had to leave the decision to ministers. When the Cabinet reviewed the proposal, Chamberlain repeated his objection to an embargo, which had been delivered at the previous meeting. Regarding the policy for the Brussels Conference, he suggested that they would say:

> we had come to the Conference in the interests of peace and were not going to think of compulsion until conciliation had been exhausted. That would not commit us on the ultimate issue . . .

Eden said that:

> He endorsed the Prime Minister's description of the effect of sanctions. He himself would never agree to the imposition of sanctions without the agreement of the United States . . . to support those sanctions by the use of force, if need be. He thought that President Roosevelt's speech was a most important new factor in the situation, and that Anglo-American co-operation was vital.

Other ministers also supported Chamberlain. In the end, the Cabinet concluded that the policy should be formulated on the lines of the Prime Minister's proposal.[209]

In the light of the Cabinet discussion, the FO re-drafted its proposal, taking departmental criticism into account. In the new version, Eden instructed that they intended 'not to discourage in any way the present tendency of the United States Government to emerge from their isolation' on one hand, and avoided strengthening 'their isolationist tendencies' on the other by asking 'outright for a guarantee of military assistance'. As for the issue of the embargo, the British Counsellor in Washington should communicate with the American Government on the following lines:

> it seems to His Majesty's Government that if sanctions appeared likely to succeed in their object, there would be a very real danger of Japan taking violent action to prevent their success . . . In view of this danger . . . no country could afford to impose effective sanctions unless it first received from the other participating countries an assurance of military support in the event of violent action by Japan.

After discussion with Chamberlain, Eden approved the dispatch of the telegrams on 18 October.[210]

The British exploratory communications did not bring any encouragement. The Under-Secretary of State told Mallet on 12 October that 'quarantine' was 'a remote and vague objective'. Later that month, Bingham explained to Eden that 'quarantine did not mean sanctions at the present stage'.[211] During the Brussels Conference, the American Delegates did not want to discuss the issue of an embargo on Japan since, as Norman Davis indicated: 'America's direct interests in the Far East were not so great as those of certain other countries.' He poured cold water on Eden, saying that the maximum extent of any sanctions they might impose was that they would 'just refuse to buy Japanese goods'.[212] The three-week conference did not produce any resolution for applying coercive means against Japan, but turned down the proposal of material assistance to China instead.[213] At the Cabinet meeting on 24 November to consider the outcome of the conference, Chamberlain, 'with the general concurrence of his colleagues', pointed out that 'the main lesson to be drawn was the difficulty of securing effective co-operation from the United States'. He said: 'we could not put forceful pressure on the Japanese without co-operation of the United States and while he had no objection to the Foreign Secretary making an approach', he did not place too much hope on it.[214] Eden completely agreed with the Prime Minister, but held a more positive view about Anglo-American co-operation, as he wrote in a secret document of 18 November, which was deliberately concealed from the Cabinet:

> I naturally wish to take all possible steps which may lead to closer Anglo-American co-operation, whether in Europe or in the Far East. Any suggestion that we are lukewarm in the matter of joint action might fatally impair the good will of President Roosevelt, and we should be made to appear once more as having rebuffed an American offer of co-operation as in the case of Manchukuo . . . If the United States Government are prepared and are able to take such action, even though modest and probably ineffective, . . . such joint action might be the foundation for later co-operation in Europe and it might be a capital error to discourage it.[215]

That month, Italy joined the Anti-Comintern Pact signed by Germany and Japan the previous year, forming the Berlin-Rome-Tokyo Axis. After the FO had diagnosed the situation, Collier, Counsellor at the FO, criticised in his memo of 10 November the deduction that Britain could weaken this bloc 'by offering special concessions to one of them' or by buying them off with economic concessions. He argued that the methods proposed would not work, on the grounds that the aims of these aggressive powers were 'incompatible with vital British interests'. Therefore, the Government must set up 'a state of armed truce based upon a balance of power'. To reach this end, Britain should co-operate with France and America, and 'give the lead to all those countries whose interests are threatened by this new "Holy Alliance"'. His memo was reviewed by Vansittart, Orde and other officials, such as Norton and Ingram.[216]

Two days later, the Chiefs of Staff submitted their report comparing the strengths of the great powers. After observing the situation in Europe, the Mediterranean and the Far East, they concluded:

> the outstanding feature of the present situation is the increasing probability that a war started in any one of these three areas may extend to one or both of the other two . . . we cannot foresee the time when our defence forces will be strong enough to safeguard our territory, trade and vital interests against Germany, Italy and Japan simultaneously. We cannot, therefore, exaggerate the importance, from the point of view of Imperial defence, of any

political or international action that can be taken to reduce the numbers of our potential enemies and to gain the support of potential allies.[217]

During his preparations for the reply to the above report, Eden had a discussion with Collier and took the latter's gist 'in a milder form' in his own memo of 26 November, namely to strengthen relations with France, America and other potential allies. On the other hand, Eden agreed with the Chiefs of Staff's conclusion, and wrote:

> There is no reason why contacts should not be maintained between His Majesty's Government and the three Governments in question, and why, in spite of the fundamental divergence that exists between these three Governments and ourselves as to the principles of international conduct, His Majesty's Government should not try to seek a settlement of outstanding issues and the establishment of harmonious relations . . .

His conclusion was somewhat vague and self-contradictory:

> it would . . . be a mistake to try to detach any one member of the German-Italian-Japanese *bloc* by offers of support or acquiescence in the fulfilment of their aims . . . I do not say that we . . . are necessarily in a position to prevent the attainment of the aims of Germany, Italy and Japan . . . We may, indeed have to acquiesce perforce in more than one *fait accompli*. But it would . . . be, in my view, a mistake in the present tense state of Europe to risk opening the floodgates of territorial change by open and express acquiescence in German, Italian or Japanese expansion before it occurs.[218]

At the Committee for Imperial Reference meeting on 1 December, he repeated: 'it was clear that we should make every possible effort to come to terms with each or all of our potential enemies'. He was completely in accordance with Chamberlain and other ministers on the argument that diplomacy should be applied to improve relationships with potential enemies, aiming to balance the British military weakness caused by the limited rearmament budget. He was currently working on preparations for a settlement with Germany and Italy. As for Japan, he told his colleagues at the Cabinet meeting of 8 December:

before the trouble had arisen in the Far East, we had been making great efforts to improve our relations with Japan and that considerable progress had been made. Owing to recent events, we had been compelled to break off these negotiations, but we had tried to keep open the position of resuming them later on.[219]

However, the Japanese did not stop their provocation because of the Western Powers' accommodation in the Far East. In mid-December, two British ships, *Ladybird* and *Bee*, and an American one, *Panay*, were fired upon by the Japanese at Wuhu.[220] After consultation with Chamberlain, Eden sent a message to Washington on 14 December, asking whether the American Government would like to take joint action to defend its interests in the Far East.[221] The next day, the Cabinet discussed the possibility of dispatching a fleet to Far Eastern waters on condition that America was willing to do the same. Duff Cooper, the First Lord of the Admiralty, expressed doubt as to whether it was necessary to make this inquiry of America because of her lukewarm attitude towards co-operation. He suggested that they should ask France to look after the Mediterranean if the British fleet went to the Far East. Both Eden and Chamberlain agreed that further inquiries should not be made until American intentions were clarified. After the meeting, Eden instructed the British Ambassador in Washington to seek the American view as to whether they would make 'an equivalent effort' if Britain sent eight or nine capital ships to the Far East.[222] On 17 December, Roosevelt had a secret meeting with the Ambassador. He turned down the British proposal for a naval mobilisation, but suggested opening Anglo-American Staff talks.[223]

On 12 January 1938, the US President initiated a secret approach to Chamberlain, in which he proposed to work with relevant democratic countries, and to establish the foundation for restoration of world peace and international order. He hoped to receive the British reply by 17 January.[224]

At the moment of the arrival of Roosevelt's plan, Eden was away on holiday in France. Cadogan, now Permanent Under-Secretary, suggested not to discourage the President, 'although the prospects of the success of his scheme are problematical and the risks, maybe, great'. The Prime Minister instructed him to discuss it with Horace Wilson, Chamberlain's confidential adviser, who was 'very anti-Roosevelt'. They agreed that Roosevelt 'was taking and holding over our heads rather a hasty decision without full light on the situation here'. Cadogan, however, intended to add a sentence at the end of the draft reply, that if the President insisted on his plan, 'we should . . . give it our whole-hearted support'. When he brought the draft to Chamberlain, who 'hates R.'s idea', the Prime Minister ignored Cadogan's intention of attaching an encouraging ending. Without consultation with Eden, Chamberlain dispatched the message the next day, saying that he considered Roosevelt's plan as 'cutting across' their efforts to search for settlement with Italy and Germany, and asking the President to hold 'his hand for a short while'.[225]

On his return on 15 January, Eden was 'outraged and uneasy' at all these developments, since he thought 'we must accept Roosevelt's offer outright'.[226] The reaction from Washington over the following days indicated that the President felt 'a little disappointed' and held reservations about the British proposal of offering Mussolini *de jure* recognition of the Italian conquest of Abyssinia. The President said: 'A surrender by His Majesty's Government of the principle of non-recognition at this time would have a serious effect upon public opinion in this country.'[227]

In the mean time, Eden tried to persuade the Prime Minister to adopt 'parallel lines', arguing:

I really do not feel that this initiative of President Roosevelt need necessarily injure the attempts which we are making to improve relations with Germany, nor even have any repercussions on the conversations which I know you are so anxious to start with Italy.

He warned that *de jure* recognition 'might produce constant friction and would make collaboration between the United States and ourselves in the Far East more difficult'.

However, he was not very successful in persuasion. Chamberlain believed that negotiations with Germany and Italy 'were likely to lead very soon to real settlements'.[228]

From 19 to 21 January, the Cabinet Foreign Policy Committee (FPC) held a meeting every day. Chamberlain, Halifax, Simon and Inskip (Minister for Co-ordination of Defence) were 'strong against Roosevelt's plan'. Eden stuck to his argument, to the extent of implying he would resign. Under his pressure, ministers opposed became 'noticeably less stiff'. Chamberlain made concessions too, and agreed to parallel action. Cadogan thought that Eden 'has won a great victory'.[229] Following the agreed lines of the FPC, Eden sent four telegrams to Washington on 21 January, asking Roosevelt to 'go ahead' with his plan. He instructed Lindsay to explain that *de jure* recognition would remove Italian hostility, which limited 'the freedom of His Majesty's Government to take action in the Far East'. The Ambassador should emphasise the accordance between European appeasement and the President's plan:

> The effort therefore which we urgently need to make to find some prompt means of reducing the strain in Europe, which is becoming intolerable, has for its object a measure of political appeasement without which proposals of a more general character for improving international relationships are likely to fall on deaf ears. It is in effect not a divergence from the President's own proposals but a contribution which should assist their realisation.[230]

In the American reply on 24 January, Roosevelt was 'deeply gratified' by the British communications,[231] but he never revived his plan.

Comparison of Eden and Chamberlain's attitude towards Anglo-American co-operation shows that they both considered it essential, as without it they could not apply any coercive measures against Japan. However, Chamberlain thought that Roosevelt's plan would cut across their current efforts to search for a settlement with Germany and Italy, while Eden considered it a parallel line which would benefit European appeasement. Their divergence was only on the matter of methods, not the basic principle of appeasement.

Since February 1938, a series of European developments had placed the Far Eastern problem very much in the background, but without diminishing the problem itself. Late in October, after they occupied Hankow, the Japanese military authorities imposed restrictions on shipping on the lower part of the Yangtze, which violated the Western Powers' rights of freedom of navigation on the river. On 3 November, the American Embassy in London informed the British Government that the US Government had decided to make 'strong representation' to Japan, and inquired whether Britain would take similar action. It also asked what further counter-measures the British would consider if Japan's reply to their protests was unfavourable. Four days later, along similar lines to those of the Americans, the British Ambassador in Tokyo handed a note to the Japanese Government.[232] Meanwhile, the Cabinet discussed the matter on 9 November. Halifax, the Foreign Secretary, thought that 'this action was somewhat significant'. The issue of navigation had bothered them for a year, and 'if the United States were now prepared to act with us', he said, 'the position might be different'. Chamberlain, however, wanted to put the repeated question to America. He said:

> Suppose that we joined with the United States in economic pressure . . . the next step might be a Japanese attack on Hong-Kong. Might we not at some stage have to ask the United States Government what action they would be prepared to take in that event?[233]

The Japanese reply on 18 November indicated, as Sumner Welles, Under-Secretary at the State Department, interpreted: 'the Japanese had every intention of excluding the United States, Great Britain and France from those possibilities of commence in China which should be secured by the observance of the Open Door principle'. The American Government therefore suggested that the Western Powers should consult each other about 'economic action in their defence'.[234] Having undertaken 'a detailed study' of this American suggestion, British policy-makers came to the conclusion, as Halifax telegraphed to Washington, that 'in the present state of Europe, the right policy for the present is not to embark on retaliation'.[235]

In mid-December, Craigie, the British Ambassador in Tokyo, pointed out in his letter to Halifax that 'conciliatoriness, unless backed at least by a modicum of force, is liable to be mistaken for weakness'. The Government should consider the dispatch of battle cruisers – even just one or two – to the Far East, 'manifesting as it would our determination to play our own part in our own defence', which would certainly encourage America. This argument was shared by Crosby, HM Minister at Bangkok, and Clark Kerr, the British representative at Shanghai.[236] Halifax also agreed. Under his instruction, the FO produced a report on 27 January 1939, which came to the same conclusion as Craigie. On 13 February, they enclosed a memo to the Admiralty for its comments. In its reply of 29 March, the Admiralty turned down the FO's suggestion of stationing a capital ship in the Far East simply because 'with our restricted number of capital ships and with heavy commitments in the Mediterranean, it is impossible to do so', and reminded its colleagues in the FO that 'a reduction in the number of our potential enemies is as definite an accretion to our strength as is an increase in the number of our battleships'.[237]

However, the Tientsin incident in April increased tensions in the Far East. On 9 April, Cheng Lien-shih, the manager of the Tientsin Branch of the Federal Reserve Bank, was killed by an anti-Japanese soldier of the Chinese Ninth Route Army in the British Concession. In the joint raids arranged by the British and Japanese Consul-Generals, four Chinese, who were suspected by the Japanese of complicity, were arrested by the British Municipal Police.[238] The Japanese demanded that the four men must be handed over to them. On 1 June, they asked the British Concession authority to give 'a definite reply' by noon on 7 June. It was too much like 'blackmail', as Clark Kerr complained. The British authorities at first refused the demand, on the grounds that the Japanese could not provide sufficient evidence to accuse these four of complicity. On 14 June, the Japanese set up a blockade of the British Concession.[239]

On the same day, the Tientsin problem was discussed at the Cabinet meeting. Halifax confessed: 'it was difficult to hold the balance between action which might involve us in serious difficulties and action which would result in our being subjected to further pressure from the Japanese'.[240] He was preparing a memo, 'Retaliation for the Tientsin Blockade', for the FPC, in which he gave three alternatives: to compromise and co-operate with Japan; to do nothing, or to adopt specific retaliatory measures. He ruled out the first two on the grounds that they would lead to the downfall of China, and would encourage Japan and other aggressive powers. Regarding the third option, he suggested that they should warn the Japanese Government that 'certain action is contemplated and will be taken unless Japan ceases her attacks on British interests in China and gives adequate assurances in that respect for the future'.[241]

The Chiefs of Staff also submitted their report 'The Situation in the Far East' to the FPC on 18 June. The military experts drew the ministers' attention to their view, which had been 'frequently reiterated' since November 1937, that the naval forces were not strong enough to safeguard British interests against Germany, Italy and Japan simultaneously. They concluded that to deal with Japan would require at least eight capital ships, but the maximum force they could send to the Far East was no more than two, while maintaining adequate naval forces at home and in the Mediterranean. Therefore, they did not recommend dispatching such a small fleet (two capital ships) to the Far East unless they could obtain 'the active co-operation' of America, or unless it was in the event of war with Japan.[242]

On the same day, in his dispatch, Craigie suggested that the Government should open negotiations with Japan to resolve the Tientsin issue.[243] Indeed, on 19 June, the FPC met to consider Halifax's memo and the report of the Chiefs of Staff. Chatfield, Minister for the Co-ordination of Defence, thought that 'if a fleet had to be sent, it would be necessary to send a larger fleet'. He reminded the Cabinet of the previous view given by military experts, that while she was at war with these three powers, Britain 'should abandon the Mediterranean rather than sacrifice the command of the sea in home water or the Far East'. But recently, the Staff had changed that view, as he conveyed:

> The sound strategic policy, if faced with several enemies, was to attack the weakest enemy first, and to endeavour to knock him out, before others could come to his assistance . . . we should endeavour at the outset of a war to knock Italy out, hoping that Japan would not join our enemies at the outset.

In the course of the discussion, weighing 'the dangers inherent in the present European situation and in the Far Eastern position', Halifax 'fully shared the anxiety' of the Staff. He did not raise the question of reprisal, but intended to take Craigie's proposal of negotiation with Japan, which actually was part of the alternative of concession that he had opposed in his memo, although he realised that 'in doing so we should increase our political difficulties at home as the critics would at once say that this was another example of the Government's condoning aggression'.

Oliver Stanley, the President of the Board of Trade, delivered a critical opinion:

> if we had to make a very humiliating surrender to the Japanese the reactions on the European situation would be extremely bad, and might indeed lead to the outbreak of a general war. In the result we might have got into the worst possible position, namely, war simultaneously against Germany, Italy and Japan, and at the same time have lost American sympathy and support.

However, the Prime Minister, based on the Staff's report, was in favour of negotiations, pointing out that:

> our best course would have been to endeavour to reach some settlement with the Japanese on the most favourable terms

obtainable, though, no doubt in so doing we should open ourselves to considerable humiliation and criticism.[244]

That afternoon, Halifax instructed Craigie to open negotiations with the Japanese, on the grounds that the Government was 'impressed with the difficulty of retaliatory action'.[245] Starting on 15 July, the Anglo-Japanese negotiations soon came to a first-stage agreement on 23 July, which actually accepted the Japanese invasion of China. It reads

His Majesty's Government . . . fully recognise the actual situation in China where hostilities on a large scale are in progress and note that, as long as that state of affairs continues to exist, the Japanese forces in China have special requirements for the purpose of safeguarding their own security and maintaining public order in regions under their control, and that they have to suppress or remove any such acts or causes as will obstruct them or benefit their enemy. His Majesty's Government have no intention of countenancing any act or measures prejudicial to attainment of the above-mentioned objects by Japanese forces and they will take this opportunity to confirm their policy in this respect . . . [246]

On 23 August, Halifax instructed the British Concession authorities in Tientsin to hand the four Chinese over to the Japanese.[247]

Although the Tokyo negotiations had been still going on, it was obvious that they would not solve problems resulting from Britain's and Japan's incompatible interests. Early in August, Sir G. Sansom, Commercial Counsellor in the Tokyo Embassy, suggested in a memo that the Government should adopt 'a policy of non-resistance' in the Far East. He explained:

we should not attempt to penetrate the home front in Japan by announcing openly that we are prepared, in the proper conditions, to surrender a great deal of what we have hitherto held in China . . .

A policy of non-resistance . . . might have to be prepared in advance so as to give the impression not of a hasty scuttle from danger but of a strategic retreat according to plan.

When he reviewed the document, Cadogan agreed with Sansom's argument to a certain extent.[248] He was preparing a proposal for the Cabinet, in which he pointed out that 'in view of the European situation the only course open to His Majesty's Government' would be a combination of non-resistance and Resistance. His suggestions for combining these two methods included:

1   denunciation of the Commercial Treaty with Japan;
2   the evacuation from the Japanese occupied regions;
3   the recommendation of 'leaving our hands free to take further economic steps';
4   consideration of financial assistance to China.

In his final suggestion, he formulated future policy:

> The Japanese have repeatedly explained that they have been driven to their present policy of seeking a self-sufficient economic *bloc* with their neighbours on the mainland by their exclusion from the markets of the British Empire and other countries. It might therefore be possible for His Majesty's Government to offer to contribute to a general settlement of Far Eastern problems by trying . . . to remove this alleged grievance . . . At a suitable opportunity an intimation of His Majesty's Government's willingness to act on these lines might be conveyed informally to the Japanese Government as an earnest of His Majesty's Government's desire to offer some more constructive way out of Japan's difficulties than the prolongation of a destructive campaign in China and a sterile competition in reprisals with her principal commercial customers.[249]

On 2 August, the Cabinet held a meeting to consider the situation, but ministers could suggest nothing effective to cope with the Japanese, except that they would 'exhaust every device to prevent a breakdown of the negotiations' in Tokyo. However, if the negotiations broke down, Halifax advised that 'the wisest course would be to denounce our Commercial Treaty with Japan'. He confessed that: 'If . . . we could reach some general agreement with the Japanese, he would be prepared to put up with certain indignities . . .'[250]

In the last month before the Second World War, British policy-makers could not produce any effective policy to get them out of this diplomatic blind alley. Faced with actual and immediate danger of fighting three enemies simultaneously, the only thing they could do was to accommodate Japan, and to hold on in this hopeless situation as long as possible.

CONCLUSION

In past and current studies of British Far Eastern policy in the 1930s, there are two major arguments, as mentioned at the beginning of this chapter: whether the policy was one of appeasement, and whether there existed a fundamental relationship between crises in the Far East and Europe. These two arguments are in fact related: neglect of appeasement in the Far East easily leads to the conclusion that there was no fundamental relationship between the Far Eastern crisis and that in Europe. On the other hand, failure to find the underlying relationship between the two supports denial of Far Eastern appeasement.

The substantial evidence in this chapter has proven that the above arguments are incorrect. In the Manchurian episode, the British Government made every effort to buy off the Japanese aggressor by helping the latter 'ward off' charges of aggression. Despite being a leading power in the League, Britain sacrificed the principle of the Covenant by misinterpreting it, emphasising the complexity and particularity of the Manchurian case as an excuse for not employing the principles and methods of the League. Britain attempted to find a way round the conflict between the League and Japan, rather than taking a firm stand to defend the Covenant. Pretending to be fair and impartial to both sides, Britain tried to argue in favour of the aggressor by implying that China's failure to set her house in order provoked the Japanese invasion. The resolution to the crisis, in the Government's opinion, was not to take any anti-aggressive measure, but to 'promote conciliation'.[251] Instead of opposing Japan, the Government tried to restore Anglo-Japanese friendship, which was, in its view, the only assurance for British interest in the Far East. Baldwin said to Thomas Jones during the Shanghai incident:

> The very people like Bob Cecil . . . are now urging us forward to take action. But where will action lead us to? If we withdraw Ambassadors that's only the first step. What's the next? and the next? If you enforce an economic boycott you'll have war declared by Japan and she will seize Singapore and Hongkong and we can't, as we are placed, stop her.[252]

After they revised the DRC policy in May–June 1934, ministers completely ruled out defending the Pacific by force, and decided to accommodate Japan without setting any limits. Chamberlain and Simon went further, devising a proposal for a Munich-like resolution in the Far East, in which they considered that by keeping the status quo in Manchuria, they could invite Japan to enter into 'a new and specific assurance which would guarantee the integrity of China proper' within the Great Wall.[253] British policy after the outbreak of the war in China was a continuation of her Manchuria policy, in the sense that it bore all the consequences of the previous conciliatory course and ran along the road of accommodation with Japan. During this period, the Japanese had jeopardised vital British interests in China, which forced the policy-makers to consider the possibility of retaliatory measures. Nevertheless, whenever they reviewed the problem, the British leaders came to the same conclusion: that they were unable to take any reprisals against Japan due to the European situation, lack of Anglo-American co-operation, and military weakness. Instead of imposing sanctions, they tried to ease tensions by coming to terms with three aggressive powers, including Japan. During the Tokyo negotiations, they made it clear that they would never intervene in a Japanese invasion of China. Although they realised that the Japanese aim was incompatible with British interests, they could do nothing but prepare the policy of 'non-resistance', hoping for future opportunities to reach settlement with Japan by satisfying her appetite further. However, there was a notable difference between British policy in the Manchurian episode and in the period 1937–9: in the former situation, Britain wanted to appease Japan, but in the latter, to a certain extent, she had to do so.

The British policy-makers did not succeed in selling China physically to Japan as they sold Czechoslovakia to Hitler because the situation did not allow it. Unlike Hitler, the Japanese seized Manchuria in 1931 and launched a total war on China in 1937 without consulting the Western Powers beforehand. In other words, the Japanese did not give Britain the time and opportunity to arrange any sale. They aimed not only to control China, but also to expel British influence from East Asia, treating Britain as a loser rather than a business partner. On the other hand, China, unlike Czechoslovakia, did not accept any arrangement which involved selling herself, and she resisted Japanese invasion, even with little help from the Western Powers, rather than surrender. All this had spoiled the Munich-like design in the Far East, but it did not change the nature of Far Eastern appeasement.

There were various reasons for which Britain was on the road to Far Eastern appeasement in the 1930s. Apart from the background discussed in the Introduction, the following points should be emphasised.

First, despite discrediting the League, the Japanese invasion of Manchuria had not yet jeopardised British interests in the Far East. In order to save British interests in China without running any risk of war, the policy-makers thought that the best – and perhaps the only – way was to reach a settlement with the Japanese by sacrificing the Covenant. Wellesley summarised: 'the success of our Far Eastern policy and the prosperity of our economic interests are largely dependent on Japanese good will'.[254] After the beginning of the Sino–Japanese War, the British Government somewhat hardened its attitude towards Japan, due to the fact that the Japanese acceleration of expansion had seriously damaged vital British interests in China. However, limited by the consequences of its earlier conciliatory policy, it had to continue accommodating Japan, whether it liked it or not. During this period, British policy shifted to a certain degree from 'want-to' appeasement, taking the initiative, to 'have-to', due to the deteriorating situation.

Second, during the Manchurian crisis, the British leaders intended to accommodate Japan in order to concentrate on the potential German menace in Europe. Later, whenever they considered applying sanctions on Japan, they were disturbed by European developments. They were hopelessly stuck on the assumption that if Britain were involved in war in the Far East, Germany and Italy would launch their adventures in Europe and the Mediterranean. But leaving Japan unchecked in the Far East made it impossible for Britain to concentrate on Europe either. It deterred policy-makers from taking a firm stand against aggressors in Europe for the same reason that if Britain was engaged in a quarrel with European aggressors, the Japanese would seize the chance to strike in the Far East. This was one of the most fundamental factors leading to European appeasement.[255] In addition, appeasement towards Japan weakened Russia's counterpoise to Germany, and the failure of Anglo-American co-operation worsened the British position, both in the Far East and in Europe. On the other hand, the Japanese success in Manchuria not only encouraged Germany and Italy to put into practice their ambitious plans, but also made a Tokyo-Berlin Axis possible,[256] which increased the danger of Britain being involved in a three-front war. In the face of so much complication and uncertainty in the links between the Far East and Europe, the British leaders thought that appeasement was the best policy to cope with the situation.

Third, British military weakness – in particular, deficient naval forces – took away the basis of strong policy in the Far East. Giving priority to economic recovery at home, ministers cut defence budgets despite the Chiefs of Staff's warning that the Navy was unable to defend British interests against three enemies simultaneously. Faced with the danger of fighting a three-front war, policy-makers preferred to reduce the number of potential enemies by buying off one or all of them, rather than producing sufficient armaments to deter aggression.

Fourth, the British Government hesitated to apply any coercive measures in Japan owing to the failure of Anglo-American co-operation. It emphasised that Britain could not check Japan unless America used force. Since it was not certain that the Americans would use force, they would not check Japan in any way. Both Britain and America were half-hearted in their collaboration. The British Government was afraid that America would leave it with 'the brunt of the work and of the blame', while the latter feared that 'we might go along with the British for a certain distance and they would then leave us holding the bag'.[257] Neither Britain nor America was prepared to take the lead. However, in the Manchurian crisis, it is Britain which should bear the bulk of the blame for weakening Anglo-American co-operation through her hesitation in joining the American action under the Nine Power Treaty and her too conciliatory and unprincipled attitude towards Japan. The failure of Anglo-American co-operation discouraged America, so that she showed a more isolationist attitude towards later developments.[258] Although they had made efforts to gain American co-operation in the years 1937–9, neither Chamberlain nor Eden was prepared to consider sanctions against Japan without an American guarantee, in advance, of full support. In other words, they still intended to push the Americans to the front, instead of playing their own part independently in the Far East to set an example for the latter. Above all, one of the aims of obtaining American co-operation was, as Eden indicated, that American involvement in the Far East 'might be the foundation for later co-operation in Europe'.[259] It was a 'parallel line' which would benefit European appeasement.

Based on these observations, the reply to the arguments at the beginning of this section can be summarised: as a component part of British general appeasement-making, which was an organic whole, Far Eastern policy was one hundred per cent appeasement. This policy not only was a parallel line closely related to European appeasement, but also, to a great extent, caused the latter. Although the Far Eastern crisis itself did not *cause* Mussolini and Hitler's invasion, European appeasement, led by Far Eastern appeasement, offered favourable conditions which, to a large extent, caused the European aggressors' success, just as appeasement had contributed to the Japanese success in the Far East.

In the Manchurian episode, Sir John Simon was a key person in policy-making because he was in a position to sum up the proposals of his subordinates and report the conclusion to his colleagues as the basis for shaping policy, which was generally taken by the Cabinet. His hesitant personality increased the powerlessness that was characteristic of British foreign policy of this period. MacDonald's decline, both in his political career and in health, coincidentally mirrored the decline of Britain. The impact of his personality on policy-making was negative and passive. In the first years of the Sino–Japanese War, Chamberlain and Eden played more important roles in policy-making than anyone else. Although they had minor divergences on the issue of American co-operation, they were completely in agreement on searching for a settlement with the three aggressive powers.

Public opinion in the early 1930s seemed generally pro-League, and Simon was often criticised for having 'let down the League'.[260] However, the public had no way of influencing policy-making. The appeasers turned a deaf ear to the calls for taking a firm line against aggression, and they evaded or suppressed questions which would embarrass them in the House. Within the Government, they also dismissed Cecil's dissenting views. In conspiring to deceive the public, they insisted on this powerless policy. As a result, they missed the first chance to stop aggression. The documents show that the British leaders did not change their methods of dealing with dissenting views throughout later developments in the Far East.

In 1931, the anti-fascist powers were in a favourable position to stop the Japanese aggression. Danger from Germany was still remote, and Mussolini had probably not even thought about his adventure in Abyssinia.[261] Had Japan been checked in time, it would have discouraged the other aggressors, and enabled Britain to gain relief from being confronted with a double danger both in the Far East and Europe later. In fact, according to Lampson's estimate (which even the Japanese Minister admitted), Japan had lost 38 per cent of her trade due to the Chinese boycott, and it might well have brought industrial trouble upon her more quickly than she anticipated.[262] If Britain had taken a vigorous line, it would have been effective even without the imposition of a direct blockade or other military measures.[263] Compared with the total loss of British interests in the Far East later, this risk – if there was any – was worth taking. If a firm line had been adopted, Britain would not have suffered so much from the disastrous consequences of earlier appeasement on the eve of the Second World War.

British Far Eastern policy in the 1930s was a failure, not only because it was unable to check Japan, but also because it aggravated the situation in the Far East:

1   The British policy of appeasement did not satisfy Japan. Instead, it nourished her ambition to such an extent that nothing could satisfy her until she had got whatever she wanted. She instigated a source of war in the world, which made war in the Far East inevitable and world war possible.

2   Not only were British interests in the Far East lost, the League of Nations was not saved either. Failure to settle the Chinese–Japanese dispute in accordance with the principles of the Covenant fore-shadowed the collapse of the League. It also became unavoidable that Britain would soon be deprived of her Far Eastern interests by Japan.

In short, following the Manchurian crisis, British foreign policy-making had been based on appeasement, which was used not only to deal with the Japanese, but also with Mussolini and Hitler.

2

THE FATE OF ABYSSINIA

THE ITALO–ABYSSINIAN DISPUTE

While Japan had become a potential enemy since the Manchurian crisis, Italy was still considered as a friendly power by British policy-makers. On 9 November 1933, the Committee of Imperial Defence discussed the Annual Report of the Chiefs of Staff. Laying stress on Anglo-Japanese *rapprochement* in the Far East, ministers agreed:

> No expenditure should for the present be incurred on measures of defence required to provide exclusively against attack by the United States, France or Italy . . .[1]

In British global strategy, a friendly Italy would insure the British route of communication through the Mediterranean to the Far East, and would be a deterrent to German expansion in Central Europe. This consideration was not in doubt until after the Walwal incident.

Walwal belonged to Abyssinia, but had been poached by Italian forces in the late 1920s. However, Haile Selassie, the Abyssinian Emperor, intended to take back control of the zone because of the importance of the freshwater wells, which were regarded as a source of life there. In November 1934, when an Abyssinian escort went to guard the wells, military confrontations occurred between the Abyssinian and Italian forces. After 5 December, these escalated into general fighting. On 3 January 1935, the Abyssinians invoked Article 11 of the Covenant, and the League Council, with the participation of the British and French delegates, arranged direct negotiation between both disputants. Although the agreement about the establishment of a neutral zone had been reached late in February, deadlock persisted due to the uncompromising attitude of both sides. For example, the Abyssinians declared that since Walwal was within their territory, they had the right to defend it, even using force. They insisted that the dispute should be arbitrated by the League, but the Italians considered that the Walwal incident was evidence of Abyssinian aggression, and they refused to lay down the case for arbitration. In the meantime, they increased their military force in their East African colonies.[2]

On 3 September, the Conciliation Committee decided unanimously that neither Italy nor Abyssinia could be held responsible for the Walwal incident.[3] The Committee of Five worked out a plan on 18 September whereby the independence and territorial integrity of Abyssinia would be respected, the administrative reorganisation should be put into force, and 'a special Italian interest' in the economic development of Abyssinia would be recognised. In addition, the British and French Governments had intimated that they were prepared to facilitate, by common sacrifices, 'territorial adjustments' between Italy and Abyssinia.[4] This plan was accepted by Abyssinia, but rejected by Italy.

On 3 October, Italy, after long-term preparations, went to war against Abyssinia. In light of the Italian act of aggression, the Council Committee decided a few days later that sanctions should be imposed on Italy. Ignoring the League's resolution, the Italians accelerated their military campaign. After they had occupied Abyssinia's capital, Addis Ababa, on 5 May 1936, they declared the annexation of the country.

It is unanimously agreed, as Thorne and Carr comment, that 'the Abyssinian affair was to provide a final, major test' to the League, and 'the Italian victory was a grave blow to the League'.[5] Some historians consider it 'the first great act of appeasement' and 'a turning-point on the road to war'.[6] However, although the Hoare–Laval Plan was generally criticised as a diplomatic scandal at that time, A.J.P. Taylor argues:

> this was a perfectly sensible plan, in line with the League's previous acts of conciliation from Corfu to Manchuria. It would have ended the war; satisfied Italy; and left Abyssinia with a more workable, national territory.

He implies that failure of the plan resulted in the breakdown of the Stresa Front that was a deterrent to Hitler's expansion.[7] Eubank also justifies Britain's acquiescence to the Italian invasion, on the grounds that 'Had British soldiers battled Italian armies in Africa in 1935, Hitler would have been free to move troops into Central Europe'.[8] It is therefore necessary to review the process of British policy-making during this period, to see whether there is any basis for these arguments.

THE IMPORTANT POLICY-MAKERS IN BALDWIN'S GOVERNMENT

During the early stages of the Abyssinian crisis, MacDonald was still Prime Minister, but he 'was already a tired man', contemplating an exchange of posts with Baldwin.[9] In June 1935, Baldwin succeeded him as Prime Minister, following Sir Samuel Hoare's succession to Simon as Foreign Secretary.

Baldwin had the image of being easy-going and humble, with a nature of 'shrewdness, kindness and decisiveness'. 'He was slow to move and act', being criticised for his appetite for leisure, and lack of clear instructions on foreign policy, in which he was not interested. Like his predecessor, he had a fear of war and declining health. However, Hoare commented: 'Baldwin, in fact, was exactly the man for keeping together a Three-Party Government'.[10]

As soon as he took over, Baldwin realised that since his 'first duty' was 'to groom the Party for an election, any Minister who had erred would have to be asked to go'.[11] Due to the Peace Ballot of 1935, which showed that the majority of people held a positive attitude to standing by the Covenant and countering aggression by military and non-military means,[12] he gathered many votes from the electorates in his campaign by declaring that the Government's manifesto was that 'the League of Nations will remain as heretofore the keystone of British foreign policy'.[13] However, he did not really want to fight for the Covenant. During the Abyssinian crisis, his repeated and emphasised underlying assumption in foreign policy-making was to keep Britain out of war. Since he thought sanctions might lead to war, he told the House: 'the moment you are up against sanctions you are up against war'.[14]

In the Cabinet, Neville Chamberlain, Chancellor of the Exchequer, had a stronger and stronger influence on foreign policy after 1933. Regarding the Abyssinian problem, he wrote in his diary on 5 July 1935:

> If we and France together determined that we would take any measures necessary to stop him [Mussolini], we could do so, and quite easily. We could e.g. stop the passage of his supplies through the Suez Canal . . . If the French would not play . . . we should not attempt to take on our shoulders the whole burden of keeping the peace.

He was one of the advocates who 'nailed the British flag to collective security', but he was also the first minister to appeal openly for this policy to be abandoned. He supported the appointment by the Prime Minister of Hoare as Foreign Secretary and Eden as Minister for League of Nations Affairs with a seat in the Cabinet, because he believed that this partnership would make 'a powerful structure'.[15]

As Foreign Secretary, Hoare was 'a shrewd and tough politician' with 'a somewhat prim personality', which 'was combined with an intense and often all-too obvious ambition'. He admired Baldwin's leadership generally, and enjoyed the closest relationship with Chamberlain, with whom he shared more common tastes and mutual understanding. However, he and his partner, Eden, 'were by no means ideally suited in temperament and experience for a close ministerial relationship'. Although Hoare desired some help from the young minister, Eden thought, as he reflected years later, that the appointment of two heads in the FO was a mistake.

Due to Baldwin's lack of interest in foreign policy, Hoare took full responsibility for the conduct of policy-making.[16] His resignation due to the Hoare–Laval Plan showed that he would sacrifice himself rather than betray his colleagues. Perhaps because of this and his determination for appeasement, as well as his good relations with Chamberlain, he continued to make an impact on foreign policy as one of the Big Four, when he was appointed as Home Secretary in Chamberlain's Cabinet in the late 1930s. As for the Abyssinian crisis, Hoare thought the course that Britain should pursue should be the dual policy of 'negotiation with Italy and respect for our collective obligations under the Covenant, based on Anglo-French co-operation'.[17] He disliked the Abyssinians,[18] but sympathised with Italian expansion, and rejected coercive measures such as oil sanctions on the grounds that they might drive Mussolini to desperate acts, or at least make him 'more, rather than less, intransigent'.[19] He believed that Britain could make Italy face up to reality by putting pressure on the Anglo-Italian friendship, and through fomenting suspicion between Italy and Germany.[20]

Being the youngest minister in the Cabinet, Eden succeeded Hoare as the Foreign Secretary after the scandal of the Hoare–Laval Plan. He thought that his appointment was not welcome to his elder colleagues in the Cabinet, so had to prevent some of them intervening in foreign affairs.[21] His general policy was little different from Hoare's.[22] However, weighing the League with the peace of Europe against Anglo-

Italian friendship, he favoured the former.[23] In theory, he laid stress on British international obligations and firm measures such as the imposition of an oil embargo on Italy, by which, he believed, Mussolini would be brought to heel.[24] In practice, although he advocated a pro-League policy in Geneva to a certain extent, he went along with appeasement. He was one of the creators of the Zeila Offer, and after he replaced Hoare as Foreign Secretary, he hesitated to impose an oil embargo on Italy too.

As to Vansittart, his role in policy-making was more important than that which he had played in the Manchurian crisis, since he was one of the principal creators of the Zeila Offer as well as the Hoare–Laval Plan.[25] The key point that he always bore in mind was, as he said:

> My real trouble was that we should all have to choose between Austria and Abyssinia . . .
>
> I was already resigned to choosing Austria . . . because it was the first point of Hitler's expansion . . .[26]

He was in favour of making 'some extensive concession' to Italy in Abyssinia as a solution to the dispute,[27] and he could usually get Hoare 'under the influence of his singleness of purpose'.[28] However, his relationship with Eden was not cordial.[29]

Apart from them, there were other members of the FO who also played a part in policy-shaping, such as R.I. Campbell, Head of the Egyptian Department; Maurice Peterson, Head of the Abyssinian Department (which was newly formed in August, 1935), dealing with the Abyssinian problem; G. Thompson, Expert on Abyssinian affairs; Drummond, the British Ambassador in Rome; and Barton, the British Ambassador in Addis Ababa.

SIMON'S MEASURES: DECEMBER 1934–JUNE 1935

Called 'the acid test' for the League, the Abyssinian case had a more significant impact on British opinion than did the Manchurian crisis, on the grounds that it was related to the anti-German front in Europe. In any case, Italy was, after all, a European power, and Britain had long-standing interests in both the Middle East and East Africa. The tendency of the press, represented by *The Times*, the *Manchester Guardian* and the *Morning Post*, was to appeal to both disputants to moderate their positions, because war, though it was quite unlikely at that time, would do no good to either side.[30] In the House, the Labour Leader, Attlee, believed: 'there is . . . a great opportunity in this incident for re-establishing the authority of the League and the rule of law in Europe'. The Opposition demanded that in the face of Mussolini's unreasonable ambitions, the Government should 'up-hold the Covenant against an aggressor State . . . it is a matter that affects our honour and our vital interests'.[31]

Like the Manchurian crisis, the Italo–Abyssinian dispute posed the British Government with a dilemma: the obligation to the Covenant of the League on one hand, and friendship with Italy on the other. Simon, who was still in the seat at the FO at the time, denied in the House on 19 February 1935 that the Government had put pressure on Abyssinia 'in the direction of conceding the Italian demands'.[32] On the other hand, he was actively pursuing an all-purpose course, which would 'satisfy the due discharge of the duty of the United Kingdom as a member of the Council without impairing in the least degree the friendly co-operation between the United Kingdom and Italy in all matters'.[33]

At the beginning of the Walwal incident, the British Government played the role of mediator, but the Italian attitude remained so 'inelastic' that Simon soon agreed that 'the disputes will go to the League'.[34]

To cope with the problem, various proposals were contemplated. Thompson, in spite of sympathy for the Abyssinians, advised on 12 December:

> . . . on the general political grounds it is essential for us to avoid a squabble with the Italians over the boundaries of Ethiopia . . . we have two objectives, namely (1) to safeguard the watering and grazing rights of our tribes in what is admittedly an Italian zone of influence, and (2) to bring about a détente between Italy and Ethiopia without allowing our existing relations with either country to be affected . . .[35]

Vansittart emphasised in late December:

> Apart altogether from the desirability of easing the situation as soon as possible on colonial grounds, it is very essential that it should not be allowed at the present critical juncture to react in any way upon the relations between Italy and the League and thereby to affect the European question . . . The question must be seen as a whole.[36]

He told Drummond, who shared his idea:

> the last thing we, the Foreign Office generally, and I in particular, desire is to have any bickering with Italy over Ethiopia or colonial matters.[37]
>
> With a little goodwill there would be plenty of ways out and a détente could, I am sure, be secured by mutual expressions of regret and a demarcation which might give substantial satisfaction to the Italians in the long run . . .[38]

He suggested to Simon that 'an amicable settlement out of court at Geneva' was not only 'the best solution available', but one that 'should be easily possible', which, without the Council intervening, would have the great advantage of 'face-saving potentialities for both sides'.[39] But Eden reported from Geneva on 16 December that Mussolini's attitude had made a further attempt for direct settlement out of court 'unavailing'. The FO realised its mediation was 'at an end'.[40]

In late February, it was almost certain that Mussolini would continue the adventure in Abyssinia. In his memo dated 25 February, Vansittart expounded the course that Britain should take:

> (1) We should endeavour to dissuade Italy from going the full length, firstly because it can hardly suit her, when she ought to have her hands free for graver matters in Europe; secondly because of the further, and perhaps deadly, blow that this must deal the League . . . thirdly on account of the consequent reaction on a large section of public opinion . . .
>
> (2) But all this must be done in the quietest, most friendly way. We must not be manoeuvred into playing an isolated and futile role of opposition. Both those epithets are now certain, seeing the attitude of France . . . we cannot afford to quarrel with Italy and drive her back into German embraces.

He asked Simon to explain these points, particularly the second one, to the ministers.[41]

Eden also set down his opinion in a memo to the Foreign Secretary, in which he raised: 'in an acute form the responsibility of H.M. Government as a member of the League, and more particularly of the Council, in respect of recent developments in the Italian-Ethiopian dispute'. He wrote:

Italy aims at no less than the absorption of Ethiopia morsel by morsel . . . unless some hint, and a pretty strong hint, is given to the Italians that we should not view with indifference the dismemberment of Ethiopia, then this dismemberment will take place . . . a clear indication from ourselves and from France . . . might effectively discourage Italy from the more ambitious of her plans.

The Egyptian Department, under Campbell's instruction, suggested taking a standpoint that was in accordance with Eden's.[42]

On 26 February, Vansittart, Eden and Campbell jointly drafted telegrams to Rome and Paris – an urgent attempt to persuade Italy to use moderation and honour her understanding with the Council – which were based on Eden's paper but represented the common views. Simon fully approved of their proposals, and reported this to the Cabinet the next day.[43]

In April, Britain, France and Italy held the Stresa Conference, aiming to consolidate their anti-German front, so the Abyssinian problem was deliberately 'excluded from the formal agenda'.[44] The British and French statesmen completely agreed with Mussolini's expression that the maintenance of peace meant 'the peace of Europe'.[45] Informal conversations about the Italo–Abyssinian dispute, however, showed that the gap between Britain and Italy was far from bridged.[46] When Thompson told the Italian official Guarnaschelli that he hoped that the rumour of an Italian attack on Abyssinia was without foundation, and warned that British public opinion would not tolerate any Italian aggression, his Italian colleague replied: 'the possibility of an offensive could not be entirely dismissed', and he went on to say, ironically, that British public opinion 'had not taken very kindly to Japan's policy in Manchuria, but that this would doubtless not prevent the eventual recognition by His Majesty's Government of the existence of the new State of Manchukuo'.[47]

It was very clear that Italy was contemplating large-scale military operations in Abyssinia as soon as the rainy season ceased, and that the Italians would not accept the resolution from the Council as Japan had done in Manchuria. Facing this grave situation, Simon completed a memo, with Thompson's assistance, for the Cabinet on 11 May, appraising the dilemma:

If they support against Italy a practical application of League principles, their action is bound greatly to compromise Anglo-

Italian relations and perhaps even to break the close association at
present existing between France, Italy and the United Kingdom . . .
the European situation would be most seriously affected, and it
would . . . be more welcome to Germany. On the other hand, if the
United Kingdom acquiesce in what would be a misuse of the
League machinery by acting in a manner acceptable to Italy . . . His
Majesty's Government will undoubtedly lay themselves open to
grave public criticism . . . the League itself seems bound to lose . . .
[having] before it the example of Japan . . .[48]

Considering his memo on 15 May, the ministers concluded:

His Majesty's Government could not acquiesce in a procedure
which must result, not only in nothing being done before
September to prevent hostilities, but which gave no opportunity
for anything to be done.

They thought that Eden should be allowed to use his discretion 'as to the
best course to be taken in his endeavours to secure this aim', and should
discuss the question with the representatives of other countries,
'especially from the point of view of the risks to the League' at Geneva.[49]

HOARE'S DUAL POLICY: JUNE–DECEMBER 1935

Public Opinion and the Appeasers

During the period that Baldwin had held his seat in the Cabinet, the
tide of public opinion was turning against Mussolini. The newspapers,
such as the *Daily Mail* and the *Manchester Guardian*, showed more
and more sympathy with Abyssinia, and support for an economic
embargo against Italy. Churchill told Grandi, the Italian Ambassador in
London, in September:

since Parliament rose, there had been a strong development of
public opinion. England, and indeed the British Empire, could act
unitedly on the basis of the League of Nations, and all parties
thought that that instruction was the most powerful protection
against future dangers wherever they might arise.[50]

A most significant development in public opinion was that the League
of Nations Union organised the Peace Ballot, with the purpose of

investigating public opinion about the issue of peace versus war. The Ballot started on 12 November 1934, and its results came out on June 27 of the following year. It revealed that the British public was strongly pro-League, and intended to take firm action, including economic sanctions and military means, to defeat aggression.[51] Whatever comments might come from various quarters, the Ballot recorded the views of 11 million people, so the Government dared not ignore its effects, particularly during the campaign period. Baldwin pleased his electorate by declaring that Britain would firmly support the League in the struggle against aggression:

> Judgement may lead to action, cautionary action, restraining action, at the extreme to coercive action. We mean nothing by the League if we are not prepared, after trial, to take action to enforce its judgement.[52]

But privately, he 'had always thought the ballot misleading, the questions tendentious and over-simplified, and the picture of collective security divorced from reality'.[53] Baldwin and Hoare repeated in the House that Britain would stand by the League, and was prepared to fulfil her obligation bound by the Covenant. But at the same time, they declared: 'We are not unsympathetic to the Italian need for expansion, and our actions since the War show that our sympathy is more than a sympathy of idle words.'[54] Hoare simply turned down the suggestion, put forward by Lord Cecil that Britain should vote for a general withdrawal of ambassadors from Italy if Abyssinia was attacked.[55] In his telegraph of 24 August 1935 to Clerk, the British Ambassador in Paris, he confessed: 'most people are still convinced that if we stick to the Covenant and apply collective sanctions, Italy must give in and there will be no war'. However, he thought that 'the world will have to face the fact that sanctions are impractical'. But he instructed the Ambassador: 'we must, however, on no account assume the impracticability of sanctions . . . and the British Government must on no account lay itself open to the charge that we have not done our utmost to make them practical'.[56]

The method policy-makers used to cope with the public was that they pretended to uphold the slogan of the League in order to obtain support from the electorate during the campaign on one hand, and fixed the dice in secret to buy the aggressor off on the other. For example, the Zeila Offer, which ceded part of British Somaliland to Abyssinia in order to entitle the latter to make territorial concessions to

Italy, had not been presented to the House for consultation before it was produced. While the Peterson–Quentin proposal was being hatched in the autumn of 1935, Clerk told Laval[57] that however the elections in Britain might go, the 'public opinion at home was such that no British Government could contemplate a solution' like that.[58] In these circumstances, the FO decided that 'as soon as the elections in this country were over a new approach should be made to the French Government'.[59] The Government believed that public opinion could be 'moulded'. Shortly before the Hoare–Laval conversation, the FO advised that 'it would take three weeks to prepare the public mind for a negotiated settlement instead of sanctions'.[60]

The Zeila Offer

When Sir Samuel Hoare replaced Simon as Foreign Secretary, he found that the measures of his predecessor had not been successful in making the Italians face reality.[61] Confronted with the grave likelihood that Italy would attack Abyssinia soon, the British Government had to clarify two important points in order to form its policy: Mussolini's price for peace,[62] and the French attitude towards the dispute, which had not been clear since the Franco-Italian agreement signed on 7 January.[63]

Regarding Mussolini's price, Drummond told the FO of his hypothesis in his dispatch of 1 June that Mussolini might consider several alternatives: some form of mandate; some scheme under which Italy should play the part in Abyssinia that Britain played in Egypt; some kind of protectorate; and outright annexation. He presumed that Britain would have to envisage the first two options if she would not take coercive measures. (He was pretty sure that she would not.) He suggested that if the British Government could show the Italians that 'within certain limits' they were prepared to help the latter, 'both at Geneva and Addis Ababa', the likelihood of any forthcoming recourse to armed conflict would be greatly reduced, although he knew that his proposal was simply a choice of the lesser of two evils.[64]

The detailed minutes showed that the FO had given his proposal serious consideration,[65] but finally rejected it on the grounds, as Vansittart said, that none of the four alternatives would work.[66] However, they inspired him with the idea that:

> if therefore we cannot satisfy Italy at Abyssinia's expense, we are, as before, confronted with the choice of satisfying her at our own

(plus some eventual Abyssinian frontier rectification) or letting things drift on their present disastrous course.[67]

During this period, the new Secretary often held long conversations with Vansittart alone, and sometimes with Eden in attendance, about what measures they should take.[68] Their discussion focused on the following problems, which stemmed, to a great extent, from the Government's Far Eastern appeasement and rearmament policy:

First, Hitler's strength was becoming daily more formidable, and his intentions more unabashed. Secondly, Japanese aggression threatened us with war in the Far East when we were not strong enough to resist Hitler in Europe and at the same time fight in the Pacific. Thirdly, it was essential to British security to have a friendly Italy in the Mediterranean that would both guarantee our lines of communication to the Far East and make it unnecessary for the French to keep an army on the Italian frontier. Fourthly, and as a favourable pointer towards the maintenance of Anglo-Italian co-operation, Mussolini was at the time on very bad terms with Hitler.[69]

Vansittart analysed that Britain had been 'over-landed' by comparison with Japan, Italy and Germany since Versailles, and British Somaliland was a real debit. Although he opposed trading Abyssinia, he opted for paying the price with British Somaliland rather than seeing 'a disastrous explosion' that would wreck the League and very possibly His Majesty's Government too, given that an election was imminent at home. He said:

I should like to see the question of Somaliland considered at least, while we can still get something for less than nothing.

His proposition is supposed to be the origin of 'the Zeila Offer'.[70]

On 16 June, when Hoare, Eden and Vansittart spent the weekend together at Trent, all three 'agreed on the offer' after discussion of Vansittart's proposal. Immediately, Vansittart drafted a note accounting for the Zeila Offer and its basic ground rules. The proposals included that the British Government should cede to Abyssinia the port of Zeila and a corridor, and in return be entitled to insist that Abyssinia should cede territory to Italy in the Ogaden country.[71] At the same time, they consulted Drummond about the proposal, with the latter's answer being favourable on the grounds that even though he could not foresee whether Mussolini would accept it, it was 'worth trying'.[72]

On 19 June, based on Vansittart's note, Hoare reported to his colleagues the details of the Zeila Offer.[73] At the beginning, with the plan being supported only by MacDonald, the Secretary of the Colonies, the Cabinet was 'reluctant to take a decision' due to the suddenness of the move. However, they came to realise that 'the only chance of persuading M. Mussolini to desist from military operations was to take action at once', and in the end they approved of both the plan and Eden's mission to Rome to explain it.[74]

Five days later, Eden had a meeting with Mussolini in which he outlined the Zeila Offer. Il Duce refused the proposal on the grounds that it would strengthen and encourage the Abyssinians. Furthermore, he made Eden understand that he wanted all four sides of Abyssinia to leave the central region intact, but under Italian control; otherwise, he would take the whole country by force.[75] Mussolini's insistence on his demand resulted in the failure of the Zeila Offer. Eden regarded this as 'the end' of the Anglo-Italian conversation for peace terms,[76] but Vansittart and Hoare were unwilling to give up.[77]

Fed by Vansittart with fears of Germany, and warned by the Admiralty of the dangers of an unfriendly Mediterranean in the face of a threat from Japan, Hoare (as he told the American Ambassador on 9 July) was determined to make every possible effort to bring about a negotiated settlement.[78]

French Uncertainty

Since the Franco-Italian Agreement included a secret concord relating to Abyssinia, the British Government had felt uncertain whether Britain could rely on French support if conflict occurred between Italy and Britain over the Abyssinian problem.

On 12 January, Laval told Simon that the Agreement aimed to guard against Germany, particularly her Austria policy. It would not prejudice British rights in East Africa under the Treaty of 1906.[79] As to the secret agreement on Abyssinia, it implied that France would 'not seek to develop any *new* concession or economic interest in Ethiopia', and both the French and Italian Governments agreed 'to give effect to the policy of friendly co-operation' which they were following 'with regard to territories adjacent to their African possessions'.[80] Although Laval explained that he had mentioned 'a free hand' to the Italians only in the economic sphere,[81] he had used this expression without any qualification.[82] In fact, the Quai d'Orsay had been ready not only to give Italy a free hand in the major part of Abyssinia, but to concede part of the French colonies in East Africa before the Franco-Italian agreement.[83] Therefore, Laval left Mussolini the impression, if not in black and white, that Italy could have a completely free hand in Abyssinia, since France had disinterested herself there.[84]

In June, Laval made another agreement with Italy – a secret Franco-Italian military understanding signed by General Gamelin and General Badoglio – by which these two countries would become a military alliance in the possible war against Germany. He said:

> This Treaty was of paramount importance; as long as Italy was France's ally we had a bridge leading to all those countries of Western and Eastern Europe which were then our allies. We could therefore not only benefit by whatever military strength Italy represented, but also by the added strength of Yugoslavia, Czechoslovakia, Poland, and Roumania.[85]

Bound by a series of agreements with Italy, he was in a 'somewhat delicate' position regarding Italian policy in Abyssinia,[86] so he did not know how to choose 'either horn of the dilemma' – the collapse of the League or the end of Franco-Italian co-operation against Germany.[87]

On 27 June, in a conversation with Eden, who had stopped briefly in Paris after his Rome mission, Laval complained that Britain had nearly deceived France by keeping the Zeila Offer secret from him. He told Eden: 'French policy was to refrain from doing anything which would disturb or make less intimate existing Franco-Italian relations.' He would not go further than 'promote a settlement by arbitration and conciliation'. 'The best solution,' according to him, might be 'the maintenance of Abyssinian integrity under Italian suzerainty'.[88]

The Three-Power Conference

In view of the fact that the gap between the Italians' minimum demand and the Abyssinians' maximum concession was too wide to be bridged, Barton suggested to Hoare on 1 July that the only means which could be used was to hold an Anglo-French-Italian discussion under the

Agreement of 1906.[89] Meanwhile, the Italian Ambassador in London had made a similar suggestion.[90] On 10 July, Hoare reported those suggestions to the other ministers, and they came to the conclusion that pending the reply of the French Government to the suggestion, it was impossible to decide on an immediate policy.[91]

On the French side, Laval agreed to the suggestion with some hesitation, and he insisted that it should be made clear what the exact object of the meeting would be; the meeting would be held in 'a realist spirit', and should search for 'possibilities of compromise'.[92] What was worse, Mussolini's attitude was so changeable that he was at first favourable to the meeting, but later showed signs of opposition on the grounds that the Three-Power Conference would get nowhere because he knew that it was impossible for Britain to support his desire to gain protectorally, or at least tutelage over the whole of Abyssinia.[93] Not until late in July did he give any assurance to the condition for the Three-Power Conference that Italian representatives should go to Geneva and state their case there.[94]

On 22 and 24 July, the Cabinet held meetings to discuss the problem. Hoare told his colleagues that if nothing came out of the Three-Power Conference, he was averse to Britain being drawn into a blind alley. He felt that 'the only card' in his hands was 'the deterrent' – 'publicity and conversations with the French in order to get them to put pressure on Italy before the Geneva discussions'.[95] His aim was to avoid 'crude questions' between Britain and France being put by either side to the other as to 'whether they were prepared to carry out their obligations under the Covenant'. 'The underlying assumption would be that both Powers realised their obligations and were therefore jointly interested in finding a way out of the difficulty' – a settlement acceptable to Abyssinia, and within the general framework of the League. Although not optimistic at the time, he believed that the difficulty Italy was confronted with might bring her to face reality.

His line was generally agreed by his colleagues, and he was instructed to continue his efforts to induce the French Government to combine with the British Government in putting pressure on the Italian Government to modify its attitude.[96]

Two weeks before the Three-Power Conference, the French Delegate at Geneva suggested to Eden that the British Government 'should make clear to the Italian Government the limits within which they were prepared to work,' but the FO was not in favour of the suggestion. Campbell said: 'If we did so earlier, M. Mussolini might make our statement an excuse for getting out of the discussion.' Mounsey, Assistant Under-Secretary, feared that the French advice seemed to aim at thrusting Britain 'into the forefront of discussion with Italy . . . in order to enable the French Govet. to keep in the back-ground and play as anodyne a part as possible'. Hoare, Vansittart and Eden all came to the same conclusion.[97] On 6 August, ministers held a meeting to decide the line that Eden would pursue at the Three Power Conference. After discussion, they concluded that in close co-operation with France, Eden should lay before the Italians the alternatives: either acceptance by Abyssinia of certain concessions within the framework of the League or the carrying out by the League of the procedure laid down in the Covenant. But in reference to the latter aspect, 'any detailed discussion of sanctions should be avoided'.[98]

Almost at the same time, Vansittart received a letter from Chatfield, the First Sea Lord, which revealed the unhappy consequence of the Government's limited naval programme of June 1934.[99] The First Sea Lord wrote that, according to the Report of the Chiefs of Staff:

> The Naval situation is bad enough . . . everything possible should be done to avoid precipitated hostilities with Italy until we are more ready . . . It would be a dangerous prospect for us to go to war with Italy with the British Fleet unmobilised and the Home Fleet on leave and scattered.[100]

In the light of these events, Vansittart told Hoare of his pessimistic estimate of the result before he accompanied Eden to the conference:

> I am therefore leaving for Paris with little hope . . . I consider that we should be very cautious as to how far and in what manner we force the pace in Paris, with an unreliable France and an unready England.

Hoare minuted on the document: 'Many thanks for this letter. I entirely agree with you.'[101]

The Three Power Conference was held on 16 August, but broke down within two days on the grounds that there was no common basis between Britain, France and Italy.[102]

Collective Security and Economic Sanctions

The Cabinet held an emergency meeting on 22 August to consider the situation arising out of the failure of the Three Power Conference. In the course of discussion, many references were made to the grave effects of the present British military weakness on diplomacy. Being anxious to avoid a war with Italy, ministers agreed that they 'should keep in step with the policy of the French Government . . . particularly in the matter of sanctions'. Also, they should carefully refrain from 'trying to force nations to go further than they were willing, and generally should make it clear that the question of sanctions was one which the members of the League had to examine in co-operation, and with a view to collective action'.[103] This policy was later known as 'collective security', described in Hoare's speech of 11 September at Geneva, having been drafted with the help of Chamberlain, Eden and Vansittart, and which Baldwin 'endorsed fully':[104]

> If the burden is to be borne, it must be borne collectively. If risks for peace are to be run, they must be run by all. The security of the many cannot be ensured solely by the efforts of a few, however powerful they may be. On behalf of His Majesty's Government in the United Kingdom I can say that in spite of these difficulties they will be second to none in their intention to fulfil, within the measure of their capacity, the obligations which the Covenant lays upon them.[105]

Being broadly supported by many important statesmen such as Austen Chamberlain, Lansbury, Lloyd George and Churchill, this policy, as Hoare explained, had a twofold purpose: to serve as a warning to Germany as well as to Italy, and to stress collective action, particularly Anglo-French co-operation, and collective responsibilities, so that Britain could avoid the risk of taking the lead in pressing the French to go further than they were really willing and then finding herself in an isolated position, facing the conflict with Italy.[106]

In their conversation in Geneva, both Hoare and Laval came to the same conclusion, that war with Italy was 'too dangerous and double-edged for the future of Europe'. Both agreed that they would try to 'avoid provoking Mussolini into open hostility'; any economic pressure on Italy should be decided collectively and applied cautiously in stages, taking full account of non-members of the League.[107]

On 3 October, the Italo-Abyssinian War began. A few days later, the Council decided to impose economic sanctions, including an arms embargo on Italy, but excluding oil and other key commodities. After all, Italy was able to get whatever she needed as long as she paid in gold.[108] Nevertheless, Vansittart still insisted that Britain should 'not proceed *at all* with sanctions' until she received from France all-aspect assurances, particularly military support.[109] Hoare initialled it and told Eden that many ministers had a feeling that he had taken 'the initiative too much at Geneva', and he should 'go slow' until the French attitude had been clarified.[110] But it was too late: Eden had already declared in favour of the imposition of economic sanctions on Italy in Geneva.[111] Under these circumstances, Eden suggested pressing the French Government, both in London and in Paris, to offer the assurances.[112] Due to this constant pressure from the British Government, 'Laval came reluctantly to heel'.[113] He replied that if Britain was attacked by Italy because of the former's collaboration with the League, the French military support of Britain was 'assured fully and in advance'.[114]

In late November, the Council stated that an oil embargo would be considered soon.[115] Vansittart believed what he had gathered from Grandi, the Italian Ambassador in London and Clerk, the British Ambassador in Paris, that if an oil embargo was provoked, Mussolini would declare war on Britain. He warned Hoare and Eden that the British Government should not proceed nor allow others to proceed at Geneva with an oil embargo until it was sure of the adequacy of its own measures of defence and supplies of munitions, and it was sure, in practice, of support from France as well as from other Mediterranean countries. Hoare agreed with his opinion. Meanwhile, Vansittart called back the Oil Paper for the Cabinet, and modified it to this end after discussion between the three. The Cabinet received the Oil Paper on 29 November, but decided to postpone discussion on it until the meeting of 2 December.[116]

The Hoare–Laval Plan

No sooner had the Zeila Offer failed than Vansittart said on 24 June 1935: 'we must have a further shot at this . . . the issues are infinitely too great to take a first no, however uncompromising, for a final one'. This comment met with immediate agreement from Hoare.[117]

At Geneva in September, Laval told Hoare and Eden that there was some room for further discussion, since Mussolini had 'a secret desire to avoid war'.[118] He suggested that the Zeila Offer might be recast with 'something new to it' – France could 'cede a strip of territory alongside the British strip'. Hoare thought it would be valuable if the experts met to work out a new proposal which satisfied Italy without striking at Abyssinia's sovereignty.[119]

On 24 September, taking Mussolini's demand into account, the FO produced a new proposal of cession of territory to Italy.[120] Before discussing it with Eden, Vansittart pointed out to Hoare that in view of 'a strong and aggressive Germany and a weak England':

> it is not to our interest either to force this burning question anywhere near a conflagration, if it can be by any means avoided . . . the Council must make a further and enlarged effort for peace . . . and that the form of the enlargement, or extra inducement, must be the change of territorial satisfaction which we have propounded. That is, Bale instead of Ogaden, plus some additional satisfaction as to advisers.

He thought that Bale, unlike Ogaden, was a fertile zone that could be sacrificed to satisfy Mussolini.[121]

Based on this proposal and discussion, he drafted a revised plan which, after Hoare had initialled it, was sent to Eden in Geneva with the request that he should consult Laval.[122] But Eden's reaction was totally negative, on the grounds that it was hard to believe that 'the offer of one additional province to Mussolini even associated with a promise of a number of other benefits would be likely to secure cessation of hostilities and negotiation of a peaceful settlement with Abyssinia'. With the dispute 'at a most critical stage' and the whole world watching to see 'how the League will acquit itself of its duty', this proposal would 'arouse suspicion' as to the integrity of the British policy. Nor did Eden agree to inform Laval, because the latter, as he said, 'would be only too glad of a hint from us . . . He will jump at any chance to delay the functioning of the League machinery and if we give him any excuse to do so we may have reason to be sorry for it.'[123] He told Hoare that Laval had already put forward a plan that included giving Italy a mandate for large portions of Abyssinia.[124] In their communication with Eden, both Hoare and Vansittart thought the French plan 'impossible' and insisted that their foregoing proposal was 'possible', and had 'a double purpose': first, 'to divert M. Laval from the unacceptable proposals'; second, and more importantly, to make 'a final attempt at peace'. They instructed Eden that the British proposal might be 'either for immediate or eventual use' in due course.[125]

Meanwhile, the British Government learnt through the French that Mussolini's peace terms included the Italian mandate over Abyssinian territories, which would be ceded to Italy.[126] In the FO there was much discussion and many suggestions about the Italian peace terms. Vansittart thought that the Italian terms were 'a distinct step in advance', and they should be given an answer in 'an encouraging tone'. Peterson held a similar standpoint.[127] Thompson suggested that Mussolini's terms should be discussed with the French on the basis of the British line as soon as possible, and that unless and until the British Government had reached agreement with the French and Italians as to the terms of settlement, they should not themselves suggest that they should be given a mandate to discuss outside Geneva. Peterson added two further points: that the first reply referred to above should, when agreed with the French, be made to Mussolini, and that the Italian peace terms were impossible to accept, on the grounds that they were not even accompanied by any promise to suspend hostilities in Abyssinia. Vansittart agreed with the substance of these suggestions, and urged Hoare and Eden to give them immediate consideration.[128] Being instructed by the Cabinet that he 'should receive any Italian overtures for negotiations for a settlement outside the League of Nations very coolly' and 'treat them with caution', Hoare had a discussion on the subject with Vansittart, Peterson and Oliphant, Peterson then being sent to Paris on 23 October, 'to explore the situation with the French Government'.[129]

Two days later, Peterson reported that he had successfully persuaded his French partner, St Quentin, to accept his idea, and drafted a proposal for the basis of a settlement which included:

(a) In the outlying zone (non-Amharic), territories under Italian mandate or any form of Italian administration.
(b) Appropriate involvement of Italy in the collective assistance system regarding the core zone (Amharic country) . . .
(a) and (b) A specific regime must be provided for the outlying provinces with non-Amharic inhabitants in which population decreased as a consequence of war, slavery and famine, etc. . . .[130]

But this draft of the Peterson–Quentin proposal was rejected by the FO on the grounds that it would be impossible to accept it either at Geneva or Addis Ababa. In Hoare's opinion, 'The right and least complicated road to a solution' should be 'by a simple exchange of territory . . . rather than by any more complicated and probably unacceptable devices such as a) and b).'[131] But Peterson held his ground, and explained that in drawing up terms of settlement:

there are two main points of departure – viz. the exchange of territory and Italian participation in the League plan of assistance . . . I still think, rightly . . . the best line of approach to a settlement was from the second point of departure rather than the first, from the point, that is, of Italian participation in the League scheme of assistance rather than from that of exchange of territory.[132]

Laval also told the British Government of his fear that a simple exchange of territory would not satisfy Italy. This was scorned by Vansittart:

M. Laval does not like our suggestion, but can suggest nothing better. He does not really know the subject. The Italians are now ready for the exchange of territory via Zeila, which they originally rejected . . . the Italians wd. now get more than Ogaden & Danakil . . .[133]

Since they were afraid that before the General Election, public opinion would not support the a Government which proposed such a plan, the FO decided that they would discuss 'a new approach' with the French Government as soon as the election was over.[134] The Government won the election on 14 November, and Peterson was sent back to Paris again a week later with 'more precise instructions'.[135] A new 'Peterson Proposal' was soon created. This time, it was accepted in principle by the FO including Eden,[136] and with a little revision, by Thompson under Vansittart's instruction. It turned out as follows:

(a) a League plan of assistance for Ethiopia, subject to (b) and (c);
(b) exchange of Adowa, Adigrat, Danakil (not including Aussa) and most of the Ogaden against a port and corridor;
(c) the endorsement by H.M. Government of some such formula as the following:
'H.M. Government undertake to use their influence in order to secure for Italy the fullest possible facilities of economic development and settlement of such areas in Southern Abyssinia as may be suitable for these purposes and as may hereafter be determined. The realisation of this programme must be effected within the framework of the plan of assistance formulated by the Committee of Five, it being understood (a) that Ethiopian sovereignty over the regions affected will be maintained intact, (b)

that the League of Nations shall be accepted by both Italy and Abyssinia as arbitrator in all cases of dispute.'[137]

Towards the end of November, Laval told Clerk that he hoped to have a meeting with Hoare as soon as possible and an appointment was made for 7 December, when Hoare would have a stop in Paris for a few hours on his way to Switzerland for a holiday.[138]

Meanwhile, some information from the Italian side attracted the attention of the British Government. On 2 November, the Italian delegate, Baron Aloisi, said, and repeated to Hoare in Geneva, that if Britain and France considered an outlet at Assab inadequate, they 'would go back to the Zeila proposal': Hoare felt it a very important suggestion.[139] Shortly before the Hoare–Laval conversation, Vansittart interviewed first the Italian General Garibaldi and then the Italian Ambassador in London, Grandi, from whom he gathered the latest Italian peace terms. Italy demanded: 1) The Bale–Ogaden cession; 2) The Adowa–Adigrat cessions; 3) A corridor only in the Danakil and in Harrar province designed to take the desired railway; 4) The economic monopoly between 37° and 40° as suggested. As its counterpart, Abyssinia could be allowed to have access to the sea.[140]

In the Cabinet meeting of 2 December – the last meeting before his departure for Paris – Hoare reported to his colleagues all of the above. He pointed out that a possible oil embargo at Geneva against Italy might raise the risk of Mussolini's 'mad dog' act – a plan of Italian attack on British interests in the Mediterranean, 'but there was no reason to get in a panic about it'.[141] As to the oil embargo, he said: 'the various countries concerned had provided a more solid front than we had reason to expect', and the United States had shown a co-operative attitude. It was almost impossible to say that the oil embargo would not be collective and effective: in the other words, Britain had no excuse to avoid taking part. Since the Government fought the election on the basis of supporting the League, any other course of action would be 'disastrous and indefensible'. Therefore, he consulted his colleagues as to 'whether sanctions ought to be brought in at once' when the League Committee met on 12 December, or whether to give the peace discussions 'a better chance' by postponing sanctions until later. He personally proposed that on the whole 'the issue depended on the prospect of the peace talks' in Paris, with an oil embargo kept hanging over Mussolini's head as pressure to bring about concessions. He told them that Peterson had been in Paris, engaged in discussions, but that satisfactory progress had not been made. He himself would see Laval on his journey, and he would 'try and press on peace talks' with Laval, and at the same time find out what the French attitude was towards Anglo-French military co-operation against possible attack from Italy.

In the course of discussions, Baldwin invited the opinion of every Cabinet member. Eyres-Monsell, of the Admiralty, and Cunliffe-Lister, the Air Minister, gave ministers the military experts' view. They emphasised that the grave situation in the Far East did not allow British forces to concentrate in the Mediterranean:

> The defences of Singapore were still incomplete, and our position in the Far East depended on the British Navy. So long as the Fleet was tied up in the Mediterranean the position would be difficult . . . if we suffered losses, whether in the Fleet or the Royal Air Force, we should lower the datum point from which the expansion of our forces (as dealt with in the Report of the Defence Requirements Committee) would start.

Therefore, military deficiencies caused by the Government's armament policy deterred it from taking a strong standpoint in the Mediterranean, as they said:

> our defence forces and defences in the Mediterranean were not in a proper condition for war, and from this point of view it was urged that an effort should be made to obtain peace, holding the threat of the oil sanction over Italy . . .

Some ministers worried that from the point of view of British trade:

> sanctions were involving very serious loss . . . Sanctions I, II and III had been agreed to because they would put pressure on Italy with the least possible cost to trade. The proposed Sanction IV was leading us further down the path. It was impossible to turn back but the proposed oil embargo made the position very serious.

They pointed out that if the oil embargo irritated Mussolini and provoked his 'mad dog' act, he would fail and 'disappear from Italian politics and there might be a Communist Government in Italy and a complete alteration in the whole European situation'. They were afraid that 'the position would be worse in the future if, having attempted sanctions, sanction failed'. Only Eden and Duff Cooper, the War Minister, seemed to express differing viewpoints. The former warned his colleagues that postponement of an oil embargo would result in breaking the common front at Geneva, and the latter thought that the importance of the shortage of anti-aircraft ammunition had been exaggerated, and postponement of an oil embargo for a few weeks or a month 'was not going to make much difference' in military preparedness. However, towards the end of the meeting, ministers generally supported Hoare's proposal, on the grounds that 'the object of oil sanctions was to stop war. If the war could be stopped by making peace that would be better'. Baldwin said: 'on broad lines there was general agreement, as proved by the discussion'. The Cabinet realised that there was only a short time for both the peace and military discussions with France, but they hoped that the issues would have been cleared up before the next League Committee Meeting on 12 December. Therefore, Hoare should press on by 'every useful means' in discussions with France, with a view to peaceful settlement, and if the basis for settlement was found before 12 December, the date of the oil sanctions should be postponed. He was instructed to bring questions back to the Cabinet only if 'the peace talks did not offer any reasonable prospect of a settlement' or if 'France was not willing to co-operate effectively'.[142]

It was apparent that when it gave its Foreign Secretary discretion to search for a basis for settlement along broad lines, the Cabinet did not classify the terms 'every useful means' or 'basis for settlement'. Nor did Hoare ask how far he could go with Laval because he did not think it necessary.[143] He once complained to Chamberlain: 'As you may imagine I have received little or no help from other quarters. Stanley would think about nothing but his holiday and the necessity of keeping out of the whole business almost at any cost.' This time, he did not obtain much help from his colleagues either. Before his journey to Paris, he discussed the matter with Baldwin. Busy with the problems that the new Government faced, the Prime Minister had little time to give him more 'implications' for the Paris discussions, and only said: 'Have a good leave, and get your health back . . . push Laval as far as you can, but on no account get this country into war.'[144]

However, Hoare foresaw the importance of the Paris trip. After making 'all arrangements for the conduct of business' in his absence, he wrote to His Majesty on 2 December, asking for leave:

> As my visit to M. Laval on Saturday may be very important, I am
> proposing to take Vansittart with me. If, as I hope, M. Laval and I
> agree upon a basis for a peace negotiation, Vansittart will stop on
> in Paris for a day or two in order to clinch the details . . . In the
> normal course the Secretary of State and the Permanent Under-
> Secretary are never absent from London at the same time. The
> special importance, however, of this meeting makes, I suggest, it
> necessary for me to take him.[145]

This letter, kept in the FO file, was not intended to be a secret to his
colleagues.

The Paris meeting was held on the afternoon of 7 December, once
Hoare had arrived.[146] During the discussions, he was terribly misled by
Laval, as Peterson reported to the Cabinet on 10 December that Hoare
had been pleased at Laval's reception of his proposal for joint Staff
discussions, though he was 'unaware that those discussions would
make what appeared to have been an inauspicious start'. He 'had been
satisfied with M. Laval's promise that France would fulfil her
engagements'. However, he doubted whether Laval could carry French
public opinion with him:

> This uncertainty as to the French attitude had perhaps been a
> factor in the discussion of the French proposals for a settlement. It
> was possible that the French might have been induced to offer
> terms that were less favourable to Italy, but in that event the
> French could not have guaranteed that they had a reasonable
> prospect of success. The French had seemed rather confident
> regarding the present proposals, which gave the impression that
> they might have taken 'soundings' in Italy.[147]

Finally, both sides came to an agreement that they must press on with
the negotiations. For the embargo to be postponed, there would have
to be a good hope of a successful outcome to the negotiations. Hoare
insisted that the proposals must be kept within the framework of the
report of the Committee of Five, and that a mandate must be
excluded.[148] Having discussed this at length, they set up the basis of the
proposals as follows.

(1) an outlet to the sea for Abyssinia,

(2) in exchange for the outlet the cession of some of the occupied territory in Tigre to Italy and a frontier rectification in the east and south-east,

(3) a large zone in the south and south-west in which Italy acting under the League will have the monopoly of economic developments.[149]

After the meeting, Hoare sent the report to the FO, where it arrived on the following day.[150]

On Sunday 8 December, the Hoare–Laval Plan, which was a synthesis of the Peterson proposal and the Italian peace terms, was 'knocked into final shape', and both Hoare and Vansittart were 'well satisfied' with it.[151] Laval kept in daily telephone communication with Mussolini during the Paris peace talks, but insisted that the Abyssinian Emperor should not be given the proposals.[152] Before he left Paris, Hoare told the press that the British Government had not yet been informed of the plan.[153]

That night, Peterson brought it back to London with a note from Hoare which urged the Cabinet to accept the plan. On the Monday morning, Eden was the first Cabinet member to read the documents, since Peterson went to him directly after arriving. He was shocked at these proposals, with their 'signs of hasty drafting' and without an English translation, which in his opinion went far beyond the resolution of the Committee of Five or the guidelines previously established by the FO.[154]

On the same day, the Cabinet held a special meeting to consider the plan. While supporting it, Eden felt bound to warn his colleagues that 'the new proposals went in some respects a good deal further than the earlier proposals of the Committee of Five'. Some features of the plan were unlikely to be favoured by the League. He suggested that the Abyssinian Emperor should be informed, and that the meeting of the Committee of eighteen on 12 December should take place as arranged, both the British and French delegates setting out the plan at the meeting. In the course of the discussion, there emerged sharp criticism that Italy's aggression had gained her more than she could have obtained otherwise. It was recognised that it would cause difficulty if any of the three sides – Italy, Abyssinia or the League – rejected the plan, particularly if Italy and the League accepted but Abyssinia refused. However, if Italy accepted it while the League and Abyssinia rejected it, the first thing they had to do would be 'to try and negotiate for a more acceptable basis'. In spite of criticism of the plan, no one censured Hoare for exceeding his authority, and no one denied that this was a possible basis for settlement either.[155]

The Cabinet finally agreed to Eden's proposal that:

peace terms ought to be communicated to Abyssinia at the same time as to Italy, and that the Emperor should be strongly pressed to accept them as a basis for discussion, or at least not to reject them.[156]

On the following day, ministers continued the discussion. They realised that 'the political difficulties which were likely to confront the Cabinet in this issue all arose from the fact that Abyssinia was likely to reject the proposals', which 'might involve the Government in a difficult situation'. It was certain that:

France would not agree to any new sanctions or to be implicated if new sanctions resulted in military consequences. In that event, in accordance with the Cabinet decisions, this country also would not be willing to involve itself in any new sanctions liable to provoke extreme action by Italy.

Chamberlain suggested:

If Italy accepts and Abyssinia refuses, His Majesty's Government would neither propose nor support the imposition of further sanctions . . .

This suggestion met with the general approval of the Cabinet.

In addition, the Prime Minister had received a question from Attlee, asking that the House be informed of 'the nature of the proposals'. The press also asked for guidance, and particularly wished to know 'whether His Majesty's Government had agreed to any proposals'. The policy-makers decided that the answer should be: 'no suggested basis has at present been submitted for the views of either Italy or Abyssinia and it would clearly be premature to make a statement on the subject at present'. At the same time, they endeavoured to avoid arranging debates before 17 December.[157]

At the Cabinet meeting of 11 December, disagreement and criticism of the plan became stronger, Eden pointing out that:

> a good many members of the League would dislike the proposals. Some would not be willing to interfere with the United Kingdom and France if they thought that peace would come of it.

He hoped that

> he would not be expected to champion the proposals made to Italy and Abyssinia in detail at Geneva. He was not likely to be successful if he made the attempt . . .

On the other hand, an oil embargo was not favoured by many ministers. Baldwin emphasised that the embargo would not be effective without American co-operation. He said: 'Until we knew what America was going to do we should hold our hand.' They instructed Eden that he:

> must not say that we would in no circumstances agree to the imposition of an oil sanction at some future date, or that recent events had removed sanctions altogether from the field of action.

They learned that there was strong reaction among public opinion, because 'a good many people had pictured an end of the dispute in which the aggressor would have lost considerably both in material and prestige'. The result of the plan 'would come as a shock to public opinion'. As to this, ministers agreed that 'public opinion ought to be gradually prepared for a different result to what it had expected'. In spite of abandoning the plan, they decided not to show any definite attitude – either positive or negative – towards it in the House.[158]

Meanwhile, leaks from Paris stirred up public opinion.[159] In Geneva, the Hoare-Laval Plan met with serious criticism from various quarters. The Abyssinian Emperor was 'bewildered' by what Britain had done.[160] In Britain, almost all the newspapers, including *The Times*, the *Daily Telegraph*, the *Herald*, the *Manchester Guardian*, the *Daily Mail* and the *Daily Express*, unusually took the same line this time in criticising the Government.[161] The *Spectator*, a weekly paper, spoke out sharply against the plan for giving:

Italy as a reward for her aggression, or as a bribe to buy her off, far more than she could have got from an award of just arbitrators before the war began. By even countenancing such a deal, let alone accepting responsibility for it, the Foreign Secretary has jettisoned in a day both his own personal reputation and his country's.

The press published a great many anti-Hoare–Laval letters from various quarters. Geoffrey Dawson, Editor of *The Times*,[162] had 'sketched out a leader trying to show the Government the strength of public feeling'.

The pressure groups also lost no time in acting. The League of Nations Union passed a resolution on 12 December, urging the Government 'to support no settlement of the Abyssinian dispute which fails to make it clear that aggression does not pay'. Its Executive Committee sent a telegraph to Eden to ask the Prime Minister to receive a deputation from the Union. Freda White, a member of staff in its Information Department, quoted the words of a Tory member: 'The whole gang must go. Baldwin and Hoare and all of them. It's a national disgrace!' In addition, the National Council of Labour pronounced an 'emphatic protest' against the Hoare–Laval Plan. At a meeting at Manchester University, a resolution calling on the Government to withdraw its support from the plan was passed by 234 votes to 2.[163]

The pressure from Parliament shook the Government more heavily. Thousands of critical letters poured in to MPs. Harold Nicolson, National Labour MP for West Leicester, wrote in his diary on 10 and 11 December:

Find the House seething because of the Abyssinian proposals. They have appeared in the Press, and Baldwin, when questioned by Attlee, made the mistake of saying that there had been a 'leakage' in Paris, thus implying that the Press reports were true in substance.

The feeling in the House is still enraged against the Laval agreement.

He said that 'Sam Hoare has completely and absolutely let us down. I feel very deeply about it and shall certainly not vote with the Government unless I am convinced that they have not done what they seem to have done. But I believe they have.'[164]

Moreover, many Conservative members were aware that they had been betrayed by their leaders, as quoted by Attlee from one of their letters:

> As a lifelong Conservative I write to you to say that I consider the difference between the Paris peace plan and the pre-Election pledges of the Government so great, that I am bitterly ashamed of having supported the Government at the last Election.[165]

On 17 December, the Parliamentary Foreign Affairs Committee held a meeting with some fifty MPs present. Most of them were opposed to the plan. They asked their Chairman, Sir Austen Chamberlain, to see the Prime Minister and convey the Committee's unfavourable view.[166] The climax came with the debates in the House on 19 December, when Attlee insisted that the resignation of the Foreign Secretary was not enough, and that the Government should resign unless they gave a satisfactory explanation.[167]

However, according to Peterson's understanding, the Government still stood by the plan on 14 December.[168] In fact, until 17 December, when it met, the Cabinet agreed that no decision could be taken in Hoare's absence. At that meeting, ministers were increasingly afraid of 'the present excited state of public opinion on the subject'. Chamberlain conveyed the message to the Cabinet from Hoare, in which the Foreign Secretary said:

> the public were thinking of peace terms which could only be obtained as the result of far greater pressure on Italy than it had as yet been possible to apply. In these circumstances the Foreign Secretary took the view that the League of Nations ought to be faced up to the realities of the situation.

Although some ministers did not agree with Hoare and suggested the plan be dropped, Chamberlain took Hoare's side. In the end, the Cabinet generally approved of the line suggested by Chamberlain, of 'boldly defending, not so much the Paris proposals themselves, as the principles on which they had been based'. It instructed Eden to make a statement in Geneva that the British Government was no longer pressing for acceptance of the plan. The Prime Minister would see Hoare after the meeting to clear up the position.[169] That day, Baldwin, Chamberlain and Eden went to see Hoare, who had returned the day before but was kept confined to bed, having broken his nose. Baldwin said to him: 'We all stand together.'[170]

The funeral bell for the Plan rolled on 18 December, when the Cabinet met again to discuss the broad lines that could be adopted for the House Debate the following day. Baldwin confessed: 'though he was not rattled, it was a worse situation in the House of Commons than he had ever known'. He had been informed that Sir Austen Chamberlain 'intended to lead the onslaught, which would then be irresistible'. It was true, as Churchill described later:

> This crisis nearly cost Mr. Baldwin his political life. It shook Parliament and the nation to its base. Mr. Baldwin fell almost overnight from his pinnacle of acclaimed national leadership to a depth where he was derided and despised. His position in the House during these days was pitiful.[171]

In the course of discussion, ministers tried to find a way out of the Cabinet crisis. Chamberlain said that due to the strength of public opinion, the Government could not adhere to the plan. He suggested some pretext that Hoare could use to ward off responsibility: such as that his 'tiredness' prevented him from making a reasonable judgement, or that he had been 'greatly misled by his staff'. But Stanley, the President of the Board of Education, feared that the effect of such a speech would be disastrous to the future of the Government, because the public 'had been let in for this issue at the Election without being told what the real position was'. Simon quoted the Motion on the Order Paper:

> That the terms put forward by His Majesty's Government as a basis for an Italo-Abyssinian settlement reward the declared aggressor at the expense of the victim, destroy collective security, and conflict with the expressed will of the country and with the Covenant of the League of Nations, to the support of which the honour of Great Britain is pledged; this House, therefore, demands that these terms be immediately repudiated.

He sought to influence his colleagues by saying:

> The public were under the impression the Foreign Secretary had gone out to Paris with instructions from the Cabinet to negotiate a

peace. This was not the case. The position would be improved if the Secretary of State were to say that he went to Paris not with instructions to negotiate, but that things developed in this way and that he had then sent the proposals home.

Cunliffe-Lister, the Air Minister, suggested:

The Government were bound to admit that they regarded the Paris proposals as dead. They would never have approved negotiations on those lines if they had been asked to do so before the Foreign Secretary went to Paris; nor could they ever agree in the Paris *Communiqué* expressing satisfaction with the terms.

Although Baldwin had not made up his mind as to whether Hoare should resign or not, ministers generally agreed, as Halifax, the Lord Privy Seal, said, that 'while it was possible to make a case against the worst attacks, this could not be done without admitting a mistake'. In this event, *'the Foreign Secretary ought to resign'*. This seemed the best means to save the Cabinet from the crisis.[172] Knowing that it would be 'something he had hardly ever done before', Chamberlain went to Hoare after the meeting and gave him an account of the Cabinet decision. Hoare was determined to defend the plan and in consequence, to resign.[173]

In his resignation speech on 19 December, Hoare told the House that his reason for resigning was that:

I feel that I have not got the confidence of the great body of opinion in the country, and I feel that it is essential for the Foreign Secretary, more than any other Minister in the Government, to have behind him the general approval of his fellow countrymen. I have not got that general approval behind me to-day, and as soon as I realised that fact . . . *without any suggestion from any one*, I asked the Prime Minister to accept my resignation.[174] [author's italics]

The real reason behind his resignation remains unknown, because no one knows what Chamberlain told him that day.[175] However, one thing is clear: the Foreign Minister was made a scapegoat, partly due to being misled by Laval, partly due to a misunderstanding between him and his colleagues, and partly due to abandonment by his friends.[176]

EDEN'S ATTEMPTS: DECEMBER 1935–MAY 1936

As Hoare's successor, Eden's explanation to Sir Barton, differed little from the double policy, being 'twofold':

> While the Members of the League continue to apply such measures of economic and financial pressure . . . the League must neglect no opportunity of trying to find a settlement of the dispute by agreement between the parties.[177]

Having been terribly delayed by the Hoare Plan, oil sanctions were now placed on the agenda of the League again, and would still be effective.[178] However, in their exchange of views, Vansittart, concerned about the imminence of an oil embargo, told Eden that he did not think the British delegate should in any case 'propose', but only 'support' the enquiry. Taking his suggestion into account, Eden reported to the Cabinet on 9 January that the British delegate at Geneva 'should not oppose, but should support, though, if possible, not himself proposing,' that the Committee should consider probable effectiveness of oil embargo'.[179]

Meanwhile, the Japanese had continuously pricked British interests in the Far East, and the Chief of the Imperial General Staff warned the Cabinet on 17 January that:

> With a hostile Italy . . . our Lines of Communication through the Mediterranean would, in time of war, become precarious if not impossible . . . It seems unlikely, in the present unsettled and inflammable state of affairs in Europe, that any British Government would allow the fleet to get so far away from the vital area in Europe.

Their conclusion was that:

> so long as affairs in Europe remain unsettled, our interests in the Far East . . . are at the mercy of the Japanese. It would seem a reasonable precaution, therefore, to try, by every means and even at some cost, to safeguard, by an amicable agreement with Japan, interests which we are unable to protect by military measures.

Although they knew that there were some major obstacles, including, the issue of 'Manchukuo', and the attitude of the League and America, they argued that:

In view, however, of our extremely weak military situation in the Far East, it is felt to be essential on strategical grounds that every possible effort should be made to overcome these political difficulties.

As for Italy, they estimated:

it is probable that after the present crisis is over, Italy will find it convenient for financial or other reasons to abandon her hostile attitude towards us.[180]

When the Cabinet considered this memo together with the FO's comment on it on 29 January, a minister (perhaps Chamberlain) suggested some possibility of carrying out the suggestions of the Chiefs of Staff. However, Eden, representing the view of the FO, pointed out that 'it was easier to desire them, however, than to find in current events a good opportunity for promoting them in the general interests'. The Government, he said, had done its 'best in recent years to cultivate friendship with Japan, stopping only where the price has been too high'. Based on these debates, the Cabinet instructed the Chiefs of Staff and the FO to have further discussions on 'whether better opportunities could not be found'.[181]

The Italian troubles were thus entangled with the Japanese disturbances. British policy-makers, while they had to appease Japan further, found that it was more difficult for them to take a firm line towards Italy. Having favoured the oil embargo in the past, Eden now became very hesitant to take action, due to the following factors: Abyssinian military collapse was in sight,[182] the Hoare Plan had compromised world opinion, particularly the good will of America in co-operating with the oil embargo,[183] and the French showed more unwillingness to co-operate over extending sanctions after the failure of the attempt to buy peace.[184] He was quite uncertain as to whether the oil embargo was too late to be effective and what line Britain would adopt in the League meeting of 2 March.[185] He first agreed that if the oil embargo 'was deemed ineffective', the League should pass 'a resolution re-affirming its willingness to apply an oil sanction', but with a report referring to the fact that the United States would probably take umbrage at it.[186] However, a few days later, when he met with the French Ambassador in London, he abandoned this idea, saying: 'it would be very difficult for us all to meet in Geneva to take note of the fact that we could not expect United States co-operation in the oil sanction, say therefore we would not apply that sanction, and all come home again'. Having set out the pros and cons, he suggested in the Cabinet meeting of 26 February that the League ought to impose oil sanctions. In the discussion, all arguments were considered. Opinions against the proposal were based on the grounds that the principal burden of sanctions would fall upon Britain, owing to her vast trade links. By contrast, the main arguments in favour of the sanctions stressed that imposition of the oil embargo would save the League's face and the Government's reputation. Convinced by the second opinion, Baldwin shifted to the side in favour of sanctions. In the end, it was decided that Britain should support the imposition of the oil embargo on the basis of the co-operation of other members of the League (essential in the case of the French). Eden was instructed not to take the lead, however.[187]

During the Council Meeting in early March, Eden had several conversations with Flandin, who succeeded Laval as Foreign Minister on 24 January, to seek French support on the subject. But there was 'marked uneasiness' during the course of the conversation, and Flandin seemed to be 'little if at all better than M. Laval'.[188] Instead of accepting Eden's idea that the oil embargo might work and save the League's face, Flandin insisted that it would probably be ineffective, and its result would be to cause Italy to withdraw from the League, thus making it weaker. He was also very worried that the extension of sanctions would lead to war or to an Italian denouncement of the military agreement with France and *rapprochement* with Germany when the German threat was approaching.[189] Owing to the fact that Flandin was very keen to make an attempt at conciliation between Italy and Abyssinia before taking a decision on the oil embargo, Eden thought it 'best to acquiesce', though he did not presume that it would be hopeful. He reported to his colleagues that if the policy of conciliation were tried out, Flandin would probably agree to the imposition of the oil embargo.[190]

In view of the fact that the appeal for negotiation was accepted by both Italy and Abyssinia, the Committee of thirteen decided to postpone its assembly until 23 March.

In early April, after considering the situation, the Cabinet agreed that if no success in direct negotiations was achieved by 8 April, Britain was 'prepared to take part in any extension of sanctions which other nations were prepared jointly to apply'.[191] As expected, the direct negotiations led nowhere. However, the French attitude towards the oil embargo had shifted from hesitation to opposition, on the grounds that due to German re-occupation of the Rhineland on 7 March, prospects of further German action in Europe were now so imminent and so menacing that the Abyssinian question must at all costs be dropped.[192]

Most of April elapsed in endless discussions between the British and French Governments, focusing on whether negotiations on conciliation should continue, and whether the oil embargo should be imposed.[193] French inactivity barred the Council from taking any decision on the oil embargo.[194] During the period of this delay, the Italians had won their major battles, and controlled Addis Ababa by 5 May. Instead of destroying the aggressor, the oil embargo itself was killed by Anglo-French 'co-operation'.

CONCLUSION

As she had done in the Manchurian episode, Britain pursued a conciliatory policy in the Abyssinian crisis, which was an important component part of appeasement in the 1930s.

After the survey of appeasement towards Italy during 1935–6, we should be reminded of the arguments by Taylor and Eubank, namely that the Hoare–Laval Plan would satisfy Italy, keeping her as a deterrent to German expansion, and Britain's non-intervention in the Italian invasion prevented Hitler from sending his troops into Central Europe.

These arguments show that some scholars, like Taylor and Eubank, did not learn from the Second World War the basic lesson that the aggressors' ambitions were unlimited, and they believed it was wise for the appeasers to use one aggressor as a deterrent against another without organising an anti-aggression initiative under the League. Suppose the Hoare–Laval Plan had been carried out, would it have satisfied Italy completely and kept her as a deterrent to German expansion? It is highly unlikely. The plan might satisfy Mussolini temporarily, but, nobody could guarantee that he would not go on to take over the remaining part of Abyssinia, as Hitler did in Czechoslovakia in March 1939. In fact, although the plan did not come into being, Britain and France had provided him with the most favourable situation, which allowed him to succeed in his conquest of Abyssinia. Had the plan been carried out, the result would have been much the same. However, Mussolini was not satisfied, and went on to intervene in the Spanish Civil War and to invade Albania. Italy broke away from Stresa because her ambitions were similar to Germany's, in that both planned expansion by aggression, and also because the conflict of interests between herself and her Stresa partners was, in the long run, fundamentally unresolvable. Indeed, as early as the Stresa Conference in April 1935, more than half a year before the Hoare–Laval Plan, Mussolini had realised that he had to abandon Austria in order to concentrate on Abyssinia.[195] Therefore, it was an illusion for the appeasers to think that they could keep Italy on their side by offering her a deal, as later experience proved. For example, in April 1938, by signing the Anglo-Italian agreement, Britain agreed to recognise Italy's sovereignty over Abyssinia, and in return, Italy would withdraw her troops from Spain. However, after putting his signature to the agreement, il Duce sent another 4,000 volunteers to Spain. Therefore, the Hoare–Laval Plan could not have made Italy safe against an aggression, even if it had been carried out, although its failure resulted in the breakdown of Stresa. (In fact, Italy never declared an official break. Until the *Anschluss*, she was still considered a Stresa power.)

In addition, there is little evidence to support the argument that if Britain became involved in a war with Italy in 1935, Hitler would have sent troops into Central and Eastern Europe. Attention should be drawn to the following: Hitler declared conscription in May of that year, and his task was to build up an army of 600,000 by 1936. During the Rhineland episode, he could send only 20,000 troops to the zone. At that time, the second phase of German rearmament under the Second Four Year Plan had not yet started. The German Army's equipment was not up to date in either quality or quantity. The second service had the more doubtful value.[196] Under these circumstances, it was impossible for Germany to break the military resistance of countries in Central and Eastern Europe (even though the latter did not rely on French assistance). On the contrary, it was ironic that Britain was not involved in any war after the mid-1930s, but it did not form a deterrent to Germany's expansion in Central and Eastern Europe. Therefore, it was Britain's inactivity, and not her intervention, that made Hitler believe that his adventure would not be hindered by the Western Powers.[197]

Just like the Far Eastern policy, British diplomacy of 1935–6 was a failure. Although the dual policy included a strong and active aspect, British policy-makers made every effort to avoid acting on it. Had the oil embargo been imposed, and had closure of the Suez Canal been put into force, Italy would have been beaten easily.[198] Mussolini's 'mad dog' action was unlikely to have been carried out, since it would have meant nothing but suicide. In other words, Britain had a greater opportunity to win at this time. But instead of experimenting with pressurising measures, she took the line of rewarding the aggressor – from the Zeila Offer to the Hoare–Laval Plan – with a higher and higher bribe. The reasons for this contradiction between theory and practice can be found in the following factors.

First, Far Eastern appeasement led to appeasement towards Italy. When they faced the Italo-Abyssinian dispute, the appeasers found that they could not afford to offend Italy, because Japan would be left unchecked in the Far East. If Britain was involved in trouble in the Mediterranean, Japan would seize the opportunity to jeopardise British interests in the Far East. On the other hand, encouraged by the Japanese success, the Italians used Manchuria to justify their adventure in Abyssinia. Aloisi, the Italian delegate in Geneva, asked Eden straight out: 'We had swallowed *la couleuvre* of Manchuria; why was Abyssinia creating such difficulties?'[199] The Japanese, however, showed Mussolini their full sympathy and understanding. In addition, being neutral, Hitler implied that he did not mind if Italy wanted to 'swallow' up Abyssinia. In return, Mussolini stood aside when Germany reoccupied the Rhineland.[200]

Second, being confronted with an imminent German threat, British policy-makers were under the illusion that they could keep Italy on an anti-German front. They failed to see through the aggressive nature of Italy, just as they failed to perceive the unlimited ambitions of the Germans and Japanese. History has proven that sacrificing Abyssinia did not prevent Italy from approaching Germany, nor did it make British policy-makers concentrate on checking German expansion in Central Europe.

Third, French reluctance to become involved destroyed every possibility of vigorous action. Concerned about the emergence of the German threat, France was unwilling to defend Abyssinia as well as the League, at the cost of losing its Italian ally. She helped the aggressor much more than she supported Britain. The French Government made use of every possible excuse, and did its utmost to bar the League from taking any major decisions. Although she never supported France in the latter's struggle against Germany, Britain wholeheartedly followed France in pursuing joint appeasement this time. Therefore, their co-operation achieved nothing but British diplomatic failure and Italian military victory.

During the Abyssinian crisis, public opinion showed an unprecedentedly strong tendency to be pro-League and anti-aggression, which put great pressure on the Government. Although they were not prepared to take any coercive action to check Italy, British leaders deceived the electorate by declaring their support for the Covenant, aiming to gain votes. On the other hand, they secretly devised a plot to sell Abyssinia at the cost of sacrificing the principles of the League, and carried this out as soon as they had won the election. The public was misled and misinformed until the leakage of the Hoare–Laval Plan. In the face of furious public opinion, stirred up by this diplomatic scandal, Baldwin and his colleagues cleverly shuffled off responsibility onto the Foreign Secretary, to save the Cabinet. After they had passed through the Cabinet crisis, Baldwin invited Hoare back into the Cabinet a few months later. Hoare, as one of the Big Four, was still in a position to decide policy. Therefore, the public was able to prevent the Government from carrying out a particular step of appeasement, such as the Hoare–Laval Plan, but could not prevent it from formulating and pursuing the course of appeasement.

Among the British policy-makers, Hoare should certainly bear more blame for the diplomatic failure than anyone else. In spite of being a scapegoat, he himself insisted on the Hoare–Laval Plan, due to his toughness. Baldwin's responsibility was no less than Hoare's, on the grounds that although he was not interested in foreign policy, he laid down the policy that the Foreign Secretary must keep Britain out of war. In addition, his brief and ill-defined instructions to Hoare resulted in misunderstanding and confusion in policy-making. As a ministerial partner, Eden was well known for his anti-Italian and pro-League attitude. However, he was not at all heroic when it came to 'facing the dictators'. After he took over the FO, he, like Hoare, accommodated the French, and likewise hesitated to impose an oil embargo on Italy.

Furthermore, British policy-makers failed to learn their lesson. On 10 June 1936 Chamberlain spoke to the 1900 Club, 'to draw what lessons and conclusion' they could from the crisis:

I see, for instance, the other day that the President of the League of Nations Union issued a circular to its members in which he . . . urged them to commence a campaign of pressure . . . with the idea that, if we were to pursue the policy of sanctions, and even to intensify it, it is still possible to preserve the independence of Abyssinia. That seems to me the very midsummer of madness . . .

Is it not apparent that the policy of sanctions involves, I do not say war, but a risk of war? . . . is it not also apparent from what has happened that, in the presence of such a risk, nations cannot be relied upon to proceed to the last extremity unless their vital interests are threatened?

Earlier than that, Chamberlain had already pointed out, in view of the failure of collective security:

My proposal was that we should abandon the idea that the League could at present use force . . . It should be kept in being as a moral force and focus, but for peace we should depend on a system of regional pacts, to be registered and approved by the League.

Therefore, he urged Eden to reform the League. [201]

Appeasement in the Abyssinian crisis once again strengthened the aggressors and weakened the Western Powers themselves. After Italy conquered Abyssinia, Britain faced a much graver situation: apart from the chronic Far East crisis and the isolation of the United States, she had to face the collapse of the League and the intertwinement of the Italian problem and German expansion, which made it more difficult for her to formulate a firm line. However, a direct consequence of the Abyssinian crisis was that it indicated clearly to Hitler that his Rhineland campaign would not have to contend with intervention by the Western Powers.

CHAPTER 3

HITLER'S FIRST COUP

THE IMMINENCE OF THE GERMAN THREAT

In the inter-war period, the German issue was at the heart of British policy-making. Concern about the potential threat from Germany resulted in accommodation with Japan and Italy. However, until the early months of 1934, the British Government still followed the policy of providing satisfactorily for Germany's future by using the machinery of the Disarmament Conference.[1] It is obvious that policy-making towards Germany was outdated because of the deteriorating situation in Europe.

After Hitler came to power in January 1933, Germany soon announced her withdrawal from the Disarmament Conference as well as from the League. A year later, it leaked out that the number of German first-line aircraft would increase to 1,300 by October 1936, instead of the anticipated 1,000 by April 1939.[2] Moreover, Hitler openly breached the Versailles Treaty on 16 March 1935 by reintroducing conscription – the German peacetime army would consist of 500,000 men.[3] In addition, under the Anglo-German Naval Agreement signed in June 1935, Germany was allowed to build her navy up to 35 per cent of the British naval strength.

As soon as the Franco-Russian Pact was signed on 2 May, Hitler lost no time in making use of this, implying in his speech of 21 May that France had already violated Locarno.[4] However, at that time, von Neurath, the German Foreign Minister, denied that the Führer's speech was an indication that Germany would withdraw from Locarno. He said: 'Such plans are far from our thoughts.'[5] It appeared that until October, Germany had not yet made up her mind.[6]

It was apparent that in mid-February 1936, Hitler began to consider what would be the right moment for the re-occupation of the

Rhineland, and discussed this with his close subordinates.[7] Although he was previously in favour of taking action in the Spring of 1937, he realised the postponement would make matters uncertain. Since 'England was in a bad state militarily, and much hampered by other problems' and 'France was distracted by internal politics', he did not think his Rhineland coup would be answered by military action. In his eyes, the powers advocating economic sanctions seemed 'whipping boys'. In addition, the Japanese Ambassador had twice encouraged Germany to take 'some kind of action . . . in order to be able to pounce on' the Russian Pact.[8] Moreover, Mussolini had confirmed with Hassell, the German Ambassador, on various occasions, that Italy would not interfere, no matter how Germany reacted to the ratification of the Franco-Russian Pact. Hitler had learned from the Abyssinian crisis that since the Western Powers did not defend the Covenant by war, they would not prevent Germany from re-occupying the Rhineland either. In spite of this, Hitler was 'fully aware of the risk'.[9]

In another discussion with von Neurath, von Ribbentrop and Hassell on 19 February, the Führer's analysis was that:

(1) There was a danger that the demilitarized zone would gradually become a sort of inviolable institution which it would then become increasingly difficult to touch. (2) . . . the Italian successes would be more likely to stiffen the British than the reverse. (3) . . . it would be psychologically wrong to believe that, success once achieved, a man like Mussolini would be more inclined to compromise; on the contrary, he would really go all out. (4) Situated as were the two Fascist/National Socialist States, surrounded by democracies tainted by Bolshevism, passivity was, in the long run, no policy.

Therefore, he concluded that the Franco-Russian Pact should be used as a pretext for the Rhineland coup, which would be carried out 'as soon as the ratification was approved by *the [French] Chamber*'.[10]

However, his intention met with strong disagreement from the German Foreign Office and Chiefs of Staff, the latter of which warned that they 'thought and still think the risk was too great', on the grounds that France would demand the withdrawal of German troops, failing which she might attempt to drive them out by force.[11] It is obvious that if Britain and France had stood firm, the Führer would not only have been set back in the Rhineland, but his position would also have been weakened at home, or perhaps he would have been overthrown by his opposition. In that case, history might have been different.

Faced with a dual risk, Hitler took the final decision to occupy the zone two days after the French Chamber approved the Pact on 27 February. On 2 March, under Hitler's instruction, von Blomberg, the Reich War Minister, issued the Z-Day order for the occupation of the Rhineland, with the idea that if the French fought back, the Commander-in-Chief had the right to decide on 'a hasty retreat'. His executive order was given on 5 March, fixing Z-Day as 7 March.[12] On the same day, the decision was conveyed to the German Ambassadors in the Locarno States.[13] The reaction of the Western Powers proved the Führer's estimate correct. Although France wanted to take action, Britain refused to co-operate, which increased French hesitation. The Locarno Powers' failure to act brought Hitler success.

Following the policy towards Japan and Italy, this conciliatory policy towards Germany formed a major part of British appeasement. During the Rhineland crisis period, this policy had been developed and formed; from then on, it had been carried out right up to the outbreak of the Second World War. As a result, not only was the Rhineland lost, but the fate of Austria, Czechoslovakia and Poland was sealed.

In March 1936, the Western Powers had every possibility of checking Hitler. Militarily, until the end of 1935, the British still had superiority over the Germans in their Air Force.[14] In addition, excluding Belgian troops, France, even before mobilisation, had a 60,000-man army ready against about 20,000 German soldiers in the Rhineland.[15] It is widely accepted, as Churchill said, that if the Western Powers had taken action, 'Hitler would have been compelled by his own General Staff to withdraw, and a check would have been given to his pretensions which might well have proved fatal to his rule.' Failure to do so 'lost irretrievably the last chance of arresting Hitler's ambitions without a serious war'.[16] This can best be seen in Hitler's own words:

> The forty-eight hours after the march into the Rhineland were the most nerve-racking in my life . . . If the French had then marched into the Rhineland, we would have had to withdraw with our tails between our legs, for the military resources at our disposal would have been wholly inadequate for even a moderate resistance.[17]

However, some historians follow the appeasers' argument that public opinion did not allow Britain and France to be involved in war with

Germany over the Rhineland.[18] We will review this argument after we have surveyed British policy-making in this episode.

TWO FOUNDERS OF APPEASEMENT TOWARDS GERMANY

Before the Rhineland crisis, there was already a strong tendency among the chief advisers of the FO that was prepared to come to terms with Germany, allowing her to expand in Central and Eastern Europe.[19] Vansittart was the most important official in a position to sum up the proposals made by his colleagues in the FO.[20] Having proposed appeasement towards the Japanese and Italians in the Manchurian and Abyssinian crises, he now formulated the policy that the Government ought to come to terms with Germany by paying the price, and at the same time speed up rearmament, aiming to strengthen its bargaining position. After Hitler's seizure of the Rhineland, although he no longer trusted the signatures of Germany, Italy and Japan, and although he criticised the Government's policy that was partly based on his advice, Vansittart did not suggest that Britain should abandon appeasement, nor did he formulate any alternative course that might be followed. In his proposal of 31 December 1936 he wrote:

> If . . . we utilise our assets, we have much in our favour. Friendship with this country is still the official German policy, and Hitler still puts colonial after European expansion. Indeed the colonial agitation, though widespread and tenacious, is largely artificial. Moreover, the Nazi party, if only it were wisely calculating, is not really in a position to embark on great adventure.
>
> A stage has now been reached, however, when we might be well advised to keep this door ajar in the event of complete success . . .[21]

As Foreign Secretary, Eden was an ambitious and vigorous politician, having built his reputation both in Geneva and Westminster: 'His youth, his charm, his good-looks all worked to his advantage.' Being confident in his own knowledge of foreign affairs, he was very sensitive to any disagreement, and guarded against any intervention, particularly from the former foreign secretaries in the Cabinet, with whom he had a delicate relationship. However, his personal relationship with Halifax and Chamberlain (the latter before 1938) was quite harmonious.[22]

In spite of devaluing Vansittart in his memoirs,[23] Eden, as documents show, relied on his Permanent Under-Secretary very much for policy-making in the FO. Although the Chiefs of Staff warned before the crisis that loss of the demilitarised zone meant the disappearance of a weakness in German defences on their western frontier, which would result in serious consequences for the security of Central and Eastern Europe, the Foreign Secretary insisted that the Rhineland could be used as a bargaining counter to exchange in a general settlement with Germany. During the Rhineland episode, he first used the term 'appeasement' in the debates on the German occupation. Since then, appeasement 'had been freely accepted into the reputable currency of political discussion'.[24] After Hitler's coup, he was still under the illusion that the Führer wanted a deal. While discouraging France, which was inclined to take forceful action, he advised that the Government should continue to search for a general settlement with Germany by offering an air pact, colonies and so on, and by acquiescing in German expansion in Central and Eastern Europe.

As a result of Vansittart's anti-German attitude and Eden's resignation in 1938, both of them were generally considered as anti-appeasers.[25] However, there is little evidence to support this. Since 1931, Vansittart, as the Permanent Under-Secretary, had been in a key position to lay down the basis for policy-making towards Japan, Italy, and now Germany. The policy he suggested was nothing but appeasement. As for Eden, despite some unprincipled disagreements between him and Chamberlain over the issues of Italy and Anglo-American co-operation in the Far East, he was completely in accord with the latter on appeasement towards Germany. What is more, since Baldwin was not very much interested in diplomacy, the conduct of foreign affairs largely depended on Eden.[26] The process of appeasement in this period was that it was first discussed among the chief advisers of the FO, summed up by Vansittart, and decided by Eden. Eden then recommended the proposed policy to the Cabinet, which usually approved it. It could be said that without Eden and Vansittart, appeasement would not have been successfully formulated. Therefore, neither of them was an anti-appeaser; on the contrary, they were arch-appeasers, the most important founders of appeasement, particularly towards Germany. Of the two, Eden was, at ministerial level, a more influential policy-maker, who induced the Government to choose European appeasement in the mid-1930s. It was futile for him to attempt to disguise himself in his memoirs as a hero, 'facing the dictators'.

BEFORE THE CRISIS: PREPARING FOR BARGAINING

As early as the Autumn of 1933, the British policy-makers started to worry about the 'German menace' together with their consideration of Far Eastern policy. Based on the first DRC report of 1934, the Cabinet decided to continue appeasing Japan in order to concentrate on Europe.[27] However, although it did not figure out how to concentrate its efforts, there were some discernible clues to be seen in its proposals. Vansittart stated in his memo of 7 April 1934: 'There is probably no *immediate* danger . . . We have time, though not too much time, to make defensive preparations.' Personally, he doubted 'whether anything much would be gained by a weakening of Hitler – on the contrary'.[28] Chamberlain told his colleagues at the beginning of September, when they were considering a bilateral pact with Japan, that 'all our evidence indicates that it would be easier and simpler to come to an agreement with Japan than with Germany'.[29] However, at that time, it seemed that they believed, as Eden told Mussolini in their meeting on 28 February 1934, that the Germans 'appeared genuinely to desire peace in order to push on with the fifteen years' internal programme'.[30]

A year before the Rhineland coup, the Western Powers had been suspicious of Hitler's intention of expansion. Being more sensitive, since Hitler's speech of 21 May 1935, the French press had suspected that Germany would abandon the Locarno Pact because of the ratification of the Franco-Russian Pact.[31] On the British side, having carefully compared the speeches given by the German leaders from May 1934 to January 1936, Eden concluded: 'after the decree of March 1935 reintroducing Conscription the German leaders began to speak somewhat differently'. Hitler's words 'scarcely leave us room to doubt that the rearmament of Germany is not being carried out for nothing or without a purpose'.[32]

In November 1935, Phipps, the British Ambassador in Berlin, warned the Government that German ambitious attempts could 'only end in war and in a war waged by Germany', and 'the present Ethiopian embroglio is mere child's play compared to the problem that will in some not very distant future confront His Majesty's Government'.[33] According to his observations, German expansion would be in a colony and in Eastern Europe, but Hitler would not commit himself decisively until the Abyssinian problem was settled. Since 'colonial expansion will not necessarily prevent subsequent efforts for expansion in the East', he opposed offering back to Germany her former colonies. While emphasising the importance of speed in British rearmament, he held that the best way to prevent Hitler coming to terms with Russia was for Britain to come to terms with Germany.[34]

The Ambassador's warning was received with great attention.[35] The majority of the senior officials in the FO overwhelmingly advocated a policy of searching for settlement with Germany, which was best represented by the joint memo of Sargent and Wigram on 21 November. These two advisers laid down three policy alternatives: the first was 'a policy of drift', whereby the Government might simply allow the situation to develop and wait to see whether the Western Powers would come to some compromise with Germany or 'keep the German claims in bounds' by strength. The second policy was 'that of the encirclement of Germany' – Britain, as the central force, might form a counter-bloc to German expansion by uniting with France, Russia, Belgium, Italy and countries in Eastern Europe such as Czechoslovakia, Romania, Poland, Austria, Yugoslavia, Bulgaria and Hungary. However, the advisers rejected these alternatives on the grounds that these courses were 'avowedly policies of negation and despair'. In particular, it was doubtful, in their view, that the encirclement of Germany would be successful from the military point of view. What they suggested was the third policy of 'coming to terms with Germany', which was, they said, 'the only constructive policy open to Europe':

> The fundamental idea is of course that the ex-Allied Powers should come to terms with Germany in order to remove grievances by friendly arrangement and by the process of give and take, before Germany once again takes the law into her own hands.

This was the basic theory for appeasement towards Germany. They went on to argue why they must pursue it: since Britain had no 'practical means entirely to counter German expansionist policy' in Central and Eastern Europe, it would be unwise to devise a policy 'which we cannot enforce' – protecting the countries in this region from German invasion. By coming to terms with Germany, they 'might hope to keep within reasonable bounds her Eastern and Central European policy'. Not only did they not rule out the possibility of making concessions to Germany on the colonial issue, but they also considered that 'the strength and weakness of the German economic position' could be used in coming to terms with Germany. As for the Rhineland, although they realised that 'defensively also it undoubtedly constitutes a definite and important counterweight against Germany and a check on any plans which she may entertain in Central and Eastern Europe', they suggested:

> an early attempt to come to terms with Germany can only work towards rendering it less likely that this dangerous question – if . . . it is raised by Germany, will be raised in an aggressive and threatening manner.

However, they confessed that their policy would 'undoubtedly involve the sacrifice of certain vested interests and the abandonment of many a point of national prestige'. But they thought that Britain as well as Europe would benefit from the success of adopting this course. Therefore, they urged:

> we lost one opportunity after another of coming to terms with Germany in the past, when conditions were far more favourable than they are at present.
>
> The longer we wait the more probable it becomes that German demands, at present fluid, will have become crystallised into certain definite forms which will not allow of any compromise or bargaining.[36]

Yet L. Collier, Counsellor at the FO, held a different view, that the Government: 'should consider the grounds for attempting no general settlement with Germany in the present circumstances'. He pointed out that German ambitions in Central and Eastern Europe would meet with firm resistance from Eastern European countries, and to let the Germans expand there was 'even worse than giving Mussolini a free hand in Abyssinia'. He also criticised the authors of the above memorandum for their conciliatory attitude towards the German demand for colonies. He advised:

> It is therefore better to let sleeping dogs lie, and . . . not to discourage those Powers who are building barriers against the 'racial doctrine' by means of Pacts and alliances . . .
>
> Our only wise and safe course is to continue that policy by discussing specific matters such as the Air Pact with Germany, but

firmly refusing to be drawn into any discussion either on the Colonial claims . . . or on German ambitions in Eastern Europe. Above all, I would urge that there should be no attempt to tinker with the Covenant of the League of Nations, in order to provide the Nazi regime in Germany with facilities for raising the question of territorial revision at the expense of other Powers, including ourselves.[37]

His proposal was called 'a combination' of a policy of encirclement and a policy of drift, stressing the latter. However, he failed to offer a plan as to how to organise 'barriers' to deter German expansion.

Having examined these different views 'in great detail', Vansittart found them very interesting. His anti-German attitude did not bother him at all when he outlined the basis for appeasement towards Germany. As for the above proposals, he said he stood somewhere between the two, but in fact he took the proposal of Sargent and Wigram as a line of policy-making, whereas Collier's suggestion with some anti-appeasement characteristics had been put aside in the first stage of policy-making in the FO. In his memo of 1 December, Vansittart decided to recommend to the Cabinet the course of appeasement as the future Government's policy towards Germany:

> You can only come to terms with Germany at a price. Even so I would be glad to come to terms with Germany. I reject of course the policy of drift; but we must be careful not to describe or consider as a policy of encirclement anything that puts us in a stronger bargaining position.

On the other hand:

> We ought not to try a bargain with Germany until we have at least made a beginning on the requirements of the new D.R.C. report . . . We need not of course wait till the D.R.C. requirements are completed. That would take far too long . . . If we try, we must be prepared for possible failure; and for that we must be already strong or running into strength.

Vansittart hoped that he would have an opportunity to discuss those matters with Eden and Hoare. In fact, all these documents had already attracted Hoare's attention to such an extent that he hoped to take them away to read during his holiday in early December.[38]

Meanwhile, Germany had become increasingly lukewarm towards the idea of negotiating with the Western Powers.[39] In the meeting of 13 December, although Phipps was at pains to explain that the Anglo-German Air Pact should be contemplated, Hitler maintained 'the strongest objection'. He condemned the Franco-Russian Pact in a 'violent outburst', and said that he regretted that he had failed to re-occupy the Rhineland on 16 March the previous year. Von Neurath also emphasised that the Air Pact should be accompanied by 'the abandonment of the demilitarized zone'. As to the colonial problem, the Führer expressed the view that 'he was only demanding the return of what really and truly was Germany's property'.[40]

In his dispatch, Phipps warned the FO: 'I fear that zone will be re-occupied whenever a favourable excuse presents itself.'[41] The Ambassador's reports met with general agreement. Eden, who was now Foreign Secretary, thought them 'a valuable and penetrating analysis, admirably timed'.[42] Having carefully considered those reports, Wigram pointed out in his memo of 16 December:

> It now seems most unlikely that any air negotiation could be carried through without the question of the demilitarised zone being raised . . . But no consideration has been given to the matter: nor, I imagine, has anyone, either in Paris or in London, any clear idea as to what attitude ought to be taken if we were suddenly presented . . . with a serious infringement.[43]

In another memo a month later, after talking with de Margerie, First Secretary in the French Embassy in London, Wigram felt:

> Not that I think the French will fight for the zone . . .
>
> Personally, I find it difficult to believe that our interests would not best be served by the maintenance of the zone. But I regard its maintenance over anything but a very restricted future as quite impracticable; and therefore . . . what all of us had best be thinking about now is the means of securing its peaceful disappearance.
>
> If we could get some little benefit in return for its disappearance, I believe we would be wise to take it.[44]

With Vansittart's agreement, Sargent also urged that they 'lose no time in getting clear in our own minds what we want and what we are prepared to do', and that the CID should speedily submit its reports, which had been required by Eden in early January, as to the value of the zone from the military and air points of view.[45]

In late January, he and Collier had an inter-departmental meeting with representatives of the Air Ministry and War Office, and they came to the general agreement that 'an Air Pact would be valuable from the political rather than the military point of view', and it might provide 'a useful bargaining counter' – an Air Pact might be obtained from Germany in return for the abolition of the zone.[46] Their conclusion was completely in accordance with the Foreign Secretary's.[47]

Although he was disturbed by a 'doubtful factor in Germany's plans for the future', Eden, depending on the observations of the British Ambassadors in Berlin from 1933 to 1935, suggested to the Cabinet in his memo of 17 January:

> The first . . . is that it is vital to hasten and complete our own rearmament . . . My second conclusion is that . . . it will be well to consider whether it is still possible to come to some modus vivendi . . . with Hitler's Germany . . . [48]

When the Cabinet considered his memo on 29 January, he informed the ministers that, according to his understanding, France was unlikely to take action 'except where her own frontier was in danger'. In addition, the ministers had a discussion on the report of 17 January by the Chief of the Imperial General Staff, in which their attention was drawn to the formidable situation in the Far East and the possible 'combination of Germany and Japan'. The military experts quoted the observation in the Third Report of the DRC dated 21 November 1935:

> We consider it to be a cardinal requirement of our national and imperial security that our foreign policy should be so conducted as to avoid the possible development of a situation in which we might be confronted simultaneously with the hostility, open or veiled, of Japan in the Far East, Germany in the West, and any Power on the main line of communication between the two. So far as Japan is concerned . . . we emphasised strongly the importance of an ultimate policy of accommodation and neighbourliness with that country. Recent events accentuate the desirability of that policy, difficult though it may be to carry out.

The Chief of Staff strongly echoed the DRC's conclusion of making every effort to improve Anglo-Japanese relations, and suggested that 'only Anglo-Japanese friendship seems likely to deter Japan from entering into closer relations with Germany'. In the course of a short discussion, Eyres-Monsell, the First Lord of the Admiralty pointed out:

> The real danger was lest Germany and Japan should be driven together . . . If Germany were to move in Eastern Europe there was the danger that Japan might move in the Far East.

He had informed the French that the British Government thought:

> that such a move on the part of Japan would be of greater concern to this country with its vast interests in the Far East than German action in Eastern Europe.

In the end, faced with the Italian danger in the Mediterranean and the German menace in Europe, the Cabinet instructed the FO and the Chiefs of Staff to discuss the possibility of improving Anglo-Japanese relations further. As for the policy towards Germany, the ministers agreed that the question should be taken up as soon as Eden was ready.[49]

In the mean time, the shape of the policy had been developing in the hands of Vansittart, Sargent and the Department.[50] In this process, both Vansittart and Eden often consulted Phipps.[51] On 3 February, Vansittart completed his memo, which was a comprehensive analysis of the German problem.

Absorbing the main ideas from the proposals of Sargent, Wigram and Phipps, Vansittart once again emphasised the necessity of coming to terms with Germany, on the grounds that since the Versailles system had broken down, something must be put in its place to avoid 'consequent tension'. In other words, appeasement would replace Versailles as a new basis for international affairs. Not only did he criticise those 'who feel their very existence dependent on the uncompromising defence of an inelastic *status quo*', but he also thought that a policy of waiting was dangerous, on the grounds that an armed Germany, seeking the satisfaction of its ambitions, would choose her own time for asserting each of her claims, and Europe would be forced to deal with each one separately. Therefore, he proposed that the British Government should seek a broad basis for negotiations that 'must not be a temporary and local *détente* but a lasting and comprehensive settlement'. He went on:

> these changes should be made, if possible, as part of an agreed settlement and not as a result of demands formulated under the threat of military pressure.
>
> This settlement must take the form of a bargain. A bargain can only be achieved at a price . . . we have got to pay for it.

He told the British leaders that Germany aimed at the demilitarisation of the Rhineland, expansion in Central and Eastern Europe, return of the colonies and so on. He estimated that:

> the demilitarised Rhineland is not likely to persist indefinitely . . . an early attempt to come to terms with Germany can only render it less likely that this dangerous question will be thrust forward in an aggressive and dangerous manner.

As to German expansion in Europe, although he was opposed to making 'any statements of renunciation in Central Europe', he suggested that 'the problem may be solved by the creation and recognition of some kind of "special area" for German economic expansion in Central Europe'. In addition to the possibility of moderating and channelling Germany's non-military influence in Central and Eastern Europe, 'an Anglo-French settlement with Germany would be a more effective guarantee against the dangers of Russo-German co-operation'.

In light of the fact that the British Government was not prepared to consider or discuss ceding the colonies to Germany, he thought that in this case 'there is no prospect of reaching any real agreement with Germany'. He proposed that 'we could meet the German claim by the retrocession of some or all of the former German colonies' as part of a general settlement.[52]

Eden recommended Vansittart's memo to the Cabinet as 'the outcome of prolonged and anxious study in the Foreign Office of the situation'. A week later, in his paper attached to Vansittart's memo, Eden approached the necessity of appeasement from another angle in his analysis:

> The poverty of Nazi Germany, measured in that country's dwindling export trade and increase of unemployment, may be

expected to have the same effect as in Italy, and to encourage a Dictator to launch his people on some foreign venture as the only means that remain to him to distract their attention from the failure of his policy at home.

One of his suggestions for avoiding this consequence was to adopt measures of economic appeasement:

> Our purpose being to avoid war, it should follow that we should be wise to do everything in our power to assist Germany's economic recovery, thereby easing the strain upon the German rulers, and making an outbreak less likely.

He made his position clear:

> I am in favour of making some attempt to come to terms with Germany . . . We should be prepared to make concessions to Germany . . . but these concessions must only be offered as part of a final settlement which includes some further arms limitation and Germany's return to the League.

What is more, he did not stop at the point of only formulating the basis for appeasement, he went further, to urge the Government to examine 'what it is possible to offer to Germany' as 'the first step' to carry out appeasement.[53] According to his suggestion, Baldwin appointed a committee on 14 February to consider the policy towards Germany, consisting of himself, MacDonald, Chamberlain, Eden, Halifax and three other ministers, who would hold a meeting on 17 February.[54]

For this meeting, Sargent prepared a memo on the Rhineland, for the Foreign Secretary, who admired it as 'an excellent statement and exactly what was needed'.[55] In the document, Eden conveyed the view of the Chiefs of Staff about the value of the Rhineland:[56]

> the Zone has, even in the air, a certain value; whilst as regards land warfare it is a weakness and thus a disadvantage to Germany in the event of her becoming engaged in war in Central or Eastern Europe . . . At present France, by invading the Zone, could with ease come to their assistance if attacked, but once the Zone is fortified France will find it much more difficult to launch a direct land attack on Germany, and the value of the French alliances will

be proportionately reduced . . . In this way the disappearance of the Demilitarized Zone will not merely change local military values, but is likely to lead to far-reaching political repercussions of a kind which will further weaken France's influence in Eastern and Central Europe, leaving a gap which may eventually be filled either by Germany or by Russia.

Nevertheless, this correct conclusion did not persuade the Foreign Secretary to abandon the idea of bargaining, and he advised:

taking one thing with another, it seems undesirable to adopt an attitude where we would either have to fight for the Zone or abandon it in the face of a German reoccupation. It would be preferable for Great Britain and France to enter betimes into negotiations with the German Government for the surrender on conditions of our rights in the Zone while such surrender still has got a bargaining value.[57]

On 17 February, the committee members held their first meeting to discuss possible concessions to Germany, such as the return of one or more of the former German colonies, an agreement on raw materials, and the abandonment of the demilitarised zone. Since the German economic crisis might result in the Nazi Government attempting a foreign adventure as a means of distracting attention, they thought it was 'an additional reason for coming to terms quickly'.

In the course of discussions, supported by Simon, Eden suggested that a short-term policy towards Germany would be required first, whereas Halifax advised that 'it would be necessary first to go some way towards clearing our minds on long-term policy'. Differing from Eden, who thought it no use discussing an Air Pact while the Abyssinian War lasted, Ramsay MacDonald thought:

we should choose the Air Pact as our opening . . . the colonial raw materials suggestion would be a new opening . . . We must be prepared to pay a heavy price, if we were to buy Germany's return to Geneva . . .

But Chamberlain agreed with Eden's view on the colonial question, that 'the transfer of Tanganyika would be worth while if a really permanent settlement could be achieved'. However, their divergence was not fundamental because it focused merely on how to appease Hitler, rather than whether they should abandon appeasement. In the end, the Committee agreed to give further consideration when the additional information had been prepared.[58]

After the meeting, Eden instructed Phipps to use the Air Pact as the means of making a first move towards Germany. If Hitler raised the issue of the zone, Phipps should reply that Britain would also like to talk about the situation in Central and Eastern Europe, and armament limitations.[59]

Early in March, the FO consulted with the French and Belgian Governments about their attitude towards the German problem. Flandin, the French Foreign Minister, informed the British Government that if Germany re-occupied the Rhineland, France would consider taking 'any preparatory measures including measures of a military character', but she would not act alone. In addition, Flandin had reason to believe that 'Germany intends to reoccupy the zone in the very near future.'[60]

In the Cabinet meeting on 5 March – the last meeting before Hitler's seizure of the Rhineland – Eden told his colleagues that if Germany violated the demilitarised zone, 'the French Government would not proceed to isolated action, and would only act in agreement with the co-signatories of Locarno whom they would consult'. Considering immediate German violation of Versailles unlikely, the ministers discussed what would be the effect on other signatories if Germany denounced Locarno, using as an excuse the ratification of the Russian Pact.[61] They thought that the possible re-occupation of the zone by Germany 'was directed against all the signatories of the Treaty other than the aggressor'. Eden, Hailsham (Lord Chancellor) and Simon all agreed to declare that at any rate, 'we were not absolved from our obligations'. However, MacDonald added: 'we should avoid being driven back on the legal issue and keep the road open for diplomatic arrangement'. With others' agreement, Baldwin pointed out that neither France nor England was really in a position to take effective military action. Based on Eden's suggestion, the Cabinet concluded that the way to get round the difficulty was to take up the question of an Air Pact with Germany. They also authorised Eden to discuss with the French Prime Minister what to do in the changed situation.[62]

Next day, Eden called in the German Ambassador and asked him to refer again to Hitler 'the possibility of the opening of serious discussions on the Air Pact' between the Locarno Powers. Yet the Ambassador confined himself 'mainly to listening to Eden's remarks', and told the Foreign Secretary that there would be 'an important declaration' from the Führer, to be delivered the next morning.[63] In fact, Eden had learned from Phipps on the same day that 'some action is on the point of being taken by the German Government in regard to Locarno'.[64]

DURING THE CRISIS: THE BARGAIN LOST

At noon on 7 March, Hitler addressed the Reichstag, announcing the re-occupation of the Rhineland, together with a declaration in which he appealed for demilitarisation on both sides of the Rhine Frontier, a 25-year non-aggression pact between Germany, France and Belgium, a similar pact between Germany and Eastern European Powers, and an air pact.[65]

Germany's action raised confusion and conflicting views among public opinion. There were 'many gratifying indications of sympathy for the German point of view, and in general, of a tendency towards objective assessment and calm reflection' in the press. On the other hand, 'sharp criticism' of German violation was to be found in many newspapers.[66] *The Times*, the *Observer*, the *Daily Mail* and the *Daily Express* were enthusiastic about Hitler's peace offer, and the *Observer* appealed for Britain to consider Hitler's proposals 'in a spirit of sympathy and goodwill'. The *Daily Express* put forward a question: 'The Germans have reoccupied the Rhineland. What does that mean to US? . . . The question WILL BRITAIN BE INVOLVED IN WAR? The answer is NO.' The *Manchester Guardian*, however, caused some controversy: although its leader articles were pro-German, F.A. Voigt, its leader-writer, held a hard line. Differing from his own paper, he wrote on 9 March that unless Britain supported the French in opposing re-occupation, 'the Germans will have attained what Hitler has in his book *Mein Kampf* declared to be one of the chief aims of German foreign policy, namely, "the possibility of achieving the overthrow of France"'. In addition, the *Daily Telegraph* appealed that Britain should meet Hitler's challenge and expose his hypocritical peace offer:

Hitler's action and his speech have created a new and most difficult situation in Europe, and on the British Government's next step – carefully considered and, whatever it may be, we hope it will be firm and unmistakable – the course of future events must largely depend.[67]

The House, however, was 'more critical and nervous' than the press. Harold Nicolson described it thus: 'General mood of the House is one of fear. Anything to keep out of war.' In mid-March, one MP told the German Ambassador: 'A pro-French policy hasn't a hope. The whole country is pro-German.'[68] Sinclair, the leader of the Liberal Party, gave a speech on 9 March:

Let us remember that we, the States Members of the League, for too long failed to fulfil one of our obligations, our obligation to disarm. For too long we refused to recognise the equality of Germany . . . Nor, while we must condemn any violation of treaties, can we regard the occupation of German territory by German troops as so clearly indefensible, as an aggression against the territory of a member of the League. Let us then give calm and dispassionate study to these detailed constructive proposals for the removal of Germany's grievances and for securing European peace which Germany has at last tabled.[69]

On the other hand, 'criticism of the German action is very marked', as the German Ambassador in London reported to Berlin:

Indignation at Germany's alleged treaty violation is profound. This is adversely influencing the effect made by the German proposals, since doubts are felt as to the value of any future German promises and, indeed, as to whether there is any point in making fresh agreements with Germany.[70]

The House had already known that 'Hitler gambled on this coup' against the warnings of the German Foreign Office and Chiefs of Staff. It was widely accepted, even by those MPs who did not agree with intervention, that if Britain and France acted together, Germany had no chance of resistance, and that if war occurred, the Western Powers would win.[71]

On 12 March, a meeting of the Foreign Affairs Committee of the Commons took place. Sir Austen Chamberlain (the Chair) strongly recommended that 'Britain was in duty bound to support France unreservedly.' If France took immediate coercive measures against

Germany, Britain should aid France with full force. He was supported by Churchill, who warned the House later about the grave consequences that would result from the re-occupation of the Rhineland:

> The violation of the Rhineland is serious because of the menace to which it exposes Holland, Belgium and France . . . *It will be a barrier across Germany's front door which will leave her free to sally out eastwards and southwards by the other doors.*
>
> That is to us a less direct danger, but it is a more imminent danger . . . the whole aspect of middle Europe is changed.

That day, these two 'influential personages succeeded by their joint action in winning over to their side about three-quarters of the members of the Committee present'.[72] The German Ambassador assumed that if the Foreign Secretary had been Sir Austen instead of Eden, and the Minister for Defence had been Churchill instead of Inskip, 'Britain would cooperate, would have yielded to the impulse to take ultimative and, possibly, forcible action against Germany.'[73]

This evidence is fatal to the appeasers' repeated argument, voiced by Eden, that 'there is little dispute that Hitler should have been called to order, if need be forcibly, at his first breach of an accepted international engagement. But nobody was prepared to do it, in this country literally nobody'.[74] The fact was that in March 1936, there were not only favourable conditions for the British Government to take joint action with the French to check Hitler, but there also existed vociferous support both within and outside the House to press them do so.

Nonetheless, critical opinion did not influence the Government's line at all. On the contrary, it employed various methods to 'mould' public opinion. For example, in February 1935, Rex Leeper, Head of the News Department in the FO, suggested: 'We really must find some way of guiding the BBC's foreign comment more than we do.' During the Rhineland episode (on 30 March 1936), a special Cabinet Committee investigated the BBC's programmes on European affairs, and decided to 'ask the BBC to refrain from arranging for independent expressions of views on the situation'. The Government successfully imposed censorship on the BBC, which has to rely on it for the renewal of its Charter and Licence. Therefore, British radio was, as an American commentator observed, a 'constant flow of reports from the government departments', tantamount to 'gentle propaganda in favour of things as they are'.[75] In the House, Eden misled the public on 9 March by saying: 'There is . . . no reason to suppose that the present German action implies a threat of hostilities'.[76]

History has proven that the policy-makers did not consult the public at all when they worked on policy-making, because policy towards Germany had already been formulated before the public had a voice on it. They would not change their policy even though outside opinion demanded they faced up to the German challenge.

On the same day that he learned of Hitler's coup against the Rhineland (7 March), Eden drove down to Chequers to discuss the dangerous situation with Baldwin. He reported to the Prime Minister that both France and Belgium would wish to condemn Germany for a breach of the Versailles Treaty, and that the former might not take military action immediately, but would lay the case before the Council, asking for an early meeting of the Locarno Powers. Baldwin 'said little'. However, based on Eden's view, he set the tone for policy-making, saying: 'there would be no support in Britain for any military action by the French'. Eden agreed. The basis for foreign policy was thus settled between the Prime Minister and the Foreign Secretary.[77]

As soon as he returned to the FO, Eden received the report from Clerk, the British Ambassador in Paris, which confirmed his assumption.[78] In addition, the Belgians held similar views to the French, showing that they would follow the lead of the British Government.[79] Italy, however, gave no indication.[80]

Based on the information from his ambassadors, Eden set down his views for the Cabinet on 8 March:

> by reoccupying the Rhineland he [Hitler] has deprived us of the possibility of making to him a concession which might otherwise have been a useful bargaining counter in our hands in the general negotiations with Germany . . . Such negotiations are now inevitable, but we shall enter them at a disadvantage, for we have lost the bargaining counter . . .

He warned his colleagues: 'We must be prepared for him to repudiate any treaty even if freely negotiated'; on the other hand, he believed:

> it is in our interest to conclude with her [Germany] as far-reaching and enduring a settlement as possible whilst Herr Hitler is still in the mood to do so.

For a possible solution, he suggested entering into negotiations with Germany with the object of:

(a) establishing a new 'Locarno' on the lines suggested by Herr Hitler; (b) concluding an air pact on the lines suggested by us; (c) bringing about some sort of settlement in Eastern and Central Europe . . . on the basis of the bilateral non-aggression pacts offered by Herr Hitler; (d) arranging for Germany's unconditional return to the League.

In order to achieve those purposes, he thought 'the essential thing will be to induce or cajole France to accept this mandate'. Therefore, they 'must discourage any military action by France against Germany'.[81]

When he consulted Vansittart, the latter 'approved it enthusiastically', but suggested that 'our guarantee was to France and Belgium alone'.[82] Next day, the Cabinet, based on Vansittart's suggestion, redrafted the last paragraph of Eden's memo and inserted it into a statement which Eden was authorised to give in the House on the same evening. It says:

In case there should be any misunderstanding about our position as a signatory of the Locarno Treaty, His Majesty's Government think it necessary to say that, should there take place . . . any actual attack upon France or Belgium which would constitute a violation of Article 2 of Locarno, His Majesty's Government in the United Kingdom, notwithstanding the German repudiation of the Treaty, would regard themselves as in honour bound to come, in the manner provided in the Treaty, to the assistance of the country attacked.[83]

After the Parliamentary Debate, Eden, with Halifax, went to Paris for the meeting of the Locarno Powers without Germany.[84] In their conversations on 10 March, Flandin told Eden that France had brought the case to the Council of the League, and that once the Council declared German action to be in breach of the treaty, the French Government would use 'all their moral and material resources (including military, naval and air forces) in order to repress what they regarded as an attempt upon international peace'. The French would not pursue negotiation with Germany unless 'international law had been re-established in its full value'. He made it quite clear that the

French Government stressed that the Locarno Powers must take up 'a common position at the Council', and he even contemplated the Locarno Powers alone taking military action. The Belgians held a similar position. Discouraging the French by referring to the British Government's different standpoint, Eden tried to convince his Locarno partners that this was an opportunity for 'reaching a settlement with Germany', several of which, in his opinion, 'had been missed' before.[85] Eden and Halifax insisted that their policy of 'trying for a negotiation was still a right one' because 'the alternative proposed by the French Government for forcing the Germans out of the Rhineland would not produce a satisfactory settlement'.[86]

It should be noted that in the mid-1930s, the British and French governments were always at odds. The French did not fully support the British in this Italo-Abyssinian dispute, while the latter had no enthusiasm in backing up the former in the Rhineland. Apart from the divergence resulting from their national interests and strategic positions, there were strong misgivings in British political circles about the Government in France, which was influenced or led by the Popular Front, including Socialists, Communists and Radicals. The British Government often complained of misinterpretation of its role in international affairs by the French press. The French, however, grumbled not less about the British media's resentment towards them.[87] Flandin told HM Minister at Paris on 7 October 1935 that since every government in France 'must eventually depend' on 'the great masses of the Left', 'there were already too many misunderstandings between England and France'. It 'would make difficult . . . cooperation between the two countries which was essential if Germany was to be kept within bounds'.[88]

In British eyes, neither Laval nor Flandin was a friend.[89] In the light of the fact that France 'is moving slowly but ever more certainly towards the Left', Wigram summarised the view in the FO in November 1935, saying: 'A French Government based merely on Left support could not support us' and 'the best for our interests would be a Right government'.[90]

There was no doubt that they had certain grievances against their French colleagues, who had signed the Franco-Soviet Pact with communist Russia. Eden said at the Cabinet meeting of 12 February 1936: 'we had not been consulted before the signature of the pact and there appeared no reason why we should express any opinion'. It was suggested that they should tell Germany that 'we had had nothing to do with the matter'.[91] He and Vansittart warned the French Government in late 1936 that if the French attempted to supplement the pact by a military treaty or staff talks, it would gravely prejudice the forthcoming 'satisfactory agreement' with Germany.[92] It was one of the reasons the British disliked the Leftist government in France, which caused disharmony between the two governments.

After their conversations with the French, Eden and Halifax returned to London the next day (11 March). That evening, Baldwin called a special Cabinet meeting to contemplate how best to proceed. Eden reported to his colleagues the French and Belgians' firm standpoint, namely that if Germany refused to withdraw from the Rhineland, they would proceed to military measures, and asked Britain to do the same. He foresaw that 'we should be in an impossible position if we refused'. Halifax said: that 'the French and Belgians sincerely believed that the Germans would not fight if they took action'. As to what proposal the Government should adopt, Eden suggested informing the German Ambassador immediately that despite the grave situation created by the German action, the British Government were still 'anxious to obtain a peaceful settlement'. But they needed Hitler to make some reasonable contribution, for example he should state 'that he wanted to negotiate a series of new pacts as a basis for peace in Europe, and he would, as a proof of his intentions, withdraw all his forces from the Rhineland over and above the troops necessary for a symbolic occupation'. In addition, Hitler should not 'build fortifications in the demilitarised zone'. The problem was, as some ministers pointed out, that the French and Belgians 'might object to it' if they were informed. It was generally accepted that:

> it was worth taking almost any risk in order to escape from that situation. Admittedly the suggestion of the Secretary of State for Foreign Affairs involved some risks from the point of view of the attitude of Germany on the one hand, and France and Belgium on the other, but we could hardly be left in a more embarrassing position than we were in already.

They agreed that they would calm the French down by telling them that due to the British military disadvantage and public opinion, the Government could not take any military action. Baldwin thought that it seemed 'very unfriendly' of the French 'to put us in the present dilemma'. He emphasised that:

> it would be necessary to point out to the French that the action they proposed would not result only in letting loose another

great war in Europe. They might succeed in crushing Germany with the aid of Russia, but it would probably only result in Germany going Bolshevik.

In the course of discussions, there was a suggestion of imposing financial and economic sanctions against Germany, but Eden rejected this, saying that the 'proposal had been for the imposition of sanctions by successive stages culminating in military action'. The Cabinet finally came to the conclusion that Eden should tell the German Ambassador about the British proposal, and 'do it well'.[93]

That evening, without informing the French, Eden told Hoesch, the German Ambassador, about the British proposal, but the latter replied on the following day that Hitler agreed only not to increase troop numbers, not to alter their geographical position.[94]

On the night of 11 March, Flandin arrived in London for the Locarno discussions. Over the following days, apart from official meetings, he had a series of private communications with influential British statesmen, and addressed the House, aiming to gain British support. His message was summed up as follows:

If England will act now she can lead Europe . . . It is your last chance. If you do not stop Germany now, all is over. France cannot guarantee Czechoslovakia any more because that will become geographically impossible . . . If you do not stop Germany by force to-day, war is inevitable, even if you make a temporary friendship with Germany.[95]

Having heard his exhortations, Churchill urged him to see Baldwin. On 12 March, Flandin had meetings separately with Baldwin and Chamberlain. He told the British Prime Minister:

France had no wish to drag Great Britain into war; she asked for no practical aid, and she would herself undertake what would be a simple police operation, as, according to French information, the German troops in the Rhineland had orders to withdraw if opposed in a forcible manner.

Baldwin turned down his suggestion, saying: 'You may be right, but if there is even one chance in a hundred that war would follow from your police operation, I have not the right to commit England.'[96]

Chamberlain did nothing more to encourage the French Foreign Minister either, according to his diary entry of 12 March:

> talked to Flandin, emphasising that public opinion here would not support us in sanctions of any kind. His view is that if a firm front is maintained by France and England, Germany will yield without war. We cannot accept this as a reliable estimate of a mad dictator's reactions.[97]

At the official meetings, Flandin told Eden again of the French standpoint. In reply, Eden asserted:

> We were convinced that it would not be possible to secure a German withdrawal from the Rhineland, and that to make an attempt to do so was to court certain failure and a grave risk of war. In these circumstances was it not better to see whether there were not some other way out of our present difficulty?

He warned his French partners:

> we feared that were we to do this our two projects might be found to diverge at almost every point. This would be a misfortune.[98]

Since all official and private discussions led nowhere, Flandin was 'in a very depressed mood', and felt that 'his mission to London had been a failure'.[99]

Based on the latest negotiations between the Locarno Powers, Eden described the resolution in his memo for the Cabinet dated March 15, which included: condemnation of Germany's action, an invitation to France and Germany to refer to the Hague Court the question of the compatibility of the Franco-Soviet Pact with Locarno, and stationing an international force, including British troops, on either side of the frontiers between France, Belgium and Germany.[100]

Next day, the Cabinet, after discussion, approved his proposal and authorised him to communicate with the French.[101] Chamberlain also reported on another talk with Flandin. Having heard his report, Baldwin said that he was strongly in favour of sending British troops to form part of an international force in the Rhineland.[102]

Yet, when the ministers met on the evening of 18 March, they found the problems far from resolved. Eden summed up the difficulties in the

Locarno Powers' discussions the same day: as to an International Force on both sides of the frontier, Flandin could accept either a Franco-Italian force in France, or an International Force in the zone only; the French and Belgian Governments wished the British Government to address a letter to them describing the steps the British would take, including economic, financial and military sanctions, in the event of Germany's refusal to accept the terms; as to laying the case before the Hague Court, they insisted that if the judgement went against France, the Franco-Soviet Pact must be annulled, but in the event of it going against Germany, Locarno must come into force; they insisted that military talks should take place between Britain, France and Belgium. In the course of the talks, Eden suggested that 'the situation would be eased if we could agree to military conversations', relating to the obligations of the powers concerned under the Locarno Treaty if the negotiations with the Germans failed. But some ministers reminded the Cabinet 'that military conversations on that basis would be very unacceptable to public opinion in this country which was strongly opposed to any forcible action to compel the Germans to evacuate the Demilitarised Zone'. They argued that they 'were not in a position to give effective military support in any such operation as the French were well aware'. They believed that 'there was no question of immediate action as contemplated in the Treaty since the time for that had already passed'. The general tenor of the Cabinet's views on the points of difference came to be as follows:

(a) The Lord Privy Seal's proposal for the stationing of an International Force, including British troops, in the Demilitarised Zone and for British and Italian forces on the French side of the frontier, was welcomed.

(b) The proposed letter to the French and Belgian Governments as to our action in the event of Germany's refusal to accept the terms offered to her was rejected . . .

(c) The difficulty as to the attitude of the French and Belgian Governments to the suggestion that Germany should go to the Hague Court had been solved by M. Van Zeeland's [the Belgian Prime Minister] latest communication.[103]

(d) Military conversations must be strictly limited to mutual arrangements for defence in the event of German aggression against France or Belgium . . .[104]

After the Cabinet meeting, the Locarno ministers resumed their difficult talks again from 10.00 that evening until 2.00 next morning, when they finally come to an agreement, which included: the stationing of an international force in the Rhineland; asking the German Government to lay its case before the Hague Court, and to refrain from fortifying the zone during the period of negotiations.[105] When Eden informed von Ribbentrop, the German Delegate to the Locarno meeting, about these resolutions, the latter answered at once that it seemed to him that certain points of the proposals were apparently 'unacceptable'. Eden was at pains to make plain to him how difficult it had been to persuade the French to agree to a temporary compromise solution, and urged the German Government 'to make some contribution on their side', emphasising the importance of not delivering a flat rebuttal of the proposals.[106]

Following the preliminary note of 24 March,[107] Hitler's answer was finally announced on 31 March, in which he made his own 'contribution to the reconstruction of a new Europe' by refusing all three requirements of the Locarno Powers and by offering a nineteen-point 'peace plan'.[108]

Immediately after receiving this on 1 April, the Cabinet members got together to discuss the matter. They thought that 'what we wanted first was to obtain some action of a re-assuring character by Germany to restore confidence in some degree', but the German memo did not meet the requirements of the Locarno Powers in the resolution of 19 March. On the other hand, they agreed that 'the French Government must not be given any encouragement by the attitude of the British Press to reject the proposals altogether', because some points of Hitler's plan 'were interesting'.[109]

On the French side, the French Government regarded the German reply as a rebuttal of the resolution of 19 March, and showed no confidence in Hitler's peace plan.[110] Van Zeeland, the Belgian Prime Minister, also suggested that the Locarno Powers meeting and staff talks should be resumed as soon as possible.[111] In a telegram from Paris, Eden reported to his colleagues about the Locarno Powers' discussions:

> French Government will concentrate on securing our support for refusal to allow zone to be fortified. They may well ask us to join in making clear to German Government that if demand is refused sanctions by Locarno Powers will follow.

In the course of talks, the ministers felt that 'the essence of sanctions was that they must be collective and effective. Neither of these conditions would apply to sanctions imposed as proposed by the French,' and they suggested that Eden should tell the French 'that sanctions could not be imposed by the Locarno Powers'. They decided:

> if the question of the French refusal to allow the Demilitarised Zone to be fortified were raised, the Secretary of State for Foreign Affairs would be justified in refusing to admit that conciliation had failed . . . if and when the point was reached where conciliation had failed . . . our first action would be consultation with the French and Belgian Governments as to the steps to be taken to meet the new situation.

That evening, Halifax left for Paris, bringing this Cabinet conclusion to Eden.[112] At the same time, the Cabinet approved a proposal that General Staff discussions between Britain, France and Belgium should open on 15 April.[113]

When Halifax joined Eden, the two ministers, following the line above, 'strongly resisted the French view that the attempt at conciliation had failed and that it was time to begin the study of sanctions'. Taking advantage of the indication that the French were looking for 'compensation' for the fortification of the Rhineland, they pointed out:

> the German proposals were far from clear on a number of points; that some of those points, if explained in a satisfactory way, might give the French the very 'compensation' they were looking for; and that therefore the first step was to clear up these doubtful points with the Germans.

They promised to get in touch with the Germans to clear up these points. At last, the French yielded.[114]

AFTERMATH: THE ILLUSION OF SEARCHING FOR A SETTLEMENT

Even immediately after his meeting with the German Ambassador on 11 March,[115] Eden realised that 'we should not get much further in the vital conversation'. Halifax and Vansittart were in agreement.[116] Even so, discussions in the FO had revealed mixed points of view, with a tendency to appease Germany further instead of changing policy. On 17 March, Lord Cranborne, the Under-Secretary, proposed stabilising the situation in Western Europe and giving Germany a free hand in the east, to a certain extent. In order to achieve a limitation of German armaments, they should give her, economically, a free hand in Central Europe, 'by a loan, or in other ways'. 'The question of the colonies, too, might be brought up in this discussion.' He warned:

> Do not let us, at any rate, in order to find a way out of the present emergency, put ourselves under definite obligations of which we do not know the final implications.[117]

Sargent had independently written his memo on the same lines. After rejecting several alternatives, he proposed that the policy should be:

> to offer Germany economic and financial help *in return for*, and *subsequent to*, a general political settlement.
>
> It certainly would seem to be the most farsighted and statesmanlike, but only on condition that we do not delay too long, for German economics will increasingly react on, and may soon dominate, German foreign politics, with quite incalculable results.[118]

Refusing to take any German assurances at face value due to the latest incident, Vansittart at first held some different views on the long-term policy from Lord Cranborne; but after their discussion, the divergence vanished.[119] Eden remarked 'There is much force' in Cranborne's view, but he did not think 'it tells quite the whole story'. As to Sargent's view, Eden minuted: 'I agree.'[120] He did not think that the crisis had made 'any difference to our intention to probe and explore Herr Hitler's offers' and to construct 'something reliable out of them'.[121]

Late in April, on Eden's instructions, the FO drafted a questionnaire for Germany which summed up the unclear points in the German proposals.[122] Eden and Lord Cranborne examined it carefully when they spent a weekend in Dorset in late April. On 27 April, Eden showed the document to Baldwin and Chamberlain, and the Chancellor had no objection.[123] The Foreign Secretary asked his colleagues 'whether it would be advisable for a Cabinet minister, but not himself, to discuss the questions in Berlin with the German Government'.[124]

At the Cabinet meeting on 29 April, he wanted this dispatch sent to Germany soon, but he doubted 'whether there was a possibility of a *détente* between this country and Germany'. Postponing consideration of the questionnaire until the next day, 'the Cabinet entered on a preliminary review of their general policy in the new situation that was developing'. Baldwin was, with the support of Simon, inclined to send the questions to the Germans via a minister, 'for the reason that the ordinary diplomatic channels hardly seemed to function in dealing with dictators'. Other Cabinet members took a different view, on the grounds that it would lower the prestige of the Diplomatic Service as a whole. Furthermore, it 'would encourage the Germans as to our attitude, and re-awaken French suspicions and lack of confidence that was so important a feature in the present situation'. Several ministers suggested that discussion on this should be left until after the general policy had been settled. They emphasised the necessity and importance of both rearmament and appeasement:

> Time was vital for the completion of our defensive security . . . There was every advantage . . . in coming to terms with Hitler and fastening him down to keep the peace in the west . . . In the long run French interests were bound up with our own, so our line should be to try and obtain *détente* with Germany.

Being disturbed by the urgency and difficulty of the defence programmes, Inskip, the Minister for Co-ordination of Defence, requested the Government to give priority to defence programmes rather than commercial business.[125] However, this proposal was not favourably echoed by Chamberlain, the Chancellor of the Exchequer, who advocated 'the cheapest' defence, and usually kept a tight reign on the budget for all three armed services. He shelved the proposal, but avoided giving an immediate answer by saying that this question 'should be reserved until after decisions had been reached on the major policy of the Government'. In the end, the Cabinet took the Chancellor's proposal as their conclusion, and appointed a committee[126] to consider the immediate policy.[127]

The following day, Cabinet members continued to consider the draft of a questionnaire. Eden told his partners:

> the difficulty in drafting the questions had been not to give offence to the Germans and not to encourage them to make fresh claims. The paragraph relating to colonies, for example, had been re-drafted several times so as to avoid inviting the Germans to raise their maximum demands.

It was true that when the FO prepared this cowardly and humiliating document, it not only avoided condemning Hitler's violation of the treaty, but also used language that was as mild as possible. However, when they went through the draft paragraph by paragraph, the ministers still thought some to be 'somewhat provocative' or 'of rather a pin-pricking character', which 'might lead the Germans to give a reply which would increase our difficulties in bringing about the desired negotiation'. They agreed to a number of modifications, with the general aim of making the language even milder without losing the essential purpose. They asked the FO to make further revisions according to the more conciliatory tone, and the re-draft would be discussed again by the Cabinet on 4 May.[128]

The Cabinet's amendments were not at all popular in the FO. When the members of the staff (Wigram, Strang and Malkin) re-drafted the document, Wigram complained to Vansittart:

> The real difficulty arises out of the Cabinet dissatisfaction with paragraphs 7 and 8 of the original draft . . . I find it quite impossible to work in the Secretary of State's idea . . . I must re-emphasize the importance of our Questions being adequate. We *are* pledged to the French on the matter . . . I think there would be a breach of faith with the French if the Questions were not adequate . . .[129]

Nevertheless, during long discussions, they had to make revisions again and again in obedience to their masters' instructions.[130]

Therefore, at the Cabinet meeting on 4 May, according to the minute, 'Doubts were raised once more as to the wisdom of including Paragraph 8, which asked for an explanation of the distinction between the Reich and the German nation'.[131] Eden explained that this 'was a matter in which every nation in Europe was intensely interested', and 'all his advisers at the Foreign Office, whatever their general attitude towards Germany, were in favour of including Paragraph 8'. He warned that 'if the Cabinet insisted on omitting it they would be closing their eyes to a matter of great importance'. Simon and Chamberlain separately put forward their amendments for that paragraph and the latter's revision was incorporated in the final form of the document.[132]

On 6 May, Phipps was authorised to present the questionnaire to the Germans.[133] In his meeting with Hitler a week later, the Führer told him that the German reply would not be given until after the new French Government had been in the saddle – the middle of June. He also discouraged the British desire to send a minister to Berlin.[134] Subsequently, the Germans kept delaying their answer no matter how hard Phipps urged them.[135] The Ambassador reported on 15 May that Hitler had declared openly that he would build fortifications in the Rhineland,[136] which in fact had already begun.[137] According to his observation, Hitler had been 'gradually moving away from the idea of a conference or any form of general settlement'.[138] The German Chancellor was 'in great form', and had 'no intention of replying seriously to our questions'.[139] Kirkpatrick, the Ambassador's subordinate, told Wigram on 8 June:

> what in his opinion we ought to realise was that in a year's time it would not be we who would be addressing questions to Germany designed to ascertain whether it was worth negotiating with her, but the Germans who would be considering whether we were worth negotiating with, or whether they would simply dictate their desires to us.[140]

The information from the Berlin Embassy aroused 'a continuation of the mood of disillusionment'. Wigram was very pessimistic:

> In Eastern Europe I cannot see that we have anything much to gain either by agreement with Germany . . . as we have nothing to give her, she will not give us much in exchange.
> [It was] disturbing to think that British public opinion has been so misled by all these years of unreality that, lest it should misunderstand, we are now obliged to run after the Germans and expose ourselves to what are almost impertinences.

Vansittart showed his distrust of Hitler and his criticism in his minute:

> Hitler has never meant business in our sense of the word. The sooner the Cabinet realise that the better for this long misguided country. (It has received little chance of comprehension, and for this the first National Government must bear a very heavy responsibility.)

Yet he still insisted on his former policy: bargaining with Germany but supporting rearmament. This diplomatic setback did not discourage

Eden either. Based on Sargent's suggestion, he instructed the FO that 'we must continue to aim at the general agreement . . . It may be that it is unattainable, but it is we who must prove this, by making every effort to attain it . . .' Showing much more enthusiasm than his colleagues for the settlement, he suggested again 'the offer of a visit of a Minister, if only because this would make it more difficult for Herr Hitler to take refuge in evasion, & would show our public our determination to get on if we can . . .'[141] But the Cabinet generally inclined to the view that it would be mistaken 'to press Herr Hitler to receive a British Minister'. On the other hand, it was impossible to let the matter drift for long. In the course of discussion at the Cabinet meeting on 20 May, it came to the conclusion that it should attempt to obtain a meeting of all the interested powers at which the Germans could be present to give their answer, rather than to press them to reply immediately. However, it was pointed out that Britain wanted a settlement and knew that a conference was the only hope. If the French and Belgian Governments learned that Hitler intended to re-fortify the zone, all hope of negotiation would disappear. Eden said that the last French Government would never have come to a conference on those conditions, but the new French Government might be different.[142]

On 1 July, Eden had supper with Blum, the new French Prime Minister, and van Zeeland in Geneva. The two Prime Ministers expressed a desire for a meeting of the Locarno Powers.[143] The Locarno ministers later came to a decision that the three powers would prepare a meeting probably inviting Italy but not Germany.[144] After receiving Eden's telegram, Baldwin summoned the ministers, including Lord Cranborne and Vansittart, to discuss the position. They agreed that it was 'as good an arrangement as could be hoped for in all the circumstances'. The Prime Minister said that Hitler would think that 'this was another attempt to annoy Germany'.[145]

On 6 July Cabinet members held a meeting to consider the possible terms of an agreement with Germany at the proposed meeting of Locarno Powers. They found themselves having to handle three difficulties at the same time: the future of the League; British policy in Eastern Europe, and the German colonies.

As to the first problem, Eden turned down the proposal of going back to the policy of the Geneva Protocol, which Churchill and the Labour Party supported, and chose the policy 'to work for a new Locarno Treaty and at the same time to declare a situation in which Articles 10 and 16 of the Covenant would disappear'. He said:

The object was to get Germany into conference, relinquishing the British questionnaire and asking them to come practically without conditions. If this was not done there was the risk that after the Olympic Games [August] the Powers would get further demands from Germany.

He addressed British policy in Eastern Europe by summarising Phipps's observation:

it might be possible to get Germany to enter into a new Locarno Treaty, but it would be at the expense of Eastern and South-Eastern Europe, as Herr Hitler would never commit himself as regards Eastern Europe . . . If we tried to get the German Chancellor to commit himself to a settlement for Europe as a whole Herr Hitler would be sure to refuse.

Some ministers added: 'while the Government should make up its own mind to reduce its commitments in Eastern Europe we should not announce that we were unwilling or unable to help in Eastern Europe'.

Impressed by Eden's description, his colleagues decided the general policy, which resulted in a series of crises in the future:

our policy ought to be framed on the basis that we could not help Eastern Europe. We ought, however, to resist by force any attempt against our own Empire or Flanders. If these were our basis . . . our policy towards the future of the League ought to be somewhat on French lines: that is to say of regional pacts.

Regarding the colonial issue, they decided that 'if Germany raised it we should make it quite clear that we would give up nothing'. In the end, they accepted the proposal that the Locarno Power meeting should be held in Brussels on 22 July.[146]

As to the prospective meeting of Locarno Powers, Neurath, German Minister for Foreign Affairs, told Newton, HM Minister in Berlin, that Germany thought this meeting would be premature, and would welcome a conference not earlier than September. The reply to the British questionnaire 'when made might, however, throw some further light on prospects of a successful meeting'.[147] The Germans would not give any reply until autumn – or more precisely, there might not be any German reply.[148] On 19 November, the British Government made its request once more, sending a note to the Germans asking for the Agenda of the Five Power Conference.[149] It spent another four months waiting for this information. At last, the reply came on 12 March 1937 – one year after the Rhineland coup – in which the Germans actually refused the meeting, saying that they still accepted the invitation in principle, but they 'felt that ground had not yet been sufficiently prepared'.[150]

CONCLUSION

Observation of the process of British policy-making during the Rhineland episode is enough to refute the argument that public opinion did not allow the British Government to go to war with Germany over the Rhineland. This argument, which exaggerates unduly the public view of non-intervention, aims to shift the responsibility onto the public, and help appeasers evade the blame. In fact, not only did many newspapers make demands to counter the German challenge, but the Foreign Affairs Committee of the House also strongly recommended support for the French. According to the view of the German Ambassador in London, if Sir Austen Chamberlain had been the Foreign Secretary and Churchill had been Defence Minister, the British Government might have taken joint action with France. In other words, it was the Government not the public that remained inactive. In addition, without consulting the public, appeasement towards Germany had been completed before the public was alarmed by the crisis. The British leaders not only ignored outside opinion, they moulded it by various means to create an atmosphere which seemed overwhelmingly favourable to the Government's policy. Therefore, instead of influencing the Government, public opinion – as Wigram confessed – was misled by the British leaders for their own purposes.

Policy-making in this period had certain general characteristics: the majority of senior officials, in particular Sargent, Wigram and Vansittart, intended to come to terms with Germany. Even after the Rhineland was lost, they insisted on continuing the proposed policy to appease the Germans further and more quickly, rather than choosing the alternative to appeasement. The appeasers urged speedy rearmament with the purpose of obtaining a stronger position to make a deal with Germany, instead of preparing to fight. The only proposal with some anti-appeasement characteristics, by Collier, was killed at the first stage of policy-making. On the other hand, the advisers in the

FO and Chiefs of Staff had to find a basis for policy according to their bosses' views, otherwise, their advice would be either amended or ignored.

At ministerial level, Eden, as arch-appeaser, should bear most responsibility for his wrong guidance of British foreign policy at that time. Since Baldwin had little interest in foreign policy, the Foreign Secretary was the key member in the Cabinet when it came to concluding policy. His youth and his vigorous character increased his determination and power in pursuing this policy. His 'appeasement', although he denied it was the same as Chamberlain's,[151] was proven to be no different from the latter's. Appeasement, after being shaped by his hand, remained the fundamental British policy towards Germany in the remaining years of the 1930s.

In addition, attention should be drawn to another two factors which led to British inaction. First, the grave situation in the Far East as well as in the Mediterranean made it difficult for the appeasers to take a firm line against Germany. When they set up Far Eastern appeasement, the original scheme was that accommodation with Japan would allow Britain to concentrate on the German menace. Now, in the face of Hitler's adventure, they believed that if Britain was involved in any trouble with Germany or Italy, Japan would take the opportunity to harm British interests in the Far East. Their logic had thus become: continue to appease Japan in order to concentrate on Europe; on the other hand, appease Germany and Italy in order to rob Japan of any chance of destroying British interests in the Far East. Therefore, the appeasers would not fight anywhere.

Second, the British leaders were inferior to Hitler in playing a game of this kind. The German Chancellor knew them better than they knew him. He foresaw correctly that his coup against the zone would not be answered by military action. Baldwin, however, simply did not understand the dictator at all, as he said: 'We none of us know what is going on in that strange man's mind.' 'He had never been able to find anyone who could give him really reliable information about Hitler's character and designs.'[152] Before the crisis, they did not believe the French information that Hitler would strike soon; during the crisis, they turned a deaf ear to the estimate that the German troops would withdraw if other Locarno Powers interfered; and after the crisis, they were still under the illusion that Hitler was in the mood to make a deal, in spite of information that showed the reverse. Their decision, based on misunderstanding, could not be correct.

What is worse, the lessons drawn from the crisis show that the appeasers wanted to continue their impotent policy. The Chiefs of Staff reported that, bound by collective security, Britain might suddenly be involved in war without full preparation due to her world-wide interests. Therefore, they advised the Cabinet to abandon collective security, rather than strengthening it.[153] Confronted with 'the downfall of the League, the resurrection and consequent rivalry of Germany', Chamberlain affirmed in July 1936: 'we have no policy'.[154]

After the Rhineland episode, the world situation was graver: the aggressive powers came closer, and finally formed the Berlin–Rome–Tokyo Axis. In contrast, the Western Powers found themselves divergent in interests and strategic positions, facing possible aggression, and Belgium broke away from the collective security of Locarno.[155] Appeasement, with its original scheme of avoiding any risk of war, put Britain in an even worse position, in which she had to face three enemies at the same time. It could be said that if Manchuria and Abyssinia made the Second World War possible, the Rhineland made it almost inevitable. Moreover, the loss of the Rhineland offered Hitler a favourable situation for initiating his next adventure – the Anschluss.

THE ANSCHLUSS

THE ANSCHLUSS AND ITS PREPARATION

The loss of the Rhineland as a bargaining counter did not exhaust British desires to agree terms with Germany. Although Hitler had shown his aloofness to its questionnaire of May and its appeal for a Locarno Power meeting, the British Government held to its wishful thinking that 'a new Western Pact' would resolve the problem created by the German violation of the Locarno treaty on 7 March, and bring the dictator power into general settlement.[1] However, its lack of knowledge of the Führer's real ambitions in Central and Eastern Europe characterised its policy-making process as one of blindness, passiveness and hesitation in the pre-*Anschluss* period.

The Austro-German union was forbidden by the Versailles Treaty. However, it was one of the principal aims Hitler had declared in *Mein Kampf*. As soon as he came to power, his policy towards Austria was *Gleichschaltung*, which preceded the Anschluss – working for the collapse of the Austrian Government, and replacing it by the Austrian Nazi Party, which offered a basis for the Austro-German union.[2]

On 25 July 1934, the Austrian Nazis attacked the Federal Chancellory and killed Chancellor Dollfuss, declaring the formation of a new government; but the *Putsch* was immediately put down by the Federal Army and police.[3] Learning from this failure, Hitler adopted von Papen's proposal that the problem of Austrian union with Germany could only be resolved by 'evolutionary methods', namely by creating a proper international situation, and by pressure from outside.[4] He appointed von Papen as Ambassador in Vienna on a special mission to be in charge of Austrian affairs. On the other hand, he and Goering personally enforced control of the Austrian Nazi Party.

On 11 July 1936, von Papen, representing the German Government, signed an agreement with von Schuschnigg, the Austrian Chancellor. Under this agreement, the Austrian Government had to associate with the Nazi Opposition and to pursue a common foreign policy with Germany. The possible Austro-German union had become a 'family affair' between the two German States.[5] At the same time, Hitler instructed the General Staff to draw up SPECIAL OPERATION OTTO – a military plan to occupy Austria, which was renewed under his direction on 24 June 1937.[6]

In the meantime, the European situation was becoming more and more favourable to Hitler's adventure. Italy, the main obstacle to the Anschluss, split from the Stresa Front due to her quarrel with Britain and France over Abyssinia. Mussolini had realised as early as April 1935 that he had to give up Austria in order to realise his ambitions in Africa.[7] Early in 1936, il Duce on various occasions told Hassell, German Ambassador in Italy, that the Stresa Front had died and Locarno would cease.[8] As to Austria, he had a long conversation with the Ambassador on 6 January, in which he said:

If Austria, as a formally quite independent State, were thus in practice to become a German satellite, he would have no objection.[9]

It was apparent that Mussolini had left Austria to Hitler. Late in October, the Berlin-Rome axis was formed,[10] and the possibility of Italian interference had been completely dismissed.

On the British side, Simon (Foreign Secretary) and Eden (Parliamentary Under-Secretary) had shown British understanding to the Führer's desire during their visit to Berlin in March 1935. Simon told Hitler:

Britain had not the same interest in Austria, as, for example, in Belgium. She had never interfered in Austrian affairs and was still confining herself to the hope that the problems there would be solved.[11]

Halifax conveyed clearer information to him in November 1937. In their conversation, the main problems discussed were disarmament, the colonies, Austria, Czechoslovakia, Danzig and the League of Nations. The British minister implied acquiescence in the German re-occupation of the Rhineland, and went on to state on behalf of HMG that:

[the] possibility of change of the existing situation was not excluded, but that changes should only take place upon the basis of reasonable agreements reasonably reached . . . Amongst these questions were Danzig, Austria, and Czechoslovakia.[12]

He particularly emphasised 'that also applies to Austria'. When he heard this, 'Hitler again became excited.'[13]

Soon after Halifax's visit, Eden gave confirmation to von Ribbentrop, the German Ambassador in London:

He had told the French that the question of Austria was of much greater interest to Italy than to England. Furthermore, people in England recognized that a closer connection between Germany and Austria would have to come about sometime.

England and France agreed that in Central Europe (Austria and Czechoslovakia) certain changes could be made, provided, however, that the *status quo* was not changed by force.[14]

The time seemed ripe for the Führer to consider the final solution. On 5 November 1937, he summoned his subordinates (three commanders-in-chief, the war minister and foreign minister) to decide the plans for German expansion. In his opinion, Britain would never give up her colonies, so Germany could only seek this space in Europe. He analysed that Britain was not able to defend her Empire by her own power, 'but only by in alliance with other states'. France, in spite of her greater military strength, was confronted with internal political difficulties. He believed that 'Germany's problem could only be solved by means of force and this was never without attendant risk'. He estimated that action should be taken by 1943–5, because the rest of the world would not have completed its counter-measures against German invasion by that time. Therefore, the Germans 'were obliged to take the offensive'. The Führer considered that there were two cases in which there was the necessity for action – either if France was involved in serious domestic crisis, or if she was embroiled in a war with another country, for example with Italy. Hitler 'was convinced of Britain's nonparticipation, and therefore he did not believe in the probability of belligerent action by France against Germany'. Hitler concluded that the time for a German attack on the Czechs and Austria 'must be made dependent on the course of the Anglo–French–Italian war', which, he foresaw, would come nearer, probably in the summer of 1938.[15]

Nevertheless, the situation in Austria did not amuse Berlin very much. Von Schuschnigg, despite bowing to German pressure, insisted on the importance of Austrian independence and hesitated to absorb the Austrian Nazi leaders into his Cabinet. Von Neurath, the German Foreign Minister, strongly condemned him by asking did von Schuschnigg 'really think that he can proceed with ruthless measures against National Socialism in Austria and still steer a common course with the Reich in matters affecting the German peoples?'. Von Papen warned the Austrian Chancellor on 21 December: 'the Agreement of July 11 was not functioning satisfactorily . . . Germany had to demand more than mere passive assistance from Austria'.[16] With Hitler's approval, he arranged a conference of the German and Austrian Chancellors with the purpose of clarifying 'the controversial issues' between them.[17]

The meeting was held at Berchtesgaden on 12 February 1938. During the stormy discussions, Hitler threatened von Schuschnigg, saying that if his guest did not meet his demands, he would immediately order the German Army to march across the border. In order to destroy von Schuschnigg's hopes of turning to the Western Powers, he said that 'Halifax had completely approved of German's attitude towards Austria and Czechoslovakia.' In the end, von Schuschnigg yielded. Seyss-Inquast, the Austrian Nazi Leader, was to be offered a post in Schuschnigg's Cabinet as Minister of the Interior.[18]

However, the Austrians did not want to surrender completely. After he failed to gain support from the Western Powers, von Schuschnigg took a final measure to defend the independence of his Motherland, calling a plebiscite on 13 March.[19] This provoked the Führer, who was considering a final solution to the Austrian problem, either by evolutionary means or by force if necessary.[20] Information from Paris showed that France would not interfere due to her internal problems, although Flandin, the French Foreign Minister said: 'a formal "Anschluss" had to be avoided'. Britain held a more conciliatory attitude on the eve of the Anschluss, as Halifax, the successor to Eden, emphasised when he told von Ribbentrop, who was visiting London, that 'England had no intention of "blocking up Austria". England admitted that this was a problem which primarily concerned Germany.' According to the record, Henderson, the new Ambassador in Berlin, even told Hitler on 3 March that he himself 'often advocated the Anschluss'.[21]

The Führer decided to act. He first sent Keppler, his right-hand man, to Vienna 'to prevent the plebiscite', and then gave the order to execute OPERATION OTTO on 11 March.[22] On the morning of 12 March,

German troops rolled across the border. Austria had become the Ostmark province in the Third Reich.

Austria had in fact been doomed when the appeasers abandoned the Rhineland. Appeasement helped Hitler to realise his aggressive plan much earlier than he estimated. Contemporary politicians and scholars regard the *Anschluss* unanimously as an upset of the balance of power in Europe and the first step in Hitler's serious invasion plans.[23] However, Hoare argues: 'there was no chance of stopping Hitler except by war or a threat of war, and neither we nor the French were prepared to fight against what was claimed to be the unification of the German people'.[24] The best way to rebut this argument is to let history speak.

IMPORTANT PERSONNEL CHANGES IN CHAMBERLAIN'S GOVERNMENT

In 1936, Baldwin's health, which had not been very good before, was worsening. It made his retirement 'both desirable and impossible', because with his disability he could hardly deal with successive crises. It was widely thought that Chamberlain would take over.[25]

In May 1937, Chamberlain replaced Baldwin, forming 'a one-man Government'. With a nature made up of alertness, fixed opinions, self-confidence and intolerance, he immediately gave his colleagues the impression that he was a more powerful Prime Minister than his predecessor: 'His mind, once made up, was hard to change.'[26] He ran the Cabinet with an iron hand: his 'remarkable strength of character and single-minded determination' kept the majority of his colleagues at his side. He was close to Hoare, Simon and Halifax, and often consulted them about foreign policy.[27] Yet his interference in the conduct of foreign policy greatly annoyed Eden, who believed that the Prime Minister knew nothing about diplomacy.[28] This was perhaps one of the reasons that led to the breakdown of their relationship.

Chamberlain had previously made his impact on foreign policy-making as Chancellor of the Exchequer, mainly by cutting expenditure on rearmament, which had the effect of pushing foreign policy in the direction of conceding to the aggressors. Now, as Prime Minister, he was over-confident in reaching 'a reasonable understanding with both Germany and Italy', as he said:

> The dictators are too often regarded as though they were entirely inhuman. I believe this idea to be quite erroneous . . . they can be approached with the greatest hope of successful issue.[29]

Although history had proven his Munich policy wrong, for the rest of his life he never doubted the rightness of what he had done at Munich.[30] During his long premiership, British foreign policy was unfortunately pulled further and further into a disastrous abyss under his dictatorial instruction.

The first personnel change after Chamberlain took office was announced at the beginning of 1938, when Vansittart was moved from the post of Permanent Under-Secretary to Chief Diplomatic Adviser. The new appointment aimed to reduce his effect on policy-making, because he was more and more at odds with his colleagues.[31] From then on, he advised and functioned 'only if and when asked'.[32]

Vansittart's successor was Sir Alexander Cadogan, who was 'an individual of great discretion, serving men of very different stamp with apparently complete composure'. He was favoured by ministers because he held 'a less black view of German intentions', and was able to take a line which they 'naturally found more palatable than Vansittart's incessant admonitions'.[33] As for Central and Eastern Europe, the new Permanent Under-Secretary explored the idea in his diaries that German expansion in that area was inevitable, and Britain could not stop it.[34]

During this period, Sir Horace Wilson 'gained in influence'. A graduate of the London School of Economics, he had been Chief Industrial Adviser to the Government since 1930. He was an 'invaluable' civil servant to Chamberlain because he could, 'with his knowledge and his understanding', share Chamberlain's loneliness, which was the inevitable result of the Prime Minister's position. It was uncertain whether he 'shared Chamberlain's ideas, or shaped them', but it was certain that he 'promulgated them'. Becoming Chamberlain's confidential adviser, he was 'a power unequalled by any member of the Cabinet except the Prime Minister'. Not only did Chamberlain trust him, Halifax and Hoare also admired him. His role, as the German Embassy commented, was: 'the Prime Minister's closest adviser. It is well known that Sir Horace Wilson is decidedly pro-German, but he keeps himself completely in the background.'[35]

The greatest change was that Eden resigned on 20 February 1938, due to a divergence in outlook between him and Chamberlain over the issue of the *de jure* recognition of the Italian conquest of Abyssinia. The Prime Minister wanted to buy off Mussolini unconditionally by offering him this recognition so as to 'bring appeasement in the Mediterranean'.[36] Eden, however, proposed that Anglo-Italian *rapprochement* could only be reached on condition that Italy withdrew her volunteers from Spain and ceased anti-British propaganda.[37] However, until the beginning of 1938, in spite of some reservations, he accommodated himself to Chamberlain's desire regarding appeasement with Italy.[38]

This was the apparent reason that led to his resignation. However, it is difficult to find any principal divergence between the courses they wanted to pursue. Some of his colleagues simply could not understand why he decided to resign. The underlying reason perhaps was, as Halifax analysed, that Eden could not tolerate Chamberlain's interference in foreign policy any longer. His resignation was 'a result of difference of temperament and training', and a point that 'had been reached where the Prime Minister and Eden no longer saw eye to eye over the methods' that were 'desirable to use in furtherance of their common object'.[39] Therefore, it is a common misunderstanding among many statesmen and scholars to say that his resignation reflected his rift with Chamberlain over general appeasement, including the policy towards Germany.[40] In fact, his policy toward Germany was completely in accordance with Chamberlain's, as we will discuss later in this chapter.[41]

After Eden resigned, Halifax, whom Chamberlain thought the only suitable candidate, was appointed as Foreign Secretary. Halifax was 'a man of simplicity and humility'. Unlike his predecessor, he preferred to follow Chamberlain rather than to initiate foreign policy. Sometimes he did voice his differing views, but without insisting on them, he could co-operate very well with the Prime Minister. Chamberlain always admired him as 'a Cabinet mind', and relied very much on his judgement.[42]

In addition, according to Vansittart's recommendation, Eden appointed Sir Nevile Henderson, from three candidates, to be the British Ambassador in Berlin in April 1937.[43] Henderson's pro-German attitude was very well known, as his colleagues critically noted:

> Sir N. Henderson has by now created for himself such an entirely Nazi reputation everywhere that much of what he says is discounted.

Vansittart later was very angry with Henderson's behaviour in Berlin, and said: 'Henderson is a complete Nazi,' and 'the Foreign Office do not trust him to represent their real point of view.'[44] Even so, Henderson was admired as usual by Chamberlain, who even turned down ministers' proposals on the strength of the Ambassador's suggestions.[45] We will see how British foreign policy in forthcoming crises was misdirected by His Excellency.

Until the outbreak of war, although the FO was still part of the policy-making machinery, more important procedures had been shifting to the Foreign Policy Committee (FPC) of the Cabinet,[46] particularly in the hands of 'The Big Four', referring to Chamberlain, Halifax, Simon and Hoare. Whatever decision was reached, it would be the product of their complete agreement.[47] It was widely recognised that foreign policy was 'run by the P.M. and a small committee'. Some FO staff 'discussed frankly the P.M.'s dictatorship in the Cabinet'. Chamberlain, in Harvey's words, 'likes his present Cabinet of yes-men', in which he could dictate and carry out his policy with (and sometimes without) the co-operation of his team.[48]

To sum up, all these resignations and appointments meant, as Butler, Parliamentary Under-Secretary, remarked, the decline of the old pro-French foreign service and the ascendancy of pro-German diplomats in the Chamberlain Government.[49] It completed the personnel changes that paved the way for pushing appeasement further.

BRITISH POLICY-MAKING BEFORE THE ANSCHLUSS
'Non-intervention' in the Spanish Civil War

After the Rhineland crisis, apart from the Far East, the British Government faced two troublesome factors in Europe: Germany's expansion, and Italy's disturbance in the Mediterranean. What is worse, while they were enthusiastically preparing for the Locarno Power Conference, which was aimed at seeking a new Western Pact and general settlement, the Spanish Civil War broke out.

In July 1936, the fascist insurgents in Spain, under the leadership of General Franco, started their campaign against the Government, which was in the hands of communists. The rebels were militarily supported by Italy and Germany, whereas the lawful Government was helped by the Soviet Union. With strong sympathy for the Government of the Left in Spain, France communicated to Britain a draft proposal of non-intervention on 2 August, suggesting that all the countries concerned should refrain from sending military supplies to either side. The FO was of the opinion:

we must be careful about our answer. The French Government would no doubt like to draw us into some commitment to support

. . . the present Spanish Government, and then deter other foreign Governments from sending arms to the rebels in face of Anglo-French opposition.[50]

Since Baldwin was absent from office due to poor health, Eden fully controlled the conduct of policy.[51] Faced with the possibility of being drawn into conflict with the dictators, his major concern was 'the necessity for not unduly antagonising Italy (or Germany) at this stage, when we are looking forward to a five-Power meeting at which their co-operation will be essential." Therefore, he immediately showed his favour to the non-intervention proposal.[52]

On 24 August, the Chiefs of Staff reported that Italian intervention in the Spanish Civil War would threaten vital British interests in the Western Mediterranean. They advised that conclusion of a non-intervention pact with, among others, France, Russia, Italy and Germany would protect British interests there without tending 'further to alienate Italy'. A week later, the FO also submitted its conclusion that 'a Communist Spain would mean the loss of the whole of the British invested capital in Spain', whereas a fascist Government 'would naturally tend to look for support to Italy and Germany'.[53] Having summarised the above notes, the Foreign Secretary decided to adopt a policy of non-intervention because, as he wrote:

we are known to be more neutral than any other great power, & *because a compromise is in our national interest.* The victory of either extreme would be most unwelcome to us, so that we must be up & doing in favour of compromise whenever opportunity affords.[54]

Thanks to an Anglo-French arrangement, the Non-Intervention Committee held its first meeting in London on 9 September, attended by Britain, France, Italy, Germany, Russia and twenty other countries. Although a non-intervention agreement was reached between the members, it never worked. In supporting the rebels, Mussolini sent 100,000 soldiers to Spain from December 1936 to April 1937, and Hitler sent 6,000 troops with artillery and tanks in November 1936.[55] Vansittart feared that investigation of the fascist powers' violation of non-intervention might 'break up the agreement', and 'affect adversely our cooperation in regard to the Five Power Conference' as well. Eden then declared in the House on 19 November: 'so far as breaches are concerned,

I wish to state categorically that I think there are other Governments more to blame than those of Germany or Italy'.[56] After the insurgents controlled Madrid, he instructed the British Ambassador to establish *de facto* relations with General Franco in early November 1936.[57]

The Spanish episode is less important in making sense of the Second World War compared to the other crises studied in this book. The Civil War broke out because of a Spanish internal crisis, rather than Italo-German encouragement. Spain could not be taken as a victim of the Dictator Powers' invasion; although Mussolini and Hitler sent arms and volunteers to support the rebels. Franco's victory did not change the map of Europe, nor did it turn the balance of power sufficiently in favour of the dictators launching a general war. Although Franco joined the Anti-Comintern Pact in 1939, Spain did not fully participate on the Axis side during the Second World War.

However, the theme of appeasement is very clear in this episode: the British Government intended, by pursuing a non-intervention policy, to avoid conflict with the dictators, aiming to gain their co-operation at the Five Power Conference for a new Locarno Treaty and general settlement. Nevertheless, non-intervention did not bring a new Western pact: on the contrary, Franco's victory increased uncertainty in British European defence.

A Policy of 'Keeping Germany Guessing'

British appeasement of Italy, both in Abyssinia and in Spain, was not repaid by Mussolini's behaviour;[58] however, compared with the German danger, the Italian problem was of only secondary importance. Although there existed controversy about the policy towards Italy, the FO was unanimous in its conclusions about the German issue, under the guideline of Eden's speeches at Leamington and Bradford.[59]

On 4 May 1937, O'Malley, Counsellor and Head of the Southern Department, minuted that:

> if it became practicable to improve our relations with Germany, the Italians would be given much wholesome food for thought and might be expected to become more tractable.

He reminded the Government that he had suggested before that Britain should be 'ready to sell the lumber of Versailles'. Now he asked whether it was 'a vital British interest that Austria and Czechoslovakia should not (whatever the territorial and constitutional position be) fall under German domination'. One month later, he put forward another memo on the same line.[60] In the mean time, Henderson expressed a more radical view in his memo of 10 May, that none of the German aims – the absorption of Austria and part of Czechoslovakia, expansion in the east and recovery of its colonies – 'need injure purely British national interests'. Following the line in Eden's speeches, which, to his understanding, showed that Britain was only prepared to defend Western Europe, he suggested that it was unwise to oppose Germany's 'peaceful expansion' in Central and Eastern Europe, and 'Germany might well be given some colonies.' If Anglo-German understanding could be achieved by offering the above terms:

> British friendship with Germany could and would serve British national policy by restraining both Russian intrigues and ambitions . . . as well as Italian aspiration in the Mediterranean.[61]

The above proposals raised intensive discussion in the FO. Minuting on O'Malley's paper, Vansittart said: 'honour, moral principles & utility all dictate that we shd. not compromise or bargain with their independence'. He explained: 'I don't suppose it is really intended that we should assist at destruction of the independence of smaller European countries.' Sargent, Assistant Under-Secretary, despite divergence on some points in O'Malley's proposal about Italy, confessed that he did not think there was any disagreement as regards the desirability of reaching an understanding with Germany:

> it is of vital importance that an agreement with Germany should be reached at once, even at a considerable cost.

Both Eden and Vansittart supported his conclusion and the former summed up: 'Nothing could be more beneficial for the interests of H. M.G. than an improvement of Anglo-German relations even if it only proved temporary – Spain is a possible field for our collaboration.'[62]

Nevertheless, the FO was not very happy with Henderson's proposal, because, as Vansittart criticised, it was a 'full acceptance of the German attitude'.[63] However, Strang, Head of the Central Department, thought that this was 'not necessarily a decisive objection' to it, although it represented 'a very considerable departure' from the Government's policy. The main difference between the Ambassador's policy and the Government's lay:

in the terms of the intimation which he proposes to make to the German Government of our acquiescence in German expansion in Central and Eastern Europe, provided certain conditions are fulfilled. Whether or not we believe that territorial expansion by Germany is in any event inevitable, we should, by making any such intimation to the German Government, run the gravest risks of disturbing the stability of Europe.

The position so far as we are concerned is as follows: (1) any territorial change in Central and Eastern Europe, even if it comes slowly and in good order, is certain to have political effects in Europe . . . (2) we are not (though we do not publicly say so) prepared to intervene by force of arms to prevent it; (3) the object of our policy is to keep the situation as steady as we can, without bringing ourselves face to face with war.

Therefore, he opposed 'making too plain an intimation to Germany of our acquiescence in her expansion'. Vansittart and Sargent warmly admired this commentary, and the former recommended it to Eden. The Foreign Secretary sent the commentary, together with Henderson's paper, to Halifax while the Lord President was visiting Germany in mid-November.[64]

At the Imperial Conference on 19 May, Eden explained in detail the policy as set out in the Leamington–Bradford speeches:

We might disinterest ourselves altogether in Central Europe and confine ourselves strictly to our vital interests in the Low Countries and Northern France. Such a policy would be unwise and would most certainly invite aggression. Alternatively, we might declare our readiness to fight for Czecho-Slovakia or Austria if they became the victims of aggression. That would mean going far beyond our obligations under the Covenant and far beyond what the people of this country were prepared to go . . . There remained the third possibility, namely, that without undertaking any military commitment we should make it clear that we were interested in events in Central Europe.[65]

This was the so-called policy of 'keeping Germany guessing'.

The ministers, including Chamberlain, were completely in accordance with this line. From the very beginning, the new Prime Minister had been 'trying to improve relations with the 2 storm centres

Berlin and Rome'. The reason was that he did not believe that France was 'in a very strong position to give us much help', because of her serious domestic problems. America was not reliable either, owing to her isolation. Moreover, at least £1,500 million must be spent on rearmament, which 'seemed likely to be more than we could find without heavily increased taxation for an indefinite period'. In the case of the Far East and Europe, he was an unequivocal advocate of pursuing appeasement towards Japan with the purpose of allowing Britain to concentrate on Europe. Following this logic, he argued that 'if we were involved in a war with Japan or Germany, Italy might join in'. He pointed out:

> The ideal, no doubt, was to be prepared to fight Germany or Italy or Japan, either separately or in combination. That, however, was a counsel of perfection which it was impossible to follow. There were limits to our resources, both physical and financial, and it was vain to contemplate fighting single-handed the three strongest Powers in combination.

His recipe was, as he told his colleagues at the meeting of the Committee of Imperial Defence on 5 July, that: 'defensive preparations against Germany received first consideration'. However, 'the best insurance' against possible aggression from Italy 'would be a friendly Germany'.

Therefore, he was eager to make a friendly approach towards the dictator powers, particularly Germany. His general scheme included two points: Britain could offer Italy *de jure* recognition in order to restore the Stresa Front, then Italy would again be a deterrent to German expansion in Central Europe. On the other hand, he believed that:

> we ought so to direct our foreign policy that we did not quarrel with Germany. If we could do that he did not feel that we need fear any sudden attack by Italy.

His conclusion, which was the same as the FO's, was generally shared by his colleagues.[66]

Looking for an Opportunity for Rapprochement

In mid-June the British Government invited the German Foreign Minister, von Neurath, to visit London 'to discuss openly all questions affecting Anglo-German relations'.[67] Eden told his colleagues that this visit 'ought to be useful'.[68] Strang prepared a proposal for the forthcoming conference:

> Germany is in favour of change, and of drastic change. She has strengthened herself in order to secure that changes should take place to her advantage, by peaceful means if possible, but by war if necessary. We . . . have not reached any clear conclusion in our own minds as to what changes we should regard as tolerable.

Based on the policy of 'keep Germany guessing', he suggested:

> we cannot make any promise that we shall intervene by force of arms in any part of Europe other than Western Europe. As regards this, we do not say 'Yes', and we do not say 'No'.

The proposal was discussed in the FO.[69] Sargent, however, supplemented later that they should discourage Germany's ambition in Central and Eastern Europe by telling her: 'The annexation of Austria by Germany, or even a proposal to that effect, would produce in Europe a highly dangerous political crisis, and as such would at once come before the League Council.' Eden admired this suggestion.[70] Indeed, like Chamberlain, he did not think that Britain would be able to undertake a military commitment to Austria or Czechoslovakia.[71]

However, von Neurath's visit was first postponed and then cancelled, using the excuses of the *Deutschland* and *Leipzig* incidents,[72] but the real reason was that Hitler did not approve of it.[73] This disappointed the British leaders very much, but did not exhaust their wish for a *rapprochement* with Germany.

Chamberlain took 'the opportunity of making friendly references to Germany in 2 speeches but though these seemed to be appreciated they elicited no corresponding response'. He regretted to say, 'the way to Berlin was blocked'.[74] Eden found the same. During this period, the Foreign Secretary presided over four meetings of the respective Ambassadors from Germany, Italy and France, aiming to save the Non-Intervention Committee from complete collapse due to the *Leipzig* incident.[75] In addition, he persuaded Dawson, Editor of *The Times*, to hold back some articles which he assumed might damage the possibility of an impending agreement with Germany.[76] However, his efforts, like Chamberlain's, were to no avail, as he told his colleagues in September:

Hitherto all attempts to get to closer quarters with Germany have failed and for the moment nothing more can be done in that quarter.[77]

A chance seemed to come in mid-October: Halifax received an invitation to the November hunting exhibition in Berlin. It was, in Henderson's words, another chance 'to break the ice of bad relations with the Nazi Government'.[78] Halifax wrote in his memoirs that when he told Eden of this news, the latter said quite seriously:

that he was not sure whether it might not be of some advantage for me to go to Germany under this cover.[79]

Eden himself confessed that he 'was not eager, but saw no sufficient reason to oppose it'.[80] On 22 October, he informed the British Embassy in Berlin:

It would clearly be undesirable that Lord Halifax should accept this invitation unless we could be reasonably sure that he would see some persons in authority.[81]

However, in the FO, Sargent analysed some disadvantages of the proposed visit on 27 October, observing that it seemed to put Halifax on 'a special mission', but in fact his intention was 'merely to make a *tour d'horizon* on the lines of those which have taken place in the past'. In addition, Henderson was to be instructed to have conversations either with Goering or von Neurath about 'some very definite statements and proposals' from Goering which should not be allowed to 'pass unanswered'. On the other hand, Eden would probably meet von Neurath at the Brussels Conference, which might lead to the misunderstanding that Halifax was sent to Berlin to continue the conversation initiated in Brussels. Vansittart was worried about this too, and even suggested that 'it is also probable that Lord Halifax wd. not have gone to Berlin'. But Cadogan thought that as Halifax had already accepted the invitation, it was 'undesirable to cancel it', though there was some inconvenience.[82]

In the mean time, Henderson reported that it was quite unlikely that Hitler would meet the British Minister in Berlin during the exhibition: Halifax had either to wait in Berlin until after the exhibition, or propose himself to Berchtesgaden without encouragement. But even so, the Ambassador strongly recommended that the 'present opportunity is one which we should not allow to pass'.[83]

On 10 November, Cranborne, the Under-Secretary, told Chamberlain that according to Eden's telephone instruction from Brussels:

there was no great enthusiasm on the part of Herr Hitler for such a visit. This did not perhaps so much matter if the plan was to fit in a conversation merely as a side product of visit by Lord Halifax . . . Moreover, we might appear in the role of suppliant, which would be most undesirable. Under such circumstances you [Eden] were of the view that the visit would hardly be justified.

Chamberlain replied that he fully agreed that if it became necessary for Lord Halifax to ask for a meeting, the effect would be deplorable. But he did not see that this should be necessary. If Halifax were to receive an invitation to go to Berchestgarden, he would be glad to accept.[84]

As soon as he returned from Brussels on 14 November, Eden had a meeting with Chamberlain, Halifax and Vansittart. He 'by this time had come to regard Halifax's visit as not necessarily a bad thing as H. would impress Hitler, provided always visit was kept informal and no negotiations were started'.[85]

The guideline for Halifax's visit was, as Eden told Halifax and Henderson on 27 October:

The former [Halifax] will listen and confine himself to warning comment on Austria and Czecho-slovakia . . . I have impressed on Sir N. Henderson the need for doing all we can to *discourage* German initiative in these two states. We must keep Germany guessing as to our attitude.[86]

Chamberlain took a similar point of view: 'It was no part of my plan that we should make or receive any offer. What I wanted H[alifax] to do was to convince Hitler of our sincerity and to ascertain what objectives he had in mind.' He instructed Halifax that 'he would be well content to see things move slowly and that they could not be expected to do otherwise'.[87]

During his visit (17–21 November), Halifax had a meeting with the Führer and other top German leaders including Goering, von Blomberg and Goebbels.[88] When he came back to London on 22 November, he gave Eden and Chamberlain an account of the visit.[89] Two days later, he reported to the Cabinet his general impression. According to his observations, the colonies were the only outstanding issue between the two countries, but it would not lead to war. As for Central and Eastern Europe, Hitler had expressed satisfaction with the Austro-German Agreement of July 1936, and he had said that Czecho–Slovakia 'only needed to treat the Germans living within her borders well and they would be entirely happy'. Halifax's conclusion, therefore, was 'that the Germans had no policy of immediate adventure'.

Chamberlain 'expressed warm appreciation of Lord Halifax' efforts'.[90] He remarked that the visit was 'a great success'.[91] Differing from the description in his memoirs, Eden in fact 'expressed great satisfaction with the way the Lord President had dealt with each point in his conversations with the Chancellor'.[92] He thought that the visit was carried out completely in accordance with the line of the Government.[93]

Halifax's report offered a basis for the FO's study, and Eden summed up the results of their research:

> Hitler had now adopted the theme that a general settlement was not practical politics, that immediate negotiations between Great Britain and Germany were unnecessary, but that if Britain really wanted to improve relations, she could do so by satisfying German colonial claims. It was noticeable that Hitler had offered no guarantees about his policy in Central Europe.[94]

Chamberlain had a similar view, as he told his sister: 'I see clearly enough the lines on which we should aim at progress but the time required to arrive at satisfactory conclusions will be long and we must expect setbacks.'[95] According to Oliver Harvey's diaries, he and Eden 'were in absolute agreement about Germany – viz. no settlement except a general European settlement'.[96]

In the meantime, Henderson sent back a series of telegrams, in which he advised that the Government should make an offer on the subject of colonies in order to start discussion with the Germans, and he had already told Dr Schmidt, Hitler's interpreter, that Halifax's visit constituted 'a turning point from the old course on to a new one'. He conveyed the Germans' idea to the FO that 'the next move must come from us'.[97]

These despatches were received in the FO with furious criticism. Vansittart minuted: 'We made this last move . . . they also expect us to make the next.'[98] Another minute reads more sharply:

> Again and again Sir N. Henderson exceeds his functions and misunderstands the business of an Ambassador.[99]

Eden agreed with these criticisms, and said: 'I am inclined to think we might perhaps repeat our warning.'[100] After Sargent sent a critical letter to Berlin, Eden himself warned Henderson in mid-December that the Ambassador must strictly follow the Government's policy, which had been described by Halifax to Hitler, and by Chamberlain and himself to the French Ministers. Halifax's foregoing visit did not mean 'a change in direction of the policy' towards Germany, and:

> It would be a mistake, therefore, to give the German Government the impression that His Majesty's Government are impatient for some new initiative at this moment . . .[101]

Anglo-French Ministerial Discussions

Being interested in the information about Halifax's visit, the French showed their desire to meet the British Ministers.[102] On 23 November, Eden had a talk with Chamberlain and both agreed to invite Delbos, the French Foreign Minister, and Chautemps, the other French Minister, to London.[103]

Discussions between British and French Ministers were held on 29–30 November. Halifax first told the French of his visit to Germany, and then Chamberlain added that:

> the Germans wanted two things . . . first, colonies; secondly, assurances about Central and Eastern Europe. If they could get what they required without giving anything for it, that would be for them the best solution. On the other hand, His Majesty's Government were not prepared to open discussions unless the Germans were prepared to discuss the things that His Majesty's Government wanted.

The French ministers held the same attitude towards the colonies and European appeasement.

As far as Central and Eastern Europe were concerned, Eden drew attention to the point that 'neither France nor Great Britain had treaty engagements as regards Austria'. Chamberlain asked Delbos whether the treaty between France and Czechoslovakia would be brought into operation if Germany invaded Czechoslovakia. The French Foreign Minister replied: 'if there were armed intervention by Germany, it was evident that the treaty would apply'. He also emphasised that although there were no treaty engagements with Austria, 'there were certain declarations such as that made at Stresa by which Great Britain and France and Italy asserted that the maintenance of the integrity and independence of Austria was a necessary element for European peace'. Since the Italian attitude had changed, 'France and Britain might manifest a certain solicitude'. However, Eden pointed out that the Austrian question should not be dealt with in the same way as the Czech problem. The Prime Minister went further, stressing that British public opinion would not approve of Britain becoming 'entangled in a war on account of Czechoslovakia'. He agreed with Chautemps that they 'could not request Czechoslovakia to grant autonomy to the *Sudetendeutsche*. He did not, in fact, believe that the Germans would go so far in their demands as that'. Eden added with sympathy: 'Sudeten Germans had certain grievances . . . the right course would be to impress upon the Czech Government the need for doing something . . . to meet the grievances of the Sudeten Germans'.[104] In short, the French Ministers wanted to 'press the British Ministers to adopt some more forthcoming attitude in Central Europe', but 'No encouragement had been given to them'.

In the end, both sides agreed that the right course in dealing with Central and Eastern Europe was 'to interest ourselves in a spirit of conciliation', that appropriate concessions might be made by Czecho–slovakia, and that an attempt should be made to reach a general settlement with Germany. In addition, improved relations with Mussolini might have the effect of reviving his interest in Austria.[105]

On 1 December, Eden informed the German Ambassador of the Anglo-French discussions, telling him:

> As regards Austria . . . It had always been my view that Austria was even more an Italian interest than a French or British interest.[106]

Preparing The Formula for a Settlement

Although they decided not to rush into a general settlement with Germany, the British Government had never given up its efforts to work towards that end. In late December, when the Cabinet discussed the *Interim Report on Defence Expenditure in Future Years*, Halifax said:

> that brought out clearly how the limitation imposed on defence by finance threw a heavy burden on to diplomacy . . . we were faced

with the possibility of three enemies at once . . . we ought to make every possible effort to get on good terms with Germany . . . it was of great importance to make further progress in improving relations with Germany.

Being in accord with Halifax, Eden thought that the first task was for the French Government and themselves to decide what could be done in the colonial sphere. Chamberlain agreed that 'no further move could be made with Germany until after further explorations'. He recalled that the preliminary consideration of the German contribution to a settlement 'might take the form of some measure of disarmament'.[107]

At Chamberlain's request,[108] the FO studied the colonial issue, and the report of 1 January 1938 under Eden's name came to the same conclusion as Henderson had done. It says:

> The conversation between Lord Halifax and Herr Hitler showed that, if we wish for a general settlement with Germany, it will be for us, and not for the German Government, to take the next step by putting forward some concrete proposals . . . It is important, if we are really anxious to prevent the hopes created by the recent conversations from evaporating, that there should be no long delay. We must keep moving; and we must try to make some further communication on the subject not only to the French Government, but also to the Germans, as soon as we possibly can.

Eden implied that the British Government could make a concession on the colonial issue, and in return, requested a general settlement with Germany. He advised the Committee to consider what British colonial territories could be transferred to Germany, and what the term 'general settlement' really meant.[109]

On 8 January, Chamberlain met Joseph Avenol, the Secretary-General of the League, at Hever Castle. The interview inspired the Prime Minister with 'an idea' for further negotiations with Germany:

> The notion which had been developing in his mind was the possibility of a solution by the adoption of an entirely new method of presenting the problem. His suggestion was that the matter should not be treated as a restoration to Germany of territory of which she had been deprived, but the opening of an entirely new chapter in the history of African colonial development to be

introduced and accepted by the general agreement of the Powers interested in Africa. The new conception would be based on the complete equality of the Powers concerned and of their all being subjected to certain limitations in regard to the African territories to be administered by them under the scheme. Germany would be brought in to the arrangement by becoming one of the African Colonial Powers in question and by being given certain territories to administer.

If this scheme could be put forward it would not be necessary, in the first instance, to discuss and settle what particular territories should be assigned to Germany, or what compensation (if any) should be given to those Powers which assigned territory to Germany.

He did not reveal the idea, which would 'open up a hopeful prospect', to his colleagues until 24 January when the Committee meeting was held.[110]

On 13 January, with Wilson's participation, he worked out a principle for the FO to study the colonial issue further:

His Majesty's Government have realised that if such appeasement is to be achieved it will not be upon the basis of bargaining in which each side seeks to weigh up what it will get against what it will be asked to give. Our plan (both as regards Germany and Italy) rests upon the view that we and they are in a position each to make a contribution towards an objective we both desire to obtain. There would be no need to discuss whether our contribution were greater or less than theirs. What is needed is to ensure that the contribution of each will, taken with the contribution of the other, make up an agreement which will bring appeasement.

According to this principle, if Britain contributed a concession of colonies, it could ask Germany to offer assurances about the Western frontier and about Belgian neutrality, and no use of force against Austria or Czechoslovakia.[111]

On 24 January, the Cabinet Committee considered Eden's memo of 1 January. Chamberlain admired it. He thought that a *rapprochement* with Germany was urgent, because some time had elapsed since Halifax's visit and Germany might think that Britain had abandoned its original intention. Another reason was that before the opening of the Anglo-Italian conversations, the British Government needed to show its efforts to secure a general appeasement by discussions not with Italy alone, but also with Germany. He then told the Committee of his 'new method' concerning the colonial issue, which was 'promptly & even enthusiastically' accepted.

In the course of discussion, Ormsby-Gore, Colonies Secretary, said: 'the longer we waited the higher was the price that we should have to pay and that the granting to Germany of some concessions now in West Africa would heal a running sore and effect a permanent settlement'. Chamberlain concluded: 'time should not be lost . . . the Germans could be told we were ready to discuss'. Based on his instruction, the Cabinet Committee decided that Eden should consult Henderson about the formula.[112] The telegram to Henderson was drafted by Cadogan, and approved by both Eden and Chamberlain.[113]

On the following day, Eden prepared a memo, according to the principle formulated by Chamberlain, to estimate what offer might come from Germany for 'general appeasement'. As to Central and Eastern Europe, he thought that no further consideration had been given to the suggestion that Germany might renew to Britain and France the undertaking she had given regarding Austria in the German-Austrian Agreement of July 1936. In addition, 'some lesser form of autonomy should be granted to the *Sudetendeutsch*', and 'in return Czech independence should be guaranteed by one or more of the great Powers'.[114] On the same day, he went to Geneva.

Meanwhile, Chamberlain summoned Henderson back to London for consultation, and asked the Ambassador to tell the Germans that he returned 'to take part in work . . . engaged for following up Halifax's conversation'.[115] On 3 February, Henderson attended the Cabinet Committee meeting and gave the ministers his forecast of Nazi reaction to the British formula. He informed them that the German Government would certainly not be satisfied unless it was granted some territory over which it could exercise full sovereign rights and call its own colony. Germany would agree to 'some form of limitation of armaments', but she would not return to the League until the Covenant had been modified. He told the ministers that the problem of Czechoslovakia might be solved if Germany made a long-term agreement with her, while the German Government refused to give any promise to Austria.[116] After the meeting, instructions to the Ambassador were drafted and circulated to the Committee members. Simon and Halifax put forward some revising points,[117] and the final draft was sent by Eden to Henderson on 12 February. The Foreign Secretary instructed the Ambassador to inform the Germans that the British Government was ready to discuss with the German Government on all issues which had been referred to during Halifax's visit to Germany. 'Mention should be made of Czecho-slovakia and Austria as illustrative of the general principle of collaboration.'[118]

Meanwhile, however, due to personnel changes in the German Government[119] and Hitler's forthcoming speech on 20 February, Henderson suggested on 7 February that it would be a mistake to make an approach until things had settled down 'after recent convulsions'.[120] It seems that Eden was at first inclined to agree, but other senior officials, such as Vansittart, Cadogan, Sargent and Strang, were in favour of sending a communication to Hitler before his forthcoming speech, on the grounds that during the period in which Hitler was preparing his speech, he should know what HMG was prepared to offer.[121] Eden then took their view. At the Cabinet meeting of 9 February, he explained to his colleagues: 'it would be inadvisable to wait, as, if no further approach were made, Herr Hitler might express disappointment that nothing had been done to follow up the Lord President's visit'. Chamberlain's view, however, was closer to Henderson's. Halifax drew up a compromise plan, that Henderson should consult von Ribbentrop, the new Foreign Minister, first as to whether it would be advisable for him to ask for an interview with Hitler before 20 February. If the reply was negative, the Ambassador might ask von Ribbentrop to tell Hitler that HMG was ready to take the next step as soon as the Chancellor was ready to receive him. This proposal met with considerable support, while Eden seemed very impatient, and insisted on 'the minimum that the Ambassador ought to say was that he was available for a further conversations'.[122]

BRITISH POLICY-MAKING DURING THE ANSCHLUSS

Repercussions of the Hitler–von Schuschnigg Meeting at Berchtesgaden

It was apparent that without consulting the House, the Government had completed policy-making long before public opinion focused on the Austrian problem, owing to Hitler's stormy interview with von Schuschnigg on 12 February. The disturbing news about the Berchtesgaden meeting was not revealed until 15 February. When the story emerged that day, the *News Chronicle* reported: 'from the very start of the interview Chancellor Schuschnigg found himself subjected to great pressure . . . At times the discussion was extremely blunt.' On the other hand, *The Times* carefully avoided strong wording, and reported: 'Hitler used the plainest language in stating his demands and it is understood that he indicated grave consequences if they were not accepted . . . It is understood that he recommended compliance to Herr von Schuschnigg in the most emphatic terms, and expressed the view that the Austrian Government had no backing to hope for in any third quarter if they were obdurate.' Gedye, Vienna Correspondent of the *Daily Telegraph*, gave more details:

> The Führer went so far – and I can assert this positively, in the face of any subsequent denials – as to threaten that in the case of disorders in Austria, he would 'march', being unable to resist any longer the pleas of the 'downtrodden German population in Austria' . . . Actually – as I am able again to assert without fear of contradiction – Herr Hitler delivered an ultimatum.

Whatever the extent of the criticism, the general tone of the press showed that Austria was a closed case, and that it was impossible for the Western Powers to declare war on Germany over this.[123]

In the House, however, the Opposition 'tried to make a major issue out of British policy towards Austria', and Attlee led a move to 'jog the Government into action'.[124] On 16 February, Arthur Henderson, a Labour MP, asked: 'Will His Majesty's Government stand by the joint declaration of February, 1934, to the effect that they re-affirmed the interest of this country in the integrity and independence of Austria?' Eden, who was still Foreign Secretary, did not answer the question directly, only saying that the Stresa Powers needed to consult each other, and they were waiting for Italian consultation.[125]

The following day, the Foreign Affairs Committee in the House discussed the situation with the attendance of a hundred MPs. Opening the discussion, Harold Nicolson, National Labour MP for West Leicester, appealed to the Committee to 'face the fact that adventurism is now in the ascendant in Germany, and the cautious people have been proved to have been wrong'. Churchill, in support of his argument, took a firmer attitude and declared, 'we must call a halt'. The whole feeling of the meeting, as Nicolson observed, 'is very different from that of a year ago. They no longer believe that we can buy Germany off with concessions.'[126] This accorded with the report of Franckenstein, the Austrian Minister in Britain, in which he wrote that:

> a number of Members of Parliament have reexamined their views on Central Europe and found that England could not only not keep aloof from the impending chaos, but would even have to collaborate vigorously in the solution of this problem. People have come to understand that England is bound to intervene not only in the case of an unprovoked attack upon Austria or Czechoslovakia, but also in case revolts should be engineered by the N.S.D.A.P. in these two countries.[127]

However, official reaction to public opinion was very ambivalent. Before the news of Berchtesgaden broke, Eden addressed the Foreign Affairs Committee in the House on 9 December 1937:

> His general line is that there is no imminent likelihood of war and a far better prospect of appeasement than ever before. He draws attention to several favourable factors, such as the progress of our rearmament, the fact that Spain has ceased to be a real source of danger . . .

As regards Central Europe, he prevaricated, saying: 'we cannot disinterest ourselves and will enter into commitments'. From Nicolson's diary, we know that Eden successfully misled his audience.[128]

In fact, as early as during Halifax's visit to Germany, a new initiative was being arranged to curb the press. In the meeting of 21 November, Goebbels complained that the British press attacked Hitler. Halifax promised him that he would consult Chamberlain and Eden 'with a view to seeing what could be done to secure the cooperation of the British Press particularly with regard to the question of personal attacks on Herr Hitler'. He told the German Propaganda Minister that it was necessary 'for the Press to create the right atmosphere'.[129] As soon as he came back, he took a series of steps, as he wrote to Henderson:

> I have seen Steward, the Prime Minister's Press Adviser at No. 10, and discussed ways and means with him, and have also had a personal talk on the subject with Lord Southwood [of Odhams Press] who controls the *Daily Herald* and Sir Walter Layton of the

News Chronicle. The *Daily Herald* had a very objectionable cartoon on Wednesday and I immediately wrote to Southwood following our interview and have had a reply of a character which gives one to hope that we shall not have reason to complain again of this sort of thing.[130]

However, in the face of the public being alarmed by the news about the Berchtesgaden meeting, Oliver Harvey recorded: 'the Government . . . took every possible step to secure the London papers . . . The B.B.C, was told to say nothing that night about Germany and Italy.' On 28 February, Halifax (now Foreign Secretary) saw Reith, the Director of the BBC, and asked him 'not to proceed with a series of talks on . . . the German Colonies'. Reith asked Halifax 'pointblank whether H.M.G. wished him to stop them'. Halifax replied: 'that was so but he would deny it if challenged in public!'[131] Chamberlain tried to calm the public by telling the House on the eve of the *Anschluss* (2 March):

it hardly seems possible to maintain, from the juridical point of view, that because these two statesmen agreed that certain internal changes in one of their two countries were desirable in the interests of the relations between their two countries, the one country had alienated its independence to the other.[132]

In fact, information received in the FO was far from reassuring. On 15 February, the Austrian Chancellor told Palairet, the British Ambassador in Vienna, that 'he had been met by threats' in his interview with Hitler, but 'had yielded the minimum'. Von Schuschnigg hoped that the Western Powers would make Germany know that Austria had gone to 'the limits of conciliation'. He was convinced that 'absorption of Austria by Germany must lead to war'.[133] In Paris, Delbos summoned up Phipps, the British Ambassador, and said that the French Government 'strongly favour making some communication to German Government showing interest that British and French Governments take in events in Austria and in the maintenance of peace and tranquillity in Central Europe'. Two days later, he told the Ambassador that he greatly feared that sounding on the colonial question at this moment 'would give the impression to Germany that both Great Britain and France were unduly weak and unduly impressed by German violence'.[134]

When the Vienna telegrams were considered at a meeting on 15 February in the FO, Cadogan, Oliver Harvey, Eden's Private

Secretary and others thought that the Anschluss was inevitable, sooner or later and they could not help. Cadogan personally wished 'Germany would swallow Austria and get it over'. Vansittart, however, advised that Henderson should advise Hitler that the British Government 'wanted to know what was going on about Austria'. Cadogan had his suggestion 'watered down to "include Austria"', and Chamberlain 'watered it down further' because, as Cadogan explained, 'what is the good of brandishing Austria under Hitler's nose when we can't do anything about it?'[135] Eden, in Harvey's words, was 'determined not to get into the false position of giving the Austrians advice and then being saddled with the responsibility if they accept advice and the situation gets worse. We cannot fight for Austria and we must be careful not to raise false hopes in Vienna.'[136] Strang, however, was very angry that Hitler said Halifax had approved of Germany's attitude towards Austria, and suggested: 'that we should warn Herr Hitler that he must not quote H.M.G., in the person of Lord Halifax, as approving of his designs on Austria'. But Halifax was reluctant to make a complaint, because he did not want to spoil the attempt to approach Germany:

> We clearly have every right to make our position plain – provided Schuschnigg agrees – & will stick to his guns above having said it. I obviously couldn't approve Germany's attitude when I did not know what it was. But if the matter is taken up, I hope it may be so handled as not to prejudice the other side of our policy – i.e. the broad question of getting onto closer terms with the gangsters.

After further discussion, the decision says: 'No action was taken on this.'[137] The instruction to Vienna, drafted with the approval of Eden and Chamberlain, ran as follows:

> we should not put ourselves into the position of making suggestions which, if accepted or rejected, produced a major crisis of which we could be accused of being the authors.[138]

As to the French suggestion, Eden was 'extremely doubtful of the wisdom of any separate or joint communication to the German Government by the British and French Ambassadors in Berlin', because Henderson was authorised to inform Hitler that 'His Majesty's Government were considering what steps might be taken to bring about a measure of appeasement which would include *inter alia*

Austria.' The Foreign Secretary therefore instructed Phipps on 16 February: 'we do not intend ourselves to go further than this, and we should deprecate any Anglo-French warning or protest in Berlin'.[139]

On the same day, the Cabinet assembled to discuss the Austrian situation. Halifax recalled that his general impression had been that the Führer would continue his activities with regard to Austria, but in a manner, which did not enable any other country to interfere. Chamberlain thought that 'Hitler wanted peace but at his own price.' Eden told the Minister that 'he did not want to put himself in a position of suggesting a resistance which he could not, in fact, furnish'.[140]

Just two days before Eden's resignation, the French again delivered messages suggesting that it was 'illogical and even dangerous' at that moment to start discussions with Germany. They wanted a joint *démarche* of protest against the German Government, on the following lines:

(1) that the legitimate anxiety of Doctor Schuschnigg to safeguard Austrian independence will not, in the opinion of Great Britain and France, allow him to go any further;

(2) that the real and not merely verbal independence of Austria constitutes one of the major interests of European peace, and that the British and French Governments could not be indifferent spectators of any new attempts destined to destroy it.

(3) that in general we cannot tolerate any coup de main or act of war likely to bring into question the territorial status quo in Central Europe, and that in that case these events would meet with opposition on the part of the Western Powers.[141]

Tense minutes in the FO led to the conclusion that the reaction to the French proposal must be negative. Strang said that the French 'put up proposals which go well beyond what they themselves are willing (or in a position) to perform, and will place the responsibility for inaction upon us . . . neither we nor the French possess the offensive power sufficient to prevent Germany from working her will in Central Europe'. Sargent and Cadogan agreed. The latter summed up: 'the time for talking about Austria has gone by'. A reply was discussed at a meeting between Halifax, Cadogan, Plymouth (Parliamentary Under-Secretary) and Ingram (Counsellor in the FO) on 22 February, and examined by the Cabinet on 25 February. Based on the Cabinet's conclusion, the FO prepared a memo to tell the French that their suggestion:

if held in Berlin, might, if it became known in Vienna, only mislead the Austrian Chancellor by encouraging his hopes for military support from France and Great Britain, which is unlikely to be forthcoming.

The language suggested by the French Government implies a readiness on the part of the French and British Governments to have recourse to war in order to assert their will . . . His Majesty's Government have refused to undertake a decision which in present circumstances they are unable to reverse.

They made their aversion plain to their French colleagues:

His Majesty's Government contemplate following up Lord Halifax's visit by initiating further conversations through the diplomatic channel with the German Chancellor, in the course of which it is hoped to ascertain how far the German Government are prepared to go in making a concrete contribution in respect of Central Europe and disarmament. These conversations would make it clear to the German Government that in the view of His Majesty's Government recent events have aroused apprehensions in many quarters which must inevitably render more difficult the negotiation of a general settlement, and that a general appeasement depends on the restoration and maintenance of confidence and stability in Austria and Czechoslovakia.[142]

At the same time, the Cabinet instructed Henderson to carry out the proposal put forward before Eden's resignation.[143] Some telegrams even repeated Eden's instructions.[144]

On 3 March, Henderson had a conversation with the Führer. He turned down immediate Anglo-German discussions, saying that the colonial question was not ripe for settlement, and 'it would be better to wait for a few years'. His remarks on Austria were that he proposed to 'proceed with his declared policy regardless of consequences'. As regards the Czechs, his view was that the present situation was 'intolerable and must be modified by negotiation or by dictation'.[145] In the Ambassador's opinion, it was very difficult to find 'a common basis for reasonable discussion'. However, he did not believe 'that at this stage Hitler is thinking in terms of the Anschluss'.[146] Despite warning Germany, he told Hitler that he personally advocated the Anschluss.[147] Following the line set by Eden but continued by Halifax, Henderson let the Germans know that 'we had, in short, washed our hands of Austria, except to express a wish for "reasonable solutions reasonably achieved"'.[148]

The Anschluss

Although Hitler did not want to come to terms immediately, the British Government was still prepared to push things further during the forthcoming visit of von Ribbentrop to London. At the Cabinet meeting of 9 March, Halifax (now Foreign Secretary) suggested as to the line to be adopted for the future meeting, that since the Germans did not want to tie their hands through talks, he should show the German Foreign Minister 'a mixture of disappointment, reproach and warning'. In spite of this, he would say:

> that the Government would at any time be ready to join the German Government in an attempt to realise an understanding . . . We had no desire to block any peaceful agreements arrived at by peaceful means. We had not tried to block the German policy in Austria . . . His general line, therefore, was not to give the Germans the impression that we were running after them; but to show that we were not shutting the door.

In the course of discussion, admiring Halifax's suggestion, Chamberlain pointed out that 'it was not proposed to say that this was the last opportunity'. As to the German threat to Austria and Czechoslovakia, Maugham, the Lord Chancellor, said that they should remind the Germans that 'the German nation was pledged by the Treaty of Paris'. Hoare added that 'if Germany invaded Austria or Czecho-slovakia they raised dangers in Europe of which the end could not be foreseen'.[149]

That very day, news came from Vienna that von Schuschnigg had decided, as the last measure to maintain the independence of Austria, to hold a plebiscite on 13 March,[150] which caused a 'storm' in Germany.[151] Halifax warned von Ribbentrop, who was now in London, that 'if once war should start in Central Europe, it was quite impossible to say where it might not end, or who might not become involved'.[152] He also instructed Henderson to speak to Hitler along the same lines.[153]

On 11 March, German troops were moving towards the Austrian border.[154] Due to pressure from ultimatums both by the Austrian Nazi leader and by Germany, von Schuschnigg had to cancel the plebiscite and consider resignation. He asked for immediate advice from HMG because 'if he yields any semblance of Austrian independence is gone'.[155] After receiving this information, Cadogan showed the details to Chamberlain at a luncheon-party for von Ribbentrop. The Prime Minister urged von Ribbentrop to report to Hitler the serious view the British Government took of these latest developments in Austria.[156]But, in fact, nobody wanted to fight for Austria.[157]

Based on the result of discussions in the FO that day, Halifax telegraphed Vienna in the afternoon that he could not advise von Schuschnigg to 'take any course of action which might expose his country to dangers against which His Majesty's Government are unable to guarantee protection'.[158] Regarding the French enquiry on 12 March about whether the Western Powers should bring the Austrian question before the League, Halifax instructed Phipps to give them a negative answer.[159]

On the other hand, Vienna's appeal to France and Italy failed too, because the French Government had just resigned on 10 March; Italy, however, did not even want to communicate with the Western Powers over the Austrian problem.[160] Since the Austrian President refused to accept the German ultimatum, German troops moved into Austria on the night of 11–12 March.[161]

World opinion was profoundly shocked by the lightning Anschluss. In Britain, most newspapers, including *The Times*, seriously condemned the German action. Although it agreed that the Anschluss should be accepted with acquiescence, *The Times* was dismayed by Hitler's surprise initiative. The leading articles, keeping the same line as the Government, pointed out that 'the indignation of the world is not at the thing he has done, but at the manner of the doing'. Hitler's violation was incompatible with the policy of appeasement. The *News Chronicle* put forward the alternative to appeasement, namely to restore the collapsed collective security system around Czechoslovakia. Germany must be told that further aggression would be met with an overwhelming solidarity of resistance.[162] The *New Statesman* also agreed that the best hope of checking Germany lay in Churchill's proposal of a Grand Alliance.[163] The press had a tendency to emphasise the future danger, particularly the case of Czechoslovakia rather than that of Austria, which seemed too late to fight for.

On 14 March, the Cabinet received a note from the Opposition which demanded a debate. In order to cope with public opinion and to discuss the situation, Chamberlain summoned the Cabinet to meet twice, on 12 and 14 March. At the first meeting, Halifax suggested that there were two points which had to be considered: what steps should be taken to guide public opinion; how they were to prevent similar action being taken in Czechoslovakia. Chamberlain pointed out:

> The manner in which the German action in Austria had been brought about was most distressing and shocking to the world and as a typical illustration of power politics . . . There was little doubt that Hitler would represent it as another illustration of peaceful methods . . . he believed that what had happened was inevitable unless the Powers had been able to say 'If you make war on Austria you will have to deal with us.'

But he thought that 'at any rate the question was now out of the way'. He told his colleagues that 'there was probably not very much that could be done'.[164] However, they all realised that the Government must make its standpoint clear to the public when the Prime Minister spoke in the House on 14 March. At the second meeting, describing to his colleagues the general lines of a statement, Halifax consulted them on 'how far it would be wise to include in the statement on policy a condemnation of the German attitude'. In favour of stronger language, the Cabinet was reminded that it 'had already made a protest' to the Germans, and it seemed proper 'to express strong views', reflecting the deep concern of public opinion; and also 'if this was not done it would facilitate the adoption by the Germans of similar forcible action towards Czechoslovakia'. On the other hand, in favour of milder language, it was pointed out:

> it was important to avoid giving the impression that we were on the brink of war. It was equally important to avoid exacerbating the situation or giving an impression of threats which we were not in a position to carry out; and that the general public would be much more concerned with what action the Government proposed to take to develop our own defences than in verbal condemnation of Herr Hitler.

Chamberlain suggested: 'the condemnation should be applied to the methods used by Herr Hitler and the shock that had been given to world confidence by those methods'. This met with general agreement, and the draft statement was prepared by Chamberlain and Halifax.[165]

When the debate took place on 14 March, Attlee pointed out that 'this event knocks down the house of cards which the Prime Minister has been building'. He asked the Government, 'What is your policy now?' He warned:

> What we need to-day is not an attempt to build peace by separate bargainings with separate dictators, separate attempts to buy off aggression. We need a return to League principles and League policy . . . our Government should take the lead in proposing means for preventing a further descent into lawlessness.[166]

Amery, however, did not appeal to save Austria, because that country 'was not prepared to fight' for her independence, but he demanded a definite answer from the Government on the Czechoslovakia problem, which was to be a major concern of the future.[167] Churchill delivered a powerful speech:

> We await the further statement of the Government, but it is quite clear that we cannot accept as a final solution of the problem of Central Europe the event which occurred on 11th March . . . We cannot say 'The past is the past' without surrendering the future.

In support of the Opposition leaders' view, he put forward his plan for a 'Grand Alliance':

> If a number of States were assembled around Great Britain and France in a solemn treaty for mutual defence against aggression; if they had their forces marshalled in what you may call a grand alliance; if they had their staff arrangements concerted; if all this rested, as it can honourably rest, upon the Covenant of the League of Nations, agreeable with all the purposes and ideals of the League of Nations; if that were sustained, as it would be, by the moral sense of the world; and if it were done in the year 1938 – and, believe me, it may be the last chance there will be for doing it – then I say that you might even now arrest this approaching war.[168]

The critics could never change Chamberlain's mind. In his statement, the Prime Minister tried to blind the public as to what the proposed line might be. He condemned Germany's 'violent methods' on one hand, and refused to 'take action *vis-à-vis* Austria' on the other. He did not make it clear whether his policy had been dashed by Hitler's action:

> While the policy of appeasement would lead to a relaxation of the economic pressure . . . what has just occurred must inevitably retard economic recovery and, indeed, increased care will be required to ensure that marked deterioration does not set in.

As to preventing future aggression against Czechoslovakia, he avoided giving a direct answer, but only quoted Goering's assurance to that country, which stated: 'it would be the earnest endeavour of the German Government to improve German-Czech relations'.[169]

The Prime Minister's statement did not quell criticism. Harold Nicolson wrote in his diary entry of 15 March:

> the Government have betrayed the country and . . . the Tories think only of the Red danger and let the Empire slide. I am in grave doubts as to my own position. How can I continue to support a Government like this?[170]

However, Chamberlain did not want to change his policy, in spite of criticism. On the contrary, he told his colleagues at the FPC meeting on the same day that 'recent events had confirmed him in his opinion that the policy was the right one and he only regretted that it had not been adopted earlier'.[171]

CONCLUSION

History has proven the absurdity of the appeasers' formulation, as given at the beginning of this chapter, that they had no chance of stopping Hitler. Although stopping Hitler from annexing Austria was much more difficult than driving him out of the Rhineland, it was not a case of 'no chance'. If the British Government had followed the French suggestion of manifesting a 'solicitude' from the very beginning, and made a joint protest to Germany for Austria's independence before the Anschluss, the situation might have been different because the firm attitude of the Western Powers would have strengthened the position of Hitler's opposing generals, who warned the Führer that 'Germany was not in a position to undertake the risk of a major conflict.'[172] This would certainly have discouraged Hitler, or at least made it more difficult for him to win.

The British leaders' mistake over the loss of Austria was twofold: first, after the Rhineland episode, the British questionnaire was shelved by Hitler, and his appeal for a 25-year non-aggression pact and air pact was obviously an empty promise. All this did not open the appeasers' eyes to Hitler's real ambitions. They tried to fool themselves into believing that Hitler would not strike in Austria immediately, and would not go so far as to demand autonomy for the *Sudetendeutsche*. Without any assurance of future settlement from Hitler after his violation of Locarno, and without any knowledge of the dictator's real intentions in Central and Eastern Europe, they were under the illusion that general agreement would be reached by offering Germany some colonies. In order to attract Hitler's interest in a general settlement, Halifax and Henderson had revealed to the Führer in their meetings that Britain would acquiesce in the change in Central and Eastern Europe as long as it took place 'upon the basis of reasonable agreements reasonably reached'. They failed to give any definition of what 'reasonable' really meant, nor did they dare to specify what they should do if Hitler made changes by *unreasonable* means. History demonstrates that it was the British leaders – not the Germans – who were kept guessing what would happen next, because the Führer was quite sure that whatever he did, Britain would not interfere.

Second, although they realised from the *Anschluss* that Hitler would practise the same method in the future, they summed up the lessons wrongly. Cadogan wrote on 16 March:

> I shall be called 'cowardly' but after days and nights of thinking, I have come to the conclusion that is the least bad. We *must* not precipitate a conflict now – we shall be smashed. It *may* not be better later . . . [173]

Chamberlain told his colleagues that the present incident had confirmed him in his belief that appeasement was right, and he only regretted that it had not been adopted earlier. Therefore, if the Rhineland caused the ripening of appeasement towards Germany, the *Anschluss* hastened and extended this process.

During this period, the Far Eastern pin-prick still diverted the policy-makers' attention while they wanted to concentrate on the dangers nearer home. In Europe, facing the two 'storm centres' of Berlin and

Rome, Chamberlain followed a very peculiar course: if he could make friends with Italy, the Stresa Front would be restored to deter German adventures in Central Europe; on the other hand, if he could buy Hitler off, Mussolini would not dare attack Britain single-handedly. As the result of this logic, instead of fighting against the aggressive powers, Britain tried to rope them in. Chamberlain's proposal was based on an assumption that the French strength and American support were unreliable, and that successful appeasement would reduce the numbers of enemies and expenditure on rearmament.

Under Chamberlain's leadership, Eden formulated the policy of 'keeping Germany guessing' to hold the situation while preparations for negotiation with Germany were under way. It is true that he declared that 'we were interested in events in Central Europe',[174] rather than that Britain disinterested herself in that area, as Henderson suggested. However, the two intimations were no different from each other in the face of Hitler's strike. The British Government did not do anything at all for Austria except that it discouraged the French from taking any joint action. In spite of their conflicting ideas over the Italian problem, Eden and Chamberlain were completely in accord over policy towards Germany. If Eden had not resigned, he would not have favoured British action to help Austria either. Therefore, their divergence was a difference between appeasers, rather than between appeaser and anti-appeaser. Although he resigned before the *Anschluss*, Eden should bear an equal responsibility with Chamberlain for misleading British foreign policy.

Policy-makers made every effort to deceive and 'guide' public opinion, rather than listen to it. Without consulting the public, they had hatched policy long before the public discussed the Austrian crisis intensively. Public opinion was misled by the Government's promise that Britain never disinterested herself from Central and Eastern Europe without exploring the implications. However, the *Anschluss* alarmed the public. Although it perhaps did not demand war on Germany, public opinion generally hardened towards Hitler's expansion, particularly his possible invasion of Czechoslovakia in the future. MPs like Harold Nicolson, who had held a conciliatory attitude a year before, no longer believed that Hitler could be bought off. The Opposition not only criticised the Government's appeasement, it also put forward its alternative proposals, such as a suggestion of a 'return to League principles' and Churchill's 'Grand Alliance'. All this showed that public opinion was more mature than before, due to the experience of a series of events. It demonstrated a great moral and social strength, which could be used to enforce the peace front. However, the policy-makers' determination for appeasement made this impossible.

After the *Anschluss*, the appeasers had no card left to play when they found that Hitler did not even play the same game. While condemning the means used by the Germans to annex Austria, Chamberlain acquiesced in the *Anschluss*. This was tantamount to implying that Hitler could do whatever he wanted towards the Czechs in the future. Indeed, the success of the *Anschluss* encouraged the Sudeten Germans to press for Hitler's forthcoming annexation of Czechoslovakia.[175] That country had now been surrounded by Germany on three sides, which made it militarily impossible, in the appeasers' view, to save her. The unhappy consequence of appeasement convinced them that they had to appease Hitler continuously, quickly and thoroughly, and this paved the way for the German invasion of Czechoslovakia.

CHAPTER 5

MUNICH

OPERATION GREEN AND HITLER'S GAMBLE

The impact of the *Anschluss* on the process of British policy-making was twofold: it exposed a clearer picture of Hitler's ambition to the British Government on one hand, and hastened it in pursuing appeasement further on the other. It inevitably resulted in the sacrifice of Czechoslovakia for the sake of Anglo-German understanding.

On the German side, the decision to attack Czechoslovakia was taken at the same time as the *Anschluss*.[1] The plan entitled OPERATION GREEN, was first formulated by Field Marshal Blomberg on 24 June 1937.[2] However, after the *Anschluss*, Germany needed some time to digest the fruits of its victory. Goering assured Mastny, the Czech Minister in Berlin, on 11 and 12 March, that the developments in Austria would 'in no way have a detrimental influence on the relations between the German Reich and Czechoslovakia', and emphasised 'the continued earnest endeavour on the part of Germany to improve those mutual relations'.[3] However, a few weeks later, Hitler and General Keitel had a further conversation to discuss OPERATION GREEN. They agreed to the following:

Idea of strategic attack out of the blue without cause or possibility of justification is rejected.

Action after a period of diplomatic discussions which gradually lead to a crisis and to war.[4]

In the mean time, the Nazi regime instigated Konrad Henlein,[5] the Leader of the Sudeten Nazi Party, to stir up trouble. Owing to rumours of German intervention, the Czech Government ordered mobilisation on 21 May, which made Hitler furious. On 30 May, the Führer took his 'unalterable decision to smash Czechoslovakia by military action'. OPERATION GREEN was to be carried out by 1 October at the latest. In his opinion, it would be best, if possible, to avoid the Western Powers' intervention, which he thought most unlikely. However, if intervention was provoked, he would take the risk of war.[6]

His view of risking war with the Western Powers met with strong disagreement among his subordinates. Unlike Hitler, they thought that France and Russia would take the Czech side, and Britain would not stand by if Germany attacked Czechoslovakia. They had no way of winning the war, even taking into account Italian and Japanese help.[7] In order to save the country from plunging into a hopeless war, the opposing generals created a plot by which they would first force Hitler to abandon his idea, and then remove him from office.[8]

In mid-August, they sent their representative, von Kleist, to London to have a series of meetings with Vansittart, Churchill and other important persons in the political circle. His mission was: 'to obtain material with which to convince the Chancellor of the strong probability of Great Britain intervening should Germany take violent action against Czechoslovakia'.[9]

On 27 September, since war seemed unavoidable, the opposing officers fixed a date for the execution of their plot: 29 September. General Halder, their leader, confessed in 1946 that 'we were firmly convinced that we would be successful' if the plot had been carried out. However, when he was to give the order of execution on 28 September, the news arrived that Chamberlain would come for further talks, to save a peaceful settlement. The General said: 'I therefore took back the order of execution because, owing to this fact, the entire basis for the action had been taken away . . .'[10]

The Munich accord was the inevitably disastrous effect of pursuing appeasement for a long time, and not only was it the climax of appeasement, it also exceeded the scope of this policy, becoming complete surrender. It is so notorious that it has met with condemnation ever since. Carr comments that Munich was a shame for Britain, 'whose reputation had . . . been lowered by a cowardly and unworthy act'. Thorne cites a message from a British diplomat in the Far East of that time as evidence of world opinion on Munich:

The effect of the Munich accord on foreign opinion as seen from here is that perfidious Albion has been true to form and let her friends down again. The Chinese reaction . . . is that we are entirely self-seeking and have merely been keeping them in play with fair words throwing them a bone now and again hoping they would go on fighting long enough to exhaust Japan and remove a potential danger to ourselves. The Japanese reaction . . . is that we are prepared to put up with almost any indignity rather than fight. The result is that, all in all, our prestige is at a low ebb in the East . . . [11]

Even the appeasers and their supporters dared not justify it fully. Although he admired Munich as 'a triumph', A.J.P. Taylor felt: 'this was a triumph with bitter fruits . . . Appeasement had lost its moral strength.' Gilbert says with regret: 'Munich was not appeasement's finest hour, but its most perverted. It was a distortion of all that appeasement stood for.' Even Chamberlain had to confess, in his Birmingham speech of 17 March 1939: 'I have never denied that the terms which I was able to secure at Munich were not those that I myself would have desired.'[12] However, appeasers are rarely willing to bow to criticism and often try to find excuses for evading responsibility. There are a few of their arguments that should be noted: the most frequently heard clichés are, as Henderson wrote in his memoirs, that 'it was solely thanks to Mr. Chamberlain's courage and pertinacity that a futile and senseless war was averted'.[13] Another typical argument is that Chamberlain's objective at Munich was to 'gain time' for rearmament.[14] The third formulation argues that Britain was not able to save Czechoslovakia due to her own military weakness. Halifax wrote in his memoirs:

No one who had the misfortune to preside over the Foreign Office at that time could ever . . . forget that he had little or nothing in his hands with which to support his diplomatic efforts . . . thus the Foreign Secretary was like a player invited to stake, when he knew that if the fortune of the game turned against him he had nothing with which to redeem his pledge.[15]

The fourth argument is that Munich was supported by the people. Feiling quotes a number of letters to Chamberlain at that time in order to show how much individuals thanked him for bringing them peace, and that 'they would not see their children killed, crippled, blinded, made imbecile'. Chamberlain was forgivable, since his primary motive at Munich was 'simply the rightness of peace and the wrongness of war'.[16] It is worthwhile bearing the above arguments in mind when we investigate British policy-making in the Munich crisis.

POLICY-FORMULATION BEFORE MUNICH
Czechoslovakia Doomed in March

When the Cabinet summoned an emergency meeting to discuss the *Anschluss* on 12 March, the Prime Minister instructed that, in consultation with the French, Halifax should consider what measures could be taken to avert the similar threat that Germany might create in Czechoslovakia.[17]

Policy towards Czechoslovakia began to be formulated in the light of this instruction. Newton in Prague analysed the situation in his dispatch of 15 March:

> [The Czechoslovak Government] still believe they can continue with their present policy so long as they can count on France as an ally, and so long as France in her turn counts on . . . British support if she involves herself in hostilities with Germany over Czechoslovakia.

He warned:

> Should war come, nothing that we or France could do would save Czechoslovakia . . . Should France, nevertheless, think it worth while to try to perpetuate the *status quo* in her own interests, I submit that she should do so with her own strength, and His Majesty's Government are entitled to decline the risk of involving Great Britain in a fresh war . . .

The Ambassador then suggested:

> We should rather make it as easy for her [Czechoslovakia] as possible to adjust her position to the circumstance of post-war Europe while she can still do so in more favourable conditions than will obtain later.

He implied that it was quite impossible to adopt a policy of maintaining Czechoslovak independence without any impairment. This opinion was shared 'unreservedly and in all respects' by Henderson.[18] The document was submitted to the FPC for its information, attracting much attention there.[19] However, not everyone was happy with the Ambassador's telegram. Vansittart was furious, and said that he 'cannot accept' Newton's suggestion.[20]

Within the FO, Sargent, Assistant Under-Secretary, in favour of backing the Franco-Czech alliance,[21] offered his proposals, which were quite similar to Churchill's 'Grand Alliance'.[22] Considering the Anschluss benefited Germany very much and worsened the European situation, he suggested that there were two points the Government should bear in mind: first, to 'organise and strengthen the diplomatic resources of this country, not only in order to help prevent by these means a catastrophe from occurring, but also to have these resources in readiness for immediate use if a catastrophe does occur'. To do so, he said: 'We must expect that the French Government will insist, with increasing persistence and vigour, that His Majesty's Government should now declare themselves more definitely than hitherto as to the policy they intend to adopt in the face of the altered balance of power in Europe and as to the measures they propose to take to give effect to it.' In addition, he urged the British Government to open staff talks with France and Belgium immediately. Britain should also strengthen ties with Greece, Turkey, Poland, Russia and so on. Second, he asked the Government to 'consider whether, for the sake of ultimate peace, His Majesty's Government are prepared now to defend one or other position in Europe if and when it is attacked by Germany'. He warned: 'if we and [the] French do nothing, not only is Czechoslovakia likely to be dismembered for the benefit of Germany, but the whole of Central Europe will be lost to us and to France. In any future war not only will they not be allies but they won't even be neutrals.'[23]

Another typical point of view was voiced by Gladwyn Jebb, Private Secretary to the Permanent Under-Secretary. Although he thought Sargent's proposal was 'logical', he pointed out:

> there is an obvious risk that it may lead to a war for which we are not, as yet, prepared, and in which we might consequently be defeated . . . As evidence of our ability to do so, we shall attempt to organise a 'Grand Alliance', and presumably put the economy of this country on to a war footing at once. The trouble is that, once having committed ourselves to this attitude, the Dictators may 'get their blow in first'.

He laid down his alternative course, to restore the Stresa Front by taking 'immediate steps to come to a real understanding with Mussolini', although he knew very well that 'Mussolini has now gone too far in his dealings with Hitler to join in an anti-German combination'. The essential point in his alternative course was 'a tacit understanding that we would *not* support Czechoslovakia'.[24]

The third strand of opinion was represented by Strang, Head of the Central Department, who was authorised to prepare a memo for the FO according to the Cabinet decision of 12 March. He reminded the Government of Hitler's words about Czechoslovakia, that if 'internal explosions took place, Germany would not remain neutral, but would act like lightning'. Neither the German Government nor Henlein had stated with any precision what was meant by 'autonomy'; therefore, it should be assumed that not only was the Sudetenland to be autonomous and self-governing, it was also to be involved into the incorporation of the German districts in the Reich. He said:

> It has been the policy of His Majesty's Government to advise the Czechoslovak Government to make all possible concessions to the Sudetic Germans . . . as a means of depriving the German Government of any reasonable pretext for complaint or intervention.

Then, from the legal point of view, he pointed out that a treaty existed between France and Czechoslovakia. Britain, however, had no obligations to Czechoslovakia except those of the League. Although Britain had obligations to France as a signatory to the Locarno Treaty in addition to those of the League:

> If Germany were to attack Czechoslovakia, and France came to the assistance of the latter . . . Germany, for her part, would not, by becoming engaged in hostilities with France in the circumstances postulated, be committing an act of unprovoked aggression against France, and, consequently, Great Britain would be under no obligation under the Locarno Treaty to go to the assistance of France . . .

In his opinion, a new commitment to Czechoslovakia by Britain, whether undertaken directly or indirectly, 'might considerably reduce the chances of war, in that it might prove to be an effective deterrent'.

On the other hand, 'it might increase our chance of being involved in war earlier rather than later, since the possession of an undertaking from us might encourage France to take action in defence of Czechoslovakia'. If Britain were prepared to undertake a new commitment, he suggested his preferable alternative:

(I) Action at Prague to the end that the Czechoslovak Government should satisfy both Great Britain and France that she has done all that she reasonably can to remove the grievances of the Sudetendeutschen . . .

(II) An undertaking by Great Britain to France, in declaratory form, that if in the event of a German attack on Czechoslovakia, France came the assistance of Czechoslovakia after consulting with and securing the approval of His Majesty's Government, His Majesty's Government would view France's intervention with benevolent sympathy, and if in the ensuing war French territory were threatened or attacked by Germany, either by land, sea or air, then His Majesty's Government would give immediate support to France in defence of her territory.[25]

Having read all these papers, Cadogan commented:

Sargent paints a gloomy picture . . . Germany might be able to establish an *economic* domination of that part of the world. I do not see how we can stop her . . . why should we . . . try to prevent her?[26]

After nights of thinking, he 'toned down Sargent's picture and came out against a guarantee to Czechoslovakia'.[27]

As regards Jebb's proposals, the Permanent Under-Secretary said that it was 'the best hope that I can see', but he scarcely thought they could achieve it by the methods Jebb had suggested, on the grounds that 'It is too crude, both for our own people here, and for Italy.'

So he finally came to the conclusion that Strang's paper was 'the best course' compared to the other proposals. However, he could not conceal his hesitation:

Much will depend on the report of the Chiefs of Staff. Such a course obviously involves an enormous risk: it is calling a halt to Hitler at a moment when he is an exalted mood. It might precipitate the conflict that we all fear. Shall we risk a war now, when our prospects are not too bad, or shall we put it off till our prospects, maybe, will be worse, but with the hope that in the meanwhile 'something will turn up'?

But one thing was certain, as he wrote: 'unless the Chiefs of Staff can give us a much more reassuring report than I expect, we should undertake no fresh commitment in regard to Czechoslovakia'.

Synthesising different views in the FO, Cadogan made a collection of all these documents, together with his own comments.[28]

Halifax also studied these papers.[29] Based on Strang's paper, he submitted his revised memo to the FPC, in which the most important supplement was that he added another alternative, namely 'no new commitment to France'. Of this choice, he said:

> [It] is advanced not on its own positive merits, but rather on the strength of the objections to other alternative courses. It is briefly, that we should decline to undertake any fresh commitment in regard to Czechoslovakia; that we should, on the contrary, try to persuade France and Czechoslovakia that the best course would be for the latter to make the best terms she can with Germany . . . since in that event Germany would have less reason to risk the hazards of war in order to obtain what she could have some hope of obtaining by peaceful negotiation.

Despite the wide acknowledgement that Germany's superiority in arms might be greater a year or two hence than at this time, this policy alternative did not consider it 'a good argument for risking disaster now'.[30]

During these few days, Chamberlain, Halifax and Cadogan discussed on a number of occasions a guarantee to Czechoslovakia and some related points.[31] They considered: that the Chiefs of Staff should estimate the military aspect of giving a guarantee to France if she was involved in war with Germany over Czechoslovakia; Churchill's proposal of the Grand Alliance; that the FO should advise the Cabinet as to whether, on the political aspect, Czechoslovakia should allow an Anglo-French or a purely British Commission of Inquiry to visit that country and report on the Sudeten position. The Prime Minister's observations were 'apparently moving on these lines'.[32] For a while, both he and Halifax were 'rather on the line of Winston's "Grand Alliance"' as he wrote:

it is perfectly evident, surely, now that force is the only argument Germany understands, and that collective security cannot offer any prospect of preventing such events, until it can show a visible force of overwhelming strength, backed by determination to use it. And if that is so, is it not obvious that such force and determination are most effectively mobilised by alliances . . . I don't want to get back to alliances but if Germany continues to behave as she has done lately, she may drive us to it.

However, this was not what he really wanted, because he continued:

If we can avoid another violent coup in Czechoslovakia, which ought to be feasible, it may be possible for Europe to settle down again, and some day for us to start peace talks again with the Germans.[33]

With some influence from Cadogan, Chamberlain finally abandoned the idea of a Grand Alliance, as well as backing up France in connection with her obligations to Czechoslovakia on the grounds that:

nothing that France or we could do could possibly save Czechoslovakia from being overrun by the Germans . . . The Austrian frontier is practically open; the great Skoda munition works are within easy bombing distance of the German aerodromes, the railways all pass through German territory, Russia is 100 miles away. Therefore we could not help Czechoslovakia – she would simply be a pretext for going to war with Germany.

Halifax independently came to the same conclusion. He rejected the idea of a Grand Alliance, saying that 'there is one decisive objection against it for our present purposes'. It 'would afford both a provocation and an opportunity to Germany to dispose of Czechoslovakia before the grand alliance had been organised'.[34]

At the FPC meeting of 15 March, Chamberlain reaffirmed the policy of seeking terms with the dictators, saying that 'he did not think anything that had happened should cause the government to alter their present policy; on the contrary, recent events had confirmed him in his opinion that the policy was the right one and he only regretted that it had not been adopted earlier'.[35]

Three days later, the FPC held another meeting, which finally decided the Czechs' fate. Halifax submitted his memo as a basis for discussion and for the statement that the Prime Minister would make in the House in a few days.

The question raised was whether Hitler wanted only the Sudetenland or the whole of Czechoslovakia. Chamberlain obviously agreed with Newton's assumption that:

> the seizure of the whole Czechoslovakia would not be in accordance with Herr Hitler's policy, which was to include all Germans in the Reich but not to include other nationalities. It seemed most likely . . . that Germany would absorb the Sudeten German territory and reduce the rest of Czechoslovakia to a condition of dependent neutrality.

He went on to suggest: 'we should ask the German Government to give us an assurance that pending the investigation and report by the Commission of Enquiry, the German Government would not resort to force against Czechoslovakia'.

Then the Cabinet started to discuss Halifax's memo paragraph by paragraph, and was more and more inclined towards the alternative course of 'no new commitment'. Only Stanley, President of the Board of Trade, wanted to propose a simple declaration that Britain would come to France's aid if she was involved in war with Germany due to Czechoslovakia, but his proposal met with strong disagreement from others. Inskip, Minister of Co-ordination Defence, said straight away that 'he could see no reason why we should take any steps to maintain such . . . a highly artificial state'. Simon also thought, if war against Germany 'was successful, when it was over what should the victors do? . . . Czechoslovakia was a modern and very artificial creation with no real roots in the past.' Other ministers, such as Ormsby-Gore (Secretary for the Colonies) and Malcolm MacDonald (Dominion Secretary), spoke openly against any new commitment.

When he made his comment on the memo, Chamberlain said that he was disturbed by the course of new commitment too, because not only might it strengthen the French argument that 'whatever might be the position under the Locarno Treaty, we in fact could not afford to see France destroyed, and we must therefore always come to her aid', it also 'might cause Germany to fear that France would be more ready and willing to implement her treaty undertakings to Czechoslovakia'.

Therefore, rather than backing France, he suggested that the British Government should require the French to give it 'whole-hearted support in any attempt to find a peaceful solution to avoid any risk of an outbreak of war'. He wondered 'whether it would not be possible to make some arrangement which would prove more acceptable to Germany . . . this would have the advantage that it would be more likely to secure permanency'. He tended to believe Hitler's words that Germany only wanted some measure of local autonomy for the Sudeten territory. If this could be done, Germany would be prepared to guarantee the independence of Czechoslovakia. Therefore, he thought that 'at all events the possibility of some arrangement of this kind might be worth exploring'.

Following him, the Foreign Secretary offered the following analysis. First, the theory of a fresh commitment 'rested on the assumption that when Germany secured hegemony over Central Europe she would then pick a quarrel with France and ourselves'. But he 'did not agree with this argument'. Second, the more the Western Powers were plotted to encircle Germany, the more difficult it would be to make any real settlement with Germany. If the Government had decided on a policy of no further commitments, he suggested:

> We still . . . retained full liberty of action, and we could in any particular case say whether or not we would or would not come to France's assistance. This had the great advantage that we were able to keep both France and Germany guessing.

Towards the end of the meeting, although it still requested Chiefs of Staff to submit their report for further consideration, the FPC had come to the conclusion, as Halifax said, that:

> we must decline to undertake any fresh commitment in regard to Czechoslovakia and that we must try and persuade Dr. Benes and also the French Government that the best course would be for Czechoslovakia to make the best terms she could with Germany.[36]

At a full Cabinet meeting, on 22 March, the report of the Chiefs of Staff was ready to be circulated to the ministers. Strictly guided by the 'no new commitment' policy of the Prime Minister, the military advisers based their report on two hypothetical alternatives: that Britain would co-operate with France, Czechoslovakia, Yugoslavia,

Romania, Hungary, Turkey and Greece, or any of them, to resist German invasion of Czechoslovakia; and that Britain would make a guarantee to France were the latter compelled to aid Czechoslovakia by her obligations. The Chiefs of Staff could not foresee that 'our defence forces will be strong enough to safeguard our territory, trade and vital interests against Germany, Italy and Japan simultaneously' at the time when it happened, but they were certain that Britain was not ready for war in 1938. Many of her possible allies, in their opinion, were of doubtful military value in such a war. Therefore, they concluded:

> that no pressure that we and our possible allies can bring to bear, either by sea, on land or in the air, could prevent Germany from invading and overrunning Bohemia and from inflicting a decisive defeat on the Czecho-Slovakian Army. We should then be faced with the necessity of undertaking a war against Germany for the purpose of restoring Czecho-Slovakia's lost integrity and this object would only be achieved by the defeat of Germany and as the outcome of a prolonged struggle.[37]

Halifax thought the report 'an extremely melancholy document', but 'no Government could afford to overlook it'. He told the Cabinet the proposed line, which was said to be based on this report, but in fact had been decided by the FPC a few days before. He said that he was not in a position:

> to recommend a policy involving a risk of war. Consequently, he had to consider the alternatives. His suggestion was that we should endeavour to induce the Government of Czecho-Slovakia to apply themselves to producing a direct settlement with the Sudeten-Deutsch. We should also persuade the French to use their influence to obtain such a settlement . . . it might be possible for the British and French Governments to approach the German Government with a view to acceptance of the settlement in Czecho-Slovakia.

However upset the French Government might be with the above course, the Foreign Secretary said that he did not see what alternative was open to them other than to acquiesce. Moreover, he added: 'we could not accept new commitments withdrawing the decision on peace and war from our Government and leaving it in the hands of the French Government'.

The Prime Minister explained that 'they had approached the question with a bias in favour of some kind of guarantee to Czecho-Slovakia', but the FPC had changed its view because the Foreign Secretary's proposal 'was likely to be generally approved by Parliament'.

The Cabinet minutes showed that the ministers thought that 'even if we had the strength, we could not protect a country in the geographical position of Czecho-Slovakia'.[38]

At the end of the meeting, the Cabinet generally agreed to the policy proposed by the Foreign Secretary and supported by the Prime Minister. They instructed Halifax, with the help of Chamberlain, Simon, Hoare and Stanley, to draft a statement on the above lines for the Prime Minister, who would speak in the House on 24 March. In addition, Halifax would inform the French Government of the policy that the British Government had decided.[39]

On 24 March, full debates in the House on the Czechoslovak problem took place. Chamberlain again tried to confuse the public. He first reminded the House that Britain was bound by the Covenant and the Locarno Treaty towards France, and the Covenant towards Czechoslovakia, which 'might lead to the use of our arms for purposes other than our own defence'. The Government would 'stand by these declarations'. Then he said that he could not go further and give an assurance to France in the event of her being involved in war with Germany over Czechoslovakia, nor could he offer a guarantee of the independence and integrity of Czechoslovakia, because this automatic pledge might take the right of decision on peace or war away from the British Government. His policy was therefore to ask the Czech Government 'to meet the reasonable wishes of the German minority'.[40]

This speech was very unsatisfactory to the Opposition critics. Attlee, Archibald Sinclair (the Liberal Leader) and Churchill voiced sharp criticism. Attlee pointed out that Chamberlain 'yields to force all the time'. The Prime Minister was proceeding on 'a policy of negotiation with persons who have shown their belief in force and who exercise force even while he is negotiating with them'. The proposal the Labour Leader put forward was that the Government should organise collective security in the League, and 'be prepared to deal with the utmost generosity with other countries', including Russia, to prevent war. Churchill, while urging the Government to take up his proposal of a 'Grand Alliance', highlighted the ambivalence in Chamberlain's statement about guarantees to France and Czechoslovakia, saying:

with the rape of Austria before our eyes, Great Britain should have said, and should still say, 'If the German march in upon this State of Czechoslovakia without even waiting for an impartial examination, perhaps by a commission of the League of Nations, or some other body into the position of the Sudeten Deutsch and the remedies offered for their grievances : . . then we should feel, on this occasion, and in this emergency, bound to act with France in resisting it.'[41]

However, all these arguments could not move the policy-makers an inch. In defence of the Government's policy, Simon indicated that the Prime Minister's reaffirmation of the existing commitments was clear enough and good enough to deal with the present problem. He rejected the idea of a Grand Alliance, saying that it was 'contrary to' the conception of the League, and would lead to 'disaster'.[42] Halifax later explained that one should not 'give too broad an interpretation' to Chamberlain's statement regarding using British arms to defend the victims of aggression, because it was 'in the nature of a probability', but not 'in the nature of a certainty'.[43]

Anglo-French Communications in April

Shortly after the Anschluss, the French Ambassador told Halifax that France would take immediate action in the event of any aggression being perpetrated on Czechoslovakia.[44] In addition, on 17 March information from the Soviets showed that Russia also declared that she would intervene in defence of Czechoslovakia if France did.[45] Chamberlain disliked the Soviet declaration, because he thought that Russia was 'stealthily and cunningly' pulling 'all the strings behind the scenes to get us involved in war with Germany'. So he immediately turned down the Soviet proposal, telling the House that Russian intentions would spoil the establishment of European peace.[46]

As for the French enquiry, Strang drafted an answer based on the line of 'no new commitment'. Sargent then made some amendments, 'to remove all possible ambiguity'. After being submitted to Cadogan and Halifax, these papers were sent to Paris on 22 and 23 March. While vetoing the French suggestion that both Governments should issue a joint warning to Germany, they informed them of the 'no new commitment' decision made by the British Government, which required that Britain and France impose joint pressure on Czechoslovakia to obtain a peaceful settlement with Germany. This disappointed the French very much.[47] They looked forward to exchanging views with their British partners.[48]

On 27 April, the ministers discussed their policy for the impending meeting with the French. Chamberlain told his colleagues that although the War Office thought the staff talks would 'come as a severe shock' when it became clear how very limited was the amount of military assistance – two divisions – Britain could send to France at the outset of war, he thought it would be difficult to refuse if the French wanted to hold such discussions. Otherwise, it would seem 'rather churlish'. In the course of discussion, Simon said, there was 'the risk of coming so near to the point of a commitment to send two divisions that it would be assumed by the French as a definite undertaking'. Halifax insisted that they should let the French know frankly that they could not commit themselves by sending troops to France, 'but it was also important not to say that in no circumstance would Britain ever send any troops.' The Prime Minister then concluded that if in no circumstance would they allow any staff talks, 'there might be an uncomfortable jar' in Anglo-French relations. The Cabinet agreed that the Prime Minister and the Foreign Secretary should have discretion to decide whether the Army Staff talks took place separate from the current Air Staff discussions.[49]

At the invitation of the British Government, the Daladier–Bonnet team[50] came to London on 28 April, and spent two days in talks with their British partners. Both sides soon found they were at odds.

Halifax, on behalf of the British Government, told the French at the beginning that it was not necessary to hold Naval Staff talks. As to the Air Staff talks, however, he said that they could be held within a certain scope. Then he explained that the greatest help the French could hope for from Britain at the beginning of a war, would be two divisions.

On the French side, Daladier tried to persuade the British leaders to open up Naval Staff talks, but in vain. However, he felt quite satisfied with British approval of the Air Staff talks and the decision to send two divisions to France. But his satisfaction was certainly set back by Chamberlain's words:

His Majesty's Government had no desire to commit themselves to sending two British divisions to France on the outbreak of war. The most he could definitely say was that this possibility was not excluded if the Government of the day decided accordingly.

On the second day, the talks concentrated on Czechoslovakia. Halifax, at the very beginning, pointed out that Britain was different from France, since the latter was bound by very precise engagements towards Czechoslovakia, but the former was not. The British Government felt:

> that every step that was possible must be taken to avoid an outbreak which, as things now stood, might carry with it a very considerable risk for both France and Great Britain.

Therefore, he thought that pressure should be put on Benes to make a supreme effort to reach a settlement with Germany.

Although he agreed that the Czechoslovak Government should go further to meet the demands of the Sudeten Germans, Daladier warned that Henlein 'was not, in fact, seeking any concessions, and that his real object was the destruction of the present Czechoslovak State'. He implied criticism that when Hitler took the Rhineland and Austria, Britain talked a great deal, 'but nothing had been done'. Now 'we were faced with the question of Czechoslovakia'. He believed that 'war could only be avoided if Great Britain and France made their determination quite clear to maintain the peace of Europe by respecting the liberties and the rights of independent people'. He disagreed with the British view of military weakness, estimating that the Czechoslovak Army numbered 180,000 men on a peace footing, and on mobilisation it could be enlarged to 500,000, well trained, well equipped, and animated by public spirit. If Britain and France took action, he believed Romania, Yugoslavia, and perhaps even Poland would change their views and take the Czechoslovak side. Furthermore, Russia still possessed the strongest Air Force (5,000 aeroplanes) in Europe, and her potential war resources were extremely great and could easily be brought into play. Therefore, he suggested that when they asked Czechoslovakia to make reasonable concessions, if the two powers should declare at the same time that 'they could not permit the destruction of the Czechoslovak State, then the peace of Europe might be saved'. Bonnet supplemented:

> if France remained alone, the situation must be uncertain; but if solidarity existed between France and Great Britain they could ensure the success of their views . . . if . . . there were no solidarity between the French and British Governments in support of

Czechoslovakia, then he was convinced that Germany would be in a position to remove Czechoslovakia from the map . . .

After hearing the French arguments, Chamberlain said that the French proposal was a 'bluff', because Czechoslovakia was surrounded by German territory on three sides. He warned that the French 'sentimental considerations' were dangerous. He doubted 'whether the picture was really so black as M. Daladier had painted it', and 'whether Herr Hitler really desired to destroy the Czechoslovak State or rather a Czechoslovak State'. In conclusion, he told his French friends:

He had himself seen war and had seen how impossible it was for anyone engaging in any war like the last war to come out of it stronger or happier. Therefore only dire necessity would ever persuade him to wage a preventive war. He was against preventive war.

However, in spite of the British arguments, the French still insisted that pressing Czechoslovakia to make further concessions would cause the result that 'after such concessions had been offered the road would be open to Germany, who would be given a free hand to act as she wished, then we should only have precipitated a catastrophe instead of preventing it'.

At the adjournment of the meeting at noon, no agreement had been reached between the two sides.[51]

During lunchtime, Cadogan took the chance to have a talk with Chamberlain and Halifax. He regarded the French proposal as 'awful rubbish', and offered his suggestion, 'of asking Germans what it is they *want*', to persuade the French.[52] In the afternoon meeting, Halifax took this line in the discussions, and it was effective. Finally, both sides reached agreement as follows:

both Governments were agreed that there should be a *démarche* by His Majesty's Government alone in Berlin. They would explain to the German Government that they were doing their best to find a peaceful solution of the Sudeten difficulty and had asked Dr. Benes to make his contributions, but it took two to reach an agreement, and they therefore wished to know what was the position of the German Government. They wished to impress on the German Government that, in the meantime, and in view of their intervention at Prague, there was no need, nor indeed any reason, for action on the part of the German Government. Simultaneously, a *démarche* would be made at Prague by both the French and the British Governments to secure the maximum concessions from Dr. Benes.[53]

The Runciman Mission

Four days after the Anglo-French talks, Halifax instructed Henderson to inform the German Government of the *démarche* made by Britain and France. He appealed to the Germans to 'use their influence with the Sudeten Germans in the direction of moderation', while the British Government put pressure on Prague.[54] At the same time, he authorised Newton both to inform the Czechs of the Anglo-French *démarche*, and to press them to 'make a supreme effort' to meet Henlein's demands.[55] On the other hand, in an instruction to the British Ambassador in Paris on 22 May, Halifax warned the French Government that it 'should not be under any illusion as to attitude' of Britain. If France was 'the victim of unprovoked aggression by Germany,' Britain would come to her assistance. 'If, however, the French Government were to assume that His Majesty's Government would at once take joint action with them to preserve Czechoslovakia against German aggression, it is only fair to warn them that our statements do not warrant any such assumption.' Because of this fatal discouragement, the French abandoned the idea to fulfil their obligations to Czechoslovakia.[56]

Yet the negotiations between the Czech Government and Henlein over the forthcoming months were not promising. In mid-July, Halifax obtained the information that 'Henlein took an extremely pessimistic view of the situation', and he no longer trusted the Czechoslovak Government. Halifax foresaw that if the deadlock was not broken, Henlein would ask for a plebiscite.[57]

During this period, the FO had been considering sending a conciliator to bridge the gap between the two parties. Halifax thought on 8 May that it was worth keeping in mind, but that the move was 'premature'.[58] Nevertheless, he worried that negotiations might break down. He instructed Phipps to consult the French Government over the idea that the two governments should send 'an international commission' to investigate the cause of deadlock and bring 'the two parties together again'.[59] On 21 June, Newton suggested appointing 'an outstanding figure' as a mediator.[60] This suggestion met with great attention in the FO. Mallet, First Secretary, agreed with Newton, and pointed out that 'it would be better not to sound the Czechoslovak Government at present', on the grounds that it would make the Czechs less ready to reach agreement, because they would feel able to get better terms through British mediation than they would in direct negotiation with the Nazis, and that it would also give the Sudetens the impression that Britain expected negotiations to fail, therefore discouraging them from seeking to make them succeed. He went on to say: 'in any "compromise" that we are to find we shall have to induce the Czechs to make further concessions' on all or some of the Sudetens' demands. If Britain were to intervene with an offer of mediation in order to forestall a plebiscite:

> we must (1) be ready not only to mediate on internal affairs, but also to put forward a scheme for changing the international status of Czechoslovakia; and (2) to have our mediator ready.

His proposal was generally agreed with by Vansittart and Sargent. Halifax and Cadogan initialled the document.[61] On 16 June, the FPC discussed the names of candidates, but no decision was taken[62] until one month later, when Halifax 'sounded Lord Runciman as to his willingness'.[63]

Runciman would not be 'an arbitrator', as Chamberlain declared on 26 July, 'but investigator and mediator'.[64] From early August to early September, Runciman worked very hard to keep the two parties together, particularly to press Benes to go further and further to meet the SDP's demands. Under this pressure, the Czech Government offered its 'Third Plan'[65] in late August, to satisfy the SDP's points for equality and autonomy, but the SDP rejected it.[66] At the end of that month, Benes put forward the 'Fourth Plan' based on the 'Third', on which Runciman commented that 'This plan embodied almost all of the requirements' of the SDP's demands.[67] However, when both parties discussed the plan on 7 September, the SDP representatives used the incident at Moravska Ostrava to break off the negotiations for good.[68]

During this period, the press, under the influence of the Government, remained quite optimistic. It generally welcomed the announcement of the Runciman mission on one hand, while being concerned about the likelihood of failure in mediation on the other. The *Daily Telegraph* appealed for compromise from both sides. The *Manchester Guardian* proposed that Runciman should stand by the Czechs while he looked for justice. *The Times*, however, revealed a tendency to suggest that the Czech problem stood in the way of Anglo-German understanding. The FO kept the muzzle on the media to avoid alarming the public. On 5 September, it informed the BBC that no commentary should be given on the international crisis. Although it denied this was 'an instruction', it insisted that it was a 'very strong' recommendation. Under this pressure, Harold Nicolson's script, which discussed the Czechoslovak crisis, had to be re-written twice, and finally its subject became the rise in milk prices to 7*d* a quart.[69] On the very day the negotiations broke off, a leading article in *The Times* contained the following passage:

> It might be worth while for the Czechoslovak Government to consider whether they should exclude altogether the project, which has found favor in some quarters, of making Czechoslovakia a more homogeneous State by the secession of the fringe of alien populations who are contiguous to the nation with which they are united by race.

The phrase 'project, which has found favor in some quarters' could be suspected of referring to either the Cabinet or the FO. Although the Foreign Secretary immediately denied that *The Times* represented Government policy, Kordt, the German Chargé d'Affairs in London, estimated that this article possibly derived 'from a suggestion which reached *The Times* editorial staff from the Prime Minister's entourage'. Solid support for this view came from the fact that Halifax told Corbin, the French Ambassador, two days later that 'from a purely tactical point of view, he was of the same opinion' as the leading article.[70]

The Opposition was agitated by the Government's ambiguous attitude towards the Czechoslovak problem. On 8 September, National Labour Executives held a joint meeting, issuing 'The Blackpool Declaration', which was approved by the Trade Union Congress the same day. It read:

> If mediation is not now successful, a relentless and inevitable chain of events will drag the whole world into war. France and the Soviet Union are bound by Treaty to support Czechoslovakia if it is attacked. They have announced that they will at once honour their engagements . . . The British Government must leave no doubt in the mind of the German Government that they will unite

with the French and Soviet Governments to resist an attack on Czechoslovakia.

Their slogan was 'Stand by the Czechs!'

As Parliament was not in session, Attlee requested that the House be summoned for debate, but this twice met with Chamberlain's refusal. Hugh Dalton of the Labour Executive commented: 'Had such a discussion taken place a fortnight earlier, the Munich surrender could not have been made.'[71]

Churchill and Eden, however, delivered their advice. The former wrote to Halifax, suggesting that jointly Britain, France and Russia should warn Germany that the use of force would raise a 'capital issue' for the three powers. He believed that America 'would give moral support to such a declaration'. In addition, partial fleet mobilisation was necessary.[72] Eden went to the FO on 9 September to bring Halifax a similar suggestion in more moderate language. The Foreign Secretary comforted his predecessor, saying: 'Great minds are thinking alike, for my mind is moving on just such a project and indeed I was going to speak to Neville about a draft today.'[73] The Prime Minister, consulting with the Opposition leaders and with Churchill and Eden, declared on 11 September: 'Germany cannot with impunity carry out a rapid and successful military campaign against Czechoslovakia without fear of intervention by France and by Great Britain.'[74] However, this warning was soon proved to be a sham, due to the fact that before this declaration, Chamberlain had decided to go to see Hitler in person to buy peace at any price.

POLICY-MAKING DURING THE MUNICH PERIOD
Plan Z

As the Runciman mission was likely to fail, the Government was still in the dark about Hitler's real intentions. There were two different views mentioned at Cabinet meetings. The first view, with a great deal of evidence to support it, was that Hitler was determined to intervene by force. The second one was that while Hitler was determined to get the Sudeten German question settled this year, he had not yet made up his mind to use force for this purpose. Halifax felt: 'the conflict of evidence was such that it was impossible to say which view was correct'.[75] However, he was soon inclined to believe the first view. In that case, he said, 'nothing which we could do would stop him'.

The Foreign Secretary met Churchill on 11 September. The latter expressed his proposition as follows:

> we should tell Germany that if she set foot in Czechoslovakia, we should at once be at war with her . . . he thought that by taking it we should incur no added risk.

But Halifax commented that this opinion was 'at the best a very doubtful view'.[76] He suggested:

> He was not prepared to say that we would go to war on the issue of Czechoslovakia alone, since it was impossible to say in what form that issue might arise. To say without qualification that we were prepared to go to war to defend Czechoslovakia would, in fact, put the decision of peace or war in the hands of others than ourselves.[77]

Chamberlain fully supported his suggestion, although he realised that 'if we were right up against war, public opinion might well change suddenly'. In addition, he thought that although an ultimatum 'might avert war, it was not certain that it would do so'. If Hitler regarded it as a 'bluff', Britain had to choose between being shown up as bluffing, or going to war. Moreover:

> supposing the threat was made and had the desired results on this occasion; would that be the end of the story? The steps taken on the 21st May had not proved the end of the story, and people were now saying that it had produced in Herr Hitler a feeling of being thwarted.

Therefore, he reached the same conclusion as Halifax: 'we should not utter a threat to Herr Hitler, that if he went into Czechoslovakia we should declare war upon him'.[78]

But the problem was still there. During this period, Chamberlain kept racking his brains 'to try and devise some means of averting a catastrophe'.[79] Towards the end of August, he had a new idea: he would go to see Hitler himself, to save peace. He first discussed the idea with only Wilson and Henderson (who was back for consultation on the policy).[80] The crucial point was that if Hitler had decided to invade Czechoslovakia, 'this new idea might cause him to cancel that intention'. Henderson agreed: 'it might save the situation at the 11th hour'. Chamberlain then consulted Halifax, Simon and Hoare over the following days. It 'rather took Halifax's breath away'. However, all of them agreed to the proposal, which was now called 'Plan Z'.[81]

Chamberlain thought that this plan might be put into effect about 17 September,[82] on the grounds that:

> If adopted too soon it would be asked why this action had been taken before Lord Runciman had finished his task. On the other hand, if we waited too long, Herr Hitler might have taken some irrevocable action.

However, the plan was brought forward, due to two factors on 13 September. The first was information from Paris: Daladier said that at all costs, Germany must be prevented from invading Czechoslovakia, because in that case France would have to face up to her obligations. The second was that the SDP delivered an ultimatum to the Czech Government. Faced with this situation, Chamberlain, with the support of his closest colleagues, decided to put the plan into operation at once.[83] He drafted a message that indicated the Prime Minister was ready to visit Hitler, and asked the Germans to reply as soon as possible. When it had been put into a simple form, Halifax sent it to Henderson late on the night of 13 September.[84]

After all this had been done, Chamberlain informed the Cabinet of his surprise on 14 September. He explained why he had kept them unaware of the plan until then, saying that due to the fear of it leaking out, he had thought it better to delay mentioning it 'until the last moment'. He hoped that: 'the Cabinet would feel that he had not gone beyond his proper duty in taking this action on the advice of those of the colleagues . . . but without consulting the full Cabinet'.

He outlined the original scheme, that since Hitler liked to see heads of State, 'it might be agreeable to his vanity that the British Prime Minister should take so unprecedented a step'. This procedure could prevent the Führer from finding an excuse for declining. In addition, Chamberlain felt that he would have the advantage of being able to say more to Hitler face to face than he could put in a letter.

He then went on to describe the plan in detail. He would appeal to Hitler, saying that the latter 'had a great chance of obtaining fame for himself by making peace in Europe and thereafter by establishing good relations with this country'. This could be achieved by finding 'a just and equitable settlement'. If Hitler showed no confidence that Benes would carry out his promises, the Prime Minister would suggest that 'some international body should be set up to supervise the fulfilment of any agreement reached'. If Hitler retorted that no agreement had yet been reached, Chamberlain would propose as a solution that the two parties should agree to put their views before Lord Runciman, and accept Runciman as the final arbitrator. Hitler might say that nothing could now settle the matter except a plebiscite. On this issue, Chamberlain would take up Simon's suggestion as the answer:

> the Sudeten Germans should at the outset be given a wide measure of autonomy in specified areas, with the option of a Plebiscite after a given period.[85] This . . . would relate the Plebiscite to specified areas. As regards mixed areas, the only satisfactory solution seemed to be transfer.

For the rest of Czechoslovakia, Britain should join in guaranteeing its integrity together with France, Russia and Germany.

The Prime Minister thought that the proposed negotiations offered the chance of 'securing better relations between Germany and England'. This chance would be lost if Hitler 'had recourse to force now'. He believed what Goering had told Henderson, namely that after solving the problem of Czechoslovakia, Germany 'would finally become a territorially satisfied country'.[86]

In the course of discussions, no contradictory arguments were brought forward. Ministers discussed the plan along the lines the Prime Minister had drawn. However Morrison, the Minister of Agriculture, said:

> public opinion had greatly changed in the last few years, and the people who had then been loudest in opposing rearmament were now loudest in demanding that this country should take a firm line.

Halifax emphasised guidance for the media, and pointed out:

> that it was of the utmost importance that steps should be taken to ensure that the Press received the news of plan 'Z' correctly, and suggested that it might be necessary that the newspaper proprietors and editors should be seen instead of the Lobby and Diplomatic Correspondents.

Duff Cooper, of the Admiralty, pointed out that he was quite confident that if they went to war, they should win. What was really influencing them was 'hatred of war', rather than 'fear of German arms'.

Simon thought

we must be careful that it did not lead us further along the road to complete surrender. It was important to make it plain that the decision taken was not only conciliatory but was also a firm step.

In the end, the Cabinet showed 'its 'whole-hearted approval' of the plan drawn up by Chamberlain.[87] On the same day, von Ribbentrop informed Henderson that 'the Führer would naturally be pleased to receive Chamberlain' on the next day, but at Berchtesgaden instead of Berlin.[88]

Based on Halifax's suggestion of guiding the press at the Cabinet meeting, Hoare took action immediately. He organised daily meetings to give interviews to the Editor of the *Daily Herald* and the chairman of the *News Chronicle*, and persuaded them to hold their papers 'on the side of peace'. Because of his effective work, the press generally held a positive attitude towards Chamberlain's visit to Germany. *The Times* admired this 'bold move'. The *Daily Herald* commented that it was 'not only the bold but the supremely wise course'. The *News Chronicle* approved it on the grounds that it was the best way for the Prime Minister to tell Hitler in person that Britain would co-operate with France and Russia in order to prevent German demands exceeding reasonable scope.[89] Duff Cooper commented that the press reaction towards Chamberlain's visit was 'mainly favourable, including rather surprisingly that of the *Daily Herald*'.[90]

Before he left, Chamberlain had a very brief meeting with Attlee, telling the latter 'there was a chance of doing something'. The Labour Leader said that nobody was against the Prime Minister's attempt to save peace, but 'we mustn't give way to threats, we had a duty to the Czechs, and principles which all parties in Britain now adhered to must not be compromised'. The Prime Minister 'had very little to say; nothing really'.[91]

Berchtesgaden

Having never been in an aeroplane before, poor old Chamberlain, like a pilgrim, embarked on a bumpy journey to see Hitler, first by plane and then by train. At the beginning of the meeting, he opened the talk along the proposed lines. When they came to the problem of Sudetenland, Chamberlain asked 'whether this was all that Germany was demanding, or whether she was not aiming over and above this at the dismemberment of the Czechoslovak State'. Hitler replied that the demands of the Sudeten Germans alone were what he was interested in, and the Czechoslovak question would be 'the last major problem' to be solved. However, he exclaimed: 'I shall not put up with this any longer. I shall settle this question in one way or another.' To achieve this end, he 'would face any war, and even the risk of a world war'. Hearing this, Chamberlain became 'indignant', and said with serious calm: 'If . . . you are determined to proceed against Czecho-Slovakia in any case . . . why did you let me come to Berchtesgaden? . . . It is best for me return at once. Anything else now seems pointless.' It was obvious that Hitler did not want to break off the conversation. He quietened down immediately, but requested that the British Prime Minister 'must first of all state whether he could accept this basis or not, namely, the secession of the Sudeten German region by virtue of the right of self-determination'. If so, discussions could continue. Chamberlain said that although he 'personally' recognised the principle of the detachment of the Sudeten areas, he 'could give no assurance' without consultation with his Cabinet. He suggested they break off the negotiations at this point, and he would come back to meet the Führer again after consultation. The words 'breaking off' made Hitler very uneasy, 'but when he understood that Chamberlain would meet him again, he agreed with obvious relief'. At the end, both sides agreed that 'in a few days a new conversation will take place'.[92]

After the talks, Chamberlain believed that:

> I had established a certain confidence, which was my aim, and on my side . . . I got the impression that here was a man who could be relied upon when he had given his word.[93]

The Prime Minister landed at Heston in the late afternoon of 16 September. He immediately summoned the ministers to a meeting, Halifax, Simon, Hoare, Cadogan, Wilson, Vansittart and Runciman being present. He told them that Hitler wanted self-determination, and he thought it would be wrong to go to war to prevent it. However, the meeting broke up without a definite decision being taken.[94] Next day, the Cabinet met in full. Chamberlain first gave an account of his conversation with the Führer. When he came to the principle of self-determination, he said that he did not think that it was a matter of whether it was accepted or not, rather 'now the principle had been agreed, it remained to examine how it should be carried out'. If they wanted to reach a settlement with Germany, they could only make progress along these lines. He hoped 'his colleagues were prepared to express their general agreement with the proposition that we should accept the principle of self-determination'.

In the course of the discussion, Halifax, Simon and most other ministers completely supported the Prime Minister. Nevertheless, Oliver Stanley felt that it was a little difficult to reach a decision on such a vital issue. Duff Cooper worried that if this principle were accepted, 'we might be led into a complete surrender'. He implied a criticism that the Prime Minister should have put forward to Hitler 'a number of reasonable propositions', such as Simon's plan for autonomy for a period, to be followed by a plebiscite. He believed that Hitler 'was not prepared to leave any independence to Czechoslovakia'. He went on to point out:

> it was a primary interest of this country to prevent any single power dominating Europe. We are now faced with the most formidable power for a century . . . He found it difficult to believe that the self-determination of the Sudeten Germans was Hitler's last aim . . . even if a solution of the present problem was found, it would not be the end of our troubles, and that there was no chance of peace in Europe so long as there was a Nazi regime in Germany.

He drew attention to the fact that Britain 'was singularly united', and that the Dominions supported the democratic countries in 'a fight against dictators' more so than in 1914. However, he finally came over to Chamberlain's side, and agreed that the forthcoming negotiations could be based on the principle of self-determination.

Lord De La Warr, Lord Privy Seal, also had some different views. His main point was that if they accepted Hitler's terms without obtaining 'a *quid pro quo*', that would represent abject surrender. He suggested that 'we should accept the position laid down by the Prime Minister, that we should try to negotiate the best terms obtainable', for example demobilisation of the German Army.

After listening to all these arguments, Chamberlain explained, and justified himself, saying:

in certain circumstances we should have to fight, even if our armaments were weaker than they were. But in modern circumstances war was very different from what it was in 1914. To-day war affected the whole population . . . The alternatives to-day were not between abject surrender and war. Acceptance of the principle of self-determination was not an abject surrender.

Nor did he think that it was a good idea to use the acceptance of self-determination as a bargaining counter to ask Hitler to demobilise his army, on the grounds that 'the only result would be that Herr Hitler would order his troops to march straight into Czechoslovakia'.

After further discussion, the Cabinet generally agreed with the views expressed by the Prime Minister. However, it was decided that the final conclusion be postponed until after discussions with the French Government.[95]

On the same day, Chamberlain repeated the account of his visit to three Labour Council Executives: Citrine, Morrison and Dalton. The Opposition frankly pointed out: 'British prestige had been gravely lowered by Chamberlain going to see Hitler', and insisted on standing by the Blackpool Declaration. Towards the end of meeting, Dalton addressed the Prime Minister on behalf of Labour Party:

I don't believe that this will be the last of Hitler's demands. I believe that he intends to go on and on, until he dominates first all Central and South-eastern Europe, then all Europe, and then all the world. And at every future stage this situation may be repeated. When the next crisis comes, you or your successor will once again fly over to see him. You will return and say that the situation is 'desperately critical' – and it will be true. You will say that the German military machine is very formidable – and that will be still more true then than now. You will say that there is no time to lose, that the French, or whoever it may be, are weak and irresolute, and that therefore we must give in. For some time you will give in at the expense of other people, but sooner or later you will have to give in at the expense of British interests, and the end of the whole process may well be the liquidation both of the British Empire and of our British liberties. And at each stage you will have fewer friends and weaker allies to join you in any stand you may, at some late hour, decide to make.

He said to the Prime Minister: 'These opinions are not held only in the Labour Party. They are shared by a large number of your own supporters in Parliament.' Listening to his words, Chamberlain shuffled a little on his seat, and said: 'I freely admit that we are often haunted by fears like these, but we do not believe that such a course of things is inevitable. If we can avert war now, we are not certain that it will come later.'[96]

On 18 September, the Inner Cabinet members and their important advisers had three meetings at 10 Downing Street with the French statesmen. Although the French at the beginning worried about the loss of Czechoslovakia as a military ally in the East if the principle of self-determination was accepted, Chamberlain and Halifax succeeded in getting them back to the position that pressure should be put on Benes in order to save the peace. As the result of the discussions both sides agreed on a joint message to the Czech Government on 19 September, informing it that:

> both Governments have been compelled to the conclusion that the maintenance of peace and the safety of Czechoslovakia's vital interests cannot effectively be assured unless these areas [Sudetenland] are now transferred to the Reich.[97]

Naturally, this memo was rejected by the Czechs.[98] On receiving the Czech rejection, Newton warned Krofta, the Czech Foreign Minister, that 'refusal or evasion at this last moment meant the destruction of his beautiful country'. Halifax instructed Newton on 21 September: 'You should urge the Czech Government to withdraw this reply and urgently consider an alternative that takes account of realities.'[99]

Under such great pressure, Benes saw Newton and the French Ambassador that evening, told them that he had accepted the Anglo-French proposal, and left Czechoslovakia's fate in the hands of Britain and France.[100] Meanwhile, Henderson and von Ribbentrop arranged Chamberlain's next journey, and it was decided that the Prime Minister would fix the time with the Führer on 22 September at Godesberg.[101]

During the three days before that date, Chamberlain summoned full Cabinet meetings twice to have further discussions on the guarantee and method of transferring the Sudetenland. It was generally agreed that the guarantee to Czechoslovakia was a key step to prevent further aggression. However, as to the type of guarantee, Halifax raised the question:

If . . . it was decided to have a joint guarantee, and Germany, being one of the guarantor countries, committed an act of aggression, would the other guarantor countries be excused from coming to Czechoslovakia's help? If, however, the guarantee was several, and other countries failed to fulfil their obligations, this country might find itself alone in supporting Czechoslovakia.

Chamberlain felt:

it was not right to assume that the guarantee committed us to maintaining the existing boundaries of Czechoslovakia. The guarantee merely related to unprovoked aggression . . . Its main value would lie in its deterrent effect.

The right plan was to have a joint guarantee, and to provide for a meeting of the guarantors to decide in any particular case whether 'unprovoked aggression' had taken place.

He then suggested that the guarantor countries should be Britain, France and Russia, probably including Italy, and they should invite Germany to sign a separate non-aggression pact with Czechoslovakia. The ministers generally agreed with the Prime Minister. As to transferring an area with over 50 per cent German inhabitants, the Cabinet came to the conclusion that 'German troops should not be allowed to cross the frontier until an international force had reached Czechoslovak territory.'

In addition, Chamberlain was quite optimistic over obtaining some concessions from Hitler, such as the demobilisation of the German Army and Herr Henlein's Freikorps, and even 'to get Hitler to repeat his declaration that if he obtained incorporation of the Sudeten Germans in the Reich he would be satisfied'.[102]

Public opinion varied on the Anglo-French proposal of 18 September, with growing dislike of it. *The Times* and *The Sunday Times* held a standpoint close to the Government's; *The Times* maintained in its leading article on 20 September that, based on this proposal, 'the ultimate gain will be more real than the immediate sacrifice' to the Czechs, whereas the *Manchester Guardian* and the *News Chronicle* were critical of the plan, and the Diplomatic Correspondent of the *Manchester Guardian* wrote that the Anglo-French proposal was an 'ultimatum, with a short time-limit'.[103]

On the afternoon of 21 September, after a full meeting of the Labour Executive, it was decided that Attlee and Greenwood should see the

Prime Minister to examine the Anglo-French plan of 18 September in detail, because it seemed to them no details had been settled. The two Labour leaders had 'a disagreeable interview' with Chamberlain. Attlee said to him: 'You have abandoned these people [the Czechs] completely. You have made an absolute surrender. All Eastern Europe will now fall under Hitler's sway. We are full of the most profound disgust. This is one of the biggest disasters in British history.' But Chamberlain 'had become steelier and steelier, smiling less and snarling more'.[104]

The next day, Chamberlain left for Germany. When Churchill went to 10 Downing Street, the Cabinet told him that the Prime Minister would put to Hitler the terms discussed in the Cabinet meeting, including demobilisation. After his return, Churchill told his friends and supporters that if Hitler refused the terms, 'we shall have war'. However, at that very moment, while he was laying his proposal before Hitler at Godesberg, Chamberlain said nothing about demobilisation.[105]

Godesberg

On the afternoon of 22 September, Hitler met Chamberlain in Godesberg. When the Prime Minister told the Führer that he had successfully induced his Cabinet and the French and Czech Governments to agree to the principle of self-determination, and that the Sudetenland would be transferred to the Reich by an orderly operation involving the intervention of an international commission, Hitler replied that these proposals were out of date. He insisted on two new points, which had not been discussed at Berchtesgaden. One was that, due to Germany's friendship with Poland and Hungary, he must support the demands on Czech territory from these two countries. The other was that due to the urgency of the Sudeten problem, he declared that the problem should be settled 'definitely and completely' by 1 October. If he failed to do this, he would, instead of a 'peaceful solution', pursue a 'military solution', namely to establish a frontier 'not on a national but on a strategic basis'. As regards the suggestion of a non-aggression pact between Germany and Czechoslovakia, the Führer replied that he could only conclude such a pact when all problems, including Polish and Hungarian demands, had been settled.

Shocked by Hitler's fresh demands, Chamberlain felt 'both disappointed and puzzled'. He reminded Hitler of what the latter had stated at Berchtesgaden. In order to help Germany, Chamberlain 'had risked his whole political career'. Now these unexpected new demands would put him in a most embarrassing position. He begged the Führer to moderate the terms, but Hitler did not budge an inch. The first meeting broke up 'without any reference to a subsequent meeting'.[106]

In their phone conversation that evening, Chamberlain told Halifax that the meeting with Hitler was 'most unsatisfactory'.[107] However, he was not really prepared to shut the door, and nor was Hitler. In his letter to Hitler that evening, Chamberlain said that he would communicate the Führer's proposal to the Czech Government, who, in his opinion, would refuse to accept these terms. He appealed to the Führer once again that 'there must surely be alternatives to your proposal . . .'[108]

Hitler's reply came the next afternoon, in which the Führer, in spite of using moderate language, insisted on all the demands he had put forward the previous day.[109]

Nevertheless, Chamberlain's patience was 'not yet finally exhausted'.[110] During the adjournment, he wrote to Hitler again in a conciliatory tone, and asked the latter to make his proposals in the form of a memo, which he would pass to the Czech Government.[111] When the letter was handed to von Ribbentrop by Wilson and Henderson, both sides agreed that Chamberlain should come to see Hitler again that evening to discuss the memo.[112]

At the evening meeting, when he read the German memo with an illustrated map attached which planned that the operation of evacuating and handing over the Sudetenland should be completed by 28 September, the Prime Minister was outraged by its language and manner more than by its content: 'That's an ultimatum,' he exclaimed to Hitler, 'you have made no effort to assist my attempts to secure peace.' However, he told Hitler that he could neither accept nor reject the memo. The only thing he could do was pass it on to the Czech Government.[113] After a long, hard discussion, the Führer at last agreed to postpone the operation until 1 October. 'You are the only man,' he said to Chamberlain, 'to whom I have ever made a concession.'[114]

In a private talk after the meeting, Hitler assured Chamberlain that the Sudetenland was his last territorial ambition in Europe. In addition, he wanted very earnestly to be friends with England.[115]

As soon as he returned to London on 24 September, the Prime Minister summoned a ministers' meeting at 3.00 p.m. and then a Cabinet meeting at 5.30 p.m. in the same afternoon. He reported to his colleagues the Führer's new demands, including details of their private talk. Although Hitler's behaviour at Godesberg was obviously untrustworthy in other eyes, Chamberlain 'was satisfied that Hitler was speaking the truth'. He thought that 'he had now established an influence over Herr Hitler, and that the latter trusted him and was willing to work with him'.[116] Faced with disagreement from most of his ministers, including Hoare, the Prime Minister tried to persuade the Cabinet that:

> it was a wonderful opportunity to put an end to the horrible nightmare of the present armament race. That seemed to him to be the big thing in the present issue.

He continued:

> the Cabinet would examine very carefully the differences between the proposals made last Sunday and the present proposals, and would consider whether those differences justified us in going to war.

He justified his proposal of surrender by reminding his colleagues of the terrible prospect of war – particularly modern war, which should be avoided at any price at the moment.

Nonetheless, his persuasion seemed not as effective as usual. In the course of the discussion, foreseeing that Benes would refuse Hitler's proposal, Duff Cooper said that if Germany attacked Czechoslovakia, 'public opinion would bring about a position in which we should have to intervene in the war'. He warned that intervention might come 'too late' unless Britain took action promptly. He believed that if the Government made this clear to the Germans, it 'might yet result in deterring them from war'. In addition, he did not have any confidence in the promises Hitler had made to the Prime Minister.[117] Hore-Belisha, the War Secretary, reminded the Cabinet that the Chiefs of Staff 'urged the importance of early mobilisation'. Hoare also proposed that if Hitler attacked Czechoslovakia, 'France, Russia and ourselves would at once make war upon him.'

It was obvious that Chamberlain was very isolated in the Cabinet at this time, because it appeared that only Halifax shared the Prime Minister's view, saying that 'notwithstanding to political difficulties, he doubted whether the disadvantages of acceptance of Hitler's proposals were so great as to justify us in going to war'. In order to break the deadlock, he suggested that mobilisation should wait until a general policy had been decided. With Chamberlain's support, this suggestion was generally agreed by the Cabinet.[118]

That day, Cadogan 'was completely horrified' by the calmness of Chamberlain and Halifax towards 'total surrender'. He wrote Halifax a note to indicate his opposing opinion, but this had 'no effect' at first. However, it gave Halifax 'a sleepless night'. Restlessly shuffling ideas from late night to dawn, the Foreign Secretary completely changed his mind.[119] Next morning, when the Cabinet met again, Halifax, in spite of feeling 'a brute',[120] said that his opinion was 'changing':

> What made him hesitate was that it might be held that there was a distinction in principle between orderly and disorderly transfer with all that the latter implied for the minorities in the transferred areas.

He was not at all satisfied with the fact that:

> Hitler had given us nothing and that he was dictating terms, just as though he had won a war but without having had to fight . . . he did not feel that it would be right to put pressure on Czechoslovakia to accept. We should lay the case before them. If they rejected it he imagined that France would join in, and if France went in we should join with them.

He concluded that, working most closely with the Prime Minister throughout the long crisis, 'he was not quite sure that their minds were still altogether at one'.[121] His change of view was 'a horrible blow' to Chamberlain, who blamed his Foreign Secretary: 'Night conclusions are seldom taken in the right perspective.'[122]

In addition, Halifax informed the Cabinet of Amery's letter to the Prime Minister, in which he said that they were bound to tell Hitler:

> that the demand is in our opinion unreasonable, that we cannot blame the Czechs for rejecting it, and that if, instead of considering reasonable alternatives, he invades Czechoslovakia, he must realize the consequences . . .

> We all applauded your first going to Berchtesgaden. Many of us were greatly perturbed by what we understood to be the proposals forced upon the Czechs – going far beyond what I suggested to you earlier – and immensely relieved to hear that you were standing up to Hitler once you realized that even such a settle-

ment, which gave him more than he could ever have expected, was not enough for him. But if the country and the House should once suppose that you were prepared to acquiesce in or even endorse this last demand, there would be a tremendous revulsion of feeling against you.

This view was agreed with by Duff Cooper and Hore-Belisha.[123] Hoare did not entirely stand by the Prime Minister either, suggesting the 'counter proposals' that the transfer of the Sudetenland should be 'in an orderly fashion'. He went on to propose that Britain, France and Russia should open joint military conversations.[124] It was obvious, as Cadogan recorded, that the 'Cabinet anyhow wouldn't allow P.M. to make any further concessions (and I'm sure country wouldn't)'.[125] In the face of strong disagreement, Chamberlain did not want to give up. He summed up, saying that 'he did not think that it was necessary to take any immediate decision' because he thought that they should consult with the French first before a decision was made. This was generally accepted by the ministers.[126]

In the evening, the British statesmen met the Daladier–Bonnet team, which had returned to London for the consultation. Daladier thought Hitler's proposal was unacceptable, and that France would fight if Germany attacked Czechoslovakia. Chamberlain tried to move the French in the direction of concession. He explained Hitler's plan again and again in detail, to show there was no great difference between it and the Anglo-French proposal of 18 September. Simon, who was not at all an unequivocal opponent of Chamberlain's, now helped the Prime Minister to discourage the French by drawing attention to France's military inferiority *vis-à-vis* Germany if war broke out. Hoare also emphasised his disagreement with Daladier, saying that even if Britain and France were engaged in war with Germany, there was no way to prevent Czechoslovakia being overrun. Realising Daladier thought there was no other proposal to make regarding concessions except the original Anglo-French plan, Chamberlain continued to search for another way out. The meeting was adjourned that night without any encouraging result.[127]

After the Anglo-French meeting, Cabinet members met for the third time within twenty-four hours at 11.30 p.m. Maugham, the Lord Chancellor, pointed out that the French seemed not to have decided 'what they would do.' They wanted 'to keep Germany guessing, in the hope that Europe would take the view that France was fulfilling her obligations'. The Prime Minister took the chance to put forward his new idea, that he should write a personal letter[128] to the Führer and make one last appeal to him. He proposed to ask the Führer:

> to agree to the appointment of a Joint Commission, with German and Czech members and a British representative. This Commission would not start *de novo*, but would consider how the proposals accepted by the present Czech Government could be put into effect in an orderly manner and as quickly as possible, and without shocking public opinion.

He was 'unwilling to leave unexplored any possible chance of avoiding war'. He told his colleagues that he would authorise Wilson, as 'Confidential Adviser', to see the Führer and deliver the letter in person. In this way, if the letter failed to secure any response from Hitler, Wilson should be authorised to give a warning as follows:

> The French Government have informed us that, if the Czechs reject the Memorandum and Germany attacks Czechoslovakia, they will fulfil their obligations to Czechoslovakia. Should the forces of France in consequence become engaged in active hostilities against Germany, we shall feel obliged to support them.

Chamberlain thought it was a desperate attempt, and even he was not optimistic as to the result. Simon again came to Chamberlain's aid, and appealed to his colleagues that, knowing Hitler as he did, the Prime Minister thought that 'this course was a useful one', so 'the Cabinet should act on it'. Duff Cooper, who objected to any further concessions did not want to lose this last slice of hope either. In the end, the Cabinet accepted Chamberlain's proposal.[129]

Next morning (26 September), the Prime Minister first had a meeting with General Gamelin, who had come to London for consultation. The General estimated that if war broke out, the Czech Army 'would continue to exist as a fighting force', although it would not hold out against the Germans very long – probably for two weeks.[130] Then the British Ministers had another meeting with the French statesmen. Chamberlain informed Daladier of his plan for a last attempt. The latter appreciated the action the Prime Minister had taken.[131]

It was not unexpected when Wilson reported that evening from Berlin that he had a 'very violent hour' with Hitler, who did not even want to listen to Chamberlain's letter. There was no indication of 'compromise or even modification'. The Führer fixed 2 p.m. on 28 September as the deadline for Czech acceptance of his demands.[132] This being so, the Confidential Adviser had read Chamberlain's warning to the Führer before he left.[133]

Meanwhile, the Godesberg terms became known to the public. Being agitated, most newspapers hardened their attitude towards Germany. The article by the Diplomatic Correspondent of the *Daily Telegraph* said: 'The demands are as peremptory and uncompromising as if they represented, not the basis of negotiation for a peaceful settlement, but a dictation to an enemy beaten in the field – which Czechoslovakia is not yet.' *The Times* issued a warning similar to the one Wilson had read out to Hitler; on the other hand, its leading article appealed that 'it is still not too late to stop this great tragedy, and for the peoples of all nations to insist on settlement by free negotiation'.[134]

On the same day, a group of politicians gathered first in General Spears' office and then in Churchill's flat in the evening, including Churchill, Amery, Lord Cecil, George Lloyd, Lord Lloyd, Sir Edward Grigg, Sir Robert Horne, Boothing, Bracken, Law, Sinclair, Lytton, Spears and one or two others. Most of them were Conservatives, but there were also Opposition leaders and prominent League of Nations figures. 'The feeling was passionate', Churchill recorded. They all agreed: 'We must get Russia in.' Churchill told them that he had just seen the Prime Minister and the Foreign Secretary, suggesting again that the Government should make a joint declaration with France and Russia, showing 'unity of sentiment and purpose' against Hitler's aggression. He also urged the Prime Minister to mobilise the fleet at once. It seemed to have a temporary effect on policy-making, because that very evening, approved by Halifax, the Press Department of the FO issued a communiqué, which was similar to Wilson's warning to Hitler. Chamberlain also agreed to mobilise the fleet on the same night. In the end, these politicians decided: 'If Chamberlain rats again we shall form a united block against him.' But they did not think that he would rat, therefore they should 'rally behind him'.[135]

Nevertheless, the critics were too optimistic. Chamberlain's consideration of mobilisation was delayed until the next day. While a small meeting of ministers was held, Chiefs of Staff were called in. The ministers agreed with their advice that 'it was important to impress on the French Government that they should not take any offensive action until they had consulted with the British Government'. As to their suggestion of mobilising the Navy, the Prime Minister approved, with some hesitation.[136] However, he did not mention a word about this decision in his broadcast the same evening, as he had promised to do.[137]

Before his broadcast, Chamberlain had a discussion with Halifax, Cadogan and Wilson. Chamberlain instructed Wilson to draft a telegram telling the Czechs to accept Hitler's memo. Although Halifax and Cadogan showed their disagreement, the former sent the document separately to Prague, Paris and Berlin.[138] However, even in the face of this appeal, the German attitude was negative, on the grounds that the Czechs must accept the German plan 'at once'.[139]

All hope seemed gone. In his broadcast a few minutes after 8.00 p.m., the Prime Minister intoned:

> How horrible, fantastic, incredible it is that we should be digging trenches and trying on gas-masks here because of a quarrel in a far-away country between people of whom we know nothing . . . at this moment, I see nothing further that I can usefully do in the way of mediation.'[140]

Cooper criticised this broadcast, which did not mention France or offer a word of sympathy for Czechoslovakia. The only sympathy expressed was for Hitler. After listening to it, Churchill felt 'most indignant', and rang the Admiralty to say: 'we're preparing to scuttle'.[141]

Munich

Shortly after his broadcast, the Prime Minister received Hitler's reply to his private letter of 26 September. While insisting on his demand, the Führer maintained that the German Army would not march beyond the region which the Czech Government had agreed to cede, that the plebiscite would be carried out by free vote, and that Germany would participate in a joint guarantee to Czechoslovakia.[142] Reading this letter, Chamberlain reflected that differences and obscurities 'had been narrowed down still further to a point where really it was inconceivable that they could not be settled by negotiations'.[143] He immediately summoned the Cabinet, and told the ministers that Hitler's letter might 'afford some ground on which a further proposal for a peaceful settlement could be based'.[144]

On the morning of 28 September, without consulting any member of the Cabinet, not even Halifax, the Prime Minister alone made the decision to send Hitler a 'last last' appeal, after discussing it with Wilson and another intimate adviser.[145] In this 'last last' appeal, Chamberlain assured Hitler that he could get everything without fighting.[146] At the same time, he sent a personal message to Mussolini, asking il Duce to urge Hitler to agree to his proposal.[147] After receiving his letter, Mussolini immediately instructed the Italian Ambassador in Berlin to see von Ribbentrop and to say that Italy would certainly 'stand by Germany', yet in view of Chamberlain's proposal, Mussolini hoped that Hitler would postpone military action for 24 hours.[148] France also agreed to co-operate with Britain on the same lines.[149]

That morning, as Wheeler-Bennett described, men and women woke 'with an eerie feeling' that it was 'the last day' of peace.[150] However, there is little evidence to suggest that the public opposed facing war. That afternoon, the House was summoned to debate, but actually only to listen to the Prime Minister's speech. Chamberlain gave account of his visit to Germany, and said that the Führer was prepared 'to risk a world war' for the Sudeten Germans. Harold Nicolson noticed: 'as he said these words a shudder of horror passed through the House of Commons.' Chamberlain then told the MPs that Hitler had just accepted his last last appeal, and invited him, Daladier and Mussolini to Munich, to settle the Sudeten problem. 'For a second,' Harold Nicolson wrote, 'the House was hushed in absolute silence. And then the whole House burst into a roar of cheering, since they knew that this might mean peace.' The whole House rose to applaud their Prime Minister, except a few MPs such as Churchill, Amery, Eden and Harold Nicolson, who remained seated.[151] Like the House, the press greeted the announcement with enthusiasm, except a few papers such as the *Daily Telegraph*, the *Daily Herald* and the *News Chronicle*, which held reservations.[152] Harold Nicolson described the situation as 'mass hysteria'.[153]

On 29 September, at Churchill's suggestion, the critics wanted to send a telegram to the Prime Minister in Munich, asking him 'not to betray the Czechs'. The telegram was to be signed by Churchill, Lord Cecil, Attlee, Eden, Sinclair and Lloyd. But Eden refused to sign because he thought 'it would be interpreted as a vendetta against Chamberlain'. Attlee refused too without the approval of his party. The Opposition failed to act at this juncture.[154]

At midday on 29 September, the four heads of the Munich Powers met. After long discussion, an agreement was signed at midnight. The Czech evacuation of the Sudetenland would begin on 1 October, and would be complete by 10 October.[155] While they were waiting for the draftsmen, Chamberlain asked Hitler whether they could have a private talk. The Führer 'jumped at the idea'. With only the interpreter present, they talked about the issues of Spain, economic relations and disarmament. Finally, Chamberlain succeeded in inviting Hitler to sign a joint agreement, which he had prepared and brought with him. It said:

> the German Führer and Chancellor and the British Prime Minister . . . are agreed in recognising that the question of Anglo-German relations is of the first importance for the two countries and for Europe.
>
> We regard the agreement signed last night and the Anglo-German Naval Agreement as symbolic of the desire of our two peoples never to go to war with one another again. [156]

Then, Chamberlain and Daladier called for the Czech representatives, who were waiting for the result, and handed them the Munich Agreement. With this arrangement, the Czech Government announced its acceptance of the terms at 5.00 p.m. on 30 September.[157]

THE GOLDEN AGE OF APPEASEMENT
Chamberlain's Confidence in Appeasement and the Policy of Rearmament

Stepping down from the aeroplane at Heston on the afternoon of 30 September, Chamberlain waved the joint agreement – the receipt from selling Czechoslovakia – at the cheering crowds.[158] When he spoke at 10 Downing Street, he said:

> For the second time in our history, a British Prime Minister has returned from Germany bringing peace with honour. I believe it is peace for our time.[159]

The BBC created overwhelming support for the Prime Minister 'by broadcasting in numerous news bulletins information about the tremendous fan-mail received by the Premier', giving the impression that all these letters were letters of praise.[160] However, the fact was that many were letters of protest, which was not divulged to the public. Madge and Harrison investigated:

> Yet from one public meeting alone, in a provincial town where an observer happened to be present, 800 letters of protest to the

Premier were actually written, paid for and posted by members of the audience.[161]

Oliver Harvey's diaries gave further evidence, as he wrote on 30 September: 'Vast crowds in the streets – hysterical cheers and enthusiasm. P.M. on balcony at Buckingham Palace. But many feel it to be a great humiliation.'[162]

The general feeling, both in the Press and in the House was, as Eden summed up later, that some hoped that 'we were at the beginning of better things', but others, however, 'very reluctantly were convinced that we had gained nothing but a brief respite at the end of which more demands would be imposed by similar methods'.[163]

From 3 October, the House held four days of debates. The Labour and Liberal dissenters were little different from the Government supporters in feeling 'relief that war has not come this time' due to the Prime Minister's attempt.[164] However, they condemned Chamberlain for abjectly surrendering to the threat of force. Attlee pointed out;

> The events of these last few days constitute one of the greatest diplomatic defeats that this country and France have ever sustained. There can be no doubt that it is a tremendous victory for Herr Hitler. Without firing a shot, by the mere display of military force, he has achieved a dominating position in Europe which Germany failed to win after four years of war. He has overturned the balance of power in Europe. He has destroyed the last fortress of democracy in Eastern Europe which stood in the way of his ambition. He has opened his way to the food, the oil and the resources which he requires in order to consolidate his military power . . . [165]

Dalton asked: 'is it peace now, or is it only a short breathing space and a fatal worsening of strategical and economic conditions . . . before an inevitable war?' He foresaw: 'we shall not have to wait very long before Herr Hitler will dictate, first to his immediate neighbours and later to all Europe, and in the end to the British Empire and the world at large'.[166] Unlike other speakers, Churchill did not start his address with 'tributes' to the Prime Minister. He said: 'Do not suppose that this is the end. This is only the beginning of the reckoning. This is only the first sip, the first foretaste of a bitter cup which will be proffered to us . . .'. He thought that 'in future the Czechoslovak State cannot be maintained as an independent entity'.[167]

Meanwhile, the Opposition, including Churchill, Eden, Cooper, Amery, Harold Nicolson and six or seven other MPs, decided that it preferred to 'abstain', rather than that some should abstain and some vote against the Government.[168]

Although he asked the House not to read too much into the words he had spoken at 10 Downing Street, Chamberlain no doubt believed, as he wrote to the Archbishop of Canterbury on 2 October, that 'we have at last opened the way to that general appeasement which alone can save the world from chaos'.[169]

At the first Cabinet meeting after he returned (3 October), the Prime Minister was asked for his view about the argument that was strongly held within and outside of the Government:

we must never again allow ourselves to get into the position in which we had been in the last few weeks, and that every effort should be made to intensify our rearmament programme.[170]

In reply, Chamberlain said he 'would like to make his own position in the matter clear'. He analysed the relationship between appeasement and rearmament:

Ever since he had been Chancellor of the Exchequer, he had been oppressed with the sense that the burden of armaments might break our backs. This had been one of the factors which had led him to the view that it was necessary to try and resolve the causes which were responsible for the armament race.

He thought that we were now in a more hopeful position, and that the contacts which had been established with the Dictator Powers opened up the possibility that we might be able to reach some agreement with them which would stop the armament race.

On the other hand, he did not think it was right 'to stop rearming until we were convinced that other countries would act in the same way'. Nor did he agree that 'we should at once embark on a great increase in our armaments programme'.[171] A few weeks later (on 31 October), when the minister had another discussion on the issue of rearmament, Sir Kingsley Wood, the Secretary for Air warned that even from the defensive point of view, 'at the present time we were seriously deficient as compared with Germany. Indeed our weakness might be said to be likely to provoke aggression by others.' The Prime Minister once again rebutted proposed acceleration of rearmament:

Our Foreign policy was one of appeasement: We must aim at establishing relations with the Dictator Powers which will lead to a settlement in Europe and to a sense of stability.

There had been a good deal of talk in the country and in the Press about the need for rearmament by this country. In Germany and Italy it was suspected that this rearmament was directed against them, and it was important that we should not encourage these suspicions.

Our rearmament was directed to securing our own safety and not for purposes of aggression against other countries.

He emphasised that the purpose of the Munich Agreement was not to gain time for rearmament:

A good deal of false emphasis had been placed on rearmament, as though one result of the Munich Agreement had been that it would be necessary for us to add to our rearmament programmes. Acceleration of existing programmes was one thing, but increases in the scope of our programme which would lead to a new arms race was a different proposition.

It might be possible to take active steps and to follow up the Munich Agreement by other measures, aimed at securing better relations. The putting into effect of the Anglo-Italian Agreement would be one step in this direction. He also hoped that some day we should be able to secure a measure of limitation of armaments, but it was too soon to say when this would prove possible. An improvement in confidence was first necessary.[172]

This evidence demonstrates that at Munich, Chamberlain did not aim to buy time for military preparation against the dictators. With rearmament geared to the extent that would be sufficient for Britain's own safety, he was waiting for the right moment to slow it down, and enjoy the fruits of Munich. But British rearmament after Munich did not slow down, because this right moment never appeared. In the winter of 1938–9, there emerged a false alarm that Germany might invade Holland, but then Hitler raped Prague the following March instead.

A brief review may bring fresh light to the picture of rearmament. Since Chamberlain had cut one-third of expenditure on the DRC's four-year rearmament programme in 1934, British rearmament had followed his policy of 'cheapest defence'. Immediately after the *Anschluss*, at the meeting of 22 March, the Cabinet held the view that:

> there was an underlying resentment at the idea of constantly having to knuckle under to the Dictators for lack of sufficient strength. The best way to meet this view was to announce an acceleration of re-armament and opportunities for personnel service.[173]

Although rearmament had been again put on the agenda, there was little vigour and determination to carry it out. Chamberlain and Simon were 'against thorough-going rearmament because of its effect on our foreign trade'. They were very optimistic about 'the good behaviour of the Dictators'.[174] Halifax was also very ambivalent, as he said to FPC members on 21 March that he was 'in favour of a more vigorous line in rearmament but feared that it should not expose ourselves to rebuffs from Germany and so lose all hope of improving relations with her'.[175]

In 1937, the Cabinet approved the total cost of the defence programme for the next five years (1937–41) as £1,500 million, but the three Defence Departments estimated that the programme would require at least £2,000 million.[176] Simon, the Chancellor of the Exchequer, kept demanding that the defence services reduce their budgets. Duff Cooper felt that any discussion with Simon about increasing expenditure on the rearmament programme was a 'pure waste of time'. It was hardly surprising to find in a Cabinet document of that time that 'the Defence Services were working under instructions to cut down estimates', and that 'this was hardly consistent with an announcement that we were accelerating our armaments'.[177] General Sir Henry Pownall revealed the resentment of the Chiefs of Staff in his diary entry of 21 March:

> At the Cabinet this week there was much talk of speeding up and the W.O. could do this and that . . . But when the Cabinet minutes came out it appeared that all this wonderful business was to be done 'within the amount of money available for the Army' – and as that has not been settled – it has been indeterminable for months and is likely to remain so – it simply means that the

Treasury have a complete free hand, at any point and on any project, to say it can't be done.[178]

Even after the Rhineland crisis, the policy of rearmament was 'business as usual', which indicated that rearmament should not be put in the position where it was more important than normal industrial and commercial life. The rule lasted until the Spring of 1938.[179] This certainly explains why the phrase 'Britain was not ready for war' had been repeatedly heard since 1931, and why British rearmament had always lagged far behind Germany's.

On the other hand, Germany spent about three times as much on armaments as Britain in the years 1933–8.[180] As he started the second phase of rearmament in the summer of 1936 under his Second Four Year Plan, Hitler gave two principles to Goering, who was appointed as Plenipotentiary of the plan:

I. The German Army must be ready for commitment in four years.
II. The German economy must be ready for war in four years.[181]

Tables 5.1 and 5.2 explore the gap between the two sides in the years 1936–8.

Table 5.1: Rearmament Expenditure (£ Million)[182]

	UK	Germany
1936	£186	500 (RM 6 billion)
1937	£265	667 (RM 8 billion)
1938	£400	1,500 (RM 18 billion)

Table 5.2: Percentage of GNP Devoted to Military Expenditure[183]

	UK	Germany
1936	4	13
1937	6	13
1938	7	17

The peacetime strength of the German Army in August 1939 was approximately equal to the total of the British, French and Polish Armies.[184] Although it was much stronger than that of Germany, the

British Navy had to defend the whole Empire. In addition, a sea blockade would not bring Germany to her knees in a short period if war broke out.

As regards the Air Force, the number of German first-line aircraft had exceeded Britain's by the end of 1936.[185] Although rearmament in the air took almost the lion's share among the three services, the programme was not promising. From 1936 to 1939, the Air Staff worked out several schemes to improve the air strength. Immediately after Munich, 'Scheme M' was formulated, the last one before the outbreak of war, as shown in Table 5.3.

Table 5.3: Aircraft totals – Comparison Between Britain and Germany[186]

	Oct. 1938		1 Apr. 1939		1 Aug. 1939	
	First-line	*Reserve*	First-line	*Reserve*	First-line	*Reserve*
UK	1,606	*412*	1,782	*977*	1,890	*1,502*
Germany	3,200	*2,400*	3,680	*2,700*	4,030	*3,000*

According to this scheme, the total number of aircraft in the RAF would reach only less than half of Germany's total by 1 August 1939 – one month before the war. Even so, when the Cabinet discussed the scheme, Simon pointed out that this programme was 'so costly as to raise serious doubts whether it can be financed . . . without the gravest danger to the country's stability'. He suggested that only increases in the number of fighters should take priority, which was supported by Chamberlain and other ministers. In addition to financial stringency, the programme suffered from the problem that only 50 per cent of the reserve aircraft in Scheme M could be produced due to the industrial situation.[187] Under these circumstances, at the outbreak of war the RAF had only a total of 3,860 aircraft against Germany's 9,220, and the margin had not been narrowed greatly in the post-Munich period.[188]

Failure of the Guarantee to Czechoslovakia

When Chamberlain sold out the Sudetenland at the Munich Conference, the only reward he obtained from Hitler was that Germany promised to join in guaranteeing the remnant of Czech territory after the Polish and Hungarian minorities had been settled.[189] Sir Thomas Inskip,

Defence Secretary, said on behalf of the Government in the House on 4 October that although a guarantee would not be technically in force until settlement between Czechoslovakia, Poland and Hungary had been achieved:

> the Government felt under a moral obligation to Czechoslovakia to treat the guarantee as being now in force. In the event, therefore, of an act of unprovoked aggression against Czechoslovakia, His Majesty's Government would certainly feel bound to take all steps in their power to see that the integrity of Czechoslovakia is preserved.[190]

In fact, Hitler did not at all want to guarantee the new boundaries of the Czech State. A few days after Munich, he consulted with General Keitel on the plan of destroying the whole of Czechoslovakia.[191] On 21 October, he issued s directive under the title 'Liquidation of the Remainder of the Czech State'.[192] Within two months, a supplementary order to this directive was circulated to the Army Chiefs of Staff. It read:

> To the outside world also it must be made clear that this is merely an act of pacification and not an operation of war.
> For the same reasons provision for the exercise of executive power by the Commander-in-Chief of the Army is confined to the newly occupied territory and limited to a short period.[193]

Since frontier rectifications between Czechoslovakia, Poland and Hungary had been completed in November, the British Government sent a note to the German Government on 8 February 1939 concerning the matter of the joint guarantee to Czechoslovakia. In the German reply, which was received on 3 March, Hitler considered it necessary 'to await firstly a clarification of internal development of Czecho-Slovakia'.[194]

The British policy-makers were not alerted by Hitler's delay in giving a guarantee. In spite of the growing German threat to Czechoslovak independence, Henderson reported on 18 February: 'My definite impression . . . is that Herr Hitler does not contemplate any adventures at the moment and all stories and rumours to the contrary are completely without real foundation.' He urged the Government 'publicly both in press and speeches' to stress 'our full reliance on Herr

Hitler's peaceful intentions as it is harmful to show suspicion of them'.[195] Following him, Chamberlain, who had realised that 'British public opinion was now violently anti-dictator',[196] tried to soothe the public by telling the press on 10 March: 'Europe was settling down to a period of tranquillity.' Hoare also talked about the hopes of a 'Five Year Peace Plan', leading to a 'Golden Age of Prosperity'.[197]

Only five days later, Hitler ordered German troops across the German–Czech frontier on the early morning of 15 March, before he forced Hacha, the new President of Czechoslovakia, to sign an agreement that Hacha agreed to leave the Czech people and country 'under the protection of the German Reich'.[198]

The 'rape' of Prague was a nasty shock to the British Government. On the morning after the FO received Henderson's report,[199] the Cabinet was summoned. It was very important and urgent to discuss the guidelines for the statement the Prime Minister would make in the House that afternoon, in which he would try to get rid of the responsibility of the guarantee to Czechoslovakia. Simon said openly that 'the statement should make it clear that the Government no longer had any obligation, legal or moral, under the guarantee to Czechoslovakia'. Halifax held the same ground. Chamberlain tried to find excuses, saying:

> he thought the fundamental fact was that the State whose frontiers we had undertaken to guarantee against unprovoked aggression had now completely broken up.
>
> It might, no doubt, be true that the disruption of Czechoslovakia had been largely engineered by Germany, but our guarantee was not a guarantee against the exercise of moral pressure.

His argument was supported by the ministers present. In the end, the Cabinet decided to postpone the visit of the President of the Board of Trade to Berlin and authorised Chamberlain and Halifax to draft a statement along the lines that had been discussed.[200]

The public unanimously showed anger against Hitler's elimination of Czechoslovakia, with the view that appeasement was no longer suitable towards Germany. *The Times* and the *Daily Telegraph* held similar ground. They condemned Germany on one hand, and disapproved of British military intervention on the other. The *Daily Herald*, however, criticised Chamberlain for his policy of encouraging German invasion. Many newspapers appealed for co-operation with France and Russia against further aggression.[201]

On the Opposition side, Churchill's and Eden's groups had been working since Munich to enlarge the basis of Government – joining a National Government. Eden and his supporters decided that 'we must support the Government, and that Anthony should speak . . . The rest to keep silent.' Churchill 'perhaps hoping for office if he did not embarrass his leaders at this point, left the attack to Anthony Eden and his followers'.[202]

In the debates on the afternoon of 15 March, Chamberlain's policy was criticised from many quarters. Sinclair condemned Chamberlain for 'deliberately postponing Debates in this House until they could have no further influence on the course of events'. He urged the Prime Minister 'to gather our friends to us', particularly France, Russia and America, and that Britain should 'take the initiative in the world in the direction of basing policy on the principles of law'.[203] Eden, however, spoke in quite mild language. He agreed with the Government's decision to postpone the minister's visit to Berlin, and appealed that 'the situation was so serious that the time for party controversy had gone'.[204]

Based on the line proposed by the Cabinet that morning, the Prime Minister told the House that the Government could not 'accordingly hold themselves any longer' bound by guarantee, because Czechoslovakia 'has now ceased to exist'. Although he 'bitterly' regretted 'the manner and the method' of the German action, he was determined to continue appeasement:

> do not let us on that account be deflected from our course. Let us remember that the desire of all the peoples of the world still remains concentrated on the hopes of peace and a return to the atmosphere of understanding and good will which has so often been disturbed. The aim of this Government is now, as it has always been, to promote that desire and to substitute the method of discussion for the method of force in the settlement of differences. [205]

His statement left a very unsatisfactory impression. Cadogan commented that the Prime Minister 'would go on with his "policy" (? "appeasement"). Fatal!'[206]

CONCLUSION

Investigation of the Munich policy provides a good chance to clarify the appeasers' arguments at the beginning. First, did Munich really avert or postpone war?

According to German documents, Hitler had planned for a war against the Western Powers over Austria and Czechoslovakia to be fought as early as 1943–5.[207] Munich had offered him what he wanted without costing him a single shot. This not only nourished his ambitions, but also provided him with more favourable conditions to carry out his plan. He instructed the German press secretly after Munich (10 November):

> That we took advantage of the prevailing circumstances was, finally, perhaps the most decisive factor to bring about these achievements. The world situation in general appeared to me more than ever favourable to asserting our demands.[208]

His demands finally led to the Second World War in September 1939, which was three to five years earlier than he had projected.

Although the inevitability of war had been increased by the Czechoslovak crisis, it was still possible for the Western Powers to keep Hitler in check without war. At the Nuremberg trials, Marshal von Keitel was asked, if the Western Powers had stood by the Czechs, 'would the Reich have attacked Czechoslovakia?'. He answered: 'Certainly not. We were not strong enough militarily. The object of Munich . . . was to get Russia out of Europe, to gain time, and to complete the German armaments.'[209] General Halder also revealed that without Munich, the opposing generals would have overthrown the Führer if he had taken the risk of war against the West.[210] In that case, there might have been no Second World War.

If war had occurred in 1938, instead of 1939, it could have only been a limited war rather than a general war, because German armaments had not yet reached sufficient level for total war. There was a serious lack of trained reserves and essential resources. The West Wall had not been completed. The German Air Force, which relied on close ground support, was unable to execute a 'knock-out blow' to Britain without bases in the Low Countries. Hitler knew very well at that moment that he could afford only a short and limited war (ideally for a few weeks, and in no circumstances longer than a year), as he told his chief commanders and commanding generals: 'we cannot conduct a long war'. In addition, he doubted that the Japanese and Italians would follow him unconditionally.[211] On the other hand, although British military preparations were deficient, the combination of British and French forces was by no means inferior to Germany's. In addition, Russia would have certainly come to the aid of the Czechs because of her obligations to France and Czechoslovakia. Romania, Yugoslavia and perhaps even Poland would also have taken the Czech side. The Czechoslovak Army could mobilise up to 500,000 well-trained and well-equipped troops. An attack on Czechoslovakia would have meant a great loss of German forces. The Western Powers would have had the advantage if war had started in 1938. Duff Cooper had full confidence that they would win.

Therefore, the conclusion must be either or both of the following: either Munich brought forward the Second World War instead of postponing it, or Munich averted a short and limited war, but paved the way for a long and general one.

Second, did Munich aim to 'gain time' for rearmament? In fact, this argument was nullified by Chamberlain's own words at the Cabinet meetings of 3 and 31 October. The Prime Minister strongly opposed the view that during the time gained by Munich, 'it would be necessary for us to add to our rearmament programmes'. He emphasised that Munich was 'aimed at securing better relations' with the Dictator Powers. Allowing rearmament to go on for some time, he would reduce it if settlement could be achieved. He even dreamed that 'some day we should be able to secure a measure of limitation of armaments' because rearmament nearly broke Britain's back. British rearmament was not slowed down after Munich, because Hitler struck again too soon. If the appeasers and their followers really want to be loyal to Chamberlain, they should interpret his Munich doctrine correctly.

Third, was Britain unable to save Czechoslovakia? In spite of being a background for appeasement, military weakness, in a strict sense, was not the cause of Munich, because the FPC had decided Czechoslovakia's fate on 18 March before it read the report of the Chiefs of Staff. It was a fundamental belief among many FPC members that Czechoslovakia was 'an artificial country', which was not worth fighting for even if Britain had the strength. It was a view shared by the Chiefs of Staff that Central and Eastern Europe were not directly Britain's concern. They abandoned Churchill's proposal of a 'Grand Alliance' not because of military weakness, but because 'there is one decisive objection against it for our present purposes'.[212] Fourth, was Munich supported by the people? Should Chamberlain be free from charges of betrayal due to his belief in 'the rightness of peace and the wrongness of war'?[213]

It is true that some people wrote letters of praise to their Prime Minister at that moment because they believed that he had brought home 'peace for our time', and 'peace with honour'. If they had known that this 'peace' was in fact the silent prelude to a world war in which many of their children would be killed, crippled and blinded, and in particular if they had known that this war could have been prevented during the Rhineland period if the Government had taken proper action to support France, it is very doubtful they would have written these letters. Indeed, the many letters of protest against the Prime Minister's behaviour at Munich were never published or broadcast. As has been pointed out in the previous chapters, the public was kept in the dark about policy-making. The atmosphere which favoured Munich was largely manufactured, by curbing the media and by misleading the people.

In fact, the public did not want to shrink from war. From 27 to 28 September, war seemed inevitable and imminent. There was no evidence to suggest that the public were not prepared to face war against Hitler's aggression. After Munich, many people felt humiliated. Even Chamberlain found out, as he said on 22 October, that 'a lot of people seem to me to be losing their heads and talking and thinking as though Munich had made war more instead of less imminent'.[214]

He, like many statesmen of his generation, had a fear of war. They were afraid of taking the risk of fighting against the aggressive powers because they worried that modern war would destroy civilisation. However, in spite of great loss of life, the Second World War did not ruin the world, but the aggressive powers instead. Preventing war requires a strategist's clear-sightedness and the courage to face war rather than fear risk. It might be true that his hope for peace was one of the reasons Chamberlain pursued a policy of surrender at Munich. However, historical comment does not weigh personal motives very much, but considers the effects and results when it looks at policy. Therefore, no matter how genuine his motives, Chamberlain followed a policy which plunged the country (and in a certain sense, Europe and the world) into catastrophe. In other words, his policy led history in a direction which was opposite to his motives, even if they were sincere.

It is often suggested that Chamberlain danced to the German tune because he was cheated by Hitler. Halifax argued that 'no one could fairly charge him [Chamberlain] with lack of frankness'.[215] However, even through the surface phenomena, it is not difficult to discern that Chamberlain knew very well after the Anschluss that 'force is the only argument Germany understands'. At Godesberg, he was very 'disappointed' by Hitler's behaviour. Nevertheless, he regarded himself as a man who was able to set up 'a reasonable understanding' with dictators, and he still maintained that he had established an influence over Hitler in spite of all evidence that Hitler was untrustworthy. Even when later events severely challenged his belief, Chamberlain said before his death that he had 'never for one single instant' doubted 'the rightness' of what he had done at Munich, although he had lost all faith in Hitler.[216] Therefore, the conclusion can only be that Chamberlain was cheated not by Hitler, but by himself – by his own self-confidence in dealing with the dictators, and by his own delusions about appeasement. Because of these delusions, he had to believe whatever Hitler said, and turned a deaf ear to information he did not want to hear.[217] Otherwise, he would lose the basis for his policy. This was the most fundamental reason for his failure to penetrate Hitler's intentions, and because of it, Chamberlain and his supporters always made strategic mistakes.

Although appeasement was not a personal policy, Chamberlain should bear personal responsibility for Munich more than any one else, because it was he who, owing to his stubbornness and his faith in the dictators, insisted on compromising with Hitler further and further, even beyond what the Cabinet could accept. His hope for peace was at best a delusion, which blinded him to the inevitability of war. Because of this, he was unable to understand the dialectical relationship between peace and war. If he had realised that war was inevitable, and had stood firm by taking the risk of war, Hitler might have shrunk from it. The hope of peace would have been increased. However, denying the inevitability of war, he ruled out using force to defend peace, which, as a consequence, not only made war inevitable, but also brought it forward.

Apart from all the disastrous effects above, Munich started the process of Russo-German *rapprochement*. Excluded from the Munich talks, Moscow began to look for German friendship, for her own safety. On the other hand, Hitler needed Stalin's co-operation so that he could avoid war on two fronts and obtain Russian raw materials.[218] This cast a shadow on the forthcoming Anglo-Franco-Russian talks, which aimed to build up the last possible deterrent against Hitler's aggression.

6

THE LAST FUTILE EFFORT

THE END OF THE GOLDEN AGE OF APPEASEMENT

Until early March 1939, British policy-makers had spread the illusion that a European settlement was coming.[1] Hitler's sudden *coup* against Prague on 15 March marked the end of the golden age of appeasement. In the following months, the British Government had to make efforts to build up the Eastern Front, which included a guarantee to Poland and Anglo-Franco-Soviet discussions. Both of these arrangements were aimed at presenting a deterrent to further German aggression, but neither was successful.

Contemporary politicians and scholars have made various comments on these events. The guarantee to Poland is often described as 'a diplomatic revolution', marking the end of appeasement. It was, as Thorne says: 'a fundamental change, on the surface at least, of British foreign policy'. Eubank thinks that it 'was actually more a revolution in tactics than in policy'.[2] However, some historians hold a less favourable view. As Middlemas points out, the guarantee showed that 'unwillingly, half-heartedly, the British Government eventually admitted that it could not relinquish interest in the balance of power in Europe'. Bell's observation explores the essential meaning of the guarantee: 'The guarantee was designed as a deterrent, and if the deterrent worked, the guarantee would not have to be carried out . . . As it was, the guarantee was enough to bring Britain and France into a war over Poland, but not enough to deter Hitler from launching one.'[3] As regards the three-power negotiations, Churchill thinks that if Chamberlain had accepted the Russian proposal earlier and reached agreement with Stalin, 'history might have taken a different course. At least it could not have taken a worse.'[4] It is indisputable that due to the failure of these negotiations, Hitler 'was freed from the danger of a war on two fronts'. Some historians, in spite of doubt about whether or how far the tripartite pact would work, agree that its failure made the Second World War inevitable.[5]

Appeasers argue for their offer of a guarantee to Poland in 1939 but sacrificing Czechoslovakia in 1938 by saying that before the collapse of Czechoslovakia, 'Hitler's full intentions were still unknown', and nobody wanted to fight for Czechoslovakia. But then, as 'it was clear that he intended to dominate the Continent, we took up the challenge'.[6] They shuffled off responsibility for failure of the three-power negotiations onto the Soviets, as Hoare wrote that the principal divergence between the two sides was that the British Government would not allow Russia to occupy the Baltic States and Poland, using the excuse of offering them a guarantee. The German–Soviet Pact proved Russia's double face: 'It was Russian duplicity and not British prejudice that made these months of baffling discussion end in failure.'[7] Investigation of British policy-making in the last six months before the Second World War will bring light to these arguments.

THE GUARANTEE TO POLAND

The 'rape' of Prague took the British Government unprepared. The event seriously damaged the Prime Minister's authority, in the fact that his policy did not work.[8] Harold Nicolson, the National Labour MP for West Leicester, described the debates in the House on 17 March:

> the feeling in the lobbies is that Chamberlain will either have to go or completely reverse his policy. Unless in his speech tonight he admits that he was wrong, they feel that resignation is the only alternative. All the tadpoles are beginning to swim into the other camp . . . The Opposition refuse absolutely to serve under him. The idea is that Halifax should become Prime Minister and Eden Leader of the House.[9]

The press, such as the *Manchester Guardian*, held the view that if they changed the policy, the Government would absorb some dissenters, for example Churchill, Eden and Duff Cooper, into the Cabinet. This was, in the public eye, a test of whether appeasement had been abandoned.[10] After Munich, Halifax also gave Chamberlain a similar suggestion, including the appointment of some Labour leaders. Being reluctant to enlarge the Government, the Prime Minister turned a deaf ear to all this. He believed, in Harvey's words, that he could best handle any situation 'with the existing Cabinet'.[11] He particularly disliked the idea of including Churchill in the Cabinet, because, as he said:

> The nearer we get to war, the more his chances improve, and *vice versa*. If there is any possibility of easing the tension and getting back to normal relations with the dictators, I wouldn't risk it by what would certainly be regarded by them as a challenge.[12]

In fact, faced with Germany's violation of the Munich Agreement, the British policy-makers felt lost. When the Prime Minister discussed the situation with Halifax, Cadogan and other ministers, they found that owing to the imperfect information and the time limit, they could hardly 'give the matter proper consideration, or to decide how far the situation had changed'. Nor could the Chiefs of Staff offer their advice, because they had 'very little time to consider the matter, and the question involved so many considerations that it had not been possible for the Chiefs of Staff to reach any considered conclusion on the whole question'. Cadogan wrote in his diaries: '[We] don't know where we are. We ought perhaps to take a stand (whatever that may mean) . . . can we?'[13] In the end, the Prague *coup* forced them to open their eyes to Hitler's real ambitions. At a Cabinet meeting, the Prime Minister confessed that:

> up till a week ago we had proceeded on the assumption that we should be able to continue with our policy of getting on to better terms with the Dictator Powers, and that although those powers had aims, those aims were limited. We had all along had at the back of our minds the reservation that this might not prove to be the case but we had felt that it was right to try out the possibilities of this course.
>
> He had now come definitely to the conclusion that Herr Hitler's attitude made it impossible to continue to negotiate on the old basis with the Nazi regime. This did not mean that negotiations with the German people were impossible. No reliance could be placed on any of the assurances given by the Nazi leaders.[14]

Based on the above idea, which was supported by his colleagues, he gave an address at Birmingham on 17 March in an attempt to justify his Munich policy on one hand and to make a gesture that Britain would face the German challenge on the other:

> Germany, under her present regime, has sprung a series of unpleasant surprises upon the world . . . they must cause us all to be asking ourselves: 'Is this the end of an old adventure, or is it the beginning of a new? Is this the last attack upon a small State, or is it to be followed by others? Is this, in fact, a step in the direction of an attempt to dominate the world by force?' . . . with the lessons of history for all to read, it seems incredible that we should see such a challenge.

Yet he emphasised that he was not prepared to engage Britain by 'new unspecified commitments'.[15]

That day, Tilea, the Romanian Minister in London, asked to see Halifax urgently. In the meeting, Tilea informed him that his Government had received German demands for a monopoly on their exports, and to accept measures of industrial restriction inside Romania in German interests, which was, in his opinion, 'in the nature of an ultimatum'.[16] In addition, according to the information from France the next German victim could also be Poland, Memel or Hungary.[17]

On the weekend of 18 March, the Prime Minister summoned the Cabinet to discuss the Romanian emergency. He gave an account of his idea of changing his policy, and said that since Germany intended to obtain domination over the whole of South-Eastern Europe, 'we had no alternative but to take up the challenge'. 'On this basis,' he continued, 'our next course was to ascertain what friends we had who would join with us in resisting aggression.' He asked the Cabinet whether it agreed generally with the change of policy.

Halifax said that if Germany committed aggression against Romania, 'it would be very difficult for this country not to take all the action in her power to rally resistance against that aggression'. Lord Chatfield, the Secretary of Defence, told the Ministers that the Chiefs of Staff could only offer some preliminary observations before the general policy had been decided. Their diagnosis was

> if Germany could dominate Roumania economically, political domination of that country would almost certainly follow. This would have even more serious consequences, since there would be

nothing to prevent Germany from marching straight through to the Mediterranean . . .

They did not think there was anything they could do to save Romania from German domination, and the situation was 'very similar to that which had faced us in September in regard to Czechoslovakia'. They suggested:

> If, however, the support of Poland and Russia could be secured the position would be entirely changed . . . If Poland and Russia would be prepared to help us, we should join with them in resisting German aggression.

Lord Stanhope, the new Admiralty Minister, also emphasised that 'provided we could ensure Germany having to face war on two fronts, there was much less likelihood of war and we should be more likely to win if war came about'.

After discussion, the change of policy proposed by the Prime Minister was agreed by all the ministers present. Chamberlain concluded:

> the real point at issue was whether we could obtain sufficient assurances from other countries to justify us in a public pronouncement that we should resist any further act of aggression on the part of Germany . . . Poland was very likely the key to the situation . . . our communication to Poland should probably be to go somewhat further than our communications to other countries.

The Cabinet then decided to make approaches to Russia, Poland, Yugoslavia, Turkey, Greece and Romania about joint assistance against further German aggression.[18]

Next day, a ministerial meeting was held to examine the Cabinet's conclusion, with the attendance of Chamberlain, Halifax, Simon, Stanley, Cadogan and Wilson. The ministers came to a unanimous agreement that 'while it was important that some action should be taken quickly, if we attempted to do too much, we might end by achieving no positive results for a long time'. The Prime Minister wanted 'to gain time', for he could 'never accept the view that war is inevitable'. He realised that 'it was impossible to deal with Hitler after he had thrown all his own assurances to the winds'. They agreed, and concluded that 'a pronouncement of this character would by itself have a steadying effect' to deter further German aggression.[19]

By setting up a deterrent, Chamberlain intended to 'gain time' – but for what? For preparation for war against Hitler, or for a new chance of searching for a settlement with him? With the time he gained, he hoped that Britain would be in a stronger position due to the following factors: improvement of British rearmament, new guarantees to small States, Mussolini's help in the direction of peace, and a more fantastic possibility that Hitler might die or be overthrown by his opposing generals. With the stronger position, he believed that he could convince Germany, as he wrote on 30 July 1939:

> that the chances of winning a war without getting thoroughly exhausted in the process are too remote to make it worth while. But the corollary to that must be that she has a chance of getting fair and reasonable consideration and treatment from us and others, if she will give up the idea that she can force it from us, and convince us that she has given it up.

In other words, with the time he gained by setting up a deterrent, he could, rather than actually fighting a war, convince Hitler that if he continued his abuse of force, he would be resisted, but if he pursued his demands by peaceful means, he could still get the best offer. In order to meet this aim, Britain needed to increase her armaments to a level which was sufficient to defend her own safety and to warn Germany, but not necessarily enough to fight a real war. From 1938 to 1939, although defence expenditure, compared to that of previous years, had increased considerably, the total cost amounted to no more than 7 per cent of the national income. However, German armaments spending during the same period was nearly five times as much as Britain's.[20] The Treasury, in close consultation with Chamberlain, worked consistently to limit the defence budget until the outbreak of war.[21] All of this demonstrated that the deterrent was designed to seek a new settlement, instead of war. Feiling remarks, in commenting on Chamberlain's effort: 'if then his weapons had changed, his purpose had not'.[22] The evidence came immediately.

On 20 March, Chamberlain sent a letter to Mussolini, asking il Duce to use his influence on Hitler towards the direction of peace. Cadogan thought that it 'looked much too much like asking for another Munich'. However, even another Munich would not relax Chamberlain, as he explained later (in mid-July):

> That is not good enough. This is just what we tried at Munich, but Hitler broke it up when it suited him. I doubted if any solution, short of war, is practicable at present . . .

But he believed the moment for settlement would come again, as he continued:

> if dictators would have a modicum of patience, I can imagine that a way could be found of meeting German claims while safeguarding Poland's independence and economic security.[23]

On the same day, when the Cabinet members discussed the draft of the Four Power Declaration (Britain, France, Russia and Poland), Chamberlain made it clear that this declaration 'aimed at avoiding specific commitments':

> Although, therefore, the pronouncement did not involve us in any actual new commitment, public opinion would certainly attach significance to such a declaration signed by the Four Powers . . .
>
> The declaration did not constitute a guarantee of the existing frontiers and of the indefinite maintenance of the *status quo*. The declaration was concerned with a far wider issue, namely, security and political independence of European States against German domination.[24]

This policy, as Oliver Harvey, Private Secretary to the Foreign Secretary, remarked, was 'no more than reaffirmation of our existing League of Nations obligation to consult together'. The Government was 'still doubtful how far we will commit ourselves to *action*'.[25]

After the meeting, Cadogan knocked the draft into shape, and with Chamberlain's approval, the telegrams were sent to the countries concerned.[26] During the next few days, information from France showed that the French Government accepted the declaration, and Russia, in spite of some reservations, also accepted, on condition that both France and Poland would act accordingly.[27] However, Beck, the Polish Foreign Minister, was reluctant to agree to such a declaration, on the grounds that it would ' place Poland in the Soviet camp', which would cause an unprovoked German invasion. On the other hand, he implied that Poland might associate with England and France if Russia were omitted. A secret agreement could be signed between Britain and Poland.[28]

On 25 and 26 March, the FO held departmental meetings to discuss the next step, with the attendance of Halifax, Cadogan, Vansittart, Sargent, Strang and Butler (Parliamentary Under-Secretary). Cadogan for the first time confessed that the situation had become 'murky', as 'Van predicted and as I never believed it would'. He thought 'we must try to build a dam' to stem German expansion, although he realised that the 'chances of that are rather slight'. The Foreign Secretary held the view that the 'adherence of Poland is essential', and 'we cannot have Russia in the forefront of the picture'. They intended to approach a sort of guarantee to Poland and Romania, which Chamberlain agreed in principle.[29] Being full of misgivings over Russia, the Prime Minister did not want to associate with that country either, as he wrote on 26 March:

> I must confess to the most profound distrust of Russia. I have no belief whatever in her ability to maintain an effective offensive, even if she wanted to. And I distrust her motives, which seem to me to have little connection with our ideas of liberty, and to be concerned only with getting every one else by the ears. Moreover, she is both hated and suspected by many of the smaller States, notably by Poland, Roumania, and Finland.[30]

Owing to this prejudice, he told his colleagues at the FPC meeting next day that he would like to choose Poland rather than Russia as an ally on the Eastern Front, because Poland was unwilling to associate with Russia publicly. In his opinion, the dilemma was that a front against German aggression was likely to be frustrated if Russia was closely associated, but a failure to associate with the Soviets would give rise to suspicion and difficulty with the Left at home. He suggested that they had to abandon the policy of the Four-Power Declaration, and an alternative course was that if Poland or Romania were attacked and they were prepared to resist, Britain and France would support them. Moreover, it should be ascertained that Poland would come to their aid if Britain, France and Romania were involved in war with Germany. He said:

> this plan left Soviet Russia out of the picture . . . It would seem imprudent to attempt to bring Russia into the plan publicly . . . The Franco-Soviet Pact might possibly offer the means by which Russia might be indirectly and secretly brought into the scheme.

The Foreign Secretary was completely in accordance with the Prime Minister, pointing out: 'if we had to make a choice between Poland and Soviet Russia, it seemed clear that Poland would give the greater value'. He quoted from the report by the British Embassy in Moscow[31] to prove that the Russian Army was greatly weakened by recent purges, its offensive value was small, and their planes were out of date.

Regardless, Hoare and Stanley (the President of the Board of Trade) thought that Russia constituted the greatest deterrent in the East against German aggression. The exclusion of Russia was bound to have serious consequences. With a similar idea, Chatfield warned the Cabinet of the danger that 'the worst that could happen would be for us to get involved in war without any allies on the Eastern Front'. Therefore, he advised:

> it should be our objective to endeavour to obtain the maximum possible of support in Eastern Europe . . . Poland was, from the military point of view, probably the best of potential eastern allies, but . . . Soviet Russia would act as a greater deterrent so far as Germany was concerned.

On the other hand, he was concerned that they should not be drawn into any commitments with Russia, which might involve them in hostilities with Japan.

In the end, the Cabinet agreed the alternative course proposed by the Prime Minister. Halifax and Simon settled the final form of the telegrams to Warsaw and Bucharest. As to the issue of association with Russia, the Prime Minister said that it would depend on the reply from Poland.[32]

It seemed that the Cabinet had not made a final decision on a guarantee to Poland by 28 March.[33] However, this issue was urgently put on the agenda due to two pieces of information received the following day. The first was that the American Ambassador had informed the FO that his colleague in Warsaw had information of a possible German intention to execute a *coup* against Poland. The second was that Ian Colvin, the Berlin Correspondent of the *News Chronicle*, reported to Simon, Halifax, Cadogan and Chamberlain in person that he had received information from various contacts in Germany which indicated that Poland was Hitler's next victim, and an attack on her could be made very soon, perhaps around the end of March.[34] Although Cadogan was not 'entirely convinced', it left a deep impression on Chamberlain and Halifax, the latter of whom thought that 'these sources of information had been pretty accurate in the previous autumn, when we had not always been prepared to rely upon them'. Both of them agreed to issue an immediate declaration of support for Poland even without waiting for Beck's reply.[35]

At an emergency meeting on 30 March, reporting this information to the Cabinet, Halifax pointed out that Hitler might strike before Britain had made arrangements. He suggested that 'we should consider whether we could take some prior action as to forestall Herr Hitler's next step', namely to 'make a clear declaration of our intention to support Poland if Poland was attacked by Germany'. This proposal included two objectives: first, it might cause Hitler's plan to be suspended, and would thus discredit him within the German Army; second, it would 'educate' German public opinion that Hitler's ambitions would result in Germany becoming engaged in war on two fronts.[36]

The Prime Minister added that they should learn from the lesson of Czechoslovakia:

> instead of the Czech army being on our side, Czech resources were now available to Germany. It would be a very serious matter if Poland, instead of being a potential ally, also became added to the resources of Germany. If, therefore, we took no action, there was a risk that, in a short time, we should find that Poland had been over-run and that we had missed an opportunity. On the other hand, if we uttered a warning such as was now proposed, we should be committed to intervention if Germany persisted in aggression.

As a serious step, 'the actual crossing of the stream', this proposal indicated a new commitment under certain circumstances. But the Prime Minister strictly limited the responsibility that 'would not bring us up against a tremendous decision on some point which did not affect the independence of Poland'.

In the course of discussions, Lord Maugham, the Lord Chancellor, emphasised that 'we must support Poland if her independence was threatened' on one hand, and ' we should not encourage Poland to go to war with Germany about Danzig' on the other. Chatfield passed on the view of the Chiefs of Staff, that if Germany were to attack Poland, 'we should declare war on Germany'. In the end, the Cabinet agreed that the Prime Minister would declare in the House on 31 March:

in the event of any action which clearly threatened Polish independence, and which the Polish Government accordingly considered it vital to resist with their national forces, His Majesty's Government would feel themselves bound at once to lend the Polish Government all support in their power.[37]

Within two weeks, Britain also gave a similar guarantee to Greece and Romania.[38]

The guarantee to Poland, like the proposal for the Four Power Declaration, was not aimed towards war, as Chamberlain explained during the period when the guarantee was given: 'I am no more a man of war to-day than I was in September . . . I trust that our actions, begun but not concluded, will prove to be the turning-point not towards war, which wins nothing, cures nothing, ends nothing, but towards a more wholesome era, when reason will take the place of force.'[39]

THE ANGLO-FRANCO-SOVIET DISCUSSIONS
The Reluctant Decision on an Alliance with Russia: April–May

The exclusion of Russia from the alliance caused great uneasiness among the Opposition. A day before the declaration of the guarantee to Poland, three Labour leaders, Greenwood, Dalton and Alexander, saw the Prime Minister, stating their 'strong objections to any action being taken which would imply that Russia was being left on one side'. They were critical that 'the Government were prejudiced against Russia and were neglecting a possible source of help'.[40] Churchill and Eden also pushed the Government in the direction of allying itself with Russia with the need to build up a 'Peace Front', Churchill warning in the House on 19 May:

> none of these States in Eastern Europe can maintain themselves for, say, a year's war unless they have behind them the massive, solid backing of a friendly Russia . . . Without any effective Eastern front, there can be no satisfactory defence of our interests in the West, and without Russia there can be no effective Eastern front.[41]

Under such pressure, Chamberlain, concealing his own dislike of Russia, explained to the Opposition that the Government were not 'cold-shouldering Russia – it was the misgivings of Poland and others'.[42] In the end, the position of Russia in the 'Peace Front' was an issue which could not be circumvented. On 10 April, the FO received a report from Kennard, HMG's Ambassador in Warsaw, which was based on a memo by his Military Attaché about the main military considerations in Poland. After analysing Poland's weakness from a military aspect, the local production of armaments and the raw material supplies, the report concluded:

> It seems therefore unlikely that Poland can hope to defend the Corridor or her western frontier, but that she might be compelled eventually to fall back on the Vistula . . . The importance for Poland of a friendly Russia is thus of paramount importance.[43]

Meanwhile, Seeds, the British Ambassador in Moscow, warned the Government that he could not see how Russia would be able to contribute her military assistance effectively towards Poland and Romania if these two countries refused to consider co-operation with Russia. He urged the Government to find some way 'to prevail on Poland and Romania to accept the idea of some form of Soviet military assistance'. His French colleague in Moscow was 'in complete agreement' with him.[44]

In mid-April, the subject was discussed both in the Cabinet and in the FO. In spite of his distrust of Russia, Halifax was 'reluctant' to abandon his efforts to obtain some sort of assistance from Russia.[45] He tried to 'find a way round Russian difficulty' by proposing to the Russian Government that they should make a unilateral declaration of support to any particular State against aggression, if she desired. He told the Cabinet on 13 April, that 'he found it difficult to see on what grounds Russia could refuse to make a statement on these lines'.[46]

Next day, when he discussed this new approach with Cadogan and other FO staff, such as Oliphant, Maurice Ingram and Strang, he did 'not wish to proceed, at present, with his suggestion that we should invite the Polish and Roumanian Govts to give favourable considerations to any unilateral declaration that Russia might make in favourable of Poland and Roumania'. Cadogan thought that this proposal was made 'in order to placate our left wing in England, rather than to obtain any solid military advantage'. Then they worked on a draft telegram that was sent to Seeds late that night.[47] At the same time, they informed the French Government of the British proposal. In their reply, the French said that they would work along the same lines.[48]

When Seeds had meetings with Litvinov, the Soviet Commissar for Foreign Affairs, the latter said that, on considering the British proposal, his Government 'wanted to know how far Great Britain and other countries were prepared to go'. The Soviet Union wanted a treaty to protect itself from Germany, and he asked: 'How do we know that Great Britain will declare war in case of armed aggression? Will she only lodge a protest or not even that?' Besides this, he also wanted to know the attitude of Poland and Romania.[49] A few days later (18 April), Litvinov handed Seeds the Soviet reply. Regarding the British proposal acceptable in principle, the Soviets offered a counter-move that emphasised reciprocity, namely that Britain, France and Russia should make an agreement for mutual assistance, offer all help to States lying between the Baltic and Black Seas and bordering on Russia, discuss promptly the means of giving such help, sign conventions on the military and political aspects simultaneously, and agree not to conclude a separate peace.[50]

As soon as they received the Soviet proposal on the same day, Cadogan held discussions with Halifax, and then wrote a memo for the use of Butler and himself in the FPC the next day. In his memo, Cadogan weighed 'the advantage of a paper commitment by Russia . . . against the disadvantage of associating ourselves openly with Russia'. Based on the information available, he believed that Russia was unlikely to give effective assistance outside her borders, even if she wanted to. Therefore, in his opinion, the disadvantage was outweighed on the grounds that the association with Russia would lose much sympathy from Poland, Romania, Portugal, Spain and Yugoslavia. On the other hand, he realised that 'there is great difficulty in refusing the Soviet offer', because 'the Left in this country may be counted on to make the most of this'. Moreover, he feared that 'if we turn down this proposal, the Soviet might make some "non-intervention" agreement with the German Government'. Despite this, he concluded:

> it seems, on balance, better to refuse an offer that may alienate our friends and reinforce the propaganda of our enemies without bringing in exchange any real material contribution to the strength of our Front.[51]

His memo was much in line with Chamberlain's thinking, and was agreed by the FPC on 19 April.[52] At that meeting, Chatfield again mentioned the report of the Chiefs of Staff of 18 March:

If the U.S.S.R were on our side and Poland neutral, the position would alter in our favour. It should however be noted that the U.S.S.R is today militarily an uncertain quality . . . They do not think that she would take any military action outside her borders but she would strongly resist a direct invasion of her territory . . . With Russia as an ally Germany's position in the Baltic would be difficult and it would be possible to exercise considerable interference with that part of her iron ore supplies from Sweden . . .

He agreed with the British Embassy in Moscow, which had estimated Russia's military quality as being uncertain.

In the course of the discussions, Hoare expressed his opinion:

Poland would be able to offer little military resistance to a German invasion . . . it seemed as if Russia was the only possible source of munitions for Poland and the other countries of Eastern Europe.

He suggested that the Chiefs of Staff should be required to produce another report on the military value of Russian assistance. Inskip (Dominion Secretary), put forward the similar view that as a large power, Russia, if she meant business, 'would be of some considerable military value'. The Prime Minister, however, summed up that all the information suggested that Russia was of 'little military value for offensive purpose'. He did not agree that due to the need for munitions from the smaller Eastern European States, it was necessary to sign a definite military alliance between Britain, France and Russia. Not only would an alliance with Russia raise difficulties in Poland, it might also be an unnecessary provocation to Germany, which ought to be avoided. With this strong current of appeasement at the back of his mind, he suggested that in 'not turning down the Russian proposal we should endeavour to convey the impression that the time for a military alliance was not yet ripe'. In conclusion, the FPC approved Chamberlain's line, and instructed the Chiefs of Staff to submit an appreciation of Russia's military strength.[53]

Over the next few days, the British and French Governments communicated with each other about their replies to the Soviet proposal. Cadogan saw the French Ambassador, and requested that France hold onto its reply until it had consulted the British Government. On 21 April, Halifax asked Phipps to transfer to the French the draft of the British reply, which turned down the Soviet proposal on the grounds that 'it takes too little account of practical difficulties', particularly that Poland would object to a tripartite agreement providing Soviet assistance to her, whether she wanted it or not. The British Government therefore insisted on its own original proposal of 14 April: the suggestion of a Russian unilateral declaration.[54] The French reaction was somewhat confusing to the British policy-makers, because it 'entirely' agreed with the British criticism of the Soviet proposal on one hand, but supported a tripartite agreement on the other.[55]

Meanwhile, the Chiefs of Staff worked on the report under the guidelines of the FPC, which had simply asked them to estimate the Soviet military value without discussing the question of a guarantee, since political arguments against an alliance with Russia had already outweighed possible military advantages in ministers' eyes.[56] Their conclusion was circulated to the FPC and Cabinet: Russia could actively assist France and Britain in war, which would, apart from giving military aid to their allies on the Eastern Front, be by naval action in the Baltic. In theory, she could involve 130 divisions, but in practice, she could only mobilise about 30. The Chiefs of Staff therefore advised:

> the military assistance which Russia could bring to bear was not nearly as great as certain quarters represented it to be . . .
>
> We should not act in such a way as to forgo the chance of Russian help in war: we should not jeopardise the common front with Poland, and we should not jeopardise the cause of peace.

This certainly met the ministers' desires, and strengthened their arguments against an alliance with Russia.

When they considered the French proposal along with the British reply to Russia at the meetings on 25 and 26 April, neither Chamberlain nor Halifax liked the French idea. The Foreign Secretary remarked that it 'would certainly involve very great discouragement of all our potential friends', because 'a tripartite Agreement must involve at least indirect Soviet assistance to Poland'. The French proposal 'was therefore open to the objection which they had themselves argued'. Chamberlain agreed that the French proposal was unacceptable, and emphasised that the British proposals had been that Russia 'should limit its assistance to those countries which desired it, and that the desired assistance should be given in such manner as would be found most convenient'. Halifax concluded that the time was not ripe for a tripartite agreement, and they proposed to ask the Soviet Government to give further consideration to the British proposal of 14 April. 'It was most needed and did not ask the Soviet Government to do more than to come in when we were already involved.' Although he realised that this policy 'would be violently attacked', he thought that with the latest report of the Chiefs of Staff, they had 'a good case to defend'.[57]

Two days later, he informed the French Government that its proposal would 'raise serious difficulty', and asked it to support the British line. On 3 May, France agreed to the British proposal without much enthusiasm.[58]

In the meantime, he had discussions with Churchill, who 'was entirely in favour of the proposed tri-partite pact'. But Halifax told his colleague that he worried that such a pact 'would make war inevitable'. On the other hand, he was also disturbed by the danger that 'a refusal of Russia's offer might even throw her into Germany's arms'.[59]

On 5 May, the FPC considered the final draft of the reply to the Soviet proposal. The Foreign Secretary repeated his warning to ministers that 'it was most important that the negotiation should not be broken off at this juncture'. However, he insisted on the foregoing lines, on the grounds that:

> If to the somewhat loose and indefinite unilateral declaration we joined a firm and definite 'no separate peace' tripartite agreement we should be changing the whole basis of our policy and risking the alienation of our friends . . . If war was certain he would not care who helped him: but if there were a 5 per cent chance of peace, he did not wish to jeopardise it by associating with a country in whom he had no confidence.

Chamberlain agreed with Halifax, and suggested that before submitting the reply to the Soviet Government, Seeds should be asked to find out whether Soviet foreign policy had changed due to the replacement of Litvinov by Molotov.[60]

On 9 May, Seeds obtained an assurance from Molotov, the new Soviet Commissar of Foreign Affairs, that the Soviet policy was unchanged, and the Soviet proposal 'still held good', while the Ambassador handed over the British proposal.[61]

During this period, the FO received some information about a German–Russian *rapprochement*.[62] Halifax 'found it difficult to attach much credence' to these reports. He judged that it 'might be spread by persons who desired to drive us into making a pact with Russia'. Although he realised that the time might soon come for Staff talks with Russia, 'he would prefer to postpone this as long as possible'.

At the same time, Chatfield asked the Chiefs of Staff to report on the balance of strategic value to Britain in war of having Spain as an enemy or Russia as an ally. The military experts gave their observations as follows:

> The active enmity of Spain would greatly weaken our position in the Western Mediterranean and would threaten our Atlantic communications. On the other hand, Spain was suffering from war-weariness, and a blockade of her coasts would, in the long run, bring her to a stand-still.
>
> If Russia were an active and whole-hearted ally, she would be of great assistance, particularly in containing substantial enemy forces and in supplying war material to our other allies in Eastern Europe. But, on the assumption that if Russia was not with us, she was at least neutral . . . the advantages of an alliance with Russia would not offset the disadvantages of the open hostility of Spain. On the other hand, the greatest danger we had to face would be a combination of Russia and the Axis Powers.[63]

The Soviet reply arrived within a week (on 15 May). The Soviet Government concluded that the British proposal 'cannot serve as a basis' for negotiations, on the grounds that it lacked reciprocity. They required that Britain and France should join Russia in guaranteeing the Baltic States – Finland, Estonia and Latvia – as Russia joined them in guaranteeing Poland and Romania.[64]

Before the Soviet proposal was considered by the FPC, the FO prepared a new draft agreement which suggested future or immediate military consultations with Russia. On the morning of 16 May, Sargent, authorised by Halifax, asked the Minister of Defence about the view of the Chiefs of Staff on the new draft. This consultation gave the military experts a chance to make comprehensive observations on the situation. They were now moving over to the view that Soviet aid would be more effective than they had previously thought.[65] At the FPC meeting the same day, Chatfield told ministers about the new observations of the military experts:

We should enter into an agreement with Russia on a reciprocal basis for mutual support . . . Great Britain could be attached in many ways directly or indirectly, but apart from Poland and Roumania, Soviet Russia could only be attacked on the Baltic . . . Such an attack would be most difficult to undertake with any hope of success . . . In these circumstances we had much to gain and very little to lose . . .

The Chiefs of Staff warned:

Failure to reach agreement with Russia might result in Russia standing aside in a future European war and hoping thereby to secure advantages from the exhaustion of the Western nations.

They emphasised that Russia should not, in any circumstances, become allied with Germany. Chatfield drew attention to 'the weak strategical position of Poland', and 'the unlikelihood of Poland being able to put up any serious resistance to a German invasion'.

Neither Chamberlain nor Halifax liked the views of the military experts this time. The Prime Minister doubted whether their conclusion was based on an assumption that 'we were unlikely to get any agreement with Russia unless the agreement took the form of full pact such as Russia was demanding'. He was critical that their 'advice differed from the advice previously given'. Nor did the Foreign Secretary believe that Russia could give much help to the Western Powers. Moreover, he felt an alliance with Russia would offend Poland and Romania. In this case, 'while the military arguments for a pact were sound the political arguments against a pact were more formidable'. In addition, he did not want to fight for Russia over the Baltic States by arguing that these States did not want Russian assistance.

Nevertheless, many ministers, such as Chatfield, Hoare, Stanley and Cadogan, fully realised the importance of an alliance with Russia, and insisted on going further to meet her demands.[66] In spite of this strong opposing view, the Prime Minister still 'wished to limit our commitments to attacks through Poland and Romania . . . rather than consent to a triple alliance to include Russia'. However, he agreed to give further consideration to the issue.[67] Halifax held the same ground. Based on the record of a conversation between Vansittart and Maisky, the Soviet Ambassador, on 16 May, he suggested that Vansittart should have another talk with Maisky, on the following lines: the British

Government objected to including the four Baltic States within the scope of an arrangement, but it undertook to institute staff talks.[68]

According to these lines, the FO drew up a formula on 17 May for Vansittart's use in his further talk with Maisky on the same day. At that meeting, the Soviet Ambassador's reaction was 'not too unfriendly' and he promised to submit this formula to Moscow at once.[69] However, two days later, Maisky informed Halifax that the new formula was not acceptable to his government, on the grounds that the only basis on which Russia was prepared to proceed was that of a tripartite pact.[70]

On 19 May, Halifax gave the FPC an account of the Vansittart-Maisky discussions and informed it of the Russian refusal of the new formula. Obviously, it was high time it chose between alliance with Russia and a breakdown of negotiations. The FPC was now divided into two sides: those for an alliance included Hoare, Stanley, MacDonald, Inskip, Chatfield and Burgin (Minister without Portfolio), while those against were Chamberlain, Halifax, Simon and Morrison (Chancellor of the Duchy of Lancaster). The Prime Minister even said that he would 'resign rather than sign alliance with Soviet'.[71] Despite distrusting Russia, Halifax was more moderate than Chamberlain, and took the view that 'we had gone so far that the little more would not make much difference in its effect on Hitler'. Like him, Cadogan wrote: 'My opinion (much against my will) is hardening in favour of former.'[72]

In the FO Malkin (Legal Adviser) tried to draft a formula closer to Russian demands 'without being an alliance', but it was not very successful.[73] Communicating with Halifax, Cadogan started to prepare a memo on 20 May for the FPC to weigh up again the pros and cons of the proposed Anglo-Soviet Pact.[74] This time, he understood the importance of Russia more clearly than he had in April:

> there is no alternative between agreeing to a three-Power pact . . . and allowing the present negotiations to fail.
>
> . . . to build up a peace front to the East and South-east of Germany . . . Poland was the key, and Poland's position would be precarious in face of a hostile or perhaps even of a neutral Soviet Union. Our only practicable lines of communication with Poland in case of war would lie through Russian territory.
>
> We therefore wished to be assured of at least the benevolent neutrality of the Soviet Union, and better still of the probability of assistance being afforded by that country to Poland and Roumania in case of attack.

The disadvantages were, as he pointed out, that a tripartite alliance with Russia might 'mark a definite change of policy':

> His Majesty's Government had finally given up all hope of arriving at a settlement with Germany and that accordingly they had reached the conclusion that war was inevitable and were therefore marshalling their forces . . . it might be assumed that our association with the Soviet Government would still further infuriate him [Hitler] and impel him to aggressive action.

However, he concluded that an alliance with Russia might:

> be the only way to avert war. Germany is impressed only by a show of strength, and Italian policy has always been to reinsure with the stronger side.
>
> Therefore . . . a tripartite pact with the Soviet Union, if that is the only means by which we can be assured of the latter's support, is a necessary condition for the consolidation of the front which we have been trying to create.
>
> If the negotiations break down . . . the German Government may be encouraged to think that they are free to embark on adventures in Danzig or elsewhere in Eastern Europe.

The proposal he formulated was to meet the Soviet requirements in principle.[75]

On 22 May, he showed the draft to Chamberlain. The latter had now come, 'very reluctantly', to accept the idea of a tripartite pact. However, he would rather put this alliance under a 'League umbrella' suggested by Hoare, so that it 'might later be modified' and 'Britain would not be tied up for all time with the Soviet Government.' Although he did not think the idea would help very much, Cadogan promised Chamberlain that he would draft something along these lines.[76]

On 24 May, the Cabinet attended in full to consider the FO's memo and to make a final decision on the reply to Russia. Halifax diagnosed that 'reciprocity' in the Russian demands meant:

> first, they were not prepared to be put in a position of inequality as compared with the British, French and Polish Governments, which had concluded agreements on a reciprocal basis; secondly Russia feared that Roumania and Poland might collapse and that,

if this happened, the condition which we made that these countries should resist German aggression would not be fulfilled. Russia would thus be left face to face with Germany without any assurance of support from us.

He told the ministers: 'having gone so far in the negotiations, a breakdown now would have a definitely unfavourable effect'. Although he disliked Russia, he had to contemplate that 'we should be prepared to enter into a direct mutual guarantee agreement with the Soviet Government' because 'Hitler was more likely to be provoked into starting a war if we failed, as a result of a breakdown with Russia'. As to the story about *rapprochement* between Germany and Russia, he thought this time that it 'was not one which could be altogether disregarded'.[77]

Supporting Halifax's view, Chamberlain argued for himself that he had adopted the negative attitude in alliance with Russia due to 'considerable misgiving' from Poland, Romania and the Dominions. He 'now favoured, in substance, the conclusion of an agreement with Russia on the lines of her proposals'. But he added that the tripartite pact should be put under the principles of the Covenant.

However, although they had decided to ally with Russia, it did not mean that they were to abandon appeasement. Before the meeting was over, the ministers considered the suggestion:

when we had strengthened our position by making an agreement with the Russian Government, we should take the initiative in a renewal of the search for appeasement. When we had so strengthened our position as to have constituted the greatest practicable deterrent against aggression, we should be in a position to make such an approach from strength, and there was more likelihood that Germany would be willing to listen to us in such circumstances. Our approach might take the form of indicating that we had no intention to encircle Germany economically and that we were ready at any time to discuss any matters in dispute . . . if it was accepted it would constitute an important step towards appeasement.

Halifax thought that Germany should take the initiative this time. However, Inskip doubted whether Hitler could do so. He suggested: 'we could afford to take the initiative ourselves'.[78]

The next day, the new British proposal, drafted on the proposed lines, was sent to Moscow. Although it placed the tripartite agreement on the basis of reciprocity, the British Government refused to name either Poland, Romania or the Baltic States in the treaty.[79]

Conversations Dragged Out: June–July

When he studied the British proposal, of 25 May, Molotov thought it unacceptable, on the grounds that the proposal left him with the impression that co-operation depending on the League of Nations implied that the Western Powers 'were not interested in obtaining concrete results'. Although Seeds explained again and again that that only meant 'the spirit' and 'principles' of the Covenant, the Soviet leader simply did not listen.[80] On 2 June, Molotov handed the British and French Ambassadors the Soviet counter-proposal, in which the Russians modified the principle to the end that the mutual assistance should be immediate. They insisted that the Western Powers should not only extend their guarantee to Latvia, Estonia and Finland, but also that the three powers should name all guaranteed States (i.e. Belgium, Greece, Turkey, Romania, Poland and the three Baltic States) in the Treaty. In addition they demanded no separate peace, and conclusion of both a political and a military agreement simultaneously.[81]

At the meeting of the FPC on 5 June, Halifax pointed out that if Britain and France offered a guarantee to the Baltic States, Russia should guarantee Holland and Switzerland, which were vital to the security of the Western Powers. Chamberlain thought that 'we ought to refuse' the Russian demand, because the Baltic States did not desire a guarantee either from the Western Powers or from Russia.[82]

Before the meeting, the Foreign Secretary had the idea of asking Russia to send a representative to Paris or London to discuss the matter directly. Corbin, the French Ambassador, suggested that a better course might be to give their own representatives in Moscow 'precise instructions', on which they could press forward with negotiations more quickly.[83] Halifax took his idea and suggested that the FPC send some kind of mission to Moscow, and recall Seeds to London for consultation. At the Cabinet meeting of 7 June, the ministers first chose Sir William Malkin, Legal Adviser at the FO, as the representative to Moscow. However, the Foreign Secretary told the Prime Minister that since his chief legal assistant was ill, Malkin could not be spared from London. Therefore, both of them agreed to recall Seeds to receive further instructions.[84] Unfortunately, Seeds telegraphed back and said that he had succumbed to influenza and was unable to return.[85]

In the meantime, Eden went to see Halifax and suggested that the latter should go himself. Since Halifax declined, Eden volunteered to see Stalin. The Foreign Secretary 'seemed to like it', but after consultation with Chamberlain, the Prime Minister rejected the suggestion.[86] The top British leaders were insistent that they wished to appoint a junior official to Moscow, because they thought that: 'it would give the impression that no great political difficulties were outstanding but that agreement in substance had been reached and that it only remained to draft the agreement and settle the detail'. Halifax said that 'this kind of business was better handled by Ambassadors'.[87] In spite of the French disagreement and Eden's suggestion, they decided not to send a minister, but sent Strang, the Head of the Central Department, instead.[88]

Before he left, Strang attended the FPC meeting on 9 June, at which the ministers equipped him with various memos and instructions. The British representatives should tell Russia clearly of their standpoint towards the outstanding problems between the two sides: Britain and France did not agree to guarantee the Baltic States, nor did they agree to enumerate the names of all guaranteed countries in the treaty; if Russia insisted on the above the Western Powers would try to bargain for Russia to offer a guarantee to Holland and Switzerland; the Western Powers suggested that the political agreement would be signed before a military agreement; they rejected the Russian proposal regarding no separate peace agreement. The key instruction given to Strang was:

> The draft treaty should be as short and simple in its terms as possible. It is better that agreement should be quickly reached than that time should be spent in trying to cover every contingency . . . this may leave loopholes in the text . . . but those disadvantages are . . . less serious than the elaboration of detailed provisions which, if the treaty ever came to be executed, might be found, in practice, to bind His Majesty's Government more effectively than the Soviet Government.

The Prime Minister exhorted that:

> unless we showed that we were prepared to drive a hard bargain, we should necessarily get the worst of the bargain. He did not

think that Russia could now afford to break off negotiation, and we could therefore afford to take a fairly stiff line.[89]

Strang arrived in Moscow on 14 June, and the new round of negotiations started the following day. The British representatives, supported by their French colleagues, indicated the proposed line to Molotov. The Soviet Foreign Minister, on behalf of his Government, insisted on naming the guaranteed countries and no separate peace. He said that Russia 'would prefer to postpone the whole question of guarantees . . . and to confine Treaty to an arrangement of mutual assistance among the three signatories to operate in the event of direct aggression on them', if the Western Powers did not agree to name the Baltic States in the Protocol.[90] To satisfy Russia's preference, Naggiar, the French Ambassador, suggested that these names could be mentioned in a separate document which need not be published. In his telegram to London on 17 June, Seeds favoured the French view that the two Governments had better meet Russia's demands over the Baltic States.[91]

In the week from 20 June onwards, the FPC and Cabinet met several times to consider the Soviet demands. Although they unanimously agreed that a breakdown over these problems was not favourable to the British interest, the ministers had various arguments on the signature of a simple tripartite agreement. Chatfield was for such a treaty, on the grounds that it 'would at least have the effect that it would prevent Soviet Russia from making a Pact with Germany'. Hoare inclined to support his idea, while Oliver Stanley disagreed with it, pointing out that such a treaty would mean 'a complete breakdown of the negotiations'. 'If war resulted Russia would not be involved.' Therefore, it 'was bound to be inoperative, and would serve no useful purpose'. Although they thought there was something in the view that was in favour of a simple tripartite agreement, the Prime Minister and Foreign Secretary gave more weight to Stanley's argument. Chamberlain told the Committee that the disadvantage of a simple tripartite agreement was 'not only that public opinion would think that the negotiations had, in fact, failed but that Russia would be left in a very dissatisfied and sulky state'. Halifax warned that such a treaty:

would satisfy the tests of simplicity and brevity but it was open to the serious objection that in certain circumstances it would leave it in the hands of Russia to determine whether or not an act of aggression bringing the arrangement into operation had taken place.

It seemed that in order to break the deadlock, they had no choice but to meet the Russian demands. After some discussion, they agreed to accept the Russian point of view with regard to 'no separate peace', provided a settlement was reached on all other issues. As to naming the countries concerned in the treaty, Halifax told the Committee that if they did not satisfy Russia on this point, the negotiations were bound to break down. In spite of his dislike of the Russian demand, he would take Naggiar's suggestion of including these names in a secret protocol. But he proposed to do so on the condition that Russia must agree to offer a guarantee to Holland and Switzerland. His proposal was generally supported by the ministers. However, it was realised that there was little difference between enumerating the guaranteed States in the treaty itself and including them in a secret protocol, on the grounds that the contents of the protocol would soon leak out. Even so, Chamberlain stressed that 'it was very desirable, if possible, to refrain from including any names in the Treaty itself'.[92]

Being informed of the above line, Bonnet, the French Foreign Minister, suggested some changes in the wording of the proposal, and urged that 'the Agreement with Russia should be concluded at once'.[93] On 1 July, the British and French Ambassadors started to communicate with Molotov again about the latest British proposal. Molotov agreed to include the names of countries in a secret protocol, but he refused to make any commitment to Holland and Switzerland. In addition, the Soviet Foreign Minister raised a new point of 'direct or indirect' aggression in the treaty, namely that the guarantee would be applied to the countries concerned 'in the event either of direct aggression or indirect aggression, under which latter term is to be understood an internal *coup d'état* or a reversal of policy in the interest of the aggressor'.[94]

The information from Moscow made the FO staff feel that Russia had become 'incredibly tiresome'. In the course of discussions at departmental meetings, both Halifax and Cadogan were in a bad mood. The Foreign Secretary and his subordinates were 'mulish' on the Soviets.[95] On 4 July, the FPC met. Circulating the telegrams from Moscow among the Committee members, Halifax made it clear to the ministers that he firmly opposed the Russian definition of 'indirect aggression', because it 'was very dangerous and capable of very wide application'. He laid down two alternatives for negotiations before the Committee: to break off, or to fall back on the limited tripartite pact, of which he favoured the latter as 'our main object in the negotiations was to prevent Russia from engaging herself with Germany'. He criticised those who favoured continuing the negotiations, saying that they must realise that 'this would mean interminable discussions', but 'throughout the negotiations the attitude of the Soviet Government had not been helpful'. He believed that Hitler 'rated Russia low from the military point of view'. Even without Russian assistance, Germany would still have to face Poland, France and Britain. However, he tended to agree with the omission of Holland and Switzerland from the list.

In the course of the discussions, the ministers generally agreed with the view that they should ask Russia to abandon her definition of 'indirect aggression', and in return Britain would exclude Holland and Switzerland from the treaty. With regard to the signing of a limited tripartite agreement, opinions were divided. Some ministers, such as Oliver Stanley, MacDonald (the Colonies) and Morrison (Chancellor of the Duchy of Lancaster), worried that 'such a pact would be a ridiculously small mouse for the mountains to have produced'. The Prime Minister supported his Foreign Minister, however, and formulated a conclusion for the Committee:

> that the Soviet Government should drop their definition of indirect aggression and that we should abandon our insistence on the inclusion of Switzerland and the Netherlands . . . or that there should be a Tripartite Pact.[96]

After the meeting, Cadogan, Sargent and Malkin drafted the telegram to Moscow. Chamberlain dictated his own definition of 'aggression', which turned out to be:

> the word 'aggression' is to be understood as covering action accepted by the State in question under threat of force by another Power and involving the abandonment by it of its independence or neutrality (list of States).

With his approval, the telegrams were sent to Seeds on 6 July.[97]

The British and French Ambassadors took action on this instruction on 8 and 9 July. In his dispatches about the meetings with Molotov, Seeds reported that the Soviet Government not only insisted on the inclusion of indirect aggression, but also redefined it as follows:

> 'indirect aggression' covers action accepted by any of the above mentioned States under threat of force by another Power, or without

any such threat, involving the use of territory and forces of the State in question for purposes of aggression against that State or against one of the contracting parties, and consequently involving the loss of, by that State, its independence or violation of its neutrality.[98]

In addition, Molotov stressed that the political covenant and military agreement should be signed simultaneously, on the grounds that 'without a military Agreement the political Agreement would be a mere empty declaration'. As a concession, he accepted that the political agreement would be initialled and then the staff talks could start. Both Seeds and the French Ambassador observed that the Soviet Government would not be prepared to negotiate a limited tripartite agreement 'in the event of failure to conclude the wider Agreement'.[99]

The Soviet proposal provoked intensive discussions at the FPC meeting on 10 July. Halifax was completely against the new Soviet definition of 'indirect aggression' because he thought it gave the Soviet Government 'a wide right of intervention in the internal affairs of another country'. He told his colleagues that the French 'were much more elastic in regard to the question of indirect aggression', but they emphasised that if military negotiations failed, no political agreement would be signed. The Foreign Secretary suggested the possible course that the Western Powers would yield on the point that staff talks 'should be concluded before the political agreement was officially signed', on condition that Russia accepted the British definition of 'aggression'. The ministers agreed generally, and Chamberlain said that 'he himself had failed to find any satisfactory formula based on M. Molotoff's formula'. Despite his dislike of staff talks with Russia, he approved of it because he 'did not attach any very great importance' to such discussions. He tended to believe Henderson's latest viewpoint, that 'it would be quite impossible in present circumstances for Germany and Soviet Russia to come together'. Chatfield warned the Committee:

the conclusion of a military agreement with Russia might be found very difficult. Up to the present we had never made a military agreement with another country and it was a grave matter to have to decide in advance . . .

He suggested that if staff talks started, they would have to be conducted at 'high Service level' (probably the Deputy Chiefs of Staff). Halifax explained the real purpose of staff talks with Russia:

when the military conversations had begun no great progress would be made. The conversations would drag on and ultimately each side would accept a general undertaking from the other. In this way, we should have gained time and made the best of a situation from which we could not now escape.

In the end, the Committee decided that it would agree to the Russian proposal that the political and military agreements should be conducted simultaneously as a bargaining point to ask Russia to abandon her definition of 'indirect aggression'.[100]

Nevertheless, when he informed Seeds of this line, Halifax instructed the Ambassador not to offer this concession for the time being, due to 'the strong objections of the French'. Nor did the French agree to fall back on a simple tripartite agreement.[101] After eliminating divergence between Britain and France, Halifax instructed Seeds again on 15 July that the Ambassador should inform Molotov that the Western Powers were ready to start military discussions without waiting for signature of the agreement, on condition that Molotov abandoned his demand for simultaneous signing of the political and military agreements and accepted the British definition of 'aggression'.[102]

Two days later, the two ambassadors had a meeting with Molotov. Both sides persisted in their own definitions of 'aggression'. Molotov used the collapse of Czechoslovakia as an example to support his argument. However, he said that the Soviet Government placed an emphasis on a single politico-military agreement, namely that military obligations and contributions should have been clearly settled before this agreement was signed. He implied that if this desire was satisfied, the definition of 'indirect aggression' would be 'a technical matter of secondary importance'.[103] The French informed their British partners that they wanted to accept the Russian proposal for a single politico-military agreement 'without further bargaining'. They also suggested that they should go as far as possible to agree with Russia a definition of 'indirect aggression'. The most important point, they stressed, was to come to agreement with Russia at once.[104]

Nonetheless, at the FPC meeting of 19 July, the ministers were still stuck on the definition of 'indirect aggression'. Due to pressure from the Opposition, the Prime Minister realised that if no decision one way or the other was reached, considerable trouble would result. The Foreign Secretary suggested sending to Moscow 'someone of Ministerial rank', to speed up the negotiations, but the Prime Minister rejected this on the grounds that 'not only would this involve a considerable delay but it would be humiliating to us'. As for the staff talks, he warned the Committee that 'the military provisions of a treaty would be bound to cause serious trouble'. Chatfield, however, showed no objection to meeting the Russian demands. Finally, the Committee agreed to the suggestion by Chamberlain and Halifax that the military discussions with Russia should not start until agreement on the political articles had been reached.[105]

Nevertheless, in his telegram to Seeds on 21 July, Halifax seemed to exceed the Committee decision, and instructed the Ambassador:

> I would be prepared in the last resort to agree to the immediate initiation of military conversations without waiting for final agreement on Articles and Protocol now under discussion. I do not like this and should only wish to advance this suggestion if danger of breakdown after you have stated our requirements seems imminent.[106]

He left the decision to Seeds' discretion, whereas the Ambassador did not want to use 'the last resort'.[107] In their meeting of 23 July, Molotov urged the British Government that the three Powers should open staff talks in Moscow immediately. He repeated that as soon as the military negotiations began, its definition of 'indirect aggression' or the other outstanding points would not give rise to insuperable difficulties. Under these circumstances, on 25 July Halifax authorised Seeds to inform the Russians that the British Government agreed to the Soviet suggestion, but at the same time insisted that the three Powers should continue to conclude the political agreement.[108]

During this period, while discussions with the Soviets were dragging on, the British policy-makers tried to warm up relations with Germany. Various dispatches from Henderson advised the Government to press the Poles into making a concession to Germany over Danzig.[109] On 18 July, Wilson urged Wohltat, the German Commissioner of the Four Year Plan, that Germany should take an initiative to restore the friendship between the two countries, and explained that the real implication in Chamberlain's and Halifax's recent speeches was that 'there was still an opportunity for co-operation . . . so soon as conditions had been created that would make that co-operation feasible'. This was, according to Wohltat's understanding, approved by Chamberlain.[110] Meanwhile, Hudson (Secretary of the Department of

Overseas Trade) had a meeting with Wohltat, offering a large British loan to Germany if she mended her ways.[111] Yet at the same time, the British Government declined to approve a loan to Poland which the latter needed to equip her forces.[112] Moreover, during the communications of July and August, they put forward to the German representative a new proposal for an Anglo-German settlement.[113]

The Military Discussions in Moscow: August

Although it was an inevitable consequence that had long been foreseen, the staff talks with Russia had been poorly prepared before they came on the agenda. When he replied to Halifax's question about military communications with Russia at the FPC meeting of 19 July, Chamberlain said:

> he did not think that the Chiefs of Staff Committee need consider the question immediately. He understood that the Sub-Committee had other and even more urgent important questions before it.[114]

A few days later, due to the Russian demand, Halifax communicated to the French Government the proposal of embarking on staff talks with Russia. The French response was positive, and they suggested that military officers should depart in the next three or four days.[115] At the Cabinet meeting of 26 July, the Foreign Secretary said that since staff talks were regarded by Russia 'as a test of our good faith', he thought that opening these talks 'would have a good effect on world opinion'. Chamberlain instructed that 'negotiations with Russia would continue to drag on until we made it clear that we were prepared to face the risk of a breakdown'. The Cabinet generally agreed that:

> our representatives should be instructed to proceed very slowly with the conversations until a political pact had been concluded. In particularly, it would be desirable that we should not allow Russia to start the conversations by obtaining information as to our own plans, but should rather endeavour to secure that the Russians let our representatives know what they could do to help e.g. Poland.[116]

Based on these lines, the Deputy Chiefs of Staff Committee and the Committee of Imperial Defence drew up a lengthy document for the guidance of the Military Mission. The formula was that until political agreement was reached, the delegation should 'go very slowly with the conversations, watching the process of the political negotiations'. In addition, they should state policy in 'the broadest possible terms', although it was realised that the Russians were bound to want details. As for the possible question of the Polish and Romanian unwillingness to have Soviet troops on their territory, the delegation should persuade the Soviet Mission to accept the view that an invasion by Germany 'would quickly alter their outlook'.[117]

On 31 July, Chamberlain stated in the House that the British and French Military Missions were going to Moscow as soon as possible. The British Delegation was headed by Admiral Drax, and the French by General Doumenc.[118] The Anglo-French military team arrived in Moscow on 11 August. When military discussions took place on the next day, Marshal Voroshilov, Head of the Soviet Military Mission, told his Western partners that his Government had empowered him to negotiate and sign a military agreement with the British and French Delegations. He was disappointed by the fact that Admiral Drax had no written credentials, and that he was not empowered to sign a military agreement. However, the Soviet negotiators 'were really out for business' in the first few talks. They gave quite concrete details about what Russia could contribute in the event of German aggression. Under these circumstances, Admiral Drax, supported by Seeds, asked for authority to depart from vague generalities and 'go-slowly' policies, and to discuss the British plan more openly.[119] Halifax, with Chatfield's agreement, sent a dispatch to Moscow on 15 August, cancelling the 'go-slowly' instructions and allowing the delegation to explore the British military plan with certain reservations. This instruction was carried out on the following day,[120] but it did not bring a very encouraging result because the negotiations had come to deadlock two days earlier, on 14 August, when Voroshilov put forward some questions to the Western delegations: in the event of German aggression would the Soviet Forces be allowed to move through Polish territory, for example the Wilno Gap, Galicia, and would they be allowed to use Romanian territory? The Soviet Marshal demanded 'straightforward answers to these cardinal questions'. Without an unequivocal answer, he thought that 'continuance of the military conversations would be useless'.[121]

After discussions with their French colleagues, Seeds and Drax sent separate telegrams to Halifax and Chatfield on 15 August. Seeds suggested that since it was a 'fundamental problem on which military talks will succeed or fail',

> [the] French General Staff should get in touch with Polish General Staff and obtain their consent to the three delegations here working out general plans (for eventual action on something like Soviet lines in case of a war when Poland would agree to Russian assistance) to which Poles would meanwhile turn a blind eye.

The French Ambassador in Moscow also sent a strong recommendation to his Government.[122]

When the FO received these dispatches, Strang consulted with Halifax and Cadogan. The Foreign Secretary considered that Britain and France 'should now concert in an approach to the Polish and Romanian Governments and put the situation frankly to them'. In the Polish case, they 'should not press M. Beck for an immediate response', but the Polish General Staff should consider these questions. Strang sent the telegram to Warsaw which instructed the British Ambassador to support his French colleagues in approaching the Polish Government accordingly.[123] However, the Poles' reaction was unfavourable, although they agreed to further consideration.[124] On 21 August, Cambon, Minister at the French Embassy in London, informed Strang that the French Government had decided 'not to take literally the objections of M. Beck', and instructed General Doumenc to give the Soviet Delegation 'an affirmative answer in principle' to the questions. The French thought this was the only way to get around the deadlock, and asked the British Government to give the same instruction to its delegation.[125] In his minute, Strang pointed out that although they 'have gone ahead without consulting us', 'we cannot disavow the French Government'. He suggested that a similar instruction should be sent to the British Delegation, to support the French. Cadogan saw this minute, but no action was taken on it because Halifax did not feel it right to do so.[126]

On 22 August, General Doumenc asked for a meeting with Voroshilov. When he told him that he had heard from the French Government that the Polish reply to the passage of Soviet troops was 'in the affirmative', the Soviet Marshal was not convinced. Voroshilov insisted that the negotiations could not continue because 'the position of Poland, Romania and Great Britain is still unknown'.[127] On the same day, the news came out that von Ribbentrop would visit Moscow to sign a Soviet–German Non-aggression Pact, which completely surprised the Polish Government. Beck told the British and French Ambassadors in Warsaw on 23 August:

> in the event of common action against German aggression collaboration, under technical conditions to be settled subsequently between Poland and U.S.S.R., is not excluded.[128]

As for the achievement of Soviet–German *rapprochement*, Chamberlain seemed 'quite firm about its not altering things'.[129] When the Cabinet discussed the situation on 22 August, Hoare even said: 'we might be able to turn the German–Soviet Pact to good account in connection with our Far Eastern policy'. Being in accord with him, Halifax thought that 'the conclusion of the Pact might also be helpful to us in our dealings with Spain'. He commented that the pact 'was perhaps not of very great importance in itself', but its moral effect 'at the present time would be very great'. However, he realised that 'no useful purpose would be served by continuing the military conversations'.[130] That evening, Chamberlain wrote to Hitler, indicating that Britain would fight for Poland, but he could not see 'that there is anything in the questions arising between Germany and Poland which could not and should not be solved without the use of force'.[131]

From 22 to 24 August, Halifax kept asking Seeds to enquire of the Soviets whether they wanted to continue the negotiation. Molotov's reply, which came on the next day, was negative.[132]

A few days after the Three Power Negotiations broke off, the Second World War broke out.

CONCLUSION

Appeasers declare that since they discussed Hitler's real intentions in 1939, they were prepared to fight for Poland. Historical evidence shows that they do not tell the whole truth, because although they knew the German ambitions, they were not determined to fight a war. The guarantee to Poland was a hasty and ill-prepared deterrent, which aimed to convince Hitler rather than fight him. If he continued to behave as he had previously, his aggression would be resisted, but if he gave up the abuse of force, his rational demands would still be considered favourably. The deterrent had political, moral and psychological value, rather than a military one. That was why, during this period, British rearmament, despite a certain increase, amounted to only 7 per cent of the national income – one-fifth of German armament spending in the same period. Chamberlain was unwilling to prepare for a war he had never accepted as inevitable. He believed that the guarantee itself would deter Hitler, so there was no need to carry it out. As soon as Hitler was convinced, he would go on to find a way of 'meeting German claims while safeguarding Poland's independence', as he said the guarantee was: 'the turning-point not towards war . . . but towards a more wholesome era, when reason will take the place of force'.[133] Therefore, the guarantee to Poland was an attempt to make certain policy changes within the scope of appeasement. By deterring Hitler's abuse of force and convincing him to use peaceful means, it aimed to create a new and safer situation in which the Western Powers could search for and reach a settlement with Germany.

The guarantee was a failure because it did not achieve its aim of deterring Hitler. Nor did it even convince Hitler that Britain would fight. On 22 August, when he instructed his generals to launch war on Poland, the Führer said:

> I have but one worry, namely that Chamberlain or some other such pig of a fellow ('Saukerl') will come at the last moment with proposals or with ratting ('Umfall'). He will fly down the stairs, even if I shall personally have to trample on his belly in the eyes of the photographers.
>
> No, it is too late for this. The attack upon and the destruction of Poland begins Saturday [26 August], early.[134]

Partly because they did not expect to actually carry out the guarantee, the British Government did not place great weight on Soviet military assistance to Poland. This was one of the reasons for British hesitation in allying with Russia. This hesitation did major harm to the Three Power negotiations. Regarding the appeasers' argument which charges the Soviets with causing the failure of the talks, it contains only a partial truth. Churchill, known for his anti-communist standpoint, showed a thorough understanding of Soviet policy when he wrote in his memoirs:

> On the Soviet side it must be said that their vital need was to hold the deployment positions of the German armies as far to the West as possible so as to give the Russians more time for assembling

their forces from all parts of their immense empire . . . They must be in occupation of the Baltic States and a large part of Poland by force or fraud before they were attacked. If their policy was cold-blooded, it was also at the moment realistic in a high degree.[135]

Indeed, although their definition of 'indirect aggression' was right in theory, it was unrealistic in strategy, because the Western Powers could not stop Russia from interfering with the independence of the Baltic States in any way if she wanted. In the early stages of the war, they could not save any of these small countries from becoming Russian prey by applying their correct definition. After all, the British Government had agreed to include these small States in a secret protocol attached to the agreement with Russia without asking their permission. In addition, while the Soviets played their game of duplicity, Britain also arranged a series of discussions with the Germans about a future settlement between the British and German powers.[136] Therefore, the appeasers were not as pure, noble and honest as they seemed. Although Russia should be blamed for withdrawing from the negotiations, the British Government must bear a major responsibility for the breakdown, which resulted mainly from appeasement.

Since the guarantee to Poland was designed to be a political, moral and psychological deterrent, which would lead to the door of new settlement with Germany rather than a war against her, British policy-makers neglected the importance of Russian military assistance in the East, and excluded her completely from the picture at an early stage. They were never willing to face the inevitability of war, and worried that an open alliance with the Soviets would raise misgivings from Poland, Romania, the Baltic States and the Dominions (this was found to have been exaggerated),[137] and above all, would irritate Germany. Blinded by their prejudice and contempt for Russia, the British leaders misinterpreted or ignored military advice in favour of an alliance. They short-sightedly chose Poland as the key ally in the East instead of the Soviet Union, although they were well aware that Russia was one of the strongest powers and she possessed an important strategic position in Eastern Europe. (In fact, Russia possessed some other advantages, such as a vast landmass and terrible cold weather in winter, which had beaten Napoleon.)

All this caused the British to hesitate to ally with the Soviets, while the latter still considered their co-operation with the West as their first choice. Oliver Harvey commented: 'What is in the back of P.M.'s mind and especially of Horace Wilson's is that appeasement will be dead' if alliance with Russia were achieved.[138] From their first approach to Russia (on 20 March) to their final decision to ally with her (on 24 May), the British Government spent more than two months hesitating. If it had not wasted so much time, the Three-Power Agreement would have been concluded well before the Soviet–German Pact.[139]

Even the decision to ally with Russia did not change its idea of appeasement. Its purpose was, as the Cabinet minutes indicate, that 'when we had strengthened our position by making an agreement with the Russian Government, we should take the initiative in a renewal of the search for appeasement'.[140] It went further and further to meet Russian demands, not because it was prepared to set up whole-hearted co-operation with her against aggression, but because it was, under pressure from public opinion, afraid of a breakdown which might result in German–Soviet *rapprochement.*

The failure was also a serious consequence of the pursuit of appeasement in the previous years. If the British Government had started to work on the 'Peace Front' before Munich, it would have been more likely to succeed. Russia had been readier to join in. There would have been sufficient time to solve their problems. Failure to make the guarantee to Czechoslovakia shook the confidence of other countries (including Russia) in Britain. The unilateral guarantee to Poland weakened Britain's position in negotiations with Russia because the Soviets had more options than the Western Powers: they could either join the 'Peace Front' to fight against Germany, take the German side, or keep themselves out of the war. For her own security and interest, Russia was in a favourable position to raise her price again and again until she felt satisfied. The prolonged process of negotiation made the Soviets believe that the Western Powers were unwilling to satisfy Russia completely, but Germany would be able to. (Ironically, the Soviet–German honeymoon did not last very long, following a lightning attack on Russia from her former partner in 1941.)

In addition, decisions by the British policy-makers also had an unfavourable influence on the negotiations. During their discussions with Poland and Romania, their Ministers for Foreign Affairs were invited to London. However, to pursue negotiations with Russia, the FPC sent Strang, a junior official, to Moscow, rather than a minister. This put the British representatives in an unfavourable position. In their negotiations, as Butler described to the FPC: 'Molotov sat aloft enthroned with the two Ambassadors on a much lower level . . .

whenever the Ambassadors attempted to maintain a sustained argument M. Molotov interrupted them by saying that the Soviet Government had given their decision and demanding that they should pass to the next item on the Agenda'. Although the FPC realised that it should have sent a minister, it was now too late.[141] Furthermore, as Head of the British Military Mission, Admiral Drax had no written credentials, nor was he empowered to sign an agreement. His rank was lower than that of Marshal Voroshilov, who had full power to negotiate and sign an agreement. Disappointed by this, the Soviets had good reason to remain suspicious of British motives, and could close down the negotiations.[142] The military discussions were also poorly prepared. Based on the 'go-slowly' policy, the British Delegation was not allowed to explore its plans, whereas the Soviets gave military details. Stalin and Molotov commented on the Three-Power Negotiations in their meeting with von Ribbentrop on the night of 23–24 August that the British Military Mission 'had never told the Soviet Government what it really wanted'.[143] Finally, British leaders had become stuck on the definition of 'indirect aggression' for too long. If they had turned a blind eye to this definition and used it as bait to reel Russia in, rather than use it as a wedge to push her out, conclusion of the Three Power Agreement might have been achieved.

From a strategic point of view, if an alliance with Russia had been successfully concluded, it would have increased the military value of the deterrent against Germany, which might have caused Hitler to hesitate in launching war on Poland. Even if she overran Poland quickly, Germany would have been involved in a two-front war at the very beginning. Failure to build an alliance with Russia was a great strategic mistake and loss: without Russian assistance, the Polish defence was broken like a paper wall by a German lightning attack. Hitler successfully avoided risking a two-front war. On the other hand, according to the secret protocol attached to the Soviet–German Pact,[144] Russia joined Germany in the partition of Poland, and obtained a free hand to deal with the Baltic States on her western border. Through Soviet territory, Germany could communicate with Japan in the Far East, which made the British sea blockade ineffective. Turning the Eastern front into Germany's rear area, Hitler was able to concentrate his military forces on attacking France and bombing England in 1940.

To summarise, appeasement was a crucial factor which led to the failure of both the guarantee to Poland and the Three Power Negotiations. These two events were unsuccessful attempts by the

British Government to make certain changes within the scope of appeasement. Failure indicated that it was impossible for the appeasers even to make minor changes to appeasement, let alone abandon this policy. From 1931 to 1939, not only had appeasement become the foundation on which foreign policy was based, it had also served as a guideline in many other fields such as the economy, trade and rearmament. Furthermore, appeasement controlled the appeasers' minds, becoming a crucial part of their diplomatic lives. Therefore, even if they realised that they were wrong, it was as impossible for them to abandon their own policy as it was to abandon their own lives and the 'masterpiece' they had worked on for nine years. Not until after the outbreak of war did appeasement become bankrupt, because it had lost its entire basis. However, its spirit was not completely dead until Churchill took over in May 1940. A study of the policy of that period falls beyond the scope of this book, but forms the subject of the author's work, *Britain and the Phoney War: September 1939–May 1940*.[145]

CONCLUSION

It has been more than fifty years since the end of the Second World War, but debates on appeasement still continue. After the war, historians generally held a critical view of appeasement. Since the early 1960s, however, there has emerged a revisionist school which takes a radical standpoint in justifying this policy. In addition, some historians, despite being critical of appeasement, argue in favour of it to a certain extent. It is therefore necessary to review their arguments, which were mentioned in the Introduction, to see whether there is anything in them.

Their first argument is that the Versailles Treaty lacked moral basis, and for justice's sake, it had to be revised in favour of Germany.[1] According to this argument, the appeasers seemed to have a case for pursuing appeasement, because they should be fair and just to their opponent who lost the gamble of the First World War. They should also be fair and just to other 'have-not' powers, like Italy and Japan.

This moral standard seemed so high that nobody could criticise it. But how about the Austrians, the Czechs, the Abyssinians and the Chinese? Were they entitled to the same rule? Unfortunately, in the appeaser's terms, there was no room for the 'pig-head' Czechs, 'bad-neighbour' Abyssinians, and 'wretched' and 'foolish' Chinese to enjoy this treatment. It was very 'moral' too for appeasers to accept Hitler's 'principle of self-determination' for his annexation of Austria and the Sudetenland. However, they acquiesced to Hitler's violation of this principle when the dictator forced von Schuschnigg, the Austrian Chancellor, to cancel a plebiscite which would have decided whether the Austrians wanted to unite with Germany of their own free will. The British policy-makers also abandoned the idea of a plebiscite in the Sudetenland because of Hitler's demands. At the Cabinet meeting of 17 September 1938, which discussed Hitler's 'self-determination', the

Secretary for India warned that 'he was anxious not to say that we were actuated solely by the principle of self-determination. Were we to do so the Indian Congress Party would not be slow to take advantage of such a declaration on our part.' Halifax agreed with him, saying that 'it was undesirable to burn too much incense on the altar of self-determination'.[2] It was apparent that this 'fairness' and 'justice' applied only to the aggressors, not to victim nations and colonies. In spite of being members of the League, all these victim nations had no will and no rights in international affairs. Like chips on the gambling table, they were in the position of being controlled and dealt with by the Great Powers. Chamberlain and his kind certainly bore in mind this imperialist moral standard when they formulated their policy. It should be explored and criticised, but should not be used to justify the policy.

Although the Versailles Treaty was characterised by its ambivalent nature, its moral value resided in the fact that it offered a possibility of being a deterrent against further invasion of the weak powers. Appeasing the 'have-not' powers by sacrificing victim nations diminished the moral value of the League. On the contrary, preventing Germany from launching war by keeping her in a disadvantageous position might be unfair and unjust to her, but was fair and just to the majority of the countries in the world. After the Second World War, Germany was monitored by the Allies and divided for more than forty years; Japan is still dependent on the American security umbrella. However, few who underwent the disastrous experience of the Second World War have felt pity for them. People have learned more about what fairness, justice and morality should really mean, but some historians are still blind to it.

The appeasers' second argument says that Chamberlain pursued appeasement because of his love of peace and his belief that the policy would save peace for all.[3] This is another example of attempting to balance the evil result with good intentions. These laudable words, such as 'peace', 'hope for peace' or 'love' have often been used to defend appeasement. However, in concrete terms, what kind of peace were the appeasers looking for? Their peace certainly did not include China. They did not mind how many Chinese civilians had been slaughtered by the Japanese soldiers, as long as British interests in the Far East could rely on Japanese friendship. Their peace did not include Abyssinia either, because they rewarded Mussolini with the Hoare–Laval Plan to allow him to launch war on that country. What they were concerned about was that British colonial interests in East

Africa should not be harmed when Italy took over. Their peace was exactly the same as Mussolini's, namely peace 'in Europe', perhaps worse than that, because 'Europe' here only referred to Western Europe. As to the countries in Central and Eastern Europe, they were, in Chamberlain's eyes, the 'far-away nations'[4] although Chamberlain never felt they were too far away to sell them to Hitler. Therefore, the appeasers' hopes and love for peace were, at best, an illusion of peace in Western Europe, which, in their view, could be bought at the price of sacrificing peace in the rest of the world. It was certainly not 'peace for all', nor 'an honourable quest', nor even Christians' love for their neighbour. Morrison, the Labour Leader, said critically on 9 July 1938:

> Mr Chamberlain and his colleagues talk peace not because they mean [it] but because the language of pacifism is the new political technique of the Tory Central Office. On the Prime Minister's own admission, we are living under more disturbed international conditions than at any time since the outbreak of the Great War. And I charge that British government by its betrayal of the League of Nations, its sabotaging of the Disarmament Conference and its rejection of the policy of the collective organisation of peace has made a major contribution to the wars taking place and to the unsettlement of Europe.[5]

Therefore, Chamberlain's motives were as bad as the result.

Even if Chamberlain's intentions were genuine as some historians believe, his good intentions could not be used to balance the evil result of his policy, not only because historical comment emphasises results instead of motives, but also because his motives created disastrous consequences. If Chamberlain could be spared from blame because of his motives, Hitler could be considered innocent, because he also did not want to fight against the Western Powers if his aggressive plans could be realised without war. Indeed, it was the Western Powers that declared war on Germany, not vice versa. In addition, Hitler expressed hopes for peace in his speeches no less than Chamberlain. However, nobody can reduce Hitler's guilt by pointing out his 'hope for peace', and for the same reason, nobody can justify appeasement by referring to the appeasers' motives, even if these motives were well-intentioned.

In their third argument, some scholars think that appeasers were not cowardly, stupid, and shortsighted, but were 'cultivated, highly intelligent, hard-working' statesmen.[6] Examination of the process of policy-making has shown that most appeasers, like Chamberlain, were very shrewd politicians and diplomats. They foresaw many issues in international affairs which turned out to be true later. For example, they forecast that Germany would raise its demands in an aggressive manner. Hitler would re-occupy the Rhineland and make trouble for Austria and the Sudetenland. They estimated that Japan, Italy and Germany were three potential enemies, and tried to avoid facing all three simultaneously. All these factors had been considered some time before they occurred, and Chamberlain and his colleagues worked very hard to deal with them. Looking at proposals from the FO and discussions in Cabinet, it is not difficult to find that the appeasers had a marvellous capacity to overcome or get around obstacles on the road to appeasement. For example, during the Manchurian crisis, Simon cleverly 'warded off' charges against the Japanese for their aggression. They skilfully shuffled off responsibility for failure in Anglo-American co-operation upon the United States. During the Italo-Abyssinian dispute, Baldwin's Government attempted to formulate a series of proposals – the Zeila Offer, the Peterson Proposal and the Hoare–Laval Plan – to sell Abyssinia without, in theory, violation of the principle of the Covenant. The policy of 'keep the Germans guessing' seemed perfect to deal with Hitler. During the Munich period, Chamberlain inspired Plan Z, and carried it out with full courage. In addition, they discouraged the French and misled public opinion quite successfully. In this sense, the appeasers were really clever, brave and far-sighted. They were gentlemen.

The study of policy-making, however, also explores the other side of the story. In the event of a Japanese challenge in the Far East, the British policy-makers ingratiated themselves with the aggressor, because they feared that British interests in the Far East would be harmed if Britain offended Japan. Vansittart confessed: 'We must live from hand to mouth – an humiliating process' . . .[7] During the Abyssinian crisis, they abandoned oil sanctions for fear of Mussolini's 'mad dog' act, which was highly unlikely to be launched. They could not 'afford to quarrel with Italy and drive her back into German embraces'.[8] Following the same policy, the appeasers offered Hitler whatever he wanted before he asked for it, because they were afraid that if these dangerous questions were raised by the Germans, they would be 'raised in an aggressive and threatening manner'.[9] After Hitler militarised the Rhineland without giving anything in return, the Cabinet dared not even ask the dictator to explain 'the distinction between the Reich and the German nation', on the grounds that this question seemed too provocative. Although their questionnaire had been shelved by Hitler, and although they were uncertain whether Hitler's ambitions were limited or not, the appeasers hurried to offer the new deal by allowing German 'peaceful' expansion in Central and Eastern Europe because they were afraid that Hitler might be fed up with waiting. Kirkpatrick, a member of staff at the British Embassy in Berlin, wrote on 8 June 1936:

> In a year's time it would not be we who would be addressing question to Germany . . . But the Germans who would be considering whether we were worth negotiating with, or whether they would simply dictate their desires to us.[10]

This humiliating situation soon came about. When the Cabinet discussed the terms laid down by Hitler at Berchtesgaden and Godesberg, the ministers did not deny that acceptance of these terms meant 'total surrender'. Even Halifax felt it was too much. Nevertheless, Chamberlain bravely went to Munich and accepted this humiliation as a 'victory with honour'.

When they dealt with the Rhineland, according to the advice of the Chiefs of Staff, they should have foreseen that without the demilitarised zone, they would lose deterrence to Hitler's expansion in Central and Eastern Europe. When they remained inactive during the Anschluss, they should have known that if she successfully annexed Austria, Germany would surround Czechoslovakia on three sides, which would increase the difficulty of offering military assistance to the Czechs if they were attacked by the Germans. Although they formulated proposals one after another, the British policy-makers failed to work out any effective deterrent measure to prevent matters proceeding from bad to worse, due to their short-sightedness. 'Making eyes at Japan' did not keep her friendship. Roping Italy in did not result in her estrangement from Germany. Hitler was not at all puzzled by the policy of 'keeping the Germans guessing'. On the contrary, it was the appeasers who always had to second-guess Hitler's intentions. Appeasement finally created the very situation Britain wanted to avoid: facing three enemies simultaneously.

From this analysis, one can deduce that the British policy-makers had dual personalities and capabilities. As individuals, they were shrewd, intelligent, capable and courageous; but as representative leaders of

Britain, they *were* cowardly, stupid and short-sighted. The reason for this contradiction in their personalities and capabilities was that when they made policy, they were not only private individuals, but also representatives of the British Empire, which was declining. The impact of this decline caused the negative aspects of their personalities and capabilities. Since historical comment is made on their role as politicians in public life and in history, it has to emphasise the aspects of their personalities and capabilities as representatives of the British Empire.

In their fourth argument, the apologists regard appeasement as a realistic policy, denying it amounted to buying peace at any price.[11] Is this true? After the First World War, Britain, in spite of her decline, was still a first-class power in the world. On the other hand, Germany had been terribly weakened by the victor powers. Appeasement was not realistic because it was not a policy of redressing 'British weakness', but a policy that resulted in this weakness. The policy was so reasonable in the appeasers' minds that they hardly believed that Hitler 'would repudiate it'. However, it was unrealistic and unreasonable, because the appeasers had formulated this policy on the basis of a lack of awareness of Hitler's real ambitions. In other words, appeasement was realistic and reasonable to the appeasers, but unrealistic and unreasonable in dealing with Hitler. Furthermore, it was unrealistic and unreasonable on the grounds that although they were set back time after time, the appeasers were still under the illusion that they could come to terms with the aggressors by pursuing this policy. It is not an exaggeration to say that Munich was a policy to buy peace at any price. The process of policy-making indicates that before Hitler annexed the whole of Czechoslovakia, the appeasers did not set any limits in their concessions. As long as it was by peaceful means, Hitler was allowed to take the Rhineland, Austria, the Sudetenland and Danzig as well as the whole of Central and Eastern Europe. Until after the collapse of Czechoslovakia, the British Government declared a guarantee to Poland. Even so, Danzig was not unnegotiable in the appeasers' minds, nor did they really want to strengthen this deterrence by co-operating with the Soviets. This vague limit led Hitler to assume that Britain would not fight for Danzig, which encouraged him to launch war on Poland. Therefore, appeasement did not set any limits on concessions until its latest stage. When the appeasers did set limits, it was too late and they were too vague to limit Hitler. If appeasers and their supporters still consider this policy realistic and reasonable, one question should be put to them: 'Will you adopt the same policy in a similar situation in the future, which would certainly lead to a Third World War?'

The fifth argument in favour of appeasement is that Munich postponed war and gained time for rearmament.[12] This seems a great contribution to the world. However, according to Hitler's schedule, he had considered waging war with the Western Powers by 1943–5, but Munich created such favourable conditions that he successfully launched war on Poland in 1939, about three to five years ahead of schedule. What is more, if Chamberlain had taken a hard line during the Munich period, Hitler might have been overthrown by his opposition, so there might have been no Second World War. Even if Hitler had started the war owing to Britain's firm standpoint, it would have been a short and limited war rather than a general one, because Hitler had not completed his war preparations. The Western Powers, allied with Russia and other Eastern European countries, possessed the strategic and military advantage. Churchill's comment is conclusive: 'there is no merit in putting off a war for a year if, when it comes, it is a far worse war or one much harder to win'.[13]

Regarding the view that Munich aimed to gain time for rearmament, this is nullified because it was opposed by Chamberlain himself. At the Cabinet meetings in October 1938, he criticised the misinterpretation of Munich's aim as gaining time for rearmament. He emphasised that the purpose of Munich was to build up good relations with the Dictator Powers, and that rearmament would only make them suspicious. He would reduce rearmament in due course when it was more hopeful for him to reach settlement with them.[14] If Chamberlain were still alive, he would not allow his followers to propagate such a misunderstanding of his Munich doctrine. Not until after Hitler's *coup* against Prague did Chamberlain begin to gain time. However, the aim was not preparation for war, but enforcing the British position to put Chamberlain in a better situation in his search for a new settlement with Germany. Towards this end, total rearmament spending for 1938–9, despite a considerable increase, took only a small percentage (7 per cent) of the national income – one-fifth of German rearmament expenditure during the same period.[15]

The apologists' sixth argument declares that appeasement was supported by the majority of people in the 1930s.[16] This ignores two important factors. First, from the very beginning, there was a loud voice in favour of taking a firm stand against aggression, and this ran throughout the whole of 1930s. Several polls had shown that the public was not in agreement with appeasement. Second, according to research for this book, the appeasers deliberately misled and misinformed the public. The atmosphere favourable to appeasement was, to a large extent, created by the British Government itself, imposing censorship on the media.

Finally, we come to A.J.P. Taylor's argument, which favours Munich.[17] His viewpoint is that Munich was 'a triumph', on the grounds that selling Czechoslovakia saved the Czechs from being killed during the war, while supporting the Poles caused their sacrifice of six and a half million lives. He asks: 'Which was better – to be a betrayed Czech or a saved Pole?'[18] Following his argument, the conclusion would naturally be: to be a betrayed Czech who survived as a slave under Nazi's mandate was better than to be a Pole who died for independence and freedom. He did not suggest that the British people should follow this example to avoid the great loss of life during the German bombardment of Britain during the summer of 1940. If he had, even the appeasers would not have agreed with him, because they did at least fight for Britain's vital interests, independence and freedom, if and when they were forced to. Compared to Taylor's capitulation, appeasement should really be applauded on the grounds that it could not tolerate Britain living under the Nazis' protection as a junior partner or semi-colony, even though it might be very fortunate in Taylor's view.

Offering increasingly favourable conditions for the aggressors to realise their ambitions, appeasement deprived the Western Powers of their strategic initiative, increasing the danger of war step by step. Appeasement and the aggressors' ambitions were the two fundamental factors, which made the Second World War inevitable. Although there have been divergent views on the subject, few, including the appeasers, deny that appeasement was a failure. Henderson entitled his memoirs *Failure of a Mission*. Hoare recalled the age of appeasement as 'Nine Troubled Years'. Therefore, it is right for historians to ask: could failure possibly have been avoided if other alternative courses had been taken? What lessons can be drawn from this failure?

After the First World War, although America isolated herself from European affairs, although France was politically weak, and although the British Empire was declining, Germany, as a defeated nation, was much weaker than any one of them. In addition, the League, in spite of not being a military mechanism, offered principles and measures (i.e. Articles 10–17 of the Covenant) to maintain world peace. In general, the anti-fascist countries, if they united, were much stronger than the three aggressors. Conditions were favourable for these countries to defend world peace, preventing aggression, or defeating the aggressors in their adventures at an early stage.

Still a first-class power in a leading position in the League, Britain should have organised the 'Peace Front' first, rather than searching for a new settlement with the aggressors. In fact, the struggle against aggression during the 1930s offered a very good chance for the anti-fascist countries to unite. Despite its policy of isolationism, America's national interest was linked with that of the other Western Powers in the long run. If the British Government had searched for co-operation with America wholeheartedly during the Manchurian crisis, Anglo-American collaboration might have been achieved. As for France's weakness, Britain should have given her more support, rather than discouraging her from facing the danger from Germany. In the Western view, Communist Russia was an enemy. However, it was apparent that the Soviet Union had no intention to invade or threaten the West at that time. On the contrary, it was she who was afraid of subversion and invasion by what she perceived as 'imperial powers'. If Britain had accepted the Russian proposals, the 'Peace Front' would have been built up, and would have been a deterrent to German aggression. If the Second World War had been successfully avoided, Eastern Europe would not have been controlled by the Soviets later.

In order to avoid facing three enemies at the same time, Britain should, in co-operation with America, France, Russia and other powers in the League, have checked Japan, Italy and Germany one by one at the beginning of the emerging problem, rather than waiting until these three had achieved their *rapprochement*. During the Manchurian crisis, if Britain had firmly supported the Chinese struggle against Japanese invasion and had taken a decisive lead in imposing a boycott on Japan and wholeheartedly co-operated with America, the Japanese would not have held out very long. In the Italo-Abyssinian conflict, the situation was even more favourable for the anti-fascist powers to check Italian aggression. If the Japanese and Italians had been defeated, not only would it have greatly discouraged Hitler, but Britain would have been able to concentrate on the German problem without worrying about the danger in the Far East and the Mediterranean.

Since the British Government did not want to attend to its military deficiencies by means of economic sacrifices, it should have tried to prevent Germany from developing her military capabilities instead of acquiescing in her rearmament. During the Rhineland crisis, if Britain had backed up France and forced Germany to withdraw, it would have spoiled all Hitler's plans and prevented Germany from threatening world peace as well as the interests of the British Empire. If Britain had responded to France in firmly resisting the *Anschluss*, this would have seriously hindered Hitler's ambitions in Czechoslovakia. And if Chamberlain had taken a hard line at Munich, Hitler might have been overthrown by his opposition.

It is less blameworthy that the appeasers did not see through the nature of German Nazism, Italian Fascism and Japanese militarism because they were a new phenomenon in modern history. However, it is very blameworthy that they ruled out using force to defend peace, and insisted on concessions before they had full knowledge of the aggressors' ambitions. Based on their own imagination instead of solid evidence, they believed that the aggressive powers could be bought off. They followed appeasement further and further without any change in direction for nine years, even when the policy had been set back by one failure after another. One of the factors that led to this tragedy was that the top British leaders had closed their minds to opposing views from outside as well as differing opinions among the FO and the Chiefs of Staff, which should have been encouraged to give their observations more openly, more independently, and to look at the situation from every side.

When appeasement is criticised for its unrealistic and unreasonable concessions to the aggressors, it does not mean that each and every concession is wrong, nor should any policy with conciliatory factors be misnamed 'appeasement'. In fact, concession and force are two closely related aspects in international affairs. In the nuclear age, due to the danger of nuclear war, concessions become even more necessary. However, force always plays a more fundamental role than concessions even in these circumstances, because it is a desire to avoid the use of nuclear force that demands concessions from both sides, not vice versa. In a world of great power rivalry and conflict, a negotiator may not gain a satisfactory concession from his adversary unless diplomacy is backed up with sufficient force. Without being backed up by sufficient force, agreements reached as a result of concessions may not be kept, even if they can be reached.

It is always safer if concessions can be made from a position of strength. Nevertheless, how much force or concession is required depends on the individual case. It is always safer if concessions can be made from a position of strength. Nevertheless, how much force or concession is required depends on the individual case. Generally speaking, force should be strong enough to guarantee agreement, or to face the challenge if concession is in vain. A policy – no matter whether it is firm or conciliatory – can be judged only by its results, whether or not it works. The reason for criticising appeasement is that the policy did not work, nor did it achieve its own aims. On the contrary, it caused the situation to deteriorate, paving the way for the aggressors to destroy world peace.

A critical review of appeasement during the turn of the century updates the knowledge of the origins of the Second World War. From our present perspective, the twenty-first century seems not to be a very pacifist period, and hegemony is still a major threat to weaker powers and victim nations as well as to world peace. Therefore, experiences and lessons in the interwar period need to be consulted for prevention of world conflicts in future. Learning from these experiences and lessons is very important for all peace-loving countries, particularly for weaker powers and victim nations, which are vulnerable to power politics in international relations.

NOTES

INTRODUCTION

1. The Italians' demand for Fiume was turned down by President Wilson, although they obtained all that had been promised in the Secret Treaty of London, 1915. Japanese ambition in Shantung, China was naturally checked by the Chinese due to the fact that as an associate power, China would not possibly give up her own rights in her own territory.
2. R.J. Overy, *The Origins of the Second World War* (London, Longman, 1987), p.29.
3. Ibid., pp.37–8.
4. *Documents on British Foreign Policy 1919–1939*, 2nd Series, XIV (London, HMSO), N301.
5. DBFP 2nd–XIX, N349.
6. K. Middlemas, *Diplomacy of Illusion: The British Government and Germany, 1937–39* (London, Weidenfeld & Nicolson, 1972), p.137; R.A.C. Parker, *Chamberlain and Appeasement: British Policy and the Coming of the Second World War* (London, Macmillan, 1993), p.100.
7. See p.68.
8. See p.12.
9. Earl of Birkenhead, *Halifax, The Life of Lord Halifax* (London, Hamilton, 1965), p.366.
10. *Documents on German Foreign Policy 1918–1945*, Series D-I (London, HMSO), N31; P. Schmidt, *Hitler's Interpreter* (London, Heinemann, 1951), p.77. See also pp.137–8.
11. DBFP 2nd–XIX, N349.
12. Ibid., N409.
13. Earl of Avon, *Facing the Dictators* (London, Cassell, 1962), pp.346–7. Halifax held the same view: see 1st Earl of Halifax, *Fulness of Days* (London, Collins, 1957), p.197.
14. See pp.105–7.
15. F.R. Gannon, *The British Press and Nazi Germany 1936–1939* (Oxford, Clarendon Press, 1971), p.6.
16. R. Louis, *British Strategy in the Far East 1919–1939* (Oxford, Clarendon, 1971), p.186.
17. See pp.7–8; Chapter 2, note 18; M. Gilbert, *The Roots of Appeasement* (London, Weidenfeld & Nicolson, 1966), p.183; Parker, *Chamberlain and Appeasement*, p.164.
18. Some historians deny this and consider it a genuine hope for peace: K. Feiling, *The Life of Neville Chamberlain* (London, Macmillan, 1946), p.359; Gilbert, *The Roots*, p.xii; K. Eubank, *The Origins of World War II* (Arlington Heights, Ill., H. Davidson, 1969), p.79. For discussion, see pp.224, 265–6.
19. D. Marquand, *Ramsay MacDonald* (London, J. Cape, 1977), p.715.
20. R. Bassett, *Democracy and Foreign Policy: The Sino–Japanese Dispute 1931–1933* (London, Longmans, Green & Co., 1952), pp.192–3; B. Roberts, *Sir John Simon* (London, R. Hale, 1938), p.294; Feiling, *Chamberlain*, p.261.
21. K. Middlemas and J. Barnes, *Baldwin: A Biography* (London, Weidenfeld & Nicolson,

1969), pp.758–9; see also p.122.

22. Feiling, *Chamberlain*, p.320.
23. F.W. Hirst, *The Consequences of the War to Great Britain* (London, Oxford University Press, 1934), p.297.
24. D. Lloyd George, *The Truth about the Peace Treaties* (I) (London, Gollancz, 1938), p.87; Hirst, *The Consequences*, p.251.
25. Ibid., p.273; R. Muir, *The Political Consequences of the Great War* (London, T. Butterworth, 1930), pp.219–23.
26. W. Schlote, *British Overseas Trade from 1700 to the 1930s* (Oxford, Blackwell, 1952), p.51, Table II.
27. Marquand, *MacDonald*, p.715.
28. In August 1919, the Cabinet assumed 'that the British Empire will not be engaged in any great war during the next ten years, and that no Expeditionary Force is required for this purpose.' This came to be known as 'The Ten Year Rule'. N. H. Gibbs, *Grand Strategy* (I), (London, HMSO, 1976), p.3.
29. Ibid., p.80.
30. Marquand, *MacDonald*, p.757.
31. Feiling, *Chamberlain*, pp.258, 312–14.
32. Marquand, *MacDonald*, p.760.
33. Middlemas, *Diplomacy*, pp.15–16.
34. Feiling, *Chamberlain*, p.403. See also pp.233, 244 and Chapter 6, note 30 of this book.
35. Public Record Office, Cab23/83 18(36).
36. Middlemas, *Diplomacy*, p.54, footnote.
37. M. George, *The Warped Vision: British Foreign Policy 1933–1939* (Pittsburgh, University of Pittsburgh Press, 1965), p.220.
38. S. Aster, *1939: The Making of the Second World War* (London, Deutch, 1973), p.50.
39. L.C.M.S. Amery, *My Political Life: The Unforgiving Years 1929–1940* (London, Hutchinson, 1955), pp.173–5, 262; M. Cowling, *The Impact of Hitler: British Politics and British Policy 1933–1940* (London, Cambridge University Press, 1975), pp.224–7; As for Eden, see Chapter 4, note 41.
40. Parker, *Chamberlain and Appeasement*, pp.308–9, 312; K. Harris, *Attlee* (London, Weidenfeld & Nicolson, 1982), pp.115, 117, 123, 155.
41. W.R. Rock, *British Appeasement in the 1930s* (London, Edward Arnold, 1977), pp.72–3; Parker, *Chamberlain and Appeasement*, pp.307–8, 314–15.
42. Viscount Cecil, *A Great Experiment: An Autobiography* (London, J. Cape, 1941), pp.289–90, *All the Way* (London, Hodder & Stoughton, 1949), p.210.
43. Parker, *Chamberlain and Appeasement*, pp.320–1.
44. Harris, *Attlee*, p.124; H. Dalton, *The Fateful Years: Memoirs 1931–1945* (London, Frederick Huller 1957), p.88.
45. Harris, *Attlee*, p.155.
46. Rock, *Appeasement*, p.79; see also p. 211.
47. Parker, *Chamberlain and Appeasement*, p.320.
48. See Chapter 2, note 12.
49. A. Adamthwaite, 'The British Government and the Media, 1937–1938', *Journal of Contemporary History*, 18 (1983), 291–2.
50. DBFP 3rd–II, N1058.
51. Parker, *Chamberlain and Appeasement*, p.327.
52. Adamthwaite, 'The British Government', pp.281–93.
53. T. Jones, *A Diary with Letters 1931–1950* (London, Oxford University Press, 1954), p.xxxi; N. Thompson, *The Anti-appeasers: Conservative Opposition to Appeasement in the 1930s* (Oxford, Clarendon Press, 1971), p.135. See also Chapter 2, note 10.
54. Middlemas, *Diplomacy*, p.449.
55. Colvin wrote that he had reported to the FO many times that Hitler's opposition wanted to bring him down before Munich, and that Germany would attack Poland in the spring of 1939, but when he told Halifax and Chamberlain the same story in person, he found that they seemed never to have heard of it: see I. Colvin, *Vansittart in Office* (London, Gollancz,

1965), pp.303–5; *The Chamberlain Cabinet* (London, Gollancz, 1971), p.167. Hankey also said in 1943: 'When the pre-war records are opened on the origins of the war it will be found that the intelligence given was accurate and ample, the opinions sound, and the warnings, though given, were by no means always followed.' (N. Rose, *Vansittart: Study of a Diplomat* London, Heinemann, 1978, p.139, footnote).

56. See p.xvi.
57. M. Gilbert and R. Gott, *The Appeasers* (London, Weidenfeld & Nicolson, 1963), pp.xi, 76–7, 182–3.
58. Colvin, *Vansittart*, p.303; Viscount Templewood, *Nine Troubled Years* (London, Collins, 1954), p.291.
59. C. Thorne, *The Approach of War 1938–39* (London, Macmillan, 1967), p.16.
60. Middlemas and Barnes, *Baldwin*, pp.947, 950.
61. *The New Shorter Oxford English Dictionary*.
62. Gilbert and Gott, *The Appeasers*; George, *The Warped Vision*; Middlemas, *Diplomacy*.
63. Gilbert, *The Roots*, pp.4–5; R.J.Q. Adams, *British Politics and Foreign Policy in the Age of Appeasement, 1935–39* (London, Macmillan, 1993), pp.1, 14; Thompson, *The Anti-Appeasers*, p.27; George, *The Warped Vision*, p.3.
64. G. Martel (ed.), *The Origins of the Second World War Reconsidered: The A.J.P. Taylor Debate After Twenty-Five Years* (Boston, Allen & Unwin, 1986), p.1.
65. W. Churchill, *The Gathering Storm* (London, Cassell, 1948), pp.194, 381.
66. *Parliamentary Debates: Commons*, 5th Series, vol. 327, col. 76.
67. T. Taylor, *Munich: The Price of Peace* (New York, Doubleday, 1979), pp. xiii and 978.
68. L.B. Namier, *Diplomatic Prelude* (London, Macmillan, 1948), p.ix.
69. George, *The Warped Vision*, p.xv.
70. I. Maisky, *Who Helped Hitler?* (London, Hutchinson, 1964), pp.103–4, 133; B. Ponomaryov, A. Gromyko and V. Khvostov (eds), *History of Soviet Foreign Policy 1917–1945*, trans. D. Skvirsky (Moscow, Progress Publishers, 1969), p.339.
71. Parker, *Chamberlain and Appeasement*, pp.345, 347.
72. A.J.P. Taylor, *The Origins of the Second World War* (London, Hamilton, 1972), p.28; Gilbert, *The Roots*, pp. 22–3, 27–9, 52, 57,159; Eubank, *The Origins*, pp.73–4; A. Adamthwaite, *The Making of the Second World War* (London, Allen & Unwin, 1977), p.28.
73. Gilbert, *The Roots*, pp.xii, 88.
74. Eubank, *The Origins*, p.79; see also Parker, *Chamberlain and Appeasement*, p.345; Feiling, *Chamberlain*, p.359.
75. Gilbert, *The Roots*, pp.159, 177; Parker, *Chamberlain and Appeasement*, pp.1–2.
76. Middlemas, *Diplomacy*, pp.1 and 8, footnote.
77. P.M.H. Bell, *The Origins of the Second World War in Europe* (London, Longman, 1986), p.247; see also Parker, *Chamberlain and Appeasement*, p.12.
78. See pp.175, 221–3, 270.
79. Templewood, *Troubled Years*, pp.374–5; see also Taylor, *The Origins*, p.xvii; Parker, *Chamberlain and Appeasement*, p.345; Gilbert, *The Roots*, pp.4, 147.
80. Taylor, *The Origins*, pp.189 and xvii.
81. Avon, *Dictators*, p.523.

CHAPTER 1

1. A. Iriye, 'Japanese Imperialism and Aggression' in E. Robertson (ed.), *The Origins of the Second World War: Historical Interpretations* (London, Macmillan, 1971), pp.249–50.
2. *Report of the Commission of Enquiry* (Geneva, League of Nations, 1932), p.71.
3. Royal Institute of International Affairs, *Documents on International Affairs 1932* (London, Oxford University Press, 1933), pp.247–8.
4. R. Louis, *British Strategy in the Far East 1919–1939* (Oxford, Clarendon Press, 1971), pp.238–9, 266; A. Iriye, *The Asian Factor*, in Martel (ed.), *The Origins of the Second World War – Reconsideration: The A.J.P. Taylor Debate After Twenty-Five Years* (Boston, Allen & Unwin, 1986), p.230.

5. C. Thorne, *The Limits of Foreign Policy: The West, the League and the Far Eastern Crisis of 1931–1933* (London, Hamilton, 1972), pp.105–8; A. Adamthwaite, *The Making of the Second World War* (London, Allen & Unwin, 1977), pp.36–7; P.M.H. Bell, *The Origins of the Second World War in Europe* (London, Longman, 1986), p.204.
6. A.J.P. Taylor, *The Origins of the Second World War* (London, Hamilton, 1972), pp.222–3.
7. T. Jones, *A Diary with Letters, 1931–1950* (London, Oxford University Press, 1954), pp.xxvii, xxxi; Viscount Templewood, *Nine Troubled Years* (London, Collins, 1954), pp.27–9; J. Simon, *Retrospect: The Memoirs of Viscount Simon* (London, Hutchinson, 1952), p.272; D. Marquand, *Ramsay MacDonald* (London, J. Cape, 1977), p.150; K. Robbins (ed.) *The Blackwell Biographical Dictionary of British Political Life in the Twentieth Century* (Oxford, Blackwell, 1990), p.278.
8. Templewood, *Troubled Years*, p.29; Jones, *Diary*, p.xxxi.
9. Baldwin was Lord President at that time.
10. Thomas Jones was Deputy Secretary of the Cabinet before 1930, then Secretary of the Pigrim Trust. He had a close relationship with Baldwin and MacDonald.
11. Simon, *Retrospect*, p.273; Jones, *Diary*, xxxiii, p.93; Thorne, *Foreign Policy*, pp.92–3.
12. Simon, *Retrospect*, p.178; Marquand, *MacDonald*, p.175; *Documents on British Foreign Policy 1919–1939*, 2nd Series, XX (London, HMSO), N97.
13. Jones, *Diary*, p.xxxi; Templewood, *Troubled Years*, p.27; Robbins, *British Political Life*, p.277.
14. Viscount Cecil, *All the Way* (London, Hodder & Stoughton, 1949), p.198.
15. Marquand, *MacDonald*, pp.714–15; K. Middlemas and J. Barnes, *Baldwin: A Biography*, (London, Weidenfeld & Nicolson, 1969), p. 726.
16. C.B. Roberts, *Sir John Simon* (London, R. Hale, 1938), p.277; Jones, *Diary*, p.193.
17. Simon, *Retrospect*, p.273.
18. Robbins, *British Political Life*, p.375.
19. K. Feiling, *The Life of Neville Chamberlain* (London, Macmillan, 1946), p.249. As for Eden's comment, see Earl of Avon, *Facing the Dictators* (London, Cassell, 1962), pp.28, 219–20.
20. See p.143.
21. See p.xiii.
22. DBFP 2nd-VIII, N769.
23. Simon, *Retrospect*, p.177.
24. N. Rose, *Vansittart: study of a Diplomat* (London, Heinemann, 1978), p.106.
25. DBFP 2nd-IX, N238 note 2.
26. Ibid., nos 21, 216, 239; DBFP 2nd-X, N745 note 1; DBFP 2nd-XI, N453 note 8.
27. Thorne, *Foreign Policy*, pp.90, 141.
28. R. Bassett, *Democracy and Foreign Policy: the Sino-Japanese Dispute, 1931–33*, (London, Longmans, Green & Co. 1952), pp.11–13.
29. Thorne, *Foreign Policy*, p.92.
30. Ibid., pp.90, 149; Bassett, *Democracy*, pp.11–12.
31. DBFP 2nd-VIII, N593.
32. Thorne, *Foreign Policy*, p.149.
33. DBFP 2nd-VIII, N509.
34. Ibid., N569.
35. Ibid., N596.
36. Ibid., nos 522, 603.
37. Ibid., N566.
38. Thorne, *Foreign Policy*, p.150.
39. DBFP 2nd-VIII, N685.
40. Ibid., N689.
41. Ibid., nos 586, 587.
42. Ibid., nos 561, 562.
43. R.I.I.A. *Documents 1932*, pp.251–3.
44. DBFP 2nd-VIII, N573.
45. Ibid., N624 note 1, N681, note 3.

46. Ibid., N681 note 3 and N621.
47. Ibid., N689.
48. Public Record Office, Cab23/69 75(31).
49. DBFP 2nd-VIII, N746.
50. Ibid., nos 739, 746.
51. Ibid., N754.
52. Ibid., N746.
53. Ibid., nos 769, 775; PRO, Cab23/69 81(31).
54. DBFP 2nd-IX, N356.
55. Ibid., N85.
56. DBFP 2nd-VIII, N685.
57. *Foreign Relations of the United States, Japan 1931–41*, vol. I (Washington, DC, State Department), pp.34–5.
58. Ibid., pp.37, 45.
59. Ibid., p.76.
60. DBFP 2nd-IX, N53.
61. Ibid., N58 and note 3.
62. Ibid., nos 61, 66.
63. Ibid., N66, note 2.
64. H.L. Stimson, *The Far Eastern Crisis*, (New York, H. Fertig, 1974 [*c.* 1936]), pp.100–2.
65. DBFP 2nd-IX, N101, note 2.
66. Ibid., N84.
67. Bassett, *Democracy*, p.13.
68. Ibid., pp.111–12.
69. See p.16.
70. DBFP 2nd-IX, N120 and note 3.
71. FRUS 1932, vol. III, p.282.
72. DBFP 2nd-IX, N161.
73. Ibid., N216.
74. Ibid., N238, note 2.
75. Ibid., N238, note 2; N239.
76. Ibid., N216, note 1; PRO, Cab23/70 14(32).
77. DBFP 2nd-IX, N274; PRO, Cab23/70 11(32).
78. DBFP 2nd-IX, nos 300, 305, 588, 614.
79. Ibid., N347, N267 and note 4.
80. Ibid., N153; PRO, Cab23/70 10(32).
81. PRO, Cab23/70 11(32); Cab23/70 14(32).
82. PRO, Cab23/70 12(32); Cab23/70 14(32).
83. Ibid.
84. DBFP 2nd-IX, N535 and note 9.
85. Ibid., N636; FRUS 1932, vol. III, p.280.
86. DBFP 2nd-IX, N612.
87. Ibid., N114; FRUS 1932, vol. III, pp.61–3.
88. DBFP 2nd-IX, N128, note 3.
89. Ibid., N129.
90. Ibid., N154.
91. Ibid., nos 155, 156.
92. PRO, Cab23/70 10(32).
93. FRUS 1932, vol. III, pp.123–4.
94. Ibid., pp.124–8.
95. Ibid., pp.142–3.
96. Ibid., pp.136–40.
97. Ibid., p.147.
98. FRUS Japan 1931–41, vol. I, pp.169–71; DBFP 2nd-IX, N211.
99. FRUS 1932, vol. III, pp.153–5; DBFP 2nd-IX, N225.
100. Ibid., N235.

101. Ibid., N261.
102. Ibid.
103. FRUS 1932, vol. III, p.183.
104. DBFP 2nd-IX, N322.
105. FURS 1932, vol. III, pp.183, 236; DBFP 2nd-IX, N257.
106. FURS 1932, vol. III, p.236.
107. Ibid., p.261; DBFP 2nd-IX, N397.
108. FURS 1932, vol. III, p.282.
109. DBFP 2nd-IX, nos 432, 433.
110. Ibid., N455; FRUS 1932, vol. III, pp.335–40.
111. PRO, Cab23/70 14(32).
112. FRUS 1932, vol. III, p.353.
113. Ibid., p.343.
114. DBFP 2nd-IX, N469. Immediately after these words, it reads: 'Sir John Simon has already told Mr. Stimson how keenly the British Government wishes to keep in close co-operation with America over the whole field of the Far Eastern crisis and he is hopeful that the adherence of the Powers now at Geneva to the declaration proposed to be made by the Council of the League . . . might predispose those of them who are signatories to the Nine-Power Treaty to associate themselves with the American demarche also.' This cliché was quoted by Chamberlain on 5 November 1936 in a Parliamentary debate to give the House proof that the failure to co-operate did not come from British side. (*Parliamentary Debates: Commons*, 5th Series, vol. 317, Col. 379).
115. FRUS 1932, vol. III, p.353.
116. Ibid., p.373; DBFP 2nd-IX, N474.
117. Ibid., N533.
118. FRUS 1932, vol. III, pp.458–62.
119. Ibid., p.502.
120. Bassett, *Democracy*, pp.256, 263.
121. DBFP 2nd-X, N745 and note 1.
122. Ibid., N746, notes 2, 5.
123. Ibid., N746.
124. DBFP 2nd-XI, N4; *Report of the Commission*, pp.71, 97.
125. DBFP 2nd-XI, N17.
126. Ibid., N17, note 9.
127. Ibid., nos 32, 37.
128. Ibid., N53.
129. PRO, Cab23/73 62(32).
130. PRO, Cab23/73 64(32).
131. DBFP 2nd-XI, N53; PRO, Cab23/73 64(32).
132. PRO, Cab23/73 62(32).
133. As to the debates, see W.W. Willoughby, *The Sino–Japanese Controversy and the League of Nations* (Baltimore, Johns Hopkins Press, 1935), pp.438–62.
134. League of Nations, *Official Journal, Special Supplement*, N111, (Geneva, 1936), p.50.
135. DBFP 2nd-XI, nos 121, 103; L/N, O.J. ss. N111 p.50.
136. A.J. Toynbee, *Survey of International Affairs 1933* (London, Oxford University Press, 1934), p.493.
137. DBFP 2nd-XI, N155.
138. Ibid., N202.
139. Ibid., N155, note 7.
140. Ibid., N342.
141. Ibid., nos 260, 342.
142. Ibid., N285.
143. Toynbee, *Survey 1933*, pp.504–9.
144. FRUS 1932, vol. IV, p.300.
145. Ibid., p.316.
146. DBFP 2nd-XI, N23.

147. FRUS 1932, vol. IV, pp.405–6, 417.
148. Ibid., p.416.
149. Ibid., p.427.
150. Ibid., pp.428–9.
151. DBFP 2nd-XI, N206.
152. Ibid., N462, note 4; FRUS Japan 1931–41, vol. I, p.119.
153. See Introduction, note 28.
154. N.H. Gibbs, *Grand Strategy* (I) (London, HMSO, 1976), pp.78–81; R. Shay, *British Rearmament in the Thirties: Politics and Profits* (Princeton, Princeton University Press, 1977), pp.22–4.
155. Gibbs, *Strategy*, p.85; Shay, *Rearmament*, p.26; G.C. Peden, *British Rearmament and the Treasury: 1932–1939* (Edinburgh, Scottish Academic Press, 1979), Appendix III.
156. DBFP 2nd-XX, N39 and notes 1, 10.
157. Gibbs, *Strategy*, p.120.
158. DBFP 2nd-XX, N64, note 1; N77 and note 1, N92.
159. Rose, *Vansittart*, p.126; Gibbs, *Strategy*, p.94.
160. Feiling, *Chamberlain*, p.253. Fisher developed his view in his memo of 19 April 1934, which Chamberlain said represented the view of the Treasury (2nd-XIII, Appendix I and note 1).
161. Gibbs, *Strategy*, p.95.
162. DBFP 2nd-XIII, p.2.
163. DBFP 2nd-XX, N450, Gibbs, *Strategy*, pp.93–96; Rose, *Vansittart*, pp.124–6.
164. DBFP 2nd-XX, N97.
165. Ibid., N99 and note 3.
166. Gibbs, *Strategy*, pp.103, 105, 123–5.
167. Ibid., pp.115; Peden, *Rearmament and the Treasury*, p.119.
168. See also pp.216–18.
169. Peden, *Rearmament and the Treasury*, pp.8–9.
170. DBFP 2nd-XX, N149.
171. Ibid., nos 77, 92.
172. DBFP 2nd-XIII, N8 and note 1.
173. M. Beloff, *The Foreign Policy of Soviet Russia 1929–1941* (I), (London, Oxford University Press, 1956 [*c.* 1947]), p. 80; J. Haslam, *Soviet Foreign Policy, 1930–33, the Impact of the Depression* (London, Macmillan, 1983), p.9; J. Haslam, *The Soviet Union and the Struggle for Collective Security in Europe 1933–39* (London, Macmillan, 1984), pp. 10–11; B. Ponomaryov, A. Gromyko, and V. Khvostov (eds), *History of Soviet Foreign Policy 1917–1945*, tr. D. Skvirsky (Moscow, Progress Publishers, 1969), pp.294–5.
174. R.O. Paxton, *Europe in the 20th Century*, 2nd edn (Orlando, Harcourt Brace Jovanovich, 1985), p. 389.
175. Haslam, *Soviet Foreign Policy*, pp.86–8.
176. J. Fyrth, 'Introduction: In the Thirties' and T. Atienza, 'What the Papers Said', in J. Fyrth (ed.), *Britain, Fascism and the Popular Front* (London, Lawrence & Wishart, 1985), pp.13, 65.
177. Beloff, *Foreign Policy*, pp.108–10.
178. K. Morgan, *Against Fascism and War: Ruptures and Continuities in British Communist Politics 1935–41* (Manchester, Manchester University Press, 1989), p.25.
179. T. Atienza, 'What' in J. Fyrth (ed.), *Britain*, p.64.
180. Haslam, *Soviet Foreign Policy*, p.83.
181. Ponomaryov, *History of Soviet*, pp.296–7, 418; Haslam, *Soviet Foreign Policy*, p.81.
182. DBFP 2nd-XIII, N15.
183. Ibid., N8.
184. Ibid., N14.
185. Ibid., N26.
186. Ibid., N29.
187. Ibid., N29, note 1.
188. DBFP 2nd-XVII, N268.
189. See pp.233, 244, Chapter 6, n.30.

190. DBFP 2nd-XXI, N106.
191. Ibid., N207 note 3.
192. Ibid., N136.
193. Ibid., N142.
194. Ibid., N135 note 2, N142 note 1, N140; Avon, Dictators, p.532.
195. DBFP 2nd-XXI, nos 116, 139.
196. Ibid., N151.
197. Ibid., nos 204, 210.
198. Ibid., N215 and note 1.
199. Ibid., N238.
200. Ibid., N271 and note 3, N274.
201. Ibid., N201 and note 1; N207 note 3; N279, N283, note 6.
202. Ibid., N269.
203. Ibid., N272 and note 2, N281; Avon, *Dictators*, pp.534–5; J. Harvey (ed.) *The Diplomatic Diaries of Oliver Harvey, 1937–1940* (London, Collins, 1970), pp.48–9.
204. DBFP 2nd-XXI, nos 286, 287; DBFP 2nd-XIX, N222; Royal Institute of International Affairs, *Documents on International Affairs 1937* (London, Oxford University Press, 1939), p.586.
205. DBFP 2nd-XIX, N222, note 2; DBFP 2nd-XXI, N286, note 6.
206. Ibid., N291 and note 3.
207. Ibid., N291, N283 and notes 6, 7.
208. Ibid., N287. note 3; N291, N300 and note 1; N304 note 7.
209. Ibid., N304 and note 1.
210. Ibid., N311 and note 2, N312.
211. Ibid., nos 301, 323.
212. Ibid., nos 332, 339; Avon, *Dictators*, p.538; Harvey, *Harvey's Diaries*, pp.56–7.
213. DBFP 2nd-XXI, nos 364, 391; DBFP 2nd-XIX, N347 and note 3.
214. Ibid., N347, DBFP 2nd-XXI, N388.
215. Ibid., N346 and note 1.
216. DBFP 2nd-XIX, N311 and note 6.
217. Ibid., N316.
218. Ibid., N311, note 6; N348.
219. Ibid., N378 and note 3, N401.
220. DBFP 2nd-XXI, nos 407, 410.
221. Ibid., N419.
222. Ibid., nos 427, 429.
223. Ibid., N433.
224. DBFP 2nd-XIX, nos. 422, 423, 424.
225. Ibid., nos 428, 430, 434; D. Dilks, *The Diaries of Sir Alexander Cadogan 1938–1945* (London, Cassell,   1971), p.36; Avon, *Dictators*, p.551.
226. Ibid., p.552.
227. DBFP 2nd-XIX, nos 441, 446.
228. Ibid., nos 445, 449; Avon., *Dictators*, pp.554–5, 559–60; Harvey, *Harvey's Diaries*, pp.71, 73.
229. Avon. *Dictators*, pp.560–3; Harvey, *Harvey's Diaries*, pp.75–6; Dilks, *Cadogan's Diaries*, pp.39–40.
230. DBFP 2nd-XIX, N457, also nos 455, 456, 458.
231. Ibid., N463.
232. DBFP 3rd-VIII, nos 210, 214, 440.
233. PRO, Cab23/96 54(38).
234. DBFP 3rd-VIII, N256, N298 and note 1.
235. Ibid., N440.
236. Ibid., N338 and notes 1, 2.
237. Ibid., Appendix I, pp. 549–50.
238. A.J. Toynbee, *Survey of International Affairs 1939–1945: The Eve of War, 1939* (London, Oxford University Press, 1951), pp.639–40.

239. DBFP 3rd-IX, nos 137, 191, 196, 203.
240. PRO, Cab23/99 32(39).
241. PRO, Cab27/627 F.P. (36)95.
242. PRO, Cab27/627 F.P. (36)96.
243. DBFP 3rd-IX, N227.
244. PRO, Cab27/625 F.P. (36) 52nd Mtg. 19 June 1939.
245. DBFP 3rd-IX, N230.
246. Ibid., N365.
247. Ibid., N579.
248. Ibid., Appendix I and notes 1, 3, 4, 5.
249. Ibid., N568.
250. PRO, Cab23/100 40(39).
251. L/N, O.J. ss. N111, p.51.
252. Jones, *Diary*, p.30.
253. See p.34.
254. See p.13.
255. See pp.27–8, 70, 81, 91–2, 109–10, 148.
256. When Eden met the Italian delegate Aloisi in Geneva in May 1935, the latter asked him, since 'we had swallowed *la couleuvre* of Manchuria; why was Abyssinia creating such difficulties?' [Avon, *Dictators*, p.208.] The Japanese Military Attaché in Berlin said on 20 February 1933, 'Japan was now at a decisive turning point in her entire policy which could also be important for Germany . . . The trend in Japan that was pro-German and had always demanded that one stand by Germany in her fight against the Versailles Treaty . . . Now the way was becoming clear for cooperation with Germany. From now on Japan . . . could fight against Versailles together with Germany.' (*Documents on German Foreign Policy 1918–1945*, Series C, vol. I, London, HMSO, N28).
257. DBFP 2nd-IX, N153; PRO, Cab23/70 10(32); FRUS 1932, vol. III, p.197.
258. Jones, *Diary*, p.398.
259. DBFP 2nd-XXI, N346.
260. R.A.C. Parker, *Chamberlain and Appeasement: British Policy and the Coming of the Second World War* (London, Macmillan, 1993), pp.40, 45.
261. G.W. Baer, *The Coming of The Italian-Ethiopian War* (Cambridge, Harvard University Press, 1967), p.35.
262. DBFP 2nd-VIII, N823.
263. DBFP 2nd-IX, N267.

CHAPTER 2

1. *Documents on British Foreign Policy 1919–1939*, 2nd Series, XX (London, HMSO), N39.
2. A.J. Toynbee (ed.), *Survey of International Affairs 1935* (II) (London, Oxford University Press, 1936), pp.113–43.
3. Royal Institute of International Affairs, *Documents on International Affairs 1935* (II) (London, Oxford University Press, 1937), pp.55–60.
4. Ibid., pp.106–10, 134.
5. C. Thorne, *The Limits of Foreign Policy: The West, the League and the Far Eastern Crisis of 1931–1933* (London, Hamilton, 1972), p.388; E.H. Carr, *International Relations between the Two World Wars (1919–1939)* (London, Macmillan, 1959), p.228; G.W. Baer, *Test Case: Italy, Ethiopia and the League of Nations* (Stanford, Hoover Institution Press, 1976), p.xiii; R.A.C. Parker, *Chamberlain and Appeasement: British Policy and the Coming of the Second World War* (London, Macmillan, 1993), p.56.
6. F. Hardie, *The Abyssinian Crisis* (Hamden, Archon Books, 1974), p.3; A. Adamthwaite, *The Making of the Second World War* (London, Allen & Unwin, 1977), pp.37, 47, 52.
7. A.J.P. Taylor, *The Origins of the Second World War* (London, Hamilton, 1972), pp.96–7, 108.

8. K. Eubank, *The Origins of World War II* (Arlington Heights, Ill., H. Davidson, 1969), p.56.
9. J. Simon, *Retrospect: The Memoirs of Viscount Simon* (London, Hutchinson, 1952), pp.205–6; Viscount Templewood, *Nine Troubled Years* (London, Collins, 1954), pp.28–29.
10. K. Middlemas & J. Barnes, Baldwin: *A Biography* (London, Weidenfeld & Nicolson, 1969), pp.22, 24, 759, 806, 929–30, 960, 962–4; T. Jones, *A Diary with Letters, 1931–1950* (London, Oxford University Press, 1954), pp.xxiv, xxx, 175, 190; Templewood, *Troubled Years*, pp.30–1, 64, 164, 291; Simon, *Retrospect*, p.275. Captain Macnamara, a Conservative back-bencher, wrote about his personality. 'Lord Baldwin, the defender of democracy, was in reality a dictator. His personality was very strong and almost irresistible. It permeated into every cranny of the building (the palace of Westminster) and oozed out into the whole land. He built up around him a camarilla that did not disturb the atmosphere; to some fog, to others restful dream clouds.' (N. Thompson, *The Anti-Appeasers: Conservative Opposition to Appeasement in the 1930s*, Oxford, Clarendon Press, 1971, p.135).
11. Middlemas and Barnes, *Baldwin*, p.807.
12. The Peace Ballot of 1935 asked people to vote upon five questions: 1. Should Great Britain remain a member of the League of Nations? 2. Are you in favour of an all-round reduction in armaments by international agreement? 3. Are you in favour of an all-round abolition of national military and naval aircraft by international agreement? 4. Should the manufacture and sale of armaments for private profit be prohibited by international agreement? 5. Do you consider that, if a nation insists on attacking another, the other nations should combine to compel it to stop by (a) Economic and non-military measures? (b) If necessary, military measures? Its result is shown in the table below.

Question	Yes	No	Doubtful	Abstentions
1 11,090,387	355,883	10,470	102,425	
2 10,470,489	862,775	12,062	213,839	
3 9,533,558	1,689,786	16,976	318,845	
4 10,417,329	775,415	15,076	315,345	
5(a)	10,027,608	635,074	27,255	855,107
5(b)	6,784,368	2,351,981	40,893	2,364,441

Total number of voters for all 5 questions: 11,559,165.
See Toynbee, Survey 1935 (II), pp.48–51.
13. H. Dalton, *The Fateful Years: Memoirs 1931–1945* (London, Frederick Huller, 1957), p.72; Toynbee, *Survey 1935* (II), pp.54–5.
14. Middlemas and Barnes, *Baldwin*, p.836.
15. K. Feiling, *The Life of Neville Chamberlain* (London, Macmillan, 1946), pp.243–4, 264–5, 268–9.
16. K. Robbins (ed.), *The Blackwell Biographical Dictionary of British Political Life in the Twentieth Century* (Oxford, Blackwell, 1990), pp.206–7; N. Rose, *Vansittart: Study of a Diplomat* (London, Heinemann, 1978), pp.163; Templewood, *Troubled Years*, pp.30–6; J.A. Cross, *Sir Samuel Hoare: A Political Biography* (London, J. Cape, 1977), pp.111, 112, 186; Earl of Avon, *Facing the Dictators* (London, Cassell, 1962), pp.217–18.
17. Templewood, *Troubled Years*, pp.160–1.
18. Hoare wrote in his memoirs: 'We also had found the Abyssinians bad neighbours. The Amharic Government of Addis Ababa had little authority over the tribes and races of the south and west, Gallas, Somalis, Leiba and Shifta wandering gangs, disloyal Rases, anti-Christian Moslems, Arab slave traders and intriguing adventurers, who one and all did much as they liked in this remnant of medieval Africa.' (Templewood, *Troubled Years*, p.150).
19. Avon, *Dictators*, p.294; RIIA *Documents 1935* (II), p.48.
20. Templewood, *Troubled Years*, p.152.
21. Avon, *Dictators*, pp.318–20.
22. See p.91.
23. Avon, *Dictators*, p.244.
24. DBFP 2nd-XIV, N175, note 4; DBFP 2nd-XV, N557; Avon, *Dictators*, pp.198–200.

25. Templewood, *Troubled Years*, pp.152–5; R. Vansittart, *The Mist Procession* (London, Hutchinson, 1958), p.530; DBFP 2nd-XIV, N301 note 7; N639 note 6, nos 662, 664; DBFP 2nd-XV, N293.
26. Vansittart, *Mist*, p.522.
27. DBFP 2nd-XIV, N295, note 7.
28. Templewood, *Troubled Years*, p.138.
29. See Chapter 4, note 31.
30. D. Waley, *British Public Opinion and the Abyssinian War, 1935–6* (London, Maurice Temple Smith, 1975), pp.17–19.
31. *Parliamentary Debates: Commons,* 5th Series, vol. 302, col. 2194.
32. Ibid., vol. 298, col. 325.
33. DBFP 2nd-XIV, N273.
34. Ibid., N80.
35. Ibid., N41, note 2.
36. Ibid., N58.
37. Ibid., N78.
38. Ibid., N64.
39. Ibid., N89.
40. Ibid., N115 and note 3.
41. Ibid., N175.
42. Ibid., N175, note 4; Avon, *Dictators*, pp.198–200.
43. DBFP 2nd-XIV, N178, note 1; Avon, *Dictators*, p.200.
44. DBFP 2nd-XIV, N218, note 2.
45. Parker, *Chamberlain and Appeasement*, p.29; G. Warner, *Pierre Laval and the Eclipse of France* (London, Eyre & Spottiswoode, 1968), p.78.
46. DBFP 2nd-XIV, nos 230, 231, 232, 233, 234.
47. Ibid., N230.
48. Ibid., N253.
49. Ibid., N270, note 3.
50. W. Churchill, *The Gathering Storm* (London, Cassell, 1948), p.533; Waley, *Public Opinion*, pp.30–3.
51. See Chapter 2, note 12.
52. M. George, *The Warped Vision: British Foreign Policy 1933–1939* (Pittsburgh, University of Pittsburgh Press, 1965), p.60.
53. Middlemas and Barnes, *Baldwin*, pp.835–6.
54. RIIA, *Documents 1935* (II), pp.47–50.
55. Waley, *Public Opinion*, p.113.
56. DBFP 2nd-XIV, N493.
57. Pierre Laval was French Minister for Foreign Affairs 1934–5, President of the Council 1935–6.
58. DBFP 2nd-XV, N219.
59. Ibid., N215.
60. Waley, *Public Opinion*, p.13.
61. DBFP 2nd-XIV, N295, note 7.
62. Ibid., N296 and note 3.
63. PRO, Cab23/82 36(35).
64. DBFP 2nd-XIV, N296.
65. Ibid., N296, note 24, N304.
66. Ibid., N309. Thompson minuted on 11 June that the 'weakness of these suggestions is that each one implies the disappearance of Ethiopian independence . . . the people of that country . . . fully appreciate that in the present crisis they have only one thing to lose – their freedom. For this they will fight' (Ibid., N296, note 24).
67. Ibid.
68. Templewood, *Troubled Years*, pp.152–3; Avon, *Dictators*, p.220.
69. Templewood, *Troubled Years*, p.153.
70. DBFP 2nd-XIV, N301 and note 7.

71. Templewood, *Troubled Years*, p.155; DBFP 2nd-XIV, N308 and note 1.
72. Ibid., nos 309, 312, 315.
73. Ibid., N308, note 7.
74. PRO, Cab23/82 33(35).
75. DBFP 2nd-XIV, N325.
76. Ibid., N330.
77. Ibid., N320, note 8.
78. Middlemas and Barnes, *Baldwin*, p.841.
79. DBFP 2nd-XII, N335.
80. DBFP 2nd-XIV, N145.
81. Ibid., N327.
82. Adamthwaite, *The Making*, Document 27, pp.150–1; L. Villari, *Italian Foreign Policy Under Mussolini* (New York, Devin-Adair, 1956), p.124.
83. F.D. Laurens, *France and the Italo-Ethiopian Crisis 1935–1936* (Paris, Mouton, 1967), p.18.
84. DBFP 2nd-XIV, N320; Warner, *Pierre Laval*, pp.67–8.
85. P. Laval, *The Unpublished Diary of Pierre Laval* (London, Falcon Press, 1948), p.34; DBFP 2nd-XIV, N326, note 4.
86. Ibid., N121.
87. Ibid., N310
88. Ibid., N327.
89. Ibid., nos 329, 335.
90. Ibid., N346.
91. PRO, Cab23/82 36(35).
92. DBFP 2nd-XIV, nos 354, 348.
93. PRO, Cab23/82 39(35); DBFP 2nd-XIV, nos 366, 372.
94. Ibid., N380.
95. PRO, Cab23/82 39(35).
96. PRO, Cab 23/82 40(35).
97. DBFP 2nd-XIV, N420 and note 4.
98. Ibid., N426.
99. See p.30.
100. DBFP 2nd-XIV, N426, note 6; N431.
101. Ibid., N434 and note 8.
102. Ibid., nos 456, 465.
103. PRO, Cab23/82 42(35).
104. DBFP 2nd-XIV, Appendix IV; Templewood, *Troubled Years*, p.166; Feiling, *Chamberlain*, p.268; Middlemas and Barnes, *Baldwin*, p.855.
105. DBFP 2nd-XIV, Appendix IV.
106. Ibid., nos 477, 480, 481, 483, N555, note 1.
107. Templewood, *Troubled Years*, pp.168–9; DBFP 2nd-XIV, nos 553, 554, 564.
108. Toynbee, *Survey 1935* (II), pp.221–2.
109. DBFP 2nd-XV, N83, note 4; N27, note 5.
110. Ibid., N83, note 4; N86 and note 2; N87, note 2.
111. Avon, *Dictators*, p.283.
112. DBFP 2nd-XV, N77.
113. Avon, *Dictators*, p.283.
114. DBFP 2nd-XV, N115.
115. Ibid., nos 237, 270.
116. Ibid., N251 and note 12; N270, note 1. The 'Oil Paper' by Hoare and Eden indicated that on 21 November, M. Vasconcellos, Chairman of the Co-ordination Committee at Geneva, advocated to the Committee of eighteen that the proposal of the extension of the embargo to oil, coal, iron and steel should be considered without delay. Among the countries from which Italy received oil, the Soviet Union, Romania, India, Iraq and Netherlands had replied agreeing to the proposal. In addition, the US Secretary of State Cordell Hull said on 15 November that export of oil for war purposes was directly contrary to the general spirit of the recent Neutrality

Act. If an oil embargo had been imposed, it might at least have hampered Italy's war in Abyssinia, even if it were not decisive. (Ibid., nos 237, 270).

117. DBFP 2nd-XIV, N320, note 8.
118. Ibid., N553.
119. Ibid., N564.
120. Ibid., N639.
121. Ibid., N662; N639, note 6.
122. Ibid., N664 and note 4.
123. DBFP 2nd-XV, N29.
124. Ibid., N7.
125. Ibid., N29, note 2; N36.
126. Ibid., nos 91, 108.
127. Ibid., N108, note 3.
128. Ibid., N122, N120, note 6.
129. PRO, Cab23/82 45(35); DBFP 2nd-XV, N134; M. Peterson, *Both Sides of the Curtain: An autobiography* (London, Constable, 1950), p.115.
130. DBFP 2nd-XV, N151. The document was written in French.
131. Ibid., N162.
132. Ibid., N177.
133. Ibid., N166 and note 5.
134. Ibid., nos 215, 219.
135. Ibid., N233; Peterson, *Both Sides*, pp.116–17.
136. DBFP 2nd-XV, N254 and note 4, N292. Eden minuted on 6 December: 'I agree that we cannot go beyond the basis proposed by Mr. Peterson, and though I do not carry its terms definitely in my head, I have my doubts as to whether the Emperor could be expected to accept it with any enthusiasm' (Ibid., N314, note 7).
137. Ibid., N292.
138. Ibid., N274; Templewood, *Troubled Years*, pp.177–8.
139. DBFP 2nd-XV, N175 and note 3.
140. Ibid., nos 314, 258. As for Hoare's interview with General Garibaldi, see Ibid., N278.
141. The documents of the FO showed that the ratio between the British and Italian naval strengths in the Mediterranean was about 3:2. Eden, as well as some other ministers, thought that the danger of 'mad dog' action was 'very remote', because it would cause the isolation of the Italian forces in Abyssinia. If the Italians had attacked the British fleet in the Mediterranean, it would have been nothing but 'suicide'. (DBFP 2nd-XV, N185; PRO, Cab23/82 50(35); Avon, *Dictators*, p.296).
142. PRO, Cab23/82 50(35).
143. Hoare wrote: 'I had no intention of committing the Government to any final plan. Even if Laval and I were able to agree, we were only, at the request of the League, and in continuation of the recommendations of a League Committee, making a purely provisional scheme for bringing together the two disputants that would be referred to Geneva for final approval or rejection' (Templewood, *Troubled Years*, p.178).
144. Ibid., pp.164, 178.
145. DBFP 2nd-XV, N293.
146. On the British side, Hoare, Clerk, Vansittart and Peterson attended the meeting, and the French partners included Laval, Leger, St Quentin and Massigli.
147. PRO, Cab23/82 53(35); for a record of the conversation, see DBFP 2nd-XV, N338.
148. Ibid., N330.
149. Ibid., N337.
150. Ibid., N330.
151. Templewood, *Troubled Years*, p.185; Peterson, *Both Sides*, p.121; Avon, *Dictators*, p.299.
152. Peterson, *Both Sides*, p.119; DBFP 2nd-XV, N347. Obviously, Peterson did not tell the truth in his memoirs. He said that they did not inform the Abyssinians because there were 'no telephone lines to Addis Ababa', and furthermore, the Emperor was fighting on the northern front far away from the capital (Peterson, *Both Sides*, p.120).
153. DBFP 2nd-XV, N335.

154. Ibid., N337; Avon, *Dictators*, p.300; Peterson, *Both Sides*, p.121.
155. PRO, Cab23/82 52(35). Eden said in the House on 10 December ' If Italy and Abyssinia and the League accept to discuss on the basis of the suggestions made in Paris, there is nobody here who is going to say No, even if some of those proposals may not be particularly appealing to us' (RIIA *Documents 1935* (II), p.354).]
156. Ibid., Cab23/82 52(35); see also Eden's telegrams to Barton: (DBFP 2nd-XV, nos 353, 352).
157. Ibid., Cab23/82 53(35).
158. Ibid., Cab23/82 54(35).
159. Waley, *Public Opinion*, p.48; Peterson, *Both Sides*, p.121; N. Nicolson (ed.), *Harold Nicolson: Diaries and Letters 1930–1939* (London, Collins, 1966), p.230.
160. DBFP 2nd-XV, nos 363, 365, 380, 384, 389, 403.
161. H.C. Debs 5th series vol. 307, col. 2019.
162. Dawson was an intimate friend of Baldwin, Chamberlain and Halifax, and a strong supporter of their appeasement policy. There was very often an exchange of views between him and the top British leaders on the Government's policy and the international affairs. 'By the mid 1930s, *The Times* had gained the reputation of being an official spokesman for the British Government.' (F.R. Gannon, *The British Press and Nazi Germany 1936–1939* Oxford, Clarendon Press, 1971, p.70; Office of *The Times*, *The History of The Times 1912–1948* (II), London, Office of *The Times*, 1952, pp. 863, 870–1, 892–3, 923).
163. Waley, *Public Opinion*, pp.54–63.
164. Nicolson, *Harold Nicolson's Diaries*, pp.230, 232.
165. H.C. Debs 5th series vol. 307, cols 2019–2020.
166. Waley, *Public Opinion*, p.65.
167. H.C. Debs 5th series vol. 307, cols 2017–2018.
168. Peterson, *Both Sides*, p.121.
169. DBFP 2nd-XV, Appendix III (a).
170. Ibid; Templewood, *Troubled Years*, p.185. Chamberlain did not want Hoare to leave either. A few days earlier when D.W. Gunston, his Parliamentary Private Secretary, said to him that it looked as though 'Hoare would have to go', he replied indignantly: 'He can't, he's the Foreign Secretary!'. (Waley, *Public Opinion*, p.63).
171. DBFP 2nd-XV, Appendix III (b); C. Petrie, *The Life and Letters of the Right Hon. Sir Austen Chamberlain* (II) (London, Cassell, 1940), p.404; Churchill, *Storm*, p.143.
172. DBFP 2nd-XV, Appendix II (b).
173. Ibid; Templewood, *Troubled Years*, p.185.
174. RIIA *Documents 1935* (II), pp.392–3.
175. It seemed that there was some agreement between him and his colleagues because: (1) it was not true that he said that he decided to resign 'without any suggestion from any one'. this apparently showed the purpose of saving the Cabinet from the crisis by scarifying himself; (2) it could be considered as a reward to him that in only a few months, he returned to the Cabinet as the Admiralty representative.
176. From the Cabinet conclusion of 2 December, Hoare understood that in the Paris discussions, Laval and he would 'agree upon a basis for a peace negotiation', which was of 'special importance', although the Cabinet did not discuss the peace terms in detail. He stayed in Paris for about two days, instead of a few hours, as planned. All Cabinet members knew the urgency and importance of the forthcoming discussions and the possible peace terms – the Peterson–Quentin Proposal and the latest Italian demands. But they seemed to have a different explanation. Eden said: 'We did not, however, discuss any possible terms of peace, either at Cabinet or, so far as I know, between Ministers because the meeting with Laval was not expected to reach conclusions about them . . . Hoare, however, gave no indication, publicly or privately, that he was intending to embark on a serious negotiation with Laval . . . I certainly did not get the impression that any decision of importance had been taken' (Avon, *Dictators*, pp.297–8). Chamberlain denied the importance of the Paris conversation too, and said: 'I believed . . . my colleagues believed also, that he was going to stop off at Paris for a few hours on his way to Switzerland, to get the discussions with the French into such a condition that we could say to the League, 'don't prejudice the chances of a favourable issue by thrusting in a particularly provocative extra sanction at this moment.' Instead of that, a set of proposals was

agreed to, and enough was allowed by the French to leak out to the press to make it impossible for us to amend the proposals, or even to defer accepting them, without throwing over our own Foreign Secretary . . .' What Halifax wrote to Chamberlain on 26 December might explain more. 'the initial mistake was Sam's, in publishing his (and therefore, except at great price, *our*) assent in the Paris communiqué. And what of course explains – but doesn't justify – what we did was the habit of immense confidence we had rightly developed in him.' (Feiling, *Chamberlain*, pp.274–5). The above quotations show that on one hand ministers understood the Cabinet conclusion differently; on the other hand, they were anxious to avoid the blame when the plan failed.

177. DBFP 2nd-XVI, N16.
178. DBFP 2nd-XV, N442. On 12 February, the Petroleum Committee submitted a report showing that a universal oil embargo would be fully effective within three months. (Ibid., N514). On the eve of the Munich Conference in 1938, Mussolini told Hitler about 'the catastrophic consequences that would have ensued for Italy at the time of the Abyssinian war, if the League of Nations had extended its sanctions to oil, even if only for a week' (P. Schmidt, *Hitler's Interpreter*, London, Heinemann, 1951, p.112).
179. DBFP 2nd-XV, N442 and note 4.
180. Ibid., 2nd-XX, N450.
181. Ibid., nos 450, 454, 457.
182. DBFP 2nd-XV, N526.
183. Ibid., N545.
184. Ibid., nos 459, 463.
185. Ibid., N536.
186. Ibid., N526, note 1.
187. Ibid., N545 and note 3.
188. DBFP 2nd-XVI, N3 and note 10.
189. Ibid., nos 3, 6, 11, 13, 14, 20.
190. PRO, Cab23/83 15(36).
191. DBFP 2nd-XVI, N207, note 2.
192. Ibid., nos 197, 243.
193. Ibid., nos 221, 223, 243.
194. Ibid., N263.
195. J. Gehl, *Austria, Germany and the Anschluss, 1931–1938* (London, Oxford University Press, 1963), p.116, note 6 and p.117.
196. E. Haraszti, *The Invaders: Hitler Occupies the Rhineland* (Budapest, Akademiaikiado, 1983), pp.85–8.
197. See p.100.
198. Avon, *Dictators*, pp.296–7; Feiling, *Chamberlain*, p.265; Schmidt, *Hitler's*, p.112.
199. Avon, *Dictators*, p.208.
200. DBFP 2nd-XIV, nos 160, 276; *Documents on German Foreign Policy 1918–1945*, Series C, IV, (London, HMSO), N579.
201. Feiling, *Chamberlain*, pp.295–6. He had discussed this idea with Eden, and won the latter's agreement (H. Gibbs, *Grand Strategy* (I) London, HMSO, 1976, p.258, footnote).

CHAPTER 3

1. *Documents on British Foreign Policy 1919–1939*, 2nd Series, XII (London, HMSO), p.v.
2. N.H. Gibbs, *Grand Strategy* (I) (London, HMSO, 1976), p.135.
3. N.H. Baynes (ed.), *The Speeches of Adolf Hitler, April 1922–August 1939* (London, Oxford University Press, 1942), pp.1208–11; DBFP 2nd-XII, N570.
4. *Documents on German Foreign Policy 1918–1945*, Series C, IV (London, HMSO), pp.171–8.
5. Ibid., N107.
6. On 7 August, von Neurath, the German Foreign Minister, wrote to State Secretary von Bülow that it was undesirable and premature to discuss the Pact questions with Britain and

France at that stage. He would not advise Hitler to make a definitive statement, and 'no German views can be expected before October' (Ibid., N252).

7. Hitler had only expressed his consideration to von Neurath, the Foreign Minister; von Blomberg, Colonel General and War Minister; von Fritsch, General and Commander-in-Chief of the Army; von Ribbentrop, Ambassador Extraordinary; Goering, General and President of the Reich; von Bülow, State Secretary; Hassell, German Ambassador in Italy, and Dr Forster, Counsellor at the German Embassy in France on several occasions (Ibid., N564 and note 3; N575; E.H. Haraszti, *The Invaders: Hitler Occupies the Rhineland*, Budapest, Akademiaikiado, 1983, Appendix VIII: Forester, Details of the Rhineland Occupation).

8. DGFP C-IV, N564.

9. Ibid., N579; Haraszti, *The Invaders*, Appendix VIII; N. Nicolson, *Harold Nicolson: Diaries and Letters, 1930–1939* (London, Collins, 1966), p.247.

10. DGFP C-IV, N575.

11. Nicolson, *Nicolson's Diaries*, p.249; DBFP 2nd-XVI, N27, N52 note 2.

12. W.L. Shirer, *The Rise and Fall of The Third Reich* (New York, Simon & Schuster, 1960), p.291; W. Churchill, *The Gathering Storm* (London, Cassell, 1948), p.154; DGFP C-IV, p.1218.

13. DGFP C-V, N3.

14. Gibbs, *Strategy*, pp.139–40; DBFP 2nd-XVII, N386 and notes 1, 4.

15. DBFP 2nd-XVI, nos 82, 112.

16. Churchill, *Storm*, p.152.

17. P. Schmidt, *Hitler's Interpreter* (London, Heinemann, 1951), p.41.

18. K. Eubank, *The Origins of World War II* (Arlington Heights, Ill, H. Davidson, 1969), pp.56–7; P.M.H. Bell, *The Origins of the Second World War in Europe* (London, Longman, 1986), p.211; R.J.Q. Adams, *British Politics and Foreign Policy in the Age of Appeasement 1935–39* (London, Macmillan, 1993), p.47; Earl of Avon, *Facing the Dictators* (London, Cassell, 1962), p.376.

19. For example, apart from Eden and Vansittart, many other members of staff, such as Carr, Wigram, Head of the Central Department, Sargent, Counsellor at the FO, W. Strang, Counsellor at the FO, Lord Stanhope, Parliamentary Under-Secretary, and Lord Cranborne, Under-Secretary held this point of view (DBFP 2nd-XV, N490 and notes 2, 3, N493).

20. Vansittart also had a strong influence on his bosses. He was Baldwin's private secretary before he became Permanent Under-Secretary (PUS). He was close to MacDonald, and his advice had great weight in the latter's decision and the latter's cabinet. Being a long time in his post as PUS, he worked with three Foreign Secretaries, and Simon relied on him. Hoare was perhaps the Foreign Secretary on whom Vansittart had most influence. It was generally accepted in the Cabinet that Hoare had been misled by his official Vansittart during the Hoare–Laval affair. Eden usually took Vansittart's suggestions too although their personal relationship was poor. Chamberlain disliked this, and said 'Van had the effect of multiplying the extent of Anthony's natural vibrations . . .', DBFP 2nd-XV, Appendix III (b); N. Rose, *Vansittart: Study of a Diplomat* (London, Heinemann, 1978), pp.63–4, 109, 164, 165, 167, 168; Avon, *Dictators*, pp.187, 521; I. Colvin, *Vansittart in Office* (London, Gollancz, 1965), pp.21, 148; J. Simon, *Retrospect: the memoirs of Viscount Simon* (London, Hutchinson, 1952), p.177; T. Jones, *A Diary with Letters 1931–1950* (London, Oxford University Press, 1954), pp.158–60; K. Middlemas, *Diplomacy of Illusion: The British Government and Germany, 1937–39* (London, Weidenfeld & Nicolson, 1972), p.78.

21. DBFP 2nd-XVII, Appendix II, pp.794, 796.

22. Viscount Templewood, *Nine Troubled Years* (London, Collins, 1954), pp.136, 202, 256–7; D. Dutton, 'Simon and Eden at the Foreign Office 1931–1935', *Review of International Studies* 20 (1994) 42–3; 1st Earl of Halifax, *Fulness of Days* (London, Collins, 1957), pp.194–5; Avon, *Dictators*, pp.319, 383, 445.

23. Ibid., p.242.

24. Templewood, *Troubled Years*, p.373.

25. M. Gilbert and R. Gott, *The Appeasers*, (London, Weidenfeld & Nicolson, 1963), pp.xi, 76–77; Rose, *Vansittart*, p.vii.

26. Simon, *Retrospect*, p.178.

27. See pp.27–8.
28. DBFP 2nd-VI, Appendix III.
29. Ibid., 2nd-XIII, N14.
30. Ibid., 2nd-VI, N322.
31. DGFP C-IV, N107.
32. DBFP 2nd-XV, N507.
33. Ibid., N213.
34. Ibid., N271 and note 3.
35. A collection of Phipps' dispatches from 1933 to 1935 was circulated to the Cabinet as an important reference source for the German problem (Ibid., N460).
36. Ibid., Appendix I (a).
37. Ibid., Appendix I (b).
38. Ibid., Appendix I (c) and note 16.
39. Ibid., N241.
40. Ibid., N383; DGFP C-IV, nos 460, 462.
41. DBFP 2nd-XV, N383, note 7; N404.
42. Ibid., N404, note 5.
43. Ibid., N382.
44. Ibid., N455.
45. Ibid., N455, note 3; N476; Gibbs, *Strategy*, p.230. Among the Cabinet members, there used to exist different opinions towards the Zone. Baldwin said to the House on 30 July 1934: 'When you think of the defence of England, you no longer think of the chalk cliffs of Dover; you think of the Rhine'. Simon also suggested to the Cabinet in early 1935 that the demilitarisation of the Rhineland should still be considered 'a vital British interest'. But after discussion, the Cabinet drew the opposite conclusion (Ibid., pp.107, 228).
46. DBFP 2nd-XV, N476.
47. Ibid., N521 and note 1.
48. Ibid., N460.
49. Public Record Office, Cab23/83 3(36); DBFP 2nd-XV, N460, note 3; DBFP 2nd-XX, nos 450, 457; see also pp.105–6.
50. DBFP 2nd-XV, N382.
51. Ibid., N471; N493 note 7; N497, Appendix IV (b).
52. Ibid., Appendix IV (b).
53. Ibid., N509.
54. Ibid., N509, note 3.
55. Ibid., N521, note 1.
56. Ibid., nos 482, 483.
57. Ibid., N521.
58. Ibid., N524.
59. Ibid., N541.
60. DBFP 2nd-XVI, nos 9, 10, 12.
61. The Franco-Russian Pact was ratified by 353 votes to 164 in the French Chamber on 27 February 1936.
62. PRO, Cab23/83 15(36).
63. DBFP 2nd-XVI, N29 and note 5; DGFP C-V, N8.
64. DBFP 2nd-XVI, N24.
65 Baynes, *Hitler's Speeches*, pp.1271–302.
66. DGFP C-V, N66.
67. F.R. Gannon, *The British Press and Nazy Germany 1936–1939* (Oxford, Clarendon, 1971), pp.93–9.
68. Nicolson, *Nicolson's Diaries*, p.248; DGFP C-V, nos 66, 178.
69. *Parliamentary Debates: Commons*, 5th Series, vol. 309, col. 1863.
70. DGFP C-V, nos 66, 178.
71. Nicolson, *Nicolson's Diaries*, pp.249–50.
72. Churchill, *Storm*, pp.159–60; DGFP C-V, N178.
73. DGFP C-V, N178. It was generally accepted that Churchill would be appointed as Minister

for Co-ordination of Defence. However, to everyone's surprise, Inskip instead was announced as Defence Minister on 13 March by the Cabinet, which thought that appointment of Churchill would be 'provocative' to Hitler (Ibid., N178, note 9; K. Middlemas and J. Barnes, *Baldwin: A Biography*, London, Weidenfeld & Nicolson, 1969, pp.916–17).

74. Avon, *Dictators*, p.367.
75. A. Adamthwaite, 'The British Government and the Media, 1937–1938', *Journal of Contemporary History*, 18 (1983) 282–3.
76. H.C. Debs 5th Series, vol. 309, col. 1812.
77. Avon, *Dictators*, p.343.
78. Ibid., p.344; DBFP 2nd-XVI, N39.
79. Ibid., nos 40, 47.
80. Ibid., N48. At the Locarno Power meeting of 10 March Italy declared that being 'a State subject to sanctions' due to the Abyssinian problem, she 'could not agree in advance to any action of political, economic, or military character' (Ibid., N63).
81. Ibid., N48.
82. Avon, *Dictators*, p.346.
83. H.C. Debs 5th Series, vol. 309, col. 1812.
84. DBFP 2nd-XVI, N49 and note 3; Avon, *Dictators*, p.347.
85. DBFP 2nd-XVI, N63.
86. Ibid., N70, note 1; PRO, Cab23/83 18(36).
87. DBFP 2nd-XV, nos 21, 74, 101, 109.
88. Ibid., N43.
89. Ibid., N43, note 4.
90. Ibid., N192 and notes 1, 2.
91. Ibid., N516, note 3.
92. DBFP 2nd-XVII, N453 and note 4.
93. PRO, Cab23/83 18(36).
94. DBFP 2nd-XVI, nos 70, 74, 78, note 7; DGFP C-V, N85.
95. Churchill, *Storm*, p.153; Nicolson, *Nicolson's Diaries*, pp.250–1.
96. Churchill, *Storm*, p.154; see also the possible record of this conversation in DBFP 2nd-XVI, N78.
97. K. Feiling, *Life of Neville Chamberlain* (London, Macmillan, 1946), p.279.
98. DBFP 2nd-XVI, N109; see also nos 82, 91.
99. Ibid., N119.
100. Ibid., N110.
101. Ibid., N110, note 5.
102. Ibid., N115 and note 2.
103 The final resolution of 19 March, says: 'decide to invite the German Government to lay before the Permanent Court of International Justice at the Hague the argument which it claims to draw from the incompatibility between the Franco-Soviet Pact of Mutual Assistance and the Treaty of Locarno, and to undertake to accept as final the decision of the said court, without prejudice to the operation of paragraph 7(2) below [i.e. revision of the status of the Rhineland. – Author]' (Ibid., N144).
104. PRO, Cab23/83 21(36).
105. DBFP 2nd-XVI, N132, note 5, N144; Avon, *Dictators*, p.360.
106. DBFP 2nd-XVI, N145; DGFP C-V, N162.
107. DBFP 2nd-XVI, N163; DGFP C-V, N207.
108. DBFP 2nd-XVI, N193; DGFP C-V, N242.
109. PRO, Cab23/83 26(36).
110. DBFP 2nd-XVI, p.228, nos 222, 223.
111. Ibid., N202.
112. PRO, Cab23/83 28(36).
113. DBFP 2nd-XVI, N219.
114. Ibid., nos 234, 277.
115. See p.122.
116. DBFP 2nd-XVI, N74; DGFP C-V, N85.

117. DBFP 2nd-XVI, N122.
118. Ibid., N135.
119. Ibid., N121; N122, note 4.
120. Ibid., N122, note 4; N135, note 5.
121. Ibid., N272.
122. Ibid., N277.
123. Avon, *Dictators*, p.371.
124. DBFP 2nd-XVI, N277, note 10.
125. Duff Cooper said at the Cabinet meeting of 11 March: 'in three years' time, though we should have reconditioned at any rate to some extent our small forces, yet by that time Germany would have 100 divisions and a powerful fleet. We should not relatively, therefore, be in a better position' (see PRO, Cab23/83 18(36)). As to the policy of rearmament, see pp.25–31, 214–18.
126. The Cabinet Committee was composed of Baldwin (Chair), MacDonald, Chamberlain, Lord Hailsham, Simon, Eden, Halifax and Inskip.
127. DBFP 2nd-XVI, Appendix I (a) *Extract from Cabinet Minutes of April 29, 1936*.
128. Ibid., Appendix I (b) *Extract from Cabinet Minutes of April 30, 1936*.
129. Ibid., N283.
130. Ibid., nos 283, 304, 306.
131. Ibid., N304, note 2.
132. Ibid., N304 and notes 2, 3; N307.
133. Ibid., N277, note 10; N310.
134. Ibid., N324.
135. Ibid., nos 340, 369, 374, 394. On 16 June, von Neurath told Phipps that he had drafted the reply some time ago and submitted it to the Führer. It should have been handed to the British Ambassador on 19 June, but Hitler held on to the document, 'in view of the impending meeting of remaining Locarno Powers' (Ibid., nos 374, 369; DGFP C-V, N466).
136. DBFP 2nd-XVI, N328.
137. Ibid., nos 320, 414.
138. Ibid., N339.
139. Ibid., N371.
140. Ibid., N356.
141. Ibid., N328, note 3; N339, note 2.
142. PRO, Cab23/83 38(36).
143. DBFP 2nd-XVI, N393.
144. Ibid., N404.
145 Ibid., N407, note 4.
146. Ibid., Appendix II, *Extract from Cabinet Minutes of July 6, 1936*. The Three Power conference was held in London on 23 July, at the British Government's suggestion. Italy refused the invitation with some reluctance (Ibid., nos 420, 429, 432, 436).
147. Ibid., N417.
148. A.J. Toynbee (ed.) *Survey of International Affairs 1936* (London, Oxford University Press, 1937), p.341.
149. DBFP 2nd-XVII, N389.
150. DBFP 2nd-XVIII, N274.
151. Avon, *Dictators*, p.324.
152. Middlemas and Barnes, *Baldwin*, pp.947, 950.
153. Gibbs, *Strategy*, p.252.
154. Feiling, *Chamberlain*, p.295.
155. Toynbee, *Survey 1936*, pp.351–60

CHAPTER 4

1. *Documents on British Foreign Policy 1919–1939*, 2nd Series, XVII (London, HMSO), nos 114, 134, 321, 349, Appendix I, p.760.

2. J. Gehl, *Austria, Germany, and the Anschluss 1931–1938* (London, Oxford University Press, 1963), p.53.
3. *Documents on German Foreign Policy 1918–1945*, Series C, III (London, HMSO), nos 115, 119.
4. Franz von Papen, *Memoirs*, trans. B. Connell (New York, Dutton, 1953), pp.340–2; DGFP C-III, N167; Gehl, *Austria*, p.102.
5. *Documents on German Foreign Policy 1918–1945*, Series D, I (London, HMSO), N152.
6. W. Churchill, *The Gathering Storm* (London, Cassell, 1948), p.202; E. Robertson, *Hitler's Pre-war Policy and Military Plan* (London, Longman, 1963), p.91 and note 1; DGFP D-I, pp.433–4.
7. Gehl, *Austria*, p.116, note 6 and p.117.
8. DGFP C-IV, nos 579, 603.
9. Ibid., N485.
10. M. Muggeridge (ed.), *Ciano's Diplomatic Papers* (London, Odham's Press, 1948), pp.56–60; DGFP C-V, N624.
11. DGFP C-III, N555.
12. DGFP D-I, N31.
13. P. Schmidt, *Hitler's Interpreter* (London, Heinemann, 1951), pp.76–7.
14. DGFP D-I, nos 50, 59.
15. Ibid., N19. However, Hitler's strategy was not popular among his generals, nor with his Foreign Minister. After this meeting, von Neurath discussed with Generals Fritsch and Beck what could be done 'to get Hitler to change his ideas' (W.L. Shirer, *The Rise and Fall of the Third Reich*, New York, Simon & Schuster, 1960, pp.309–10). In the face of opposition, Hitler made 'sweeping changes in the German hierarchy' in early February 1938. They included the resignation of the War Minister, General von Blomberg (precipitated by his marriage), and General von Fritsch, Commander-in-Chief of the Army. Hitler himself took over the War Ministry and command of the Army. Von Ribbentrop replaced von Neurath as the Foreign Minister (DBFP 2nd-XIX, N492, note 1; N496; G. Brook-Shepherd, *Anschluss: The Rape of Austria*, London, Macmillan, 1963, pp.30–2).
16. Von Papen, *Memoirs*, pp.380–1; DGFP D-I, N273.
17. Gehl, *Austria*, p.166.
18. Shirer, *The Rise*, pp.325–30; DGFP D-I, nos 294, 295; DBFP 2nd-XIX, nos 513, 516, 517.
19. DGFP D-I, N340.
20. Ibid., N328.
21. Ibid., nos 132, 133, 138, 147. Henderson later explained: 'I never said that I had spoken here in favour of the Anschluss. What I did say was that I had sometimes expressed personal views which may not have been entirely in accordance with those of my Government (Ibid., N139).
22. Ibid., N339 and p.568.
23. Churchill, *Storm*, pp.212–13; A.J.P. Taylor, *The Origins of the Second World War* (London, Hamilton, 1972), pp.149–50; K. Eubank, *The Origins of World War II* (Arlington Heights, Ill., H. Davidson, 1969), p.98; P.M.H. Bell, *The Origins of the Second World War In Europe* (London, Longman, 1986), p.229.
24. Viscount Templewood, *Nine Troubled Years* (London, Collins, 1954), p.283.
25 K. Middlemas and J. Barnes, *Baldwin: A Biography* (London, Weidenfeld and Nicolson, 1969), pp.926, 929–31, 962–5; Earl of Avon., *Facing the Dictators* (London, Cassell, 1962), pp.403, 445, 479; Templewood, *Troubled Years*, pp.26, 223.
26. K. Feiling, *Life of Neville Chamberlain* (London, Macmillan, 1946), pp.303, 305; Templewood, *Troubled Years*, pp.37, 257; Churchill, *Storm*, p.173.
27. Templewood, *Troubled Years*, pp.36, 259–60; The Earl of Birkenhead, *Halifax: The Life of Lord Halifax* (London, Hamilton, 1965), p.422.
28. Once, in front of Eden, Sir Austen, Chamberlain's half-brother, said, 'Neville, you must remember you don't know anything about foreign affairs' (Avon, *Dictators*, p.445). Cadogan remarked in his diaries that Eden was unlucky in his chiefs: 'Chamberlain took too much.' (D. Dilks (ed.) *The Diaries of Sir Alexander Cadogan, 1938–1945* (London, Cassell, 1971), p.54.

29. Feiling, *Chamberlain*, p.324.
30. Ibid., p.456.
31. Since the end of 1936, Eden and Baldwin had considered some new appointment for Vansittart because his position had been shaken by the Abyssinian crisis. Early in 1937, Eden told Oliver Harvey, his Private Secretary, 'about his lack of confidence in Van's judgement' and belief that he was no longer 'in a fit state of health for his work'. In the Autumn, Eden finally decided that Cadogan was to be PUS, and created the new office of Chief Diplomatic Adviser for Vansittart. Chamberlain supported this decision, and he himself informed Vansittart of the appointment (J. Harvey (ed.) *The Diplomatic Diaries of Oliver Harvey, 1937–1940* (London, Collins, 1970), p.22; Avon, *Dictators*, p.521; DBFP 2nd-XVII, p.xiv; DBFP 2nd-XIX, N408 note 2).

It was generally accepted that Vansittart was 'kicked upstairs' because he did not agree with the Government's policy towards the Dictator Powers (I. Colvin, *The Chamberlain Cabinet* (London, Gollancz, 1971), p.264, footnote 1; N. Rose, *Vansittart: Study of a Diplomat* (London, Heinemann, 1978), pp.206–7; Avon, *Dictators*, pp.447, 448, 576; DGFP D-I, N95). However, as we discuss in Chapter 3, there was no fundamental difference between his policy and the Government's. In fact, many of the Cabinet's decisions were based on his proposals, recommended by Eden. The reason for his losing power and influence resulted from his poor relationship with his colleagues, as Eden said: 'Van had been a long time in his post and he was becoming ineffective – no longer getting along with the other heads of Departments in Whitehall.' (Colvin, *Vansittart in Office* (London, Gollancz, 1965), p.149; Avon, *Dictators*, p.521).

Other solid evidence can be found from his colleagues' comments, which were negative and controversial. For example, Eden generally took Vansittart's proposal as the basis of policy-making, but he wrote in his memoirs: 'I have never known one to compare with Sir Robert as a relentless, not say ruthless, worker for the views he held strongly himself. The truth is that Vansittart was seldom an official giving cool and disinterested advice based on study and experience. He was himself a sincere, almost fanatical, crusader, and much more a Secretary of State in mentality than a permanent official.' (Avon, *Dictators*, p.242). Cadogan remarked: 'if he has any ideas or impressions, why can't he put them down straight on paper, instead of dancing literary hornpipes?', 'He pretends to be very slick and cute but I can't see that he does, or has any idea of doing, *anything*'. (Dilks, *Cadogan's Diaries*, p.13). However, Sir Warren Fisher, head of the Civil Service, asked Lady Vansittart at a party to persuade her husband 'not to write these long papers for the Cabinet. They don't like it . . . He's exceeding his functions'. (Colvin, *Vansittart*, pp.147–8). Removal of Vansittart was not only welcomed by his colleagues, but also by his bosses. Chamberlain told his sister: 'After all the months that S[tanley] B[aldwin] wasted in futile attempts to push Van out of the FO it is amazing to record that I have done it in 3 days' (DBFP 2nd-XIX, N408, note 2; K. Middlemas, *Diplomacy of Illusion: The British Government and Germany, 1937–39* (London, Weidenfeld & Nicolson, 1972), p.78).

It is fair to say that, not being a 'yes-man', Vansittart spoke out over his distrust of dictators. His dismissal indicated that Chamberlain's Government did not tolerate any kind of opposite view within its circle.

32. Harvey, *Harvey's Diaries*, p.66.
33. Dilks, *Cadogan's Diaries*, p.29; K. Robbins (ed.), *The Blackwell Biographical Dictionary of British Political Life in the Twentieth Century* (Oxford, Blackwell, 1990), p.77. Chamberlain said: 'when Anthony can work out his ideas with a sane, slow man, like Alick Cadogan, he will be much steadier'. (Middlemas, *Diplomacy*, p.78).
34. Dilks, *Cadogan's Diaries*, pp.47, 62, 63.
35. Colvin, *Vansittart*, p.199; M. Gilbert and R. Gott, *The Appeasers* (London, Weidenfeld & Nicolson, 1963), pp.68–9, 376–7; 1st Earl of Halifax, *Fulness of Days* (London, Collins, 1957), p.231; Templewood, *Troubled Years*, pp.260–1; DGFP D-I, N128.
36. DBFP 2nd-XIX, N433 and Appendix I.
37. Ibid., N79, note 1; nos 115, 484, 493; Avon, *Dictators*, pp.572–3.
38. DBFP 2nd-XIX, N410, Appendix I, p.1139; Templewood, *Troubled Years*, p.258.
39. Halifax, *Fulness*, pp.193–5; Birkenhead, *Halifax*, pp.379–80. Their divergence, as Eden said

in his resignation speech, was 'not of aim, but of outlook', which implied that he resigned due to 'a matter of procedure rather than a major part of policy' (Parliamentary Debates: Commons, 5th series, vol. 332, cols 45–50; A.R. Peters, *Anthony Eden at The Foreign Office, 1931–1938* (New York, St Martin's Press, 1986), p.360).

40. DGFP D-I, nos 120, 127; Brook-Shepherd, *Anschluss*, pp.82, 93; N. Nicolson (ed.) *Harold Nicolson: Diaries and Letters 1930–1939* (London, Collins, 1966), pp. 319–20.

41. Eden was far from an unequivocal opponent of the Government's policy, because even after his resignation, he held an idea of rejoining the Cabinet, and kept attempting this until the outbreak of war, when he was offered a post as Dominions Secretary in the War Cabinet (D. Carlton, *Anthony Eden: A Biography* London, Allen Lane, 1981, pp.132–53; Harvey, *Harvey's Diaries*, pp.249, 256–7, 279–80, 284–6, 295, 299, 305). During the Munich crisis, he visited Halifax on 11 September, expressing 'complete agreement with the line taken' (Public Record Office, Cab23/95 37(38); Harvey, *Harvey's Diaries*, p.175). When Chamberlain came back from Munich, Eden saluted him: 'We all owe him, and every citizen owes him, a measureless debt of gratitude for the sincerity and pertinacity which he has devoted in the final phase of the crisis to averting the supreme calamity of war' (H.C. Debs. 5th Series vol. 339, col. 78, 3 Oct. 1938). Therefore, Eden's resignation by no means erased his reputation as an arch-appeaser.

42. Feiling, *Chamberlain*, pp.305, 339, 398; Robbins, *British Political Life*, pp.224–5; Dilks, *Cadogan's Diaries*, pp.54, 105–6; Birkenhead, *Halifax*, pp.364, 381, 418–20; PRO, Cab23/95 43(38).

43. Avon, *Dictators*, p.504; Colvin, *Vansittart*, p.146.

44. DBFP 2nd-XIX, N334, note 5; Nicolson, *Nicolson's Diaries*, p.334.

45. PRO, Cab23/95 37(38); D. Cooper, *Old Men Forget: The Autobiography of Duff Cooper* (London, Hart-Davis, 1953), p.227.

46. The FPC usually included the Inner Cabinet Members, such as Chamberlain, Halifax, Simon, Hoare and some other principal ministers. Wilson and Cadogan often attended meetings. Vansittart, however, was called only when ministers needed to consult him.

47. Templewood, *Troubled Years*, pp.257, 290; Colvin, *Vansittart*, p.303.

48. Harvey, *Harvey's Diaries*, pp.86, 212–3.

49. DGFP D-I, N128.

50. DBFP 2nd–XVII, N45 and note 3.

51. Avon, *Dictators*, pp.403–4.

52. Ibid., p.401; DBFP 2nd–XVII, nos 115, 52.

53. Ibid., nos 126, 157.

54. Ibid., N157 note 1, N126 note 5.

55. R.O. Paxton, *Europe in the 20th Century*, 2nd edn (Orlando, Harcourt Brace Jovanovich, 1985c), pp.404–5.

56. DBFP 2nd–XVII, N272, N395 note 1.

57. Ibid., N359.

58. The Anglo-Italian Agreement was signed on 16 April 1938, under which Mussolini agreed to withdraw Italian troops from Spain, and in return the British Government would 'remove such obstacles as might be held to impede the freedom of States members of the League as regards the recognition of Italian sovereignty over Ethiopia' (DBFP 2nd-XIX nos 643, 660, 662). However, in spite of 'his solemn engagement', il Duce sent another 4,000 volunteers in June and July. Because of this, the Agreement did not come into force (Nicolson, *Nicolson's Diaries*, p.347, footnote 3). Chamberlain, however, failed to learn any lesson from this, and trusted the dictators as much as usual.

59. In his Leamington and Bradford speeches on 20 November and 14 December, 1936, Eden said: 'If our vital interests are situated in certain clearly definable areas, our interest in peace is world-wide.' While he declared that Britain must bring her defences up to a standard commensurate with her world-wide interests and responsibility, he emphasised Britain's obligation to France and Belgium. He told his audience that apart from being used in defence of British vital interests, British arms might be used in bringing help to a victim of aggression in any case under the covenant, but 'in such an instance there is no automatic obligation to take military action.' He appealed for co-operation with the dictator powers, particularly

Germany: 'So far are we from wishing to encircle Germany that we seek for her co-operation with other nations in the economic and financial as well as in the political sphere. We want neither *blocs* nor barriers in Europe.' (Royal Institute of International Affairs, *Documents on International Affairs 1936* (London, Oxford University Press, 1937), pp.260–7).

60. DBFP 2nd–XVIII, N479, note 1; N566.
61. Ibid., 2nd–XIX, N53.
62. Ibid., 2nd–XVIII, N479, note 1; N566 and all notes.
63. Ibid., 2nd–XIX, N53, notes.
64. Ibid., N319 and note 11.
65. Ibid., 2nd–XVIII, N510.
66. Ibid., 2nd–XIX, N15, Appendix I.
67. Ibid., 2nd–XVIII, nos 611, 624.
68. Ibid., N619.
69. Ibid., N623 and note 1.
70. Ibid., N639 and notes.
71. Peters, *Eden at Office*, p.275; Carlton, *Eden*, pp.102–4.
72. In these incidents, the German warships were bombed in the waters off Spain.
73. DBFP 2nd–XVIII, nos 600, 627, 630, 660; N. Henderson, *Failure of A Mission* (New York, G. P. Putnam's Sons, 1940), pp.62–4.
74. DBFP 2nd–XIX, Appendix I.
75. Ibid., 2nd–XVIII, nos 628, 636, 638, 641; Peters, *Eden*, pp.277–8.
76. F.R. Gannon, *The British Press and Nazi Germany 1936–1939* (Oxford, Clarendon Press, 1971), p.71; Peters, *Eden at Office*, p.278.
77. DBFP 2nd–XIX, N115.
78. Henderson, *A Mission*, p.93.
79. Halifax, *Fulness*, p.184.
80. Avon, *Dictators*, p.509.
81. DBFP 2nd–XIX, N264.
82. Ibid., N272 and note 5.
83. Ibid., nos 298, 306, 307.
84. Ibid., N310. Chamberlain intimated 'very strongly' to Halifax on 27 October that the latter 'ought to manage to see Hitler – even if it meant going to Berchtergaten [*sic*] – or whatever the place is' (Ibid., N273, note 3).
85. Ibid., N319, note 11; Harvey, *Oliver Harvey's Diaries*, p.60.
86. DBFP 2nd–XIX, N273.
87. Ibid., nos 349, 395.
88. Ibid., nos 332, 336, 337, 338. See also pp.137–8.
89. Harvey, *Harvey's Diaries*, pp.61–2.
90. DBFP 2nd–XIX, N346.
91. Ibid., N349.
92. Ibid., N346. In *Facing the Dictators*, Eden described the Halifax–Hitler conversation as a 'rather aimless and therefore hazardous discussion', 'I wish that Halifax had warned Hitler more strongly against intervention in Central Europe.' (Avon, *Dictators*, p.515).
93. DBFP 2nd–XIX, nos 394, 395.
94. Avon, *Dictators*, p.516
95. DBFP 2nd–XIX, N349.
96. Harvey, *Harvey's Diaries*, pp.62–3. Chamberlain wrote to his sister: 'I saw Anthony on Friday morning [11 February 1938] and we were in complete agreement, more complete perhaps than we have sometimes been in the past.' (Dilks, *Cadogan's Diaries*, p.47, footnote 2).
97. DBFP 2nd–XIX, nos 334, 337, 365, 374, 375, 380.
98. Ibid., N337, note 3.
99. Ibid., N334, note 5.
100. Ibid., N301, note 2.
101. Ibid., nos 325, 394, 395.
102. Ibid., N335, 341.
103. Harvey, *Harvey's Diaries*, p.62.

104. DBFP 2nd–XIX, N354.
105. Ibid., N358.
106. Ibid., N360.
107. Ibid., N401.
108. Harvey, *Harvey's Diaries*, p.62.
109. DBFP 2nd–XIX, N409.
110. Ibid., N465 and note 4, Appendix I.
111. Ibid., N439 and note 1, N433.
112. Ibid., N465 and note 4.
113. Ibid., N468, notes 3, 5; Dilks, *Cadogan's Diaries*, p.41.
114. DBFP 2nd–XIX, N469.
115. Ibid., N477.
116. Ibid., N488.
117. Ibid., N488 and notes 16, 17.
118. Ibid., N512.
119. See Chapter 4, note 15.
120. DBFP 2nd–XIX, N500.
121. Ibid., N500, note 3; Dilks, *Cadogan's Diaries*, p.45.
122. DBFP 2nd–XIX, N503.
123. Gannon, *British Press*, pp.143–5.
124. Brook-Shepherd, *Anschluss*, p.87.
125. H.C. Debs. 5th Series vol. 331, col. 1863, 16 Feb. 1938.
126. Nicolson, *Nicolson's Diaries*, p.323.
127. DGFP D–I, N274.
128. Nicolson, *Nicolson's Diaries*, pp.314–15.
129. DBFP 2nd–XIX, N343.
130. A. Adamthwaite, 'The British Government and the Media 1937–1938', *Journal of Contemporary History*, 18 (1983), 284.
131. Harvey, *Harvey's Diaries*, pp.102, 108.
132. H.C. Debs 5th Series vol. 332, col. 1248, 2 Mar. 1938.
133. DBFP 2nd–XIX, N517.
134. Ibid., N523, note 1, N541.
135. Dilks, *Cadogan's Diaries*, pp.46–7; Harvey, *Harvey's Diaries*, p.91.
136. Ibid., p.90.
137. DBFP 2nd–XIX, N517, note 3.
138. Ibid., N517, note 5.
139. Ibid., N534.
140. Ibid., N522, note 4.
141. Ibid., nos 554, 557.
142. Ibid., N557, note 5; nos 580, 592.
143. Ibid., N606.
144. Ibid., N605
145. Ibid., nos 609, 610, 611.
146. Ibid., N615.
147. See p. 139, Chapter 4, note 21.
148. Feiling, *Chamberlain*, p.341.
149. PRO, Cab23/92 11(38) 9 Mar. 1938.
150. Ibid., FO371/22313 R2271/137/3; PRO, FO371/22314 R2272/137/3, R2273/137/3.
151. Ibid., FO371/22314 R2286/137/3.
152. Ibid., FO371/21656 C1664/42/18.
153. Ibid., FO371/22314 R2340/137/3.
154. Ibid., FO371/22314 R2325/137/3.
155. Ibid., FO371/22314 R2342/137/3, R2354/137/3, R2368/137/3, R2382/137/3.
156. Ibid., FO371/22314 R2394/137/3; Dilks, *Cadogan's Diaries*, p.60.
157. In the course of discussion in the FO, Cadogan asked Vansittart, 'Will you fight?' The latter said 'No', although he did not want to give up. Cadogan went on to say ironically, 'It seems

a most cowardly thing to do to urge a small man to fight a big if you won't help the former.' (Dilks, *Cadogan's Diaries*, p.60).

158. Ibid., p.60; PRO, FO371/22314 R2354/137/3.
159. PRO, FO371/22315 R2458/137/3, R2459/137/3.
160. PRO, FO371/22314 R2353/137/3, R2369/137/3, R2393/137/3.
161. PRO, FO371/22314 R2383/137/3.
162. Gannon, *British Press*, pp.149–50, 158–9.
163. N. Thompson, *The Anti-appeasers: Conservative Opposition to Appeasement in the 1930s* (Oxford, Clarendon Press, 1971), pp.156–7, footnote 3.
164. PRO, Cab23/92 12(38); Cab23/92 13(38). A minute in the FO on the same day showed the official attitude towards the Anschluss: 'Alas all is over.' (DBFP 2nd-XIX, N587, note 2).
165. PRO, Cab23/92 12(38); Cab23/92 13(38).
166. H.C. Debs 5th Series vol. 333, Col. 55.
167. Ibid., cols 85–6.
168. Ibid., cols 93–100.
169. Ibid., cols 45–52. On the same day, Corbin told Halifax that the French Government feared that if the Prime Minister's statement on the present crisis 'contained no indication of the intentions of His Majesty's Government in the event of such an attack, their silence might be interpreted, not merely in Germany but throughout Europe, as implying that they were disinterested and were prepared to acquiesce in whatever happened. This might have disastrous results . . .' Although Chamberlain read this message before his speech, he did not alter the wording of the part of the statement concerning Czechoslovakia. (DBFP 3rd-I, N82; PRO, FO371/22337 R2610/162/12).
170. Nicolson, *Nicolson's Diaries*, p.331.
171. R.A.C. Parker, *Chamberlain and Appeasement: British Policy and the Coming of the Second World War* (London, Macmillan, 1993), p.133.
172. Churchill, *Storm*, p.211.
173. Dilks, *Cadogan's Diaries*, p.63.
174. See p.147.
175. FO371/21713 C2115/1941/18.

CHAPTER 5

1. See p.138.
2. W.L. Shirer, *Rise and Fall of the Third Reich: A History of Nazi Germany* (New York, Simon & Schuster, 1960), p.303 and footnote.
3. Public Record Office, FO371/22337 R2524/162/12.
4. *Documents on German Foreign Policy, 1918–1945*, Series D, II (London, HMSO), N133.
5. Konrad Henlein began to organise the Sudeten Germans politically in 1933. In the same year, his Sudeten German Party emerged as the second strongest in Parliament. Closely co-operating with Hitler, he continued to impose pressure on the Czech Government for the cession of the Sudeten region to Germany until Munich, 1938. (*The Encyclopedia American International Edition*, vol. 14, p.92.)
6. DGFP D-II, N221; Shirer, *The Third Reich*, p.364.
7. Ibid., D-II, nos 259, 304. Hitler was told at the end of May that the West Wall could not be held for longer than three weeks (E. Robertson, *Hitler's Pre-war Policy and Military Plan 1933–1939* (London, Longman, 1963), p.131).
8. Ibid., p.127; Shirer, *The Third Reich*, p.405.
9. *Documents on British Foreign Policy, 1919–1939*, 3rd Series, II (London, HMSO), Appendix IV, p.683.
10. Shirer, *The Third Reich*, pp.407, 411.
11. E.H. Carr, *The Twenty Years' Crisis, 1919–1939* (London, Macmillan, 1962 [c. 1939]), pp.150–1; C. Thorne, *The Approach of War, 1938–39* (London, Macmillan, 1967), p.87; DBFP 3rd-VIII, N152.
12. A.J.P. Taylor, *The Origins of the Second World War* (London, Hamilton, 1972), pp.184,

189; M. Gilbert, *The Roots of Appeasement* (London, Weidenfeld & Nicolson, 1966), p.186; K. Feiling, *The Life of Neville Chamberlain* (London, Macmillan, 1946), p.400.

13. N. Henderson, *Failure of a Mission, Berlin 1937–1939* (New York, G.P. Putnam's Sons, 1940), pp.172–3.

14. I. Colvin, *The Chamberlain Cabinet* (London, Gollancz, 1971), p.168; Feiling, *Chamberlain*, pp.359, 382.

15. 1st Earl of Halifax, *Fulness of Days* (London, Collins, 1957), p.196. See also Henderson, *A Mission*, p.151.

16. Feiling, *Chamberlain*, pp.378–81, 359.

17. Public Record Office, Cab23/92 12(38).

18. DBFP 3rd-I, N86 and note 2.

19. PRO, Cab27/623 FP (36) 26th mtg., 18 Mar. 1938.

20. PRO, FO 371/22337 R2755/162/12.

21. D. Dilks (ed.), *The Diaries of Sir Alexander Cadogan, 1938–45* (London, Cassell, 1971), pp.62–3.

22. *Parliamentary Debates: Commons*, 5th Series, vol. 333, cols 99–100.

23. PRO, FO 371/21674 C1866/132/18.

24. Ibid.

25. Ibid.

26. Ibid.

27. Dilks, *Cadogan's Diaries*, p.63.

28. PRO, FO 371/21674 C1866/132/18.

29. R.A.C. Parker, *Chamberlain and Appeasement: British Policy and the Coming of the Second World War* (London, Macmillan, 1993), p.135.

30. PRO, FO 371/21674 C1865/132/18.

31. Dilks, *Cadogan's Diaries*, pp.62–3.

32. J. Harvey (ed.), *The Diplomatic Diaries of Oliver Harvey 1937–1940* (London, Collins, 1970), p.119.

33. Dilks, *Cadogan's Diaries*, p.62; Feiling, *Chamberlain*, pp.341–2.

34. PRO, FO371/21674 C1865/132/18; Dilks, *Cadogan's Diaries*, p.65; Feiling, *Chamberlain*, pp.347–8.

35. Parker, *Chamberlain and Appeasement*, p.133.

36. PRO, Cab27/623 F.P.(36) 26th mtg.

37. N.H. Gibbs, *Grand Strategy* (I) (London, HMSO, 1976), pp.642–3; T. Taylor, *Munich: the Price of Peace* (New York, Doubleday, 1979), pp.629–33; PRO, Cab23/93 15(38).

38. Hoare confessed in his memoirs: 'It would not be correct to say that our military weakness was the principal cause of the Munich Agreement. The overriding consideration with Chamberlain and his colleagues was that the very complicated problem of Czechoslovakia ought not to lead to a world war, and must at almost any price be settled by peaceful means.' (Viscount Templewood, *Nine Troubled Years*, London, Collins, 1954, p.289).

39. PRO, Cab23/93 15(38).

40. H.C. Debs 5th Series vol. 333, cols 1404–7.

41. Ibid., cols 1413, 1421, 1447.

42   Ibid., cols 1508–14.

43. PRO, FO371/21715 C2770/1941/18.

44. PRO, FO371/22337 R2672/162/12. See also PRO, FO371/22337 R2610/162/12; R2650/162/12.

45. PRO, FO371/21626 C1935/95/62; PRO, FO371/22337 R2855/162/12.

46. Feiling, *Chamberlain*, p.347; H.C. Debs 5th Series vol. 333, col 1406. Halifax did not think that the Russian note had 'great value' either. (PRO, FO371/21674 C2033/132/18).

47. PRO, FO371/21674 C1933/132/18.

48. Ibid., FO371/21715 C2924/1941/18.

49. Colvin, *Cabinet*, pp.121–2.

50. In the new French Government, Daladier was the Prime Minister, and Bonnet the Foreign Minister.

51. PRO, FO371/21591 C3687/13/17.

52. Dilks, *Cadogan's Diaries*, p.73.
53. PRO, FO371/21591 C3687/13/17.
54. Ibid., FO371/21717 C3837/1941/18.
55. Ibid.
56. PRO, FO371/21720 C4695/1941/18; A. Adamthwaite, *The Making of the Second World War* (London, Allen & Unwin, 1977), Doc. 51, pp.188–9.
57. Ibid., FO371/21727 C6920/1941/18.
58. DBFP 3rd-I, N347, note 1.
59. Ibid., N347. Bonnet told Phipps that he was in general agreement with Halifax's view (Ibid., N347, note 3).
60. PRO, FO371/21725 C6167/1941/18; PRO, FO371/21723 C5297/1941/18; PRO, FO371/21724 C5674/1941/18.
61. PRO, FO371/21725 C6167/1941/18.
62. PRO, Cab27/624 FP(36) 31st mtg. On 22 June, Wilson prepared the list of possible names: Runciman, Fisher, Macmillan, Riverdale and Raeburn (K. Middlemas, *Diplomacy of Illusion: The British Government and Germany, 1937–39* (London, Weidenfeld & Nicolson, 1972), p.266 footnote).
63. PRO, FO371/21728 C7204/1941/18. Lord Runciman was former President of the Board of Trade.
64. DBFP 3rd-II, N546.
65. PRO, FO371/21733 C8854/1941/18; A.J. Toynbee (ed.), *Survey of International Affairs 1938* (II) (London, Oxford University Press, 1951), p.225.
66. Ibid., p.233.
67. Ibid., p.248.
68. Ibid., p.253. On 7 September, there was a clash between an SDP demonstrator and a Czech counter-demonstrator in the Czech town of Moravska Ostrava. When a policeman tried to stop the two disputants, he struck the SDP member slightly, by chance. Using this excuse, the SDP leader declared that there was no point in negotiating with the Czech Government, whose subordinate officials deliberately mistreated the Germans (Ibid., pp.253 and 257).
69. F.R. Gannon, *The British Press and Nazi Germany, 1936–1939* (Oxford, Clarendon Press, 1971), pp.172–3, 191, 198–9; A. Adamthwaite, 'The British Government and the Media, 1937–1938', *Journal of Contemporary History*, 18 (1983) 286–7.
70. DGFP D-II, N443 and footnotes, N450; Office of *The Times*, *History of The Times 1912–1948* (II) (London, Office of *The Times*, 1952), p.933; W.S. Churchill, *The Gathering Storm*, (London, Cassell, 1948), p.232.
71. H. Dalton, *The Fateful Years: Memoirs 1931–1945* (London, Frederick Huller 1957), pp.174–5, 195.
72. Churchill, *Storm*, pp.228–30.
73. Earl of Avon, *The Reckoning*, (London, Cassell, 1965), pp.21–2.
74. J.W. Wheeler-Bennett, *Munich: Prologue to Tragedy* (London, Macmillan, 1948), p.97.
75. PRO, Cab23/94 30 Aug. 1938.
76. Ibid., Cab23/95 37(38). Halifax also saw Eden, who was completely in accordance with the policy the Government had adopted (ibid.).
77. Ibid.
78. PRO, Cab23/94 30 Aug. 1938.
79. Feiling, *Chamberlain*, p.357.
80. Parker, *Chamberlain and Appeasement*, p.154; Colvin, *Cabinet*, p.143, footnote; PRO, Cab23/95 38(38).
81. Ibid; Feiling, *Chamberlain*, p.357.
82. DBFP 3rd-II, N862 note 2.
83. PRO, Cab23/95 38(38).
84. Dilks, *Cadogan's Diaries*, p.98; PRO, FO371/21737 C9708/1941/18; DGFP D-II, N480. note 3.
85. It was suggested at that Cabinet meeting that the given period should be six months.
86. PRO, Cab23/95 38(38); PRO, FO371/21675 C3325/132/18; PRO, FO371/21719 C4233/1941/18.

87. PRO, Cab23/95 38(38).
88. Ibid., FO371/21737 C9802/1941/18; DGFP D-II, N480.
89. Adamthwaite, 'The British Government', p.288; Gannon, *The British Press*, pp.184, 193–4, 209, 216.
90. D. Cooper, *Old Men Forget: The Autobiography of Duff Cooper* (London, Hart-Davis, 1953), p.231.
91. K. Harris, *Attlee* (London, Weidenfeld & Nicolson, 1982), p.153.
92. P. Schmidt, *Hitler's Interpreter* (London, Heinemann, 1951), pp.90–4; Feiling, *Chamberlain*, pp.366–7; DGFP D-II, N487.
93. Feiling, *Chamberlain*, p.367.
94. PRO, Cab27/646 C.S.(38)5; Dilks, *Cadogan's Diaries*, p.99.
95. Ibid., Cab23/95 39(38).
96. Dalton, *The Fateful*, pp.176–81.
97. PRO, FO371/21741 C10729/1941/18; PRO, FO371/21738 C10026/1941/18.
98 Ibid., FO371/21739 C10215/1941/18, C10257/1941/18.
99. Ibid., FO371/21739 C10243/1941/18, C10214/1941/18.
100. Ibid., FO371/21739 C10289/1941/18.
101. DBFP 3rd-II, nos 971, 972.
102. PRO, Cab23/95 40(38); PRO, Cab23/95 41(38).
103. Gannon, *The British Press*, pp.185, 201, 210, 222.
104. Dalton, *The Fateful*, pp.187–8.
105. N. Nicolson (ed.) *Harold Nicolson: Diary and Letters, 1930–1939* (London, Collins, 1966), p.364 and note 1.
106. PRO, FO371/21785 C11970/11169/18; DGFP D-II, N562; Henderson, *A Mission*, p.160.
107. PRO, FO371/21740 C10511/ 1941/18.
108. PRO, FO371/21740 C10497/1941/18.
109. Ibid., FO371/21740 C10501/1941/18; DGFP D-II, N573.
110. Henderson, *A Mission*, p.160.
111. PRO, FO371/21740 C10593/1941/18.
112. Henderson, *A Mission*, pp.160–1; Schmidt, *Hitler's*, p.100.
113. Ibid., pp.100–1; PRO, FO371/21785 C11970/11169/18.
114. Henderson, *A Mission*, p.161.
115. N. Chamberlain, *In Search of Peace, by the Rt. Hon. Neville Chamberlain* (New York, G. P. Putnam's Sons, 1939), p.194; PRO, Cab23/95 42(38); Schmidt, *Hitler's*, p.102.
116. PRO, Cab27/646 C.S.(38)13; PRO, Cab23/95 42(38).
117. Lord Hailsham, the Lord President of the Council, put forward the same view at the meeting of 25 September. He mentioned several examples where Hitler had always given empty promises before he wanted to strike as evidence that Hitler could not be trusted (PRO, Cab23/95 43(38)).
118. Dilks, *Cadogan's Diaries*, p.103; PRO, Cab27/646 C.S.(38)13; PRO, Cab23/95 42(38).
119. Dilks, *Cadogan's Diaries*, pp.103, 105.
120. Ibid., p.105.
121 PRO, Cab23/95 43(38).
122. Dilks, *Cadogan's Diaries*, pp.l05–6.
123. L.C.M.S. Amery, *My Political Life: The Unforgiving Years 1929–1940* (London, Hutchinson, 1955), pp.273–5.
124. PRO, Cab23/95 43(38).
125. Dilks, *Cadogan's Diaries*, p.105.
126. PRO, Cab23/95 43(38).
127. Ibid., FO371/21744 C11264/1941/18.
128. For the text of the letter, see PRO, FO371/21745 C11493/1941/18.
129. PRO, Cab23/95 44(38); PRO, Cab23/95 45(38).
130. DBFP 3rd-II, N1143, note 1.
131. PRO, FO371/21744 C11264/1941/18.
132. Ibid., FO371/21741 C10787/1941/18; PRO, FO371/21785 C11970/11169/18.
133. Ibid., FO371/21743 C11050/1941/18.

134. Gannon, *The British Press*, pp.187, 195.
135. Churchill, *Storm*, pp.242–3; Amery, *Political Life*, pp.277–8; Nicolson, *Nicolson's Diaries*, pp.366–7. Halifax told Churchill later (24 July 1947) that Chamberlain was 'vexed' at Halifax's approval of this communiqué 'with not having submitted it to him before publication.' (Adamthwaite, 'The British Government', p.290).
136. PRO, Cab27/646 C.S.(38)15; Dilks, *Cadogan's Diaries*, pp.107–8.
137. Cooper, *Old Men*, pp.238–9.
138. Dilks, *Cadogan's Diaries*, p.107; PRO, FO371/21743 C11015/1941/18, C11030/1941/18.
139. PRO, FO371/21742 C10884/1941/18.
140. Chamberlain, *In Search*, pp.174–5.
141. Cooper, *Old Men*, pp.238–9.
142. PRO, FO371/21742 C10883/1941/18.
143. Chamberlain, *In Search*, p.197.
144. PRO, Cab23/95 46(38).
145. George Steward, previously of the News Department of the FO, a member of the Prime Minister's Office, told Dirksen, German Ambassador in London on 12 October 1938: 'During the recent critical days the Prime Minister had actually made decisions entirely alone with his two intimate advisers and in the last decisions had no longer asked the opinion of any member of the Cabinet, not even of Lord Halifax, the Foreign Secretary. The reason for this was that Chamberlain believed he ought to bear his extremely heavy responsibilities alone. In the end the Prime Minister had not received assistance or support of any kind from the Foreign Office, which on the contrary had striven during the last 3 days to sabotage his plans and commit Great Britain to warlike action against Germany. The final outcome was therefore due exclusively to Chamberlain, who had however thereby ignored the provisions of the British Constitution and customary Cabinet usage.' (DGFP D-IV, N251). See also Churchill, *Storm*, p.247; Amery, *Political Life*, p.280.
146. PRO, FO371/21742 C10883/1941/18.
147. Ibid.
148. Ibid., FO371/21742 C10916/1941/18.
149. Ibid., FO371/21742 C10921/1941/18. The Czech Government was also informed, and was forced to accept the British plan and the timetable for ceding the Sudetenland (PRO, FO371/21743 C11030/1941/18, C11026/1941/18).
150. Wheeler-Bennett, *Munich*, p.167.
151. Nicolson, *Nicolson's Diaries*, pp.370–1; Amery, *Political Life*, p.280, note 1; N. Thompson, *The Anti-appeasers: Conservative Opposition to Appeasement in the 1930s* (Oxford, Clarendon Press, 1971), p.181.
152. Gannon, *The British Press*, pp.187–8, 196, 202–4, 211, 218, 222, 225.
153. Thompson, *Anti-appeasers*, p.181.
154. Nicolson, *Nicolson's Diaries*, pp.371–2.
155. PRO, FO371/21743 C11118/1941/18; PRO, FO371/21745 C11970/1941/18.
156. Feiling, *Chamberlain*, pp.376–7; DBFP 3rd-II, N1228.
157. PRO, FO371/21744 C11244/1941/18.
158. As for the popular enthusiasm of the moment, Chamberlain said to Halifax: 'All this will be over in three months.' (Halifax, *Fulness*, p.199).
159. Chamberlain, in Bartlett, John, *Familiar Quotations* (Boston, Little Brown & Co., 1980, 15th and 125th anniversary edn), p.727.
160. Some of these letters can be seen in Feiling, *Chamberlain*, pp.378–81.
161. C. Madge and I. Harrison, *Britain by Mass Observation* (London, Penguin, 1939), p.106.
162. Harvey, *Harvey's Diaries*, p.203.
163. H.C. Debs 5th Series vol. 345, col. 460.
164. Ibid., vol. 339, cols 51, 66.
165. Ibid., col. 52.
166. Ibid., cols 136–40.
167. Ibid., cols 365, 373.
168. Nicolson, *Nicolson's Diaries*, p.375.
169. Feiling, *Chamberlain*, pp.375, 381.

170. PRO, Cab23/95 48(38). Halifax wrote to Phipps on 1 November: 'the greatest lesson of the crisis has been the unwisdom of basing a foreign policy on insufficient armed strength.' DBFP 3rd-III, N285).

171. Ibid., Cab23/95 48(38).

172. Ibid., Cab23/96 Cabinet minutes, 31 October 1938.

173. Ibid., Cab23/93 15(38).

174. T. Jones, *A Diary with Letters, 1931–1950* (London, Oxford University Press, 1954), p.418.

175. PRO, Cab27/623 F.P.(36) 27th mtg.

176. Gibbs, *Strategy*, pp.289–90; DBFP 2nd-XIX, N401 and notes 1, 2.

177. Cooper, *Old Men*, pp.215, 220; PRO, Cab23/93 15(38).

178. B. Bond (ed.), *Chief of Staff: The Diaries of Lt-General Sir Henry Pownall, Volume One: 1933–1940* (London, Leo Cooper, 1972), p.140.

179. Gibbs, *Strategy*, p.302.

180. G.C. Peden, *British Rearmament and the Treasury 1932–1939* (Edinburgh, Scottish Academic Press, 1979), p.8.

181. B.H. Klein, *Germany's Economic Preparations for War* (Cambridge, Harvard University Press, 1959), p.18.

182. Peden, *British Rearmament*, p.205, Appendix III; Klein, *Preparations for War,* p.16. Exchange rate against RM was approximately £1=RM12, which is calculated from Churchill's estimation. He estimated that German expenditure on rearmament (1933–5) was RM24 billion, or roughly £2 billion. (Churchill, *Storm*, p.177).

183. Peden, *British Rearmament*, p.8.

184. Adamthwaite, *The Making*, Appendix, p.227.

185. Churchill estimated on 29 November 1935 that the German Air Force was at least as strong as Britain's. By end of 1936, it would be 50 per cent stronger than the RAF. However, Baldwin disagreed with his estimate, and pointed out that Germany's 'real strength is not 50 per cent of our strength in Europe today'. With the current rates of expansion maintained on both sides, then a year hence, the British margin of superiority would still be 50 per cent. The truth is that the Government knew at that time that by November 1936, Germany would have a margin of superiority of 100–200 first line aircraft (Gibbs, *Strategy*, pp.138–40).

186. Ibid., p.584.

187. Ibid., pp.584, 587–8.

188. Ibid., p.599.

189. PRO, FO371/21743 C11118/1941/18.

190. H.C. Debs 5th Series vol. 339, col. 303.

191. A.J. Toynbee, *Survey of International Affairs, 1938* (III) (London, Oxford University Press, 1953), p.41.

192. DGFP D-IV, N81.

193. Royal Institute of International Affairs, *Documents on International Affairs 1939–1946* (I) (London, Oxford University Press, 1951), p.40.

194. Toynbee, *Survey 1938* (III), pp.66–7, 111–12; PRO, FO371/22991 C1780/17/18; DGFP D-IV, nos 91, l67.

195. PRO, FO371/22965 C2139/15/18.

196. Harvey, *Harvey's Diaries*, pp.237–8.

197. Harris, *Attlee*, p.159; Amery, *Political Life*, p.307; Churchill, *Storm*, pp.267–8.

198. Toynbee, *Survey 1938* (III), pp.266–9; DGFP D-IV, N229.

199. PRO, FO371/22993 C3085/19/18.

200. Ibid., Cab23/98 11(39).

201. Gannon, *The British Press*, pp.235–7, 239–40, 256–7.

202. Nicolson, *Nicolson's Diaries*, p.392; Thompson, *Anti-appeasers*, p.203. Since Munich, there had been a lot of talk about forming a National Government, including the appointment of Churchill, Eden, Duff Cooper and some Labour leaders if they wanted to co-operate. Halifax gave Chamberlain a similar suggestion. (Harvey, *Harvey's Diaries*, pp.212, 213, 215; Halifax, *Fulness*, p.200). Amery discussed with Attlee on 21 October 1938 the possibility of Labour co-operation with the National Government (Amery, *Political Life*,

pp.298–9). However, Chamberlain turned a deaf ear to all the suggestions. (See also pp.227–8).
203. H.C. Debs. 5th Series vol. 345, col. 457.
204. Ibid., cols 458–62.
205. R.I.I.A. *Documents 1939–1946* (I) pp.60, 62.
206. Dilks, *Cadogan's Diaries*, p.157.
207. DGFP D-I, N19.
208. Adamthwaite, *The Making*, Doc. 62, p.199.
209. Churchill, *Storm*, p.250.
210. See p.174.
211. PRO, FO371/22979 C12341/15/18; Adamthwaite, *The Making*, pp.73–4, 81.
212 See p.181.
213. See p.175–6.
214. Harvey, *Harvey's Diaries*, p.203; Middlemas, *Diplomacy*, pp.414–15.
215. Halifax, *Fulness*, p.199.
216 Earl of Avon, *Facing the Dictators* (London, Cassell, 1962), p.559; Feiling, *Chamberlain*, pp.341, 456; PRO, Cab23/95 43(38).
217. For example, both Vansittart and Cadogan wrote reports on the subject of the German opposition but they did not seem to obtain any attention from Chamberlain and Halifax (I. Colvin, *Vansittart in Office* (London, Gollancz, 1971), p.309). See also Introduction, note 55.
218. PRO, FO371/22979 C12341/15/18; Adamthwaite, *The Making*, pp.89–90.

CHAPTER 6

1. See pp.219–20.
2. A. Adamthwaite, *The Making of the Second World War* (London, Allen & Unwin, 1977), p.86; K. Feiling, *The Life of Neville Chamberlain* (London, Macmillan, 1946), p.409; M. George, T*he Warped Vision: British Foreign Policy 1933–1939* (Pittsburgh, University of Pittsburgh Press, 1965), pp.198–9; C. Thorne, *The Approach of War, 1938–9* (London, Macmillan, 1967), p.119; K. Eubank, *The Origins of World War II* (Arlington Heights, Ill., H. Davidson, 1969), p.140.
3. K. Middlemas, *Diplomacy of Illusion: The British Government and Germany, 1937–39* (London, Weidenfeld & Nicolson, 1972), p.457; P.M.H. Bell, *The Origins of the Second World War in Europe* (London, Longman, 1986), p.255.
4. W.S. Churchill, *The Gathering Storm* (London, Cassell, 1948), p.285.
5. Adamthwaite, *The Making*, p.88; R.A.C. Parker, *Chamberlain and Appeasement: British Policy and the Coming of the Second World War* (London, Macmillan, 1993), p.245; A.J.P. Taylor, *The Origins of the Second World War* (London, Hamilton, 1972), p.247.
6. Viscount Templewood, *Nine Troubled Years* (London, Collins, 1954), pp.349–50; 1st Earl of Halifax, *Fulness of Days* (London, Collins, 1957), pp.204–5.
7. Templewood, *Troubled Years*, pp.369–70.
8. *Parliamentary Debates: H.C.*, 5th Series, vol. 345, cols 438–564.
9. N. Nicolson (ed.), *Harold Nicolson, Diaries and Letters, 1930–1939* (London, Collins, 1966), p.393. For similar discussions, see J. Harvey (ed.) *The Diplomatic Diaries of Oliver Harvey, 1937–1940* (London, Collins, 1970), p.269.
10. N. Thompson, *The Anti-appeasers: Conservative Opposition to Appeasement in the 1930s* (Oxford, Clarendon Press, 1971), p.208.
11. Halifax, Fulness, p.200; Harvey, *Harvey's Diaries*, pp.269–70.
12. Feiling, *Chamberlain*, p.406.
13. PRO, Cab23/98 12(39); D. Dilks (ed.) *The Diaries of Sir Alexander Cadogan, 1938–1945* (London, Cassell, 1971), p.157.
14. Ibid., Cab23/98 12(39).
15. Royal Institute of International Affairs, *Documents on International Affairs 1939–1946* (I) (London, Oxford University Press, 1951), pp.70–1.

16. PRO, FO371/23060 C3356/3356/18. Although it was later proved that this information was a false alarm, Romania was no doubt one of the next possible German victims (PRO, FO371/22994 C3415/19/18; PRO, FO371/23060 C3586/3356/18).
17. Ibid., FO371/22994 C3423/19/18, C3415/19/18.
18. Ibid., Cab23/98 12(39).
19. Ibid., Cab23/98 13(39); Feiling, *Chamberlain*, p.401; Dilks, *Cadogan's Diaries*, p.161.
20. Feiling, *Chamberlain*, p.409; W.K. Hancock, *British War Economy* (London, HMSO, 1949), pp.68, 71, 75.
21. R. Shay, *British Rearmament in the Thirties: Politics and Profits* (Princeton, Princeton University Press, 1977), pp.271–2.
22. Feiling, *Chamberlain*, pp.402, 409; Adamthwaite, *The Making*, p.86.
23. PRO, FO371/22967 C3858/15/18; Dilks, *Cadogan's Diaries*, p.162; Harvey, *Harvey's Diaries*, p.265; Feiling, *Chamberlain*, p.407.
24. Ibid., Cab23/98 13(39).
25. Harvey, *Harvey's Diaries*, p.265.
26. Dilks, *Cadogan's Diaries*, p.161; PRO, FO371/23060 C3598/3356/18.
27. PRO, FO371/23061 C3775/3356/18, C3776/3356/18, C3821/3356/18.
28. Ibid., FO371/23061 C3727/3356/18, C3806/3356/18.
29. Dilks, *Cadogan's Diaries*, pp.163–4; Harvey, *Harvey's Diaries*, p.268.
30. Feiling, *Chamberlain*, p.403; N.H. Gibbs, *Grand Strategy* (I) (London, HMSO, 1976), p.697, footnote. The British policy towards the Soviet Union was generally based on a bitter anti-communist stance. The FO always felt uneasy at the idea of establishing normal relations with the Soviet Union, which seemed a permanent potential threat to the social order of Britain and of the whole Empire, because she encouraged the world communist movement by various means. In particular, since it had been decided to 'come to terms with Germany', all senior officials except Vansittart and Collier had held the idea that Anglo-Soviet *rapprochement* would spoil Anglo-German understanding because Hitler would think that alliance with Russia meant 'encirclement of Germany' (R. Manne, 'The Foreign Office and the Failure of Anglo-Soviet Rapprochement', *Journal of Contemporary History*, 16 (1981), 726, 748–9).
    In Cabinet, Baldwin feared the Bolsheviks no less than the Nazis. He often said that 'there were two great forces of evil at work in the world, the "Bolshies" and the "Nasties": fortunately the Nasties had achieved power as the instrument to destroy the Bolshies . . . If there is any fighting in Europe to be done, I should like to see the Bolsheviks and Nazis doing it.' Hoare held the same view. (K. Middlemas and J. Barnes, *Baldwin: A Biography* (London, Weidenfeld & Nicolson, 1969), pp.955, 961). Before his resignation, Eden was supposed to be a minister who held a mildly positive attitude towards the Soviets, whereas he wrote in January 1936 concerning the Russian loan proposal: 'While I want good relations with the bear, I don't want to hug him too close. I don't trust him, and am sure there is hatred in his heart for all we stand for.' (R. Manne, 'The Foreign Office', p.749). Both Chamberlain and Halifax were full of misgivings towards Russia. The former shared 'the indignation of his party against Bolshevist propaganda'. He told Maisky, the Soviet Ambassador in London, frankly in an interview in 1932 that he considered the Soviets as 'enemies'. Halifax disliked Russia due to the fact that the Soviets were 'anti-Christ.' During the Czechoslovakia crisis, they were suspicious of Russia's motives for co-operation, which were, in Chamberlain's words, to pull 'all the strings behind the scenes to get us involved in war with Germany' (Feiling, *Chamberlain*, pp.154, 347; I. Maisky, *Who Helped Hitler?* (London, Hutchinson, 1964), p.26; Harvey, *Harvey's Diaries*, pp.121, 290). Russia's help was not at all considered to be of 'great value' in British eyes (PRO, FO371/21674 C2033/132/18).
    Therefore, when the issue of alliance with Russia was raised, it was considered by the policy-makers with feelings of mistrust, misgiving and prejudice from the very beginning.
31. PRO, FO371/23684 N1292/233/38.
32. Ibid., Cab27/624 F.P.(36) 38th mtg. 27 Mar. 1939.
33. Chamberlain said in the House that day: 'I must still maintain a certain reserve on this matter.' (H.C. Debs 5th Series vol. 345, col. 1885).

34. PRO, Cab23/98 16(39); PRO, FO371/23015 C4505/54/18; I. Colvin, *Vansittart in Office* (London, Gollancz, 1965), pp.303–10.
35. Dilks, *Cadogan's Diaries*, pp.164–5; Harvey, *Harvey's Diaries*, p.271; PRO, Cab23/98 16(39).
36. In fact, it was too late to hope for this, because Colvin soon received a note which said: 'it would be unwise if Mr Colvin gave anyone in the Reich the impression that the British Government wished to enter into relations with them'. (Colvin, *Vansittart*, p.310).
37. PRO, Cab23/98 16(39); HC. Debs 5th Series vol. 345, col. 2415
38. Ibid., FO371/23063 C5136/3356/18, *Documents on British Foreign Policy 1919–1939*, 3rd Series, V (London, HMSO), N145.
39. Feiling, *Chamberlain*, p.404.
40 PRO, Cab23/98 17(39); PRO, Cab27/624 F.P.(36) 40th Mtg.
41. H.C. Debs 5th Series vol. 347, cols 1847–8.
42. Dilks, *Cadogan's Diaries*, p.163; PRO, Cab27/624 F.P.(36) 40th mtg.
43. PRO, FO371/23144 C4898/1110/55.
44. Ibid., FO371/23063 C5144/3356/18, C5330/3356/18.
45. Ibid., FO371/23063 C5144/3356/18.
46. Harvey, *Harvey's Diaries*, p.279; PRO, Cab23/98 20(39).
47. Dilks, *Cadogan's Diaries*, p.173; PRO, FO371/23063 C5281/3356/18, C5144/3356/18; PRO, FO371/22969 C5460/15/18.
48. PRO, FO371/23063 C5281/3356/18, C5337/3356/18.
49. Ibid., FO371/23063 C5382/3356/18, C5470/3356/18. The questions put forward by Litvinov were quite commonly shared in other quarters, as Oliver Harvey remarked: 'The truth is no one believes we can fulfil our new commitments.' (Harvey, *Harvey's Diaries*, p.281).
50. Ibid., FO371/22969 C5460/15/18; Dilks, *Cadogan's Diaries*, p.175.
51. Ibid., FO371/22969 C5460/15/18.
52. Ibid; Feiling, *Chamberlain*, p.408.
53. PRO, Cab27/624 F.P.(36) 43rd mtg.
54. Ibid., FO371/23064 C5682/3356/18, PRO, FO371/22969 C5460/15/18.
55. Ibid., FO371/23064 C5838/3356/18; PRO, Cab23/99 24(39).
56. Gibbs, *Strategy*, p.723.
57. PRO, Cab27/624 F.P.(36) 44th mtg; PRO, Cab23/99 24(39).
58. Ibid., FO371/23064 C5838/3356/18; PRO, FO371/23065 C6540/3356/18.
59. Ibid., Cab23/99 26(39)
60. Ibid., Cab27/624 F.P.(36) 45th mtg; PRO, FO371/23065 C6705/3356/18; PRO, FO371/23066 C7327/3356/18. Seeds analysed that one of the reasons for Litvinov's resignation was that 'it might imply the abandonment of the policy of collective security . . . and a decision to enter instead on a policy of isolation'. On the other hand, he pointed out that 'all the evidence . . . in the past week would seem to show that the Soviet Government are for the moment still prepared to pursue a policy of collaboration' (DBFP 3rd-V, N509).
61. Ibid., N421.
62. Early in May, the FO received such information from various channels, but did not think it was believable (Ibid., N377, note 2; N413 and note 2).
63. PRO, Cab23/99 27(39)
64. Ibid., FO371/23066 C7065/3356/18, C7328/3356/18.
65. R. Manne, 'The British Decision for Alliance with Russia, May 1939', *Journal of Contemporary History*, 9 (1974) 22; Gibbs, *Strategy*, p.727.
66. PRO, Cab27/625 F.P.(36) 47th mtg. Cadogan wrote on 16 May: 'our formula is so like – or can be represented as being so like – an alliance, that we'd better go the whole hog if we're to ensure that Russia doesn't go in with Germany' (see Dilks, *Cadogan's Diaries*, p.180).
67. Ibid., Cab27/625 F.P.(36) 47th mtg.
68. Ibid; PRO, Cab23/99 28(39); PRO, FO371/23066 C7268/3356/18.
69. DBFP 3rd-V, N527, note 1; N589, note 1. The French Government supported this formula, and their Ambassador in London begged Maisky to recommend the formula favourably to his Government (Ibid., N550, N589, note 1).
70. Ibid.

71. Ibid; PRO, Cab27/625 F.P.(36) 48th mtg; Dilks, *Cadogan's Diaries*, pp.181–2.
72. Harvey, *Harvey's Diaries*, p.290; Dilks, *Cadogan's Diaries*, p.181.
73. Harvey, *Harvey's Diaries*, p.290.
74. Dilks, *Cadogan's Diaries*, pp.181–2; PRO, FO371/23066 C7551/3356/18.
75. PRO, FO371/23066 C7591/3356/18.
76. Dilks, *Cadogan's Diaries*, p.182.
77. PRO, Cab23/99 30(39); Harvey, *Harvey's Diaries*, p.291; PRO, FO371/22972 C7457/15/18, C7449/15/18.
78. Ibid., Cab23/99 30(39).
79. Ibid., FO371/23066 C7661/3356/18.
80. Ibid., FO371/23066 C7682/3356/18; PRO, FO371/32067 C7936/3356/18.
81. Ibid., FO371/23067 C7970/3356/18.
82. Ibid., Cab27/625 F.P.(36) 49th mtg.
83. Ibid., FO371/23067 C8060/3356/18.
84. Ibid., Cab27/625 F.P.(36) 49th mtg.; PRO, Cab23/99 31(39).
85. Ibid., FO371/23067 C8097/3356/18.
86. Earl of Avon, *The Reckoning* (London, Cassell, 1965), p.55; Harvey, *Harvey's Diaries*, p.295.
87. PRO, Cab27/625 F.P.(36) 49th mtg; PRO, FO371/23068 C8214/3356/18.
88. Ibid., FO371/23068 C8212/3356/18; Churchill, *Storm*, pp.303–4; Harvey, *Harvey's Diaries*, pp.295–6.
89. Ibid., Cab27/625 F.P.(36) 50th mtg; ibid., Cab23/99 32(39); ibid., FO371/23068 C8440/3356/18.
90. Ibid., FO371/23068 C8599/3356/18, C8598/3356/18; ibid., FO371/23069 C8840/3356/18.
91. Ibid., FO371/23068 C8595/3356/18, C8769/3356/18.
92. Ibid., Cab27/625 F.P.(36) 53rd mtg; ibid., Cab27/625 F.P.(36) 54th mtg; ibid., Cab23/100 33(39).
93. Ibid., FO371/23069 C9081/3356/18, C9306/3356/18.
94. Ibid., FO371/23069 C9229/3356/18, C9293/3356/18, C9286/3356/18, C9295/3356/18.
95. Dilks, *Cadogan's Diaries*, p.191.
96. PRO, Cab27/625 F.P.(36) 56th mtg.
97. Dilks, *Cadogan's Diaries*, p.191; PRO, FO371/23069 C9295/3356/18.
98. PRO, FO371/23070 C9599/3356/18.
99. Ibid., FO371/23070 C9566/3356/18, C9600/3356/18.
100. Ibid., Cab27/625 F.P.(36) 57th mtg.
101. Ibid., FO371/23070 C9709/3356/18.
102. Ibid., FO371/23070 C9889/3356/18.
103. Ibid., FO371/23070 C10054/3356/18.
104. Ibid., FO371/23071 C10264/3356/18; ibid., Cab27/625 F.P.(36) 58th mtg.
105. Ibid.
106. Ibid., FO371/23070 C10054/3356/18. This instruction was sent without either a Cabinet or an FPC meeting. No record of any discussion on it can be found in the FO files either (Gibbs, *Strategy*, p.744, footnote).
107. Ibid., FO371/23071 C10277/3356/18.
108. Ibid., FO371/23071 C10319/3356/18, C10316/3356/18.
109. Ibid., FO371/23017 C6464/54/18, C6799/54/18, DBFP 3rd-V, Appendix I (ii).
110. Ibid., FO371/22990 C10521/16/18; DGFP D-VI, N716; M. Gilbert and R. Gott, *The Appeasers* (London, Weidenfeld & Nicolson, 1963), pp.219–20.
111. Dilks, *Cadogan's Diaries*, p.192; Gilbert and Gott, *The Appeasers*, pp.222–6; PRO, FO371/22990 C10371/16/18, C10359/16/18.
112. Harvey, *Harvey's Diaries*, pp.301–2; PRO, FO371/23146 C10287/1110/55.
113. Royal Institute of International Affairs, *Documents on International Affairs 1939–46* (I) (London, Oxford University Press, 1951), pp.323–31.
114. PRO, Cab27/625 F.P.(36) 58th mtg.
115. Ibid., FO371/23071 C10498/3356/18; Cab23/100 39(39).
116. Ibid.

117. Ibid., FO371/23072 C10801/3356/18.
118. H.C. Debs 5th Series vol. 350, col. 1929; DBFP 3rd-VII, Appendix II, p.562.
119. PRO, FO371/23072 C11275/3356/18; DBFP 3rd-VII, Appendix II, pp.558, 563, 575–80.
120. DBFP 3rd-VII, nos 6, 8, 22, Appendix II, pp.581–4.
121 Ibid., Appendix II, p.573.
122. PRO, FO371/23072 C11323/3356/18, C11372/3356/18.
123. DBFP 3rd-VII, N1, note 3.
124. PRO, FO371/23073 C11580/3356/18, C11581/3356/18, C11582/3356/18, C11583/3356/18.
125. Ibid., FO371/23073 C12272/3356/18.
126. DBFP 3rd-VII, N115, note 1; PRO, FO371/23073 C11814/3356/18; PRO, Cab23/100 41(39).
127. DBFP 3rd VII, Appendix II, pp.609–10.
128. PRO, FO371/22976 C11710/15/18; PRO, FO371/23973 C11814/3356/18.
129. Dilks, *Cadogan's Diaries*, p.199; DBFP 3rd-VII, N140, note 3.
130. PRO, Cab23/100 41(39).
131. Ibid., FO371/23026 C11611/54/18; Harvey, *Harvey's Diaries*, p.304.
132. Ibid., FO371/23073 C11778/3356/18, C11854/3356/18, C11999/3356/18, C12060/3356/18.
133. See p.236.
134. PRO, FO371/22979 C12341/15/18.
135 Churchill, *Storm*, pp.306–7.
136. See pp.254–5.
137. Cadogan said in his memo to the FPC on 22 May that 'neither Poland nor Roumania would object to an arrangement which, while having the disadvantage of associating them openly with the Soviet Government, would secure that the latter would, in the event of war, be ready to render assistance if desired'(PRO, FO371/23066 C7591/3356/18). Munters, the Latvian Minister for Foreign Affairs, told Halifax at Geneva on 23 May that 'the position of the Baltic countries might be eased if any arrangements reached between Great Britain, France and Russia, which covered the Baltic States' (PRO, Cab23/99 30(39); PRO, FO371/23066 C7552/3356/18). At the Cabinet meeting of 24 May, Chamberlain insisted that alliance with Russia would meet with objections from the Dominions. In his reply to this argument, Inskip, Dominion Secretary, said that apart from New Zealand, all the Dominions recognised that 'having gone so far it would be right to make an agreement rather than risk a complete breakdown' (PRO, Cab23/99 30(39)).
138. Harvey, *Harvey's Diaries*, p.290.
139. General Doumenc, Head of the French Military Mission, estimated in his interview with Voroshilov on 22 August that 'in five or six days we could have finished our work and signed the Military Convention' (DBFP 3rd-VII, Appendix II, p.611).
140. See p.246.
141. PRO, Cab27/625 F.P.(36) 58th mtg.
142. DBFP 3rd-VII, pp.558, 563.
143. DGFP D-VII, N213; R I.I.A. *Documents 1939–46* (I), p.406.
144. Ibid., nos 228, 229; R.I.I.A. *Documents, 1939–46* (I), pp.408–10.
145. P. Shen, *Britain and The Phoney War, September 1939–May 1940* (Department of History, Beijing Teachers' College, Beijing, 1988, unpublished).

CONCLUSION

1. See pp.xxvi.
2. PRO, Cab23/95 39(38)
3. See p. xxvi.
4. K. Feiling, *The Life of Neville Chamberlain* (London, Macmillan, 1946), p.361.
5. M. Cowling, *The Impact of Hitler: British Politics and British Policy 1933–1940* (London, Cambridge University Press, 1975), p.211, footnote.

6. See p.xxvi.
7. See p.13.
8. See p.65.
9. See p.106.
10. See p.130.
11. See p.xxvi.
12. See p.xxvi.
13. W. Churchill, *The Gathering Storm* (London, Cassell, 1948), p.251.
14. See pp.214–15.
15. See p.231.
16. See p.xxvi–xxvii.
17. See pp.xxvii.
18. See p.xxvii.

BIBLIOGRAPHY

DOCUMENTS

Degras, J.T. (ed.) *Soviet Documents on Foreign Policy (II), 1925–1932*
—— *Soviet Documents on Foreign Policy (III) 1933–1941* London, Oxford University Press, 1952–1953
Documents on British Foreign Policy 1919–1939
—— 2nd Series, vols VI–XXI, London, HMSO, 1957–1984
—— 3rd Series, vols I–IX, London, HMSO, 1949–1955
Documents on German Foreign Policy 1918–1945
—— Series C, vols IV–VI, London, HMSO, 1962–1983
—— Series D, vols I–VII, London, HMSO, 1949–1956
Foreign Relations of the United States (vols for 1919–1939), Washington, State Department, 1934–1956
League of Nations, *Official Journal* & Special Supplement N111, Geneva, January 1936
Parliamentary Debates: Commons, 5th Series (vols for 1931–1939)
Public Record Office, Cab23; 24; 27
Public Record Office, FO371; 800
Report of the Commission of Enquiry (The Lytton Report), Geneva, League of Nations, 1932
Royal Institute of International Affairs, *Documents on International Affairs, 1932–1943*, London, Oxford University Press, 1933–1943
Royal Institute of International Affairs, *Documents on International Affairs 1939–46*, vol. I, London, Oxford University Press, 1951

OTHER SOURCES
Books

Adams, R.J.Q., *British Politics and Foreign Policy in the Age of Appeasement, 1935–39*, London, Macmillan, 1993
Adamthwaite, A., *The Making of the Second World War*, London, Allen & Unwin, 1977
Albrecht-Carrie, R., *France, Europe and the Two World Wars*, New York, Harper, 1961
Aldcroft, D.H., *The Inter-war Economy, 1919–1939*, London, Batsford, 1970
Alexander, M.S. and Graham, H. (eds) *The French and Spanish Popular Fronts: Comparative Perspective*, Cambridge, Cambridge University Press, 1989
Alfieri, D., *Dictators Face to Face*, London, Elek, 1954
Amery, L.C.M.S., *My Political Life: The Unforgiving Years 1929–1940*, London, Hutchinson, 1955
Angell, N., *After All*, London, Hamilton, 1951

Arndt, H.W., *Economic Lessons of the Nineteen-thirties*, New York, Oxford University Press, 1944

Ashworth, W., *An Economic History of England, 1870 to 1939*, London, Methuen, 1960

Aster, S., *1939: The Making of the Second World War*, London, Deutsch, 1973

Attlee, C.R., *As it Happened*, London, Heinemann, 1954

Avon, Earl of, *Facing the Dictators*, London, Cassell, 1962

—— *The Reckoning*, London, Cassell, 1965

Baer, G.W., *The Coming of the Italian–Ethiopian War*, Cambridge, Harvard University Press, 1967

—— *Test Case: Italy, Ethiopia, and the League of Nations*, Stanford, Hoover Institution Press, 1976

Bassett, R., *Democracy and Foreign Policy: The Sino–Japanese Dispute, 1931–33*, London, Longmans, Green & Co., 1952

Baumont, M., *The Origins of the Second World War*, trans. S.D.C. Ferguson, New Haven, Yale University Press, 1978

Baynes, N.H. (ed.) *The Speeches of Adolf Hitler, April 1922–August 1939*, London, Oxford University Press, 1942

Bell, P.M.H., *The Origins of the Second World War in Europe*, London, Longman, 1986

Beloff, M., *The Foreign Policy of Soviet Russia: 1929–1941* (I) London, Oxford University Press, 1959 [*c.* 1947]

Birdsall, P., *Versailles Twenty Years After*, New York, Reynal & Hitchcock, 1941

Birkenhead, Earl of, *Halifax: The Life of Lord Halifax*, London, Hamilton, 1965

Blaazer, D., *The Popular Front and the Progressive Tradition: Socialists, Liberals, and the Quest for Unity, 1884–1939*, Cambridge, Cambridge University Press, 1992.

Bond, B., *British Military Policy Between the Two World Wars*, Oxford, Clarendon Press, 1980

—— (ed.) *Chief of Staff: The Diaries of Lt-General Sir Henry Pownall 1933–40*, London, Leo Cooper, 1972

Borg, D., *The United States and the Far Eastern Crisis of 1931–1938*, Cambridge, Harvard University Press, 1964

Bowley, A.L., *Some Economic Consequences of the War*, London, T. Butterworth, 1930

Brook-Shepherd, G., *Anschluss: The Rape of Austria*, London, Macmillan, 1963

Bullock, A., *Hitler: A Study in Tyranny*, London, Oldham's Press, 1952

Butler, J.R.M., *Grand Strategy* (II), London, HMSO, 1957

Cameron, E.R., *Prologue to Appeasement: A Study in French Foreign Policy*, Washington, American Council on Public Affairs, 1942

Carlton, David, *Anthony Eden: A Biography*, London, Allen Lane, 1981

Carr, E.H., *International Relations Between the Two World Wars*, London, Macmillan, 1959

—— *The Twenty Years' Crisis, 1919–39*, London, Macmillan, 1962

Carr, R. (ed.) *The Republic and the Civil War in Spain*, London, Macmillan, 1971

Carr, W., *Arms, Autarky and Agression: A Study in German Foreign Policy 1933–39*, London, E. Arnold, 1972

Cecil, Viscount, *A Great Experiment: An Autobiography*, London, J. Cape, 1941

—— *All the Way*, London, Hodder & Stoughton, 1949

Chamberlain, N., *In Search of Peace by the Rt. Hon. Neville Chamberlain*, New York, G.P. Putman's Sons, 1939

Churchill, W.S., *The Gathering Storm*, London, Cassell, 1948

Ciano, Count, *Ciano's Diary 1937–1938*, London, Methuen, 1952

Clubb, O.E., *20th Century China*, New York, Columbia University Press, 1972

Cockett, R., *Twilight of Truth: Chamberlain, Appeasement and the Manipulation of the Press*, New York, St Martin's Press, 1989

Colvin, I., *Vansittart in Office*, London, Gollancz, 1965

—— *The Chamberlain Cabinet*, London, Gollancz, 1971

Constantine, S., *Unemployment in Britain Between the Wars*, London, Longman, 1980

Cook, C., *A Short History of the Liberal Party, 1900–1976*, London, Macmillan, 1976

Cooper, D., *Old Men Forget: The Autobiography of Duff Cooper*, London, Hart-Davis, 1953

Cowling, M., *The Impact of Hitler: British Politics and British Policy, 1933–1940*, London, Cambridge University Press, 1975

Cross, J.A., *Sir Samuel Hoare: A Political Biography*, London, J. Cape, 1977
Crowley, J.B., *Japan's Quest for Autonomy, 1931–1938*, Princeton, Princeton University Press, 1966
Dalton, H., *The Fateful Years: Memoris, 1931–1945*, London, Frederick Huller, 1957
Deutscher, I., *Stalin: A Political Biography*, London, Oxford University Press, 1949
Dilks, D. (ed.) *The Diaries of Sir Alexander Cadogan, 1938–1945*, London, Cassell, 1971
Dutton, D., *Anthony Eden: A Life and Reputation*, London, E. Arnold, 1997
Elton, Lord, *The Life of James Ramsay MacDonald*, London, Collins, 1939
Emmerson, J.T., *The Rhineland Crisis, 7 March 1936*, Ames, Iowa State University Press, 1977
Endicott, S.L., *Diplomacy and Enterprise: British China Policy, 1933–1937*, Vancouver, University of British Columbia Press, 1975
Eubank, K., *The Origins of World War II*, Arlington Heights, Ill., H. Davidson, 1969
Feiling, K., *The Life of Neville Chamberlain*, London, Macmillan, 1946
Ferrell, R.H., *American Diplomacy in the Great Depression: Hoover-Stimson Foreign Policy, 1929–1933*, New Haven, CT, Yale University Press, 1957
Fischer, K.E., *The Foreign Office and British Foreign Policy During the Abyssinian Crisis, 1934–1935*, St Andrews, Library of University of St Andrews, 1988 (unpublished)
Fox, J.P., *Germany and the Far Eastern Crisis, 1931–1938: A Study in Diplomacy and Ideology*, Oxford, Clarendon Press, 1982
Friedman, *British Relations with China: 1931–1939*, New York, Institute of Pacific Relations, 1940
Fyrth, J. (ed.), *Britain, Fascism and the Popular Front*, London, Lawrence and Wishart, 1985
Gannon, F.R., *The British Press and Nazi Germany, 1936–39*, Oxford, Clarendon Press, 1971
Gehl, J., *Austria, Germany and the Anschluss, 1931–1938*, London, Oxford University Press, 1963
George, M., *The Warped Vision: British Foreign Policy, 1933–1939*, Pittsburgh, University of Pittsburgh Press, 1965
Gibbs, N.H., *Grand Strategy* (I), London, HMSO, 1976
Gilbert, M., *The Roots of Appeasement*, London, Weidenfeld & Nicolson, 1966
—— and Gott, R., *The Appeasers*, London, Weidenfeld & Nicolson, 1963
Graham, H. and Preston, P. (eds), *The Popular Front in Europe*, New York, St Martin's Press, 1987
Gull, E.M., *British Economic Interests in the Far East*, London, Oxford University Press, 1943
Halifax, 1st Earl of, *Fulness of Days*, London, Collins, 1957
Hancock, W.K., *British War Economy*, London, HMSO, 1949
Haraszti, E.H., *The Invaders: Hitler Occupies the Rhineland*, Budapest, Akademiai Kiado, 1983
Hardie, F., *The Abyssinian Crisis*, Hamden, Conn., Archon Books, 1974
Harris, K., *Attlee*, London, Weidenfeld & Nicolson, 1982
Harvey, J. (ed.) *The Diplomatic Diaries of Oliver Harvey, 1937–1940*, London, Collins, 1970
Haslam, J., *Soviet Foreign Policy 1930–33: The Impact of the Depression*, London, Macmillan, 1983
—— *The Soviet Union and the Struggle for Collective Security in Europe, 1933–39*, London, Macmillan, 1984
Henderson, N., *Failure of a Mission: Berlin, 1937–1939*, New York, G.P. Putnam's Sons, 1940
Hildebrand, K., *The Foreign Policy of the Third Reich*, trans. A. Fothergill, Berkeley, University of California Press, 1973
Hirst, F.W., *The Consequences of the War to Great Britain*, London, Oxford University Press, 1934
Hitler, A., *Mein Kampf*, trans. R. Manheim, Boston, Houghton Mifflin, 1971
Hoover, H., *The Memoirs of Herbert Hoover: The Cabinet and the Presidency, 1920–1933*, New York, Macmillan, 1952
Hull, C., *Memoirs of Cordell Hull*, New York, Macmillan, 1948
Hyde, H.M., *Neville Chamberlain*, London, Weidenfeld & Nicolson, 1976
Iriye, Akire, *After Imperialism: The Search for a New Order in the Far East, 1921–1931*, Cambridge, Harvard University Press, 1965
Irving, D.J.C., *Hitler's War*, New York, Viking Press, 1977

—— *The War Path: Hitler's Germany 1933–39*, London, M. Joseph, 1978

Jackson, G., *The Spanish Republic and the Civil War, 1931–1939*, Princeton, Princeton University Press, 1965

Jackson, J., *The Popular Front in France: Defending Democracy, 1934–38*, Cambridge, Cambridge University Press, 1988

Jones, T., *A Diary with Letters, 1931–1950*, London, Oxford University Press, 1954

Jordan, W.M., *Great Britain, France and the German Problem*, London, Oxford University Press, 1943

Kennan, G.F., *Soviet Foreign Policy 1917–1941*, D. Van Nostrand, Princeton, 1960

Kennedy, M.D., *The Estrangement of Great Britain and Japan, 1917–1935*, Berkeley, University of California Press, 1969

Keynes, J.M., *The Economic Consequences of the Peace*, London, Macmillan, 1971

—— *A Revision of the Treaty*, New York, Harcourt, Brace & Company, 1922

Kindleberger, C., *The World in Depression, 1929–39*, London, Allen Lane, 1973

Klein, B.H., *Germany's Economic Preparation for War*, Cambridge, Harvard University Press, 1959

Lauens, F.D., *France and the Italo–Ethiopian Crisis, 1935–1936*, Paris, Mouton, 1967

Laval, P., *The Unpublished Diary of Pierre Laval*, London, Falcon Press, 1948

Lederer, I.J. (ed.) *The Versailles Settlement: Was it Foredoomed to Failure?*, Boston, Heath, 1960

Lee, Chong-sik, *Counterinsurgency in Manchuria: The Japanese Experience, 1931–1940*, Santa Monica, Calif., Rand, 1967

Liddell Hart, B.H., *The Defence of Britain*, London, Faber & Faber, 1939

Lloyd George, D., *The Truth about Reparation and War Debts*, London, Heinemann, 1932

—— *War Memoirs of David Lloyd George*, 6 vols, London, I. Nicholson & Watson, 1933–1936

—— *The Truth about the Peace Treaties*, London, Gollancz, 1938

Longford, E.P., *Winston Churchill: A Pictorial Life Story*, Chicago, Rand McNally, 1974

Louis, R., *British Strategy in the Far East, 1919–1939*, Oxford, Clarendon Press, 1971

Lowe, C.J., *Italian Foreign Policy 1870–1940*, London, Routledge & Kegan Paul, 1975

Macleod, I., *Neville Chamberlain*, London, Muller, 1961

Madge, C. and Harrison, I., *Britain by Mass Observation*, London, Penguin, 1939

Maisky, Ivan, *Who Helped Hitler?*, London, Hutchinson, 1964

Marquand, D., *Ramsay MacDonald*, London, J. Cape, 1977

Martel, G. (ed.) *The Origins of the Second World War Reconsidered: the A.J.P. Taylor Debate after Twenty-five Years*, Boston, Allen & Unwin, 1986

Martin, L., *The Treaties of Peace, 1919–1923*, 2 vols, New York, Carnegie Endowment for International Peace, 1924

Medlicott, W.N., *The Coming of War in 1939*, London, Routledge & Kegan Paul, 1963

—— *British Foreign Policy Since Versailles*, London, Methuen, 1967

Middlemas, K., *Diplomacy of Illusion: The British Government and Germany, 1937–39*, London, Weidenfeld & Nicolson, 1972

—— and Barnes, J., *Baldwin: A Biography*, London, Weidenfeld & Nicolson, 1969

Milward, A.S., *The German Economy at War*, London, Athlone Press, 1965

Minney, R.J. (ed.) *The Private Papers of Hore-Belisla*, London, Collins, 1960

Morgan, K. *Against Fascism and War: Ruptures and Continuities in British Communist Politics 1935–41*, Manchester, Manchester University Press, 1989

Mowat, C.L., *Britain Between the Wars, 1918–1940*, London, Methuen, 1955

Muggeridge, M. (ed.) *Ciano's Diplomatic Papers*, London, Oldham's Press, 1948

Muir, R., *The Poltical Consequences of the Great War*, London, T. Butterworth, 1930

Murray, W., *The Change in the Euroepan Balance of Power, 1938–1939*, Princeton, Princeton University Press, 1984

Myers, W.S. and Newton, W.H. *The Hoover Administration: A Documented Narrative*, London, Charles Scribner's Sons, 1936

Namier, L.B., *Diplomatic Prelude, 1938–1939*, London, Macmillan, 1948

Nere, J., *The Foreign Policy of France from 1914 to 1945*, London, Routledge & Kegan Paul, 1974

Nicholls, A.J., *Weimar and the Rise of Hitler*, London, Macmillan, 1979

Nicolson, N. (ed.) *Harold Nicolson: Diaries and Letters 1930–1939*, London, Collins, 1966

Northedge, F.S., *The Troubled Giant: Britain among the Great Powers, 1916–39*, London, Bell, 1966

Office of *The Times*, *The History of The Times 1912–1948* (II), London, Office of *The Times*, 1952

Ogata, S.N., *Defiance in Manchuria: The Making of Japanese Foreign Policy, 1931–1932*, Berkeley, University of California Press, 1964

Ovendale, R., *'Appeasement' and the English Speaking World*, Cardiff, University of Wales Press, 1975

Overy, R., *The Origins of the Second World War*, London, Longham, 1987

—— *The Road to War*, London, Macmillan, 1989

Papen, Franz von, *Memoirs*, trans. B. Connell, New York, Dutton, 1953

Parker, R.A.C., *Chamberlain and Appeasement: British Policy and the Coming of the Second World War*, Basingstoke, Macmillan, 1993

Peden, G.C., *British Rearmament and the Treasury, 1932–1939* Edinburgh, Scottish Academic Press, 1979

Peters, A.R., *Anthony Eden at the Foreign Office, 1931–1938*, New York, St Martin's Press, 1986

Peterson, M., *Both Sides of the Curtain: An Autobiography*, London, Constable, 1950

Petrie, Sir Charles, *The Life and Letters of the Right Hon. Sir Austen Chamberlain* (II), London, Cassell, 1940

Ponomaryov, B., Gromyko, A. and Khvostov, V. (eds) *History of Soviet Foreign Policy, 1917–1945*, trans. D. Skvirsky, Moscow, Progress Publishers, 1969

Postan, M.M., *British War Production*, London, HMSO, 1952

Pressieisen, E.L., *Germany and Japan: A Study in Totalitarian Diplomacy, 1933–1941*, The Hague, M. Nijhoff, 1958

Quigley, H.S., *Far Eastern War, 1937–1941*, Boston, World Peace Foundation, 1942

Reynolds, P.A., *British Foreign Policy in the Inter-war Years*, London, Longmans, 1954

Rich, N., *Hitler's War Aims*, New York, Norton, 1973

Richardson, H.W., *Economic Recovery in Britain 1932–39*, London, Weidenfeld & Nicolson, 1967

Robbins, K., *Munich 1938*, London, Cassell, 1968

—— *Appeasement*, Oxford, Blackwell, 1988

—— (ed.), *The Blackwell Biographical Dictionary of British Political Life in the Twentieth Century*, Oxford, Blackwell, 1990

Roberts, C.B., *Sir John Simon*, London, R. Hale, 1938

Robertson, E., *Hitler's Pre-war Policy and Military Plan, 1933–1939*, London, Longman, 1963

—— (ed.), *The Origins of the Second World War: Historical Interpretations*, London, Macmillan, 1971

Rock, W.R., *British Appeasement in the 1930s*, New York, Norton, 1977

Rose, N., *Vansittart: Study of a Diplomat*, London, Heinemann, 1978

Rothfels, H., *The German Opposition to Hitler*, London, O. Wolff, 1961

Rowse, A.L., *All Souls and Appeasement: A Contribution to Contemporary History*, London, Macmillan, 1961

Royle, J.H., *China and Japan at War, 1937–1945: The Politics of Collaboration*, Stanford, Stanford University Press, 1972

Salvemini, G., *Prelude to World War II*, London, Gollancz, 1953

Schaefer, L.F., *The Ethiopian Crisis: Touchstone of Appeasement?*, Boston, Heath, 1961

Schlote, W., *British Overseas Trade from 1700 to the 1930s*, Oxford, Blackwell, 1952

Schmidt, G., *The Politics and Economics of Appeasement*, trans. J. Bennett-Ruete, New York, St Martin's Press, 1986

Schmidt, P., *Hitler's Interpreter*, London, Heineman, 1951

Selby, Sir Walford, *Diplomatic Twilight, 1930–1940*, London, J. Murray, 1953

Senton, A., *The German Army, 1933–45*, London, Weidenfeld and Nicolson, 1982

Seton-Watson, R.W., *Britain and the Dictators*, Cambridge, Cambridge University Press, 1938

Shay, R., *British Rearmament in the Thirties: Politics and Profits*, Princeton, Princeton University Press, 1977

Shirer, W.L., *The Rise and Fall of the Third Reich: A History of Nazi Germany*, New York, Simon & Schuster, 1960

Simon, J., *Retrospect: The Memoirs of Viscount Simon*, London, Hutchinson, 1952

Sked, A. and Chris, C. (eds) *Crisis and Controversy*, London, Macmillan, 1976

Smith, D., *Mussolini*, London, Weidenfeld & Nicolson, 1981

Smith, M., *British Air Strategy between the Wars*, Oxford, Clarendon Press, 1984

Smiths, S.R., *The Manchurian Crisis, 1931–1932: A Tragedy in International Relations*, New York, Columbia University Press, 1948

Stimson, H.L., *The Far Eastern Crisis*, New York, H. Fertig, 1974 [*c.* 1936]

Strang, Lord, *Home and Abroad*, London, A. Deutsch, 1956

Taylor, A.J.P., *The Origins of the Second World War*, London, Hamilton, 1972 [*c.* 1961]

Taylor, T., *Munich: The Price of Peace*, New York, Doubleday, 1979

Temperley, H.W.V., *History of the Peace Conference of Paris*, 6 vols, London, H. Frowde, Hodder & Stoughton, 1920–1924

Templewood, Viscount, *Nine Troubled Years*, London, Collins, 1954

Thompson, N., *The Anti-appeasers: Conservative Opposition to Appeasement in the 1930s*, Oxford, Clarendon Press, 1971

Thorne, C., *Approach of War, 1938–39*, London, Macmillan 1967

—— *The Limits of Foreign Policy: The West, the League and the Far Eastern Crisis of 1931–1933*, London, Hamilton, 1972

Toynebee, A.J. (ed.) *Survey of International Affairs, 1931–1938*, London, Oxford University Press, 1932–1953

—— *Survey of International Affairs 1939–1940: The World in March 1939*, London, Oxford University Press, 1951

—— *Survey of International Affairs 1939–1940: The Eve of the War, 1939*, London, Oxford University Press, 1958

Vansittart, Lord Robert, *Lessons of My Life*, New York, Knopf, 1943

—— *The Mist Procession*, London, Hutchinson, 1958

Villari, L., *Italian Foreign Policy Under Mussolini*, New York, Devin-Adair, 1956

Waley, D., *British Public Opinion and the Abyssinian War, 1935–1936*, London, Maurice Temple Smith, 1975

Walters, F.P., *A History of the League of Nations*, London, Oxford University Press, 1952

Warner, G., *Pierre Laval and the Eclipse of France*, London, Eyre & Spottiswoode, 1968

Warner, Max, *The Military Strength of the Powers*, London, Gollancz, 1939

Watt, D.C., *Personalities and Policies*, London, Longman, 1965

—— *Too Serious a Business: European Army Forces and the Approach to the Second World War*, Berkeley, University of California Press, 1975

—— *How War Came: The Immediate Origins of the Second World War, 1938–1939*, New York, Pantheon Books, 1989

Werth, A., *The Twilight of France, 1933–1940*, New York, H. Fertig, 1966

Wheeler-Bennett, J.W., *Munich: Prologue to Tragedy*, London, Macmillan, 1948

Wilbur, R.L. and Hyde, A.M., *The Hoover Policies*, New York, C. Scribner's Sons, 1937

Willoughby, W.W., *The Sino–Japanese Controversy and the League of Nations*, Baltimore, John Hopkins Press, 1935

—— *Japan's Case Examined*, Baltimore, Johns Hopkins Press, 1940

Wiskmann, E., *The Rome–Berlin Axis*, London, Oxford University Press, 1949

Wolfers, A., *Britain and France between Two Wars: Conflicting Strategies of Peace Since Versailles*, New York, Harcourt, Brace & Co., 1940

Young, A.N., *China and Helping Hand, 1937–1945*, Cambridge, Harvard University Press, 1963

Articles

Adamthwaite, A., 'The British Government and the Media 1937–1938', *Journal of Contemporary History*, 18 (1983) 281–93

Bosworth, R.J.B., 'The British Press, Conservatives, and Mussolini', *Journal of Contemporary*

History, 5 (1970) 163–82

Ceadel, M., 'The first English referendum: The Peace Ballot 1934–5', *English Historical Review*, 95 (1980) 810–39

Douglas, R., 'Chamberlain and Eden, 1937–1938', *Journal of Contemporary History*, 13 (1978) 97–116

Dutton, D., 'Simon and Eden at the Foreign Office, 1931–1935', *Review of International Studies*, 20 (1994) 35–52

Eatwell, R., 'Munich, Public Opinion and Popular Front', *Journal of Contemporary History*, 6 (1971) 122–39

Manne, R., 'The British Decision for Alliance with Russia, May 1939', *Journal of Contemporary History*, 9 (1974) 3–26

—— 'The Foreign Office and the Failure of Anglo-Soviet Rapprochement', *Journal of Contemporary History*, 16 (1981) 725–56

Parker, R.A.C., 'Economics, Rearmament and Foreign Policy', *Journal of Contemporary History*, 10 (1975) 637–47

Pugh, M., 'Pacifism and Politics in Britain 1931–1935', *Historical Journal*, 23 (1980) 641–56

Raack, R.C., 'Stalin's Plans for World War II', *Journal of Contemporary History*, 26 (1991) 215–27

Shai, A., 'Was There a Far Eastern Munich?', *Journal of Contemporary History*, 19 (1974) 161–9

Taylor, P.M., '"If War Should Come": Preparing the Fifth Arm for Total War 1935–1939', *Journal of Contemporary History*, 16 (1981) 27–54

INDEX